'A lovingly detailed, and long overdue, portrait of a much loved entertainer who had a remarkable career that spanned over sixty years.'

Dick Fiddy, media historian

'Robert Fairclough's book on Ian Carmichael has all the hallmarks of excellent biography — it's independent-minded, thoroughly researched and brings into vivid focus the inner and outer life of a significant player who has previously only inhabited the shadows of film and television histories. What's particularly impressive is the way he sheds light on the post-war significance of the 'silly ass' types Ian Carmichael played so well, and the larger social importance of the British comedies which were his early stock in trade. A remarkable, poignant, sharply written and fascinating tome populated with fresh tales involving co-stars and cult greats from Terry-Thomas to Arthur Lowe to Patrick Macnee. Ripping stuff.'

Pat Gilbert, music journalist and author of *Shut It! — The Inside Story of* The Sweeney

This Charming Man

This Charming Man

The Life of Ian Carmichael

Robert Fairclough

Foreword by Nicholas Parsons

First published 2011 by
Aurum Press Limited
7 Greenland Street
London NW1 0ND
www.aurumpress.co.uk

ISBN 978 1 84513 664 2

10 9 8 7 6 5 4 3 2 1
2015 2014 2013 2012 2011

Typeset by Saxon Graphics Ltd, Derby DE21 4SZ
Printed and bound in Great Britain by Clays Ltd, St Ives plc

Contents

Acknowledgements

S PECIAL THANKS, IN no particular order, to my 'minders' Alan ('there's been an ERUPTION!') Coles and Henry ('other fish to fry') Holland, without whom this book would not have been started and would certainly not have been completed; the best mum and dad in the world; Richard Berry, for incomparable IT skills; my agent Ros Edwardes, for making it all happen once again – I've said it before and I'll say it again, a writer is nothing without a brilliant agent; the legendary Leonard White for being such a goldmine of information; John Flanagan for helping very generously with *The Royal*; Jaz Wiseman for putting me in touch with Patrick Macnee; the one and only ex-Mrs Fairclough, Rachel Busch, for being such a dedicated transcriber and researcher once again; Robert Ross for permission to quote from his extensive interview with Ian; Michael Cragie, Richard Dacre and John Williams for exemplary archive research; the Read-Through Crew: Mike Kenwood, Tim Lambert, Julia Forrest and the extremely munificent and always helpful Dick Fiddy; and, last but not least, slippery genius Patrick Iolanthe Gilbert, for making the introductions and being such a repository of information and advice. He's right about *Feline*, too.

Thanks also to Sam Blake and Eleanor Fleetham at the BBC Written Archives Centre; Sarah Currant, Ayesha Khan, Iratxe Gardoqui and Vivien Jones at the British Film Institute; Stella and Steve Broster, Jonathan Cecil, Jeni Child, Gavin Collinson, John Cox, Simon Coward, Peter Crocker, Eric and Ernie and Pete Darman for the advice on British war films; Tom Dirks; Eltham and Blackfen libraries; Don Fearney; Sayer Galib; Howard Heather; Clive Jeavons; Matthew Lee; Morrissey and Marr (without whom ...); Brain McFarlane; Rupert Macnee; Tony Mechele; Chris Perry; Plum; Posh Ali; Ali Rees; Louise Simpson; The Skids; Neil Sinyard; Elaine Spooner and Phil Higgs; Suede; Ed Stradling; Grant Taylor; Transvision Vamp; The Vaccines; Ann Waterhouse; and everyone at Windmill Books.

For sharing their memories of Ian and his world: the lovely and very helpful Bridget Armstrong, Rodney Bennett, Lucy Boulting, Peter Bowles, Nick Broomfield, Richard Cottrell, Paul Darrow, Julian Dyer, Fenella Fielding, John Flanagan, Derek Fowlds, Gerald Harper, Rachel Herbert, Ken Horn, Francesca Hunt, Phyllida Law, Valerie Leon, Abigail McKern, Briony McRoberts, Patrick Macnee, Nicholas Mcardle, Nicholas Parsons, Robert Putt, Robert Rietti, David Robb, Janette Scott, William Simons, Linda Thorson, Tim Wallers, Terry Winsor, Leonard White and the late, great Susannah York.

At Aurum: Graham Coster for taking a chance on me, Barbara Phelan, Liz Somers, Melissa Smith and Seán Costello for his helpful suggestions on the text and thorough and detailed copy-editing.

I heartily recommend tracking down Ian's fascinating, funny and warm-hearted memoir *Will the Real Ian Carmichael ...*, published in 1979, which has been an invaluable source of reference, insight and anecdotes.

While every effort has been made to identify copyright material and to ask for permission to quote from it, if any item has been inadvertently overlooked, the copyright holder is asked to contact the publisher and the matter will be rectified in any future edition of the book.

Be seeing you.

Robert Fairclough
July 2011

Foreword

This Charming Man is an apt title for a biography of Ian Carmichael. If ever an actor epitomised that particular adjective it was Ian. He was the embodiment of those qualities that one associates with the typical, courteous Englishman, and this is the character he played so well on stage and particularly in films. He looked very English and he loved those things which are always associated with England: cricket and our beautiful countryside. Latterly, when he was no longer driven to prove himself as an actor, he settled in Whitby, in his beloved Yorkshire, away from the show business pressures he experienced when living in London close to the heart of the theatre and film industry.

I first met Ian when I took over one of the principal roles for a month in a new revue that was staged in 1951 by the major theatrical management at the time, H.M. Tennant, called the Lyric Revue. The title was taken from the name of the small theatre in Hammersmith where it was staged and starred all the young emerging talent of that period: Dora Bryan, Joan Heal, Graham Payne and, of course, Ian Carmichael. I owned a small car at the time, my pride and joy, and I drove Ian back to his flat every night after the show as I passed his home on my way to Hampstead where I was still living with my parents. I came to know him well and warmed to his very genuine and naturally charming personality. In the Revue, Ian was outstanding, and I believe it was his performance in the various sketches in which he took part that launched him on to the career that followed. He had the opportunity to display his ability as an actor and comedian, and slowly offers followed until he established himself as the country's most promising and popular leading man and, what is termed in show business, light comedian. A ridiculous phrase really. What is a heavy comedian? It is intended to convey that you are a comedian with a light, sophisticated touch as opposed to a broad stand-up variety performer.

In show business there is often one performance or little cameo that stands out in an actor's career and propels them forward and upward. In the follow-on show, The Globe Revue, named after the theatre in the West End in which it was staged, Ian had a solo sketch about which he was very nervous. It had no jokes or obvious funny business. In fact he was nervous to undertake it but was persuaded by Billie Chappell, the Producer of the show, to accept the challenge. It was quite simply about a shy, timid individual who attempts to undress and put on his bathing costume on the beach while wearing his mackintosh. Ian applied his creative talents to this task and with the meticulous attention to detail that he brought to every professional job, he made the sketch one of the highlights of the Revue and was probably remembered for his comic inventiveness in that one sketch to the exclusion of much of his other professional work at that time.

Following his success in these revues, Ian suffered from what a lot of versatile performers experience in this country: he became labelled as a revue artist or light entertainer, the fact that he was giving a fine acting performance in whatever sketch he was appearing was overlooked. He was rescued from this labelling when the Boulting Brothers, the dynamic film producing duo, put him under contract and he achieved incredible success in their films *Privates' Progress* and *Lucky Jim*,

He was now a leading man and was being offered a great deal of excellent work but Ian had his standards. If he did not approve of the work or script, he would turn it down or endeavour subtly to change the approach. One classic example of this was the play *Boeing-Boeing*, in which I starred in the West End. The play had been a huge success with David Tomlinson in the lead and then Leslie Phillips. The management, John Gale, took the show to

Broadway with Ian Carmichael, whom one would have assumed was ideal casting. Jack Minster, who directed the production in this country and America, told me Ian was reluctant to take the comedy into the realms of farce, he wished to keep it as a straight-forward light comedy. The play failed on Broadway and the producers blamed Ian. Ian was an intelligent actor who had high standards in his performance from which he would not deviate. Perhaps America just did not respond to the very European setting of the play.

Ian certainly did not embrace the broader comedy which was creeping into our entertainment, particularly on television: he was in the tradition of the stylish comedy that had been pioneered by Noel Coward and Terence Rattigan. The last performance I saw Ian give was in a brilliant play by Keith Waterhouse and Willis Hall, *Say Who You Are*, at Her Majesty's Theatre. He was superb and at the height of his powers. I had the good fortune to follow him in the role when the play transferred to the Vaudeville Theatre. I remember the charming note he wrote when I assumed the role wishing me good luck. Most actors are not so caring and thoughtful to their fellow thespians.

Another area in which our paths crossed was in the world of cricket. We were both members of The Lord's Taverners charity, which began in the Tavern at Lord's, where a number of actors who enjoyed watching the sport decided to put something back into the game they loved and help raise money for disadvantaged and under-privileged children. The charity was also a club. Ian and one or two others wanted to keep it small and beautiful, a club of cricketing-loving enthusiasts, while most of us felt if we were going to give up our spare time to play cricket and attend functions we wanted to raise as much money as possible. We needed to be more business-like. Our point of view prevailed and we now give away up to £3m a year to the causes we support. Ian was a man of principle, and instead of accepting the will of the majority, he resigned. That was Ian. If he believed in something he did not deviate or compromise.

Ian embodied all that was best in the traditional English way of life and he was unhappy with the more vulgar and cruder attitudes that have crept into our society in recent years. He understood the British character and portrayed this in many memorable performances on film and in the theatre. He epitomised all that we associate with the formal English gentleman in his appearance, speech and natural courtesy. To the public he was a versatile actor; in private life he came across as a typical English gentleman. He was a joy to know and it was a pleasure working with him. What a charming man!

INTRODUCTION

'Hello, Old Lad'

*'I've been fortunate to work with a lot of very charming people.
I could count the bastards on one hand.'*
— On-stage interview with Ian at the
National Film Theatre, 8 December 2002

IAN GILLETT CARMICHAEL once commented that interviewers always wanted to know about Terry-Thomas and Peter Sellers, with whom he made several films for the Boulting brothers, but never him. It was endearing of him to be self-deprecating, and his statement in many ways encapsulates the man: amiable and winningly modest about a career that the better-known Sellers and Thomas should have envied. A victim of lazy journalism that stuck him with the patronising tag of the 'silly ass' almost from the moment he first stepped into a spotlight, and which he constantly had to battle against, this charming man was the very definition of a Yorkshire renaissance gentleman. In a remarkable career that spanned a quarter of a century, he was a musician, actor, military commander, talent scout, dancer, singer, writer, director, producer and broadcaster.

Characteristically, he accomplished it all with the minimum of fuss, a lack of conceit and very often a handwritten note dropped into a fellow actor's dressing room thanking them for making him look good. In his personal life, he stood for resolutely good, solid and stylish English things: a happy marriage, cricket, an open-topped white Rolls-Royce, bespoke tailoring and country living. It says a lot that he outlived the Hollywood-feted Thomas and Sellers by nearly twenty and thirty years respectively.

His story is also, in many ways, the story of popular entertainment and the development of 'Englishness' since the Second World War. He was a humble innovator in the early days of BBC Television, on the cutting edge of 1950s film satire with the Boultings, Frank Launder and Sidney Gilliatt and, ten years later, even placed an immaculately polished shoe into the Swinging Sixties with the modish London movie *Smashing Time*. By contrast, he remained in the mainstream with his theatre work, championing comedies, farces and musicals, the kind of conservative but entertaining fare that Lindsay Anderson arrogantly dismissed as 'the middlebrow, middle-class vacuum of the West End.'[1] As British humour waxed and waned, from the style and wit of Noël Coward and Terence Rattigan to the low farce of the *Carry On* films, Ian took a discreet step back from the bawdy direction in which comedy was heading to bring P.G. Wodehouse's dim-witted dandy Bertie Wooster to an appreciative audience old, and, gratifyingly, new.

Towards the end of his life in the 2000s, he was content to star in the warm period nostalgia of the *Heartbeat* spin-off *The Royal*, set in 1969, perhaps the cut-off point for a mythical vision of a merry England. In a modern world of 24-hour shopping, bland urbanisation and the elevation of the mediocre by the internet, perhaps more than ever Britain needed to be reminded of a better time, a past when it seemed the sun always shone on the village green and people were just terribly nice to each other. Ian Gillett Carmichael always fulfilled that role admirably and, in the end, uniquely.

He still does.

Robert Fairclough
July 2011

CHAPTER 1

The Clan Carmichael

'At first the infant,
Mewling and puking in the nurse's arms.'
— William Shakespeare, *As You Like It*, Act II, Scene 7

IAN GILLETT CARMICHAEL first graced the world with his presence on 18 June 1920 in Kingston upon Hull in Yorkshire, England. Appropriately for a man who in future would always be considered reliable and composed, he was born almost exactly in the middle of the year. Fittingly, too, for a man who would also make a lot of people laugh during his lifetime, he arrived in the same month that the American postal service finally made it illegal to send children through the US mail.

At the beginning of the third decade of the twentieth century, the world was still in shock after the Great War of 1914–18, a global conflict that had turned Flanders fields into a nightmare of mud, barbed wire and trench warfare. The armistice in November 1918 had seen the resources of the European powers – the British, Austro-Hungarian and Ottoman Empires – vastly depleted, and the United States, which had stayed out of the conflict until its final stages, emerging as the new, world-leading economic superpower. In Russia, a successful Bolshevik revolution in October 1917 had brought to an end the dynasty of the Tsars and established the world's first Communist state, a landmark political change that in 1920 was still sending shockwaves throughout the rest of the world.

Kingston upon Hull, like its namesake on the banks of the River Thames near London, was a town that somehow remained insulated from these world-changing events. For several generations, the local economy had been a stable and prosperous one, due primarily to the town's status as a coastal port. Hull had played a major part in the journey of northern European settlers to the New World (America) in the sixteenth century, and in the nineteenth the Wilson Line of Hull had grown to monopolise the North Sea passenger routes to become, by 1920, the largest privately owned shipping company in the world. Latterly, the Wilson Line had been sold to the Ellerman Line owned by Sir John Ellerman, a Hull-born entrepreneur who was at that time the richest man in Great Britain. To add to the town's stature, just before the First World War, Hull had been granted city status.

However, Ian's roots lay further north. His paternal grandfather, Michael Carmichael, was born in Greenock in Scotland, the youngest of five children. He was lucky to be the product of a stable, educated, upper-middle-class environment, and by his twenties had become superintendent for the Scottish Legal Life Assurance Society. In the 1880s, Michael, together with his wife Mary and daughter, was sent to the north of England to establish a new branch of the insurance company, finally settling in Hull in 'a modest street'[1] (now demolished). Once settled in Yorkshire, Mary bore three more children, and one of them, Arthur – born in 1883 – would be Ian's father.

One of Ian's earliest memories was visiting Grandpa Michael's next, grander house on Beverley Road at Christmas, where he would play in the roomy cellars where Michael kept a record of all the heights of his grandchildren, an experience he recalled disarmingly as 'all very Robert Louis Stevenson'.[2] Master Ian also remembered an eccentric family ritual that took place underneath the large dining-room table at Vesper Lodge in the village of Kirk Ella, Grandpa Michael's subsequent impressive detached abode: 'Come pudding time, at family gatherings, all the children would get on the floor and crawl through the tunnel made by the legs of the chairs from the bottom end of the table to the top. There they would emerge to receive a spoonful of blancmange from Grandfather, who presided at the head.'[3]

Ian's early years were a privileged, pampered existence, a far cry from the harsh realities of life on the breadline in working-class or rural communities in England. He remembered being well provided for on Christmas Day with a train, stamp album and chemistry set, and for the Christmas meal enjoyed the luxury of goose, a taste that stayed with him throughout his life. His scatter-shot memories of visits to Vesper Lodge included the housekeeper Miss Ransome's home-made toffee, an orchard of plum trees and the church bells pealing on Sunday for evensong. His early life was the epitome of an idyllic childhood and helped shape his confident, unhurried attitude to life.

'I have nothing but happy memories of my paternal grandfather,' the grown-up Master Ian would recall. 'He died when I was eighteen in a way that all golfers would wish to go: he sustained a heart attack on the eighteenth green from which he never recovered. He was 83 ... He had a splendid *bonhomie*. His house was always so full of sunshine and fresh air.'[4]

The father of Ian's mother, Henry Meads Gillett, came from the same professional class as Michael and was an established tradesman in Hull, owning the firm T.B. Morley and Co. Ltd, who (according to their office stationery) were merchants in 'lead, glass, zinc, tinplate, oil, paint, colour, varnish'. The firm held offices in Jameson Street and, as late as 1979, was still being run profitably by two of Ian's cousins under the name Morco Products Ltd. (Ian's memories of the company warehouse were a jumble of lavatory furniture, boilers and electric light fitments.) Unusually for the times he lived in and his social class, Henry married twice. His first wife bore him a son and daughter, and his second spouse repeated the compliment, duly delivering Kate, Ian's mother, on 5 April 1883.

In common with a lot of men of his time, Henry sported an

H.G. Wells-style moustache (a fashion also adopted by Michael Carmichael) but his personality was more sullen than the genial character of the celebrated author of scientific romances. Living in a house called 'Ardlui' on Davenport Avenue in Hessle, a small village on the banks of the River Humber, Henry Gillett was a lay preacher and devout churchgoer, and Ian remembered that 'his homes ... were heavier and darker in furniture and décor and exuded a distinct Victorian atmosphere.'[5] Fear of burglary made Henry move to a terraced house on a Victorian street in Hull, and by the time he relocated to an even larger house just around the corner on Princes Avenue, his home was, to Master Ian's relief, considerably 'larger and sunnier.'[6]

Wealth, religion and artistic leanings combined in the Grandparents Gillett, helping to determine Ian's formative character and social ambitions. The family had two maids who were obliged to join in with prayers, and Ian recalled, 'If the milkman was delivering he was invited in too.'[7] In later life, Ian's mother would tell him that Grandfather Gillett had been tempted to be a professional actor − somewhat surprising, given his puritanical nature − and showed a gentler side to his austere demeanour in the long, 'loving'[8] letters he wrote to her at Harrogate Ladies' College, which would always be signed 'Your loving dear old Dad, H.M. Gillett.'[9] The missive dated 4 April 1909, written entirely in verse, was amusingly philosophical, if a little chauvinistic to modern eyes:

> You can talk of by-gone heroes
> And can tell off-hand their names,
> But could you clean a bedroom out
> And wash the window panes?
>
> You can tell of styles and fashions
> At a mile a minute rate,
> But if you tried to trim a hat
> Would you spoil it 'sure as fate'?

Now, whilst going in for dancing
Elocution and the like,
Try and learn a house to manage
Some day maids will go on strike![10]

Master Ian himself would often be the recipient of these jocular notes, which would always be 'written in a neat, firm hand [and] were full of humour and loving kindness.'[11] One day, after Ian had been playing enthusiastically in the garden, he took delivery of the following rhyme on his return to Grandpa Gillett's house:

Apple pie is very nice,
And so is apple pastry,
But if you eat it with dirty hands
I'm sure it's very nasty![12]

Unlike her extrovert husband, Grandmother Gillett remained a shadowy figure in Ian's recollections. He couldn't recall her personality at all, and the most distinctive things he could remember about her were that she always used a walking stick and would be absent from Hull for long periods for the good of her health at Harrogate or Matlock, where there were health spas. As far as her spouse was concerned, however, Ian felt that if he hadn't died when Ian was fourteen, 'I am sure Grandfather Gillett and I would have been great pals.'[13]

Ian's father Arthur (known to his friends as Mike) was cast from the same mould as his father and elder brothers Robert, James and Herbert. All of them were motivated and independent men, striking out to build businesses and self-employed careers of their own in Hull. (Ian clearly inherited their entrepreneurial spirit, even if it was channelled in a different direction). With some initial help from his father, Robert began his professional life as a premium collector for the Scottish Legal Life Assurance Society but developed a sideline buying and selling wristwatches. With the sideline becoming more and more profitable, Robert took on a loan to buy a small jewellers' shop, and Herbert joined him after a brief stint as an office boy at a timber merchants. Perhaps even more independent than his brothers, Arthur 'decided that he would have some specialist knowledge unallied to commerce so that he could be self-reliant'[14], and trained as an optician at the University of London, qualifying in October 1914, just after the outbreak of the Great War. A dedicated man and something of a perfectionist, at only twenty-one he was awarded the Freedom of the City on 8 December with a certificate that described him as 'Citizen and Spectacle Maker'. Returning to Hull, Arthur opened an optician's practice on the premises in George Street of his brothers' family firm, now with the grand title R.P. Carmichael and Co. Ltd, Jewellers and Silversmiths.

Herbert had become the Carmichaels' expert in gems and jewellery but the firm did not remain restricted to high street trade; it also dealt in commodities such as coal, and owned two railway trucks with Herbert and Robert's names emblazoned on the side to advertise the brothers' industrial interests. R.P. Carmichael and Co. Ltd became something of an institution in Hull; the shop eventually moved to the other side of the street and, even though it no longer bore the Carmichael name, was still trading in 1979. Writing about his family's business in later life, Ian was clearly proud of their commercial achievements in making 'the name Carmichael a synonym for distinction and class among Hull retailers.'[15]

With the arrival of a world war in August 1914, Arthur enlisted in the East Riding Royal Garrison Artillery, initially manning anti-aircraft guns in the Humber estuary before he was posted to the Western front in France. Reflecting on a man who was a resourceful businessman and committed patriot, Ian had nothing but love for his father, describing him as 'kind, thoughtful towards others, generous, forgiving and, if nothing else, a perfect gentleman ... I know full well that he inwardly admired my decision to branch out and do my own thing. I can remember him on more than one occasion saying to me that he envied me the independent life I had made for myself and that he wished he had had the courage to do the same thing when he was younger ... He was the most courageous, patient, painstaking, industrious man and made a success of everything he set his hand to in the commercial world.'[16]

'She was petite, uncomplicated, very feminine and slightly old-world,'[17] Ian would recall of his mother Kate Gillett. Rather like her son in later life she was interested in times past and collected old-fashioned china figurines and pictures of bygone days, poring over ladies in crinolines and bonnets, thatched cottages and Old English gardens. Bearing an astonishing likeness to her son, she rarely weighed more than seven stone and 'her figure was sylph-like and her complexion as per peaches and cream, the latter quality being inherited by all her children and grandchildren.'[18] The only slight blemish on her character was a selfish streak, a deficiency that to some extent would be inherited by Ian.

Kate's artistic interests were a great influence on Ian. She possessed a talent for drawing and painting and had a great love of poetry, which she shared with Ian's father. Their courtship was highly romantic and literary, as they gave each other pocket books of verse, bound in covers of coloured suede, containing poetry as diverse as Alfred Tennyson's 'Morte d'Arthur' and Matthew Arnold's 'Sohrab and Rustum'. They had met in 1915 when Kate was nursing with the St John's Ambulance Brigade. At first, Kate's father had opposed any permanent union, worried that his daughter would quickly become 'a penniless widow when she was barely 22.'[19] Arthur's parents had insisted on marriage, and Henry Gillett finally acquiesced after the couple threatened to marry without his permission, exhibiting the characteristic strong will and single-mindedness that their son would inherit.

On 14 May 1918, Arthur Carmichael and Kate Gillett were married in the Presbyterian church on Hull's Prospect Street, a venue where their three children would all be subsequently christened. The ten-day honeymoon took place at the Royal Marine Hotel in Ventnor on the Isle of Wight, then at Arthur's rented rooms in Carisbrooke near where he was stationed. Writing to his parents at the end of the honeymoon, Arthur was ecstatic, saying, 'we have never been so happy in our lives as we have during the last ten days, in fact we never knew what real happiness was until we got married.'[20] Kate, in an equally euphoric mood, described 'ten days of absolute bliss and happiness.'[21]

The harmonious union of the newlyweds was shattered ten days after the honeymoon ended by the news that Arthur's unit was being posted to France and the Western Front. Despite being involved in some of the fiercest fighting of the war, Arthur survived and returned to reopen his optician's practice and, most importantly, make a home for himself and Kate in the exclusive Sunnybank district of Hull. The patter of tiny feet wouldn't be far behind.

CHAPTER 2

Hurry On, Boys

Early schooldays and the emergence of young Ian

A S MASTER IAN, aged two, was enjoying the lavish family home at 32 Westbourne Avenue in Hull's Sunnybank district in 1922, in Italy the new, disturbing doctrine of Fascism, which preached the need for nothing less than dictatorship to regenerate a country politically, Benito Mussolini's bully-boy Blackshirts were marching on Rome. In the leafy lanes of Marlborough Park, Victoria Avenue and Salisbury Street, the first born of Arthur and Kate Carmichael was oblivious to a new, despotic poison seeping into the national wounds caused by the Great War that would ultimately dictate the path Ian's life would take.

The streets of Sunnybank fomed a rectangle similar to the grid system used in American cities, creating an ordered, agreeable and wealthy environment. 'If you were a professional man, were self-employed, or were an executive white-collar worker in the middle-income bracket and had to live in Hull, "the Avenues" were the place to drop anchor,'[1] Ian would recall much later in life. Number 32 was semi-detached and, typically, on the sunny side of the street, with a household that boasted assorted maids and a cook. On 4 December 1923 at 5.30 a.m., Ian was joined by Mary, the first of twin daughters, with Margaret born twenty minutes later. The always delicate Kate was exhausted by the birth and had to recuperate in Torquay for three months.

Like many wealthy children of the time, Ian's tonsils were removed when he was five, by one Dr Richie Rogers. He was terrified by the experience and, ever after, would have a wariness of hospitals. Afterwards, a maid hired for a special dinner at his parents' house, and dressed very formally, upset him so much he asked, 'I'm not going to have another operation, am I?'[2] When he underwent a severe growing pain when his heart swelled to 'half-an-inch on one side and three-quarters of an inch on the other',[3] he was told to stay in bed for six weeks – not even getting up to go to the toilet. His bedroom was over the front door of the house so he was able to observe the comings and goings in the street below. Showing signs of initiative at a very early age, he devised a rudimentary pulley system to the front gate, where a basket would collect the post and could be hauled back to his room; kindly neighbours also sometimes supplied chocolates and sweets.

This enjoyably permissive lifestyle came to an end when Ian was enrolled at his first school, Froebel House School on nearby Marlborough Avenue. He was removed after one term because of the alarmingly foul language he began bringing home. His education improved with his attendance at The Lodge School in Pearson's Park. Demonstrating early theatrical leanings, Ian helped to build the scale model of a set for the musical *Hiawatha*, winning a mauve bulb-bowl for growing the best hyacinths. While at The Lodge, he discovered a love for cricket as well as an early fondness for the (very) young ladies of his acquaintance. On one memorable occasion, Ian deliberately got himself out on the first bowl when he was in to bat so he could return to the boundary and continue to enjoy the company of two young women he had been sitting with.

Perhaps predictably for a cosseted child, Ian was precocious, and before he could even read or write, a party piece of his was the ability to select the records asked for by his father and play them on the family gramophone. Delighted with his son's performance, Arthur would then play along to the memorable tunes of the day on his ukulele.

Ian's slightly concerning, premature interest in the opposite sex continued when, on a family holiday in Hornsea, he 'married' Maureen, the daughter of family friends, in the front garden of her family's rented house, wearing a bucket as a top hat. He would lose touch with his early love when he left Hull. A more mature woman who also made an impression on Ian when he was a boy was the aviator Amy Johnson, who became famous when she flew solo from Britain to Australia and was honoured with a celebratory motorcade through Hull.

The 1920s were exhilarating times, and a decade that would define Ian's developing personality. The particular character of the Jazz Age, with its Oxford bags, plus fours, cloche hats, two-tone shoes, gin-and-limes, the Charleston dance and George Gershwin's languid, sweeping instrumental symphony *Rhapsody in Blue*, would later indelibly colour both Ian's personal and professional life.

Ian didn't like the austere and authoritarian regime he was forced to endure at the boarding school Scarborough College on the Filey Road in Hull from the age of seven. His father enrolled him there in 1928, from which time he spent only a third of the year at home with his parents. Surprisingly for an establishment which cost his father several hundred pounds per term, there was no hot water and no electricity in the prep school – austerity plainly going hand in hand with wealth in the private schools of the 1920s. Corporal punishment was common: usually slippering with a heavy shoe. Pupils were also made to sit on the floor facing the wall of a master's study for long periods with their hands clasped behind them. Scarborough College made such an impression on Ian, good and bad, that he was able to recall its layout in forensic detail:

> The main buildings of Scarborough College ... were two in number. The original imposing structure, very scholastic in style with colonnade-type cloisters against its front elevation and a clock-tower over its front door, looked south over its own playing-fields

and comprised classrooms, dormitories, dining-hall, library, a few studies for the senior boys, accommodation for the headmaster — and it was illuminated by gas.

The second building, which was referred to as the New Building, had three extra classrooms and an excellent modern gymnasium. This, as its name implied, was a more recent addition and was equipped with new-fangled electricity. The hall and corridors of the main building were festooned with almost as many glass cases containing specimens of stuffed wildlife as the National History Museum. The dining-hall displayed a similar number of silver cups, each under its own glass dome, and the library more wildlife, including mounted swordfish snouts and some positively horrific First World War bayonets.[4]

The college was run by two brothers: Percy Armstrong was fat, jolly and a good cricketer, only dealing in sixes to the boundary, while Laurence was tall, unsmiling and austere, and had a disturbing relish for administering corporal punishment. The uniform was all white, with Eton-style starched collars that caused boils on the neck. When pupils graduated to 'big school'[5] at Scarborough's Holbeck House when they were eight, thankfully normal collars could then be worn.

It's easy to see why the already easygoing Ian was repelled by the college; like a lot of bright children, he got by on his natural academic talent without excelling at any particular subject. The boys would be given only the occasional day's holiday, to celebrate a senior boy's success in a university examination, with visits from parents restricted to 'every third Sunday.'[6] The school also came with the requisite sneering bully, in this case a red-haired tyrant who would urinate in the bed of a boy at lights out, forcing him to sleep in the soiled bed clothes and be punished in the morning for bedwetting while his tormentor sniggered in safety.

An altogether happier event was the college's annual summer picnic, which took place every year at Goathland in North Yorkshire. On that happy day, the boys would be allowed to roam freely along Scarborough's coast, beach and cliffs. One day in

1934, Ian saw a German Graf Zeppelin floating across 'a clear blue sky'[7], a huge Nazi swastika emblazoned across its tail fins. Headed by decorated veteran of the First World War, Adolf Hitler, Germany's Nationalist Socialist (Nazi) Party had transformed the country's Weimar Republic into the Third Reich when Hitler became chancellor in 1933, largely on a Fascist doctrine of racism, warmongering and resentment at the way Germany had floundered economically after the Great War because of the crippling reparations demanded by the victorious powers. That summer day when Ian saw the Graf Zeppelin in the blue skies over England, the Nazi flagship was casting a shadow of impending tragedy across Europe.

Back in Scarborough College, Ian and his classmates were subjected to boring 'lantern-lectures'[8] in the evenings at Holbeck House, amateur slide-shows ineptly presented by one of the masters. More enjoyably, there were also amatuer theatricals, but Ian was not allowed to participate as he was too young. Music master Mr Littlewood always took the leading role, relying amusingly on prompt lines pasted rather conspicuously all over the stage. Apart from the welcome diversions of Mr Littlewood's theatrical antics, the boys were allowed to listen to the radio during the Oxford and Cambridge Boat Race and on Armistice Day – commemorating the end of the First World War – on 11 November, when the deeply respectful Cenotaph service was always transmitted.

Ian wasn't sorry to see the back of Scarborough College. He left when he was thirteen.

CHAPTER 3

All the World's a Stage

'And all the men and women merely players.
They have their exits and their entrances
And one man in his time plays many parts.'
–William Shakespeare, *As You Like It*, Act II, Scene 7

B Y THE END of the 1920s, the personal prosperity of Arthur
Carmichael had increased to the point where Ian's father
could give up ophthalmology and concentrate on the cut-
glass wholesale business he had been cultivating. At the same time,
the Carmichael retail empire continued to expand, acquiring a fully
stocked sweet shop – much to Ian and his sisters' delight – and an
off-licence, greatly increasing the shop frontage of R.P.
Carmichael's. To celebrate his ever-increasing wealth, Arthur
moved the family to an even more exclusive location. The new
Carmichael homestead was a 500-year-old stone-built house called
Elloughton Garth, nestling in two-and-three-quarter acres of
countryside, complete with one of the largest pigeon cotes in
England. Costing Arthur the prodigious price of £1,800 in the
1920s, Elloughton Garth nevertheless needed an extensive amount
of renovation to make it habitable. The building work overran so
much that Arthur had to move the family into a rented house for six
weeks until the repairs were finally done, a situation that Ian decided
contributed to his father going 'thin on top quite early in life.'[1]

Long spells at boarding school weren't conducive to many

lasting local friendships, but Ian shared an obsession with both football and cricket on the Paddock, one of Elloughton Garth's extensive lawns, with two good friends: Bobby Saunders, stepson of his 'uncle Bob',[2] and Peter Kidd, a neighbour from Westbourne Grove. Bicycles were also used incessantly by the trio for their adventures in collecting birds' eggs or butterflies. Whenever Bobby or Peter weren't around, Ian's long-suffering sisters would be cajoled into playing cricket (with a soft ball for the girls) or tennis, Ian fantasising about being the next Herbert Sutcliffe or Dixie Dean.

As Ian's age entered double figures, his artistic leanings became more evident as he became obsessed with the big-band dance music of the 1930s and begged his father for lessons in playing the drums. Advertising for a suitable tutor in the *Hull Daily Mail* to placate his son, a young 'gigster' with the colourful name of Laddie Moses was eventually engaged. Ian's thumping accompaniment to Moses's rendition of 'I Can't Give You Anything But Love' was a life-changing moment for the eager young musician. 'I'm rather square, I suppose,' Ian would admit later in life. 'I have never actually experienced an LSD trip, but had I done so I cannot believe that it would have turned me on any more than those two choruses did, accompanying a piano and not a gramophone record on a real set of skins and not some cheap toy.'[3]

This burgeoning interest in the performing arts developed into a passion for attending the concerts of the Herman Darewski orchestra, which featured a lively and instinctive drummer, in the Spa Ballroom at Bridlington during the school summer holidays. Another fixture of the concert hall was a troupe of pierrot clowns, whose act included a rather shaky tenor rendition of 'The Road to the Isles'.

By now, the cinema was also in Ian's blood. Like many boys, he went through a cowboy phase, dragging his parents and relations to the local cinemas to see Ken Maynard, Tim McCoy, Buck Jones and 'Hoot' Gibson. The magazine *Boys' Cinema* was a constant companion. Sport, too, had become a touchstone in Ian's life, with regular visits to Hull City Football Club's Anlaby Road ground. Standing below the window of Hull City's dressing room, Ian and his friends increased their rude-word power as they listened to their soccer heroes lark around in their post-match communal bath.

Perhaps uniquely among many of his later peers in the entertainment business, Ian's family life was a contented and happy one, his parents' loving devotion to each other suffusing their home and their relationship with Ian and his identical twin sisters. Only Ian and his parents could tell Mary and Peggy apart, a knack Ian would use when he could to irritate the girls' authoritarian and very humourless governess Miss Airey.

'As always in my youth, the sun was shining and the air was balmy,'[4] Ian wrote of the time when, at the age of 13 in 1933, he was sent to Bromsgrove School in Worcestershire, 160 miles from Hull, in a land where the people spoke with a fascinatingly different accent. Recalling this period later in his life, he commented,

> I was educated for five years in Scarborough … and then I was moved to a school near Birmingham … where I spent another five years. When I got there, my leg was pulled mercilessly because all the boys said that I had an appalling Yorkshire accent. After my period at Bromsgrove, I was sent to the RADA [Royal Academy of Dramatic Art], and the elocution master there said, 'Where did you get that terrible Birmingham accent from?' So, I can only assume I can pick up accents that are around me.[5]

Bromsgrove was a far more convivial establishment than Scarborough had been, bar the new boys' initial tormenting at the hands of the senior pupils. Situated near the High Street, it was built on high ground that gave the impression of entering 'another world, totally isolated from any outside influences. The whole area, including the playing fields, [covered] about fifty acres. The buildings [were] at the summit of the high ground and [were] dispersed around two large, well-tended lawns which themselves

[were] partially surrounded by a row of magnificent chestnut trees, between a plethora of yellow, mauve and white crocuses [grown] in the spring.'⁶

In an atmosphere that was a refreshing contrast to the austerity of Scarborough, Ian felt, 'the new curriculum was not arduous.'⁷ On the sports field, rugby and athletics failed to ignite his interest, but cricket certainly did, and he represented Bromsgrove in local tournaments, playing for the junior and senior colts. By this time, however, he knew that a lifetime of greasepaint and spotlights was what he aspired to; he longed to follow in the distinguished footsteps of the entertainers Noël Coward, Jack Buchanan and Fred Astaire, whom he could at last listen to on the radio, stare wide-eyed at in the cinema or, very occasionally, see in all their glory on the stage.

In such a regimented environment as an English public school in the 1930s, the pro- and anti-authoritarian sympathies of the pupil soon became apparent. Ian was very definitely of the latter persuasion, confronting first 'mediaeval bullying'⁸ by some older boys and later the frustration and exasperation of his masters, who recognised a talented student who, by his own admission, had a 'natural inclination to be bone idle.'⁹ By the end of Ian's time at Bromsgrove, he was in the contradictory position of being the elder statesman of loafing, a senior boy to be deferred to who otherwise set no discernible good example for the lower school. This curious mixture of rebelliousness and laziness, defined in the halls and classrooms of Bromsgrove, would colour his whole life.

Away from his dull academic studies, a passion for entertainment of all kinds now consumed the teenage Ian. 'I always had a bit of a buzz to do some performing,' he remembered. 'For a long time I wanted to be a musician and run a dance band, then I realised I didn't know anything about music, and I thought it'd be easier to become an actor.'¹⁰ Ian had an encyclopaedic knowledge of his obsessions, in his case the British dance bands of the 1930s. The Palace Theatre in Hull became his second home in the school holidays, and as his father knew the theatre's manager, Ian's autograph book was accorded a privileged position in the dressing rooms of his favourite touring musicians.

On his twice-weekly visits into Bromsgrove during term time, Ian would make straight for Mr Watton's record shop. The thin, stooping pensioner regularly had to contend with an enthusiastic Ian rifling through the latest releases and huddling with his friends over a radiogram to sample the latest sounds. The soundtrack to Ian's adolescence was provided by 'My Kid's a Crooner', 'Boo-Hoo', 'It's a Sin to Tell a Lie' and 'Is It True What They Say About Dixie?' among many others. The names of bands and singers that decorated his school notebooks included Harry Roy, Nat Gonella, Joe Daniels and His Hot Shots, and Fats Waller.

Possessing an impatient nature, Ian went through phases of trying to learn the piano and then the alto-saxophone. Inevitably, his extra-curricular pursuits also began to impact on his schoolwork, as one of his end-of-term reports sourly and shockingly reported: 'Ian will never make any progress with his scholastic studies until he learns to concentrate on lessons and abandons his craving for Negroid music.'[11] One thing Ian did excel at during his time at Bromsgrove was his drumming in the OTC band, a local military cadet troupe whose performances were exemplary models of martial precision.

Luckily for Ian, his artistic gifts were recognised and nurtured by a young, interested games master called Peter Hordern (brother of the famous actor Michael), who sponsored the formation of a Junior Literary and Dramatic Society for younger pupils who were too enthusiastic to wait until the fifth form, the point when they could appear in an official school play. During Ian's last year at Bromsgrove (when he scraped a pass in geography in the School Certificate at the third attempt), he was cast in his first stage role as the maid in Oliver Goldsmith's *She Stoops to Conquer* (Bromsgrove being an all-male school). Regrettably, his feet never touched the stage, as on the morning of his first appearance, he woke up with chicken pox and was ordered to stay in bed. Indeed, Bromsgrove would never witness his nascent acting ability at all.

The world Ian wanted so desperately to be a part of offered him solace in upsetting times such as the debacle of his *She Stoops to Conquer* debut. The cinema dazzled him, from Westerns to historical epics, to musicals starring Fred Astaire and Ginger Rogers, to comedies with Laurel and Hardy and Chester Conklin, and the home-grown output of film-makers like Alexander Korda. Regular nightly reading for Ian before lights out at Bromsgrove were the movie periodicals *Picturegoer*, *Picture Show* and *Film Weekly*.

A sign of how hard the entertainment bug had bitten Ian was his construction of an improvised stage in his playroom at Elloughton Garth, and his press-ganging of his sisters into performing with him. In 1936, his passionate hobby finally went professional. He placed an advert in the *Hull Daily Mail* that read:

> WANTED – anyone under seventeen join new juvenile amateur dramatic dance band during school holidays – Ian Carmichael, Elloughton Garth, Brough.[12]

With his old companion Bobby Saunders in tow as 'a budding percussionist'[13], the ensemble of drums, accordion and saxophone that eventually resulted from Ian's optimistic advertisement bashed through 'Goody, Goody', 'Alone', 'Did I Remember' and the theme to the Marx Brothers' film *A Night at the Opera* (1935) until, after several months rehearsing behind closed doors, the band went public at such venues as Hull's Victorian Hospital for Sick Children. The *Hull Daily Mail* reported, 'The band rendered a varied selection of popular melodies, played in a bright and snappy way,'[14] with, bizarrely, 'conjuring tricks by Ian Carmichael, leader and drummer of the band, who also arranged and produced the entire show, [producing] another high note.'[15]

A combination of his rising reputation as Hull's answer to Bing Crosby and volatile hormones resulted in Ian's first romantic experiences around this time. Cultivating a working relationship through a variety of duets with a strawberry-blonde named Hazel Rowe, Ian would escort the young lady to her bus stop behind the

Regal cinema in Hull after the band's concerts. On the way, young love would take its course and the couple would repair to a convenient secluded telephone box for some gauche romantic interludes. 'Hazel Rowe was, I think, the first girl I ever kissed in hot blood,'[16] Ian recalled, 'and such was the surprise at my initial assault that she promptly spilt the entire contents of her powder compact down my overcoat when attempting to repair the damage.'[17]

Despite these romantic distractions, Ian Carmichael and His Band continued to improve, playing their first professional engagement for the NSPCC at Hull's workhouse around Christmas 1937. In the same year, Ian showed himself to be years ahead of his time, striking out into independent film-making with his debut feature *What Happened at the Gables*, written and directed by the budding cinéaste using his father's prized 16mm camera. Typically for a young man obsessed with going to the 'flicks', the film was a crime drama that climaxed in a car chase involving the Morris Ten owned by his mother. His enthusiastically edited minor masterpiece fell to pieces every time it was shown.

'I can't remember the actual moment when I announced to my parents that I wanted to become an actor,'[18] Ian reflected in 1979. 'In fact, I'm not even sure there ever was such a moment. After all that had been going on during the past few years, I think it was just taken for granted. Nevertheless, since we had, as a family, no connections whatsoever with the theatrical profession, some fairly positive decisions had to be made concerning how I should go about it, so I have no doubt that at some time or other I must have made a specific declaration of my intention.'[19] Despite feeling that his decision to tread the boards must have been an 'enormous disappointment'[20] to a father hopeful of welcoming his son into a thriving family business, particularly as the two sons of his father's brothers had also decided to pursue careers away from the family firm, Ian was resolute: 'For myself, I'm ashamed to say, I never for a moment considered any other course of action. The glittering prize of a [family] inheritance tempted me not one jot or tittle. The impetuosity of youth, plus an unbelievable confidence, was my Sword of Excalibur.'[21]

Despite having no love for William Shakespeare due to his lassitude in English lessons, Ian for once took his housemaster's advice concerning his audition for the Royal Academy of Dramatic Art in London – 'admission to which did not appear to be over-selective at the time'[22] – and with Peter Hordern's help perfected the 'Is this a dagger I see before me?' speech from *Macbeth* as his audition piece. Typically, his last-minute conversion to the Bard worked, and the stultifying atmosphere of Bromsgrove fell away as Ian left Hull for RADA in January 1939, a year that would be significant for both the tyro actor and the rest of the world in more ways than one.

CHAPTER 4

Blood and (Foreign) Soil

'Yo ho ho and a bottle of rum,
Come and watch old Hitler run'
−Graffiti, 1939

A T THE END of the 1930s, only twenty years after the devastation of the First World War, all of Europe knew, with a sickening dread, that another, possibly even more destructive war was inevitable. The Third Reich, led by its indomitable Führer Adolf Hitler, had taken advantage of the European nations' terror of another war on the continent and had reunited Germany with Austria by marching its armies into Vienna on 14 March 1938. By operating a policy of appeasement, which Hitler took full advantage of, the democratic European countries stood by and watched helplessly as the modern, seemingly unstoppable German army – the fearsome *Wehrmacht* – occupied the German-speaking Sudetenland area of Czechoslovakia in October 1938, a clear statement that Hitler intended to expand his empire across Europe. As Ian walked through the doors of the Royal Academy of Dramatic Art on London's Gower Street in January 1939, it was a question of when, not if, like his father before him, he would be drafted by the British armed services for active military service against a belligerent Germany.

Ian remembered the first month of 1939 as one of the most important turning points in his life, as it preceded twenty-one months of:

unconfined joy, occasioned by my finally shaking off the shackles of school discipline and being able to mix daily with young men and young women who shared my interests and enthusiasms. This joy was, nevertheless, being tempered by the worsening European situation. The fear that now, just as I was standing on the threshold of a future that I had dreamed about for years, the whole thing might be snuffed out like a candle was too unbearable to contemplate.[1]

During his first, frugal months at RADA, Ian roomed on the Adelaide Road in Chalk Farm, in an establishment recommended in the RADA brochure that was run by an easygoing character actor called Christopher Steele. The proprietor of the 'semi-hostel'[2] was assisted by his cheerful housekeeper Miss Thorburn, whose prominent auburn hair earned her the nickname 'Carrot Top' from her cheeky charges. Other tenants at Adelaide Road when Ian arrived included 'a friendly Scotsman called, if you don't mind, Scottie,'[3] a serious, dedicated actor called David, an unnamed 'likeable young Lancastrian'[4] and an Australian named Bill Bennett, with whom Ian struck up an instant friendship 'probably because we both enjoyed our tipple.'[5]

RADA itself was a rather relaxed theatrical college in the late 1930s, but to Ian's delight the male students were outnumbered five to one by the girls. Coming from an all-male school background that had prohibited any contact with the opposite sex, 'to be transferred suddenly, at the age of eighteen, into a co-ed establishment in which the dice were so disproportionately loaded in one's favour was heady stuff.'[6] Despite having limited funds, Ian made the most of the economical opportunities afforded by the Lyons Corner House teashops, and cinemas like the Swiss Cottage and Haverstock Hill Odeons, to entertain a succession of pretty female companions.

During his first term, Ian's eyes were opened to the realities of acting in productions of Shakespeare's *The Merchant of Venice*, Richard Brinsley's Restoration comedy *The School for Scandal* (which, by some curious twist of theatrical fate, would be the last stage play Ian ever performed in, during the twilight of his career), the Greek tragedy *Iphigenia in Tauris*, J.B. Priestley's *Time and the Conways* and Thornton Wilder's Bertolt Brecht-style modern play *Our Town*. As was the penchant of many a student, actor or no, Ian would often be in the pub at lunchtime, before the afternoon performance. On one particular day, he shared one too many pints with the always alcohol-inclined Bill Bennett and a fellow student drinker called William Squire. As the 3 p.m. matinee of *Iphigenia in Tauris* approached, the tipsy trio left the pub for the Academy Little Theatre and Ian's by now very gregarious associates insisted on making him up and preparing his costume for his role as King Thoas.

As Ian recalled:

> They then pointed me in the general direction of the stage and went round to watch the result of their handiwork from the gallery. I was too sloshed to know precisely the impression I intended to make on the unsuspecting audience. The procession commenced, all the participant characters – soldiers, prisoners, handmaidens, you name them – being spaced correctly about a yard apart. I was somewhere about the middle of it all, and when it was my turn to enter I let those preceding me carry out the complete manoeuvre until they were all in position and static. Momentarily the stage was still, everyone looking up at the rostrum to see what had happened. At this point, I made the most impressive of entrances on my own. I wore a heavy black beard, a hat which resembled a peacock-blue tea-cosy and a tiger-skin cloak. Hilarity invaded the ladies of the chorus as I shakily negotiated the steps and finally took up a position on a stone bench for the rest of the act, from which I proceeded to tickle the feet of the chorus with my tiger-skin. Hilarity too, I might add, emanated from the majority of the audience, which was always rather sparse for Greek tragedy, and which was made up almost entirely of fellow students who had been apprised of an impending disaster and had been herded into the gallery by my friends, the two Bills. All quite unforgivable, of course, but it was, I suppose, all part of my effervescent irresponsibility and new-found freedom.'[7]

Even if Ian's drunken improvisation rather spoiled the intended atmosphere of Greek doom and gloom, it was nevertheless an early indication of the comic gift that was natural to him.

In his second term, Ian made his first professional stage appearance. This auspicious event took place in a production of the Czech writers Josef and Karel Čapek's science fiction play *RUR (Rossum's Universal Robots)*, a modern fable about humanoid robots who finally rebel against their human creators. In a play that was a variation on Mary Shelley's *Frankenstein* story with a theme that would become a staple of twentieth-century science fiction, Ian was cast for the key rebellion scene with seven other RADA students. For one week in the evenings, Ian made his way to the modest environs of the People's Palace Theatre on the Mile End Road in Stepney where he would 'dress up in a suit of brown dungarees, a tall tubular hat made of brown linoleum, and for the second time in my career I made up my own face, this time as instructed, with green and mauve greasepaint.'[8] Ian's one-week-only stint as a 1930s forerunner of *Doctor Who*'s Cybermen earned him '10 shillings. When I left on Saturday night, I had to change trains at Charing Cross and went into the Strand Corner House, ate a knickerbocker glory and my entire salary went.'[9]

While Ian found the promising scenario of *RUR* 'totally unmemorable'[10], in his second term he was fired up with enthusiasm when he was cast as Flute in a prestigious student production of *A Midsummer Night's Dream*, staged by the respected director Neil Porter. Ian assessed the status his new, prize role gave him in a way typical of the competitive and hormonal adolescent male: 'The men's reaction seemed to be a mixture of envy and awe, and the effect on the girls was all I could have wished.'[11]

A Midsummer Night's Dream opened at the Vanburgh Theatre on 1 September 1939, the day Hitler's blitzkrieg ('lightning war') began on Poland, an act which brought the United Kingdom into direct military conflict with Nazi Germany on behalf of the besieged Poles. As soon as the curtain fell, Ian and the rest of the cast were told that the play was now closed after only two performances. With RADA itself also closed, and mindful of the havoc being wrought on Poland's towns and cities by the Nazi hordes, Ian decided to leave London there and then and return to his family at Elloughton Garth to seek counsel from his parents and, with Britain now committed to what looked like another long and bloody war, try and decide what to do next.

While he was relatively safe in the bosom of a family deeply concerned about his inevitable call up to the armed forces, Ian received a letter from RADA informing him that the college would not be reopening on 29 September, as per the pre-war arrangement. Deciding to face the unavoidable and enlist voluntarily, Ian applied to the Officer Cadet Reserve – having acquired the relevant qualifications during his time in the OTC at Bromsgrove – in the hope of securing a commission in the army as an officer. While he waited for confirmation one way or the other, Ian kept himself fit and distracted from the war by helping to bring in the harvest on a neighbouring farm. On 2 October, he was summoned to an army interview in Leeds, enrolled and told that once he turned twenty years of age he would be conscripted to the ranks, where his suitability as officer material would be assessed during his training. Ian now had a few months' grace before the army took him.

After two months, it became apparent that the feared onslaught on the United Kingdom from the Nazi war machine wasn't coming – at least, not yet. England entered a period known as the 'phoney war', when everyday life returned to a nervous normality. As this strange, tense atmosphere permeated the country, Ian was informed that after 'a reappraisal of the situation'[12], RADA would now be reopening after all.

The sobering knowledge that a lot of his student contemporaries had already been called up was tempered for Ian by a move to Number 12 Roland Gardens in South Kensington with his old friend from Hull Geoffrey Hibbert, the pianist in the Ian Carmichael Band, now a student at the Webber Douglas School of Singing and Dramatic Art in Kensington. The warm friendship between the two young men was soon further enhanced by some of Geoffrey's other friends from Webber Douglas moving into Roland Gardens. One of them was a young man two years younger than Ian called Patrick Macnee. He was the product of a bizarre aristocratic upbringing, which had involved his mother moving her lesbian lover 'Uncle Evelyn'[13] into the family home and insisting that Master Patrick only wear kilts. Initially seeking out Ian's advice on an engagement ring, he and Macnee would over time become close friends, sharing a love of stylish *haute couture* and cricket.

During the Christmas holidays of 1939, Ian left the capital to become assistant stage manager on a production of Noël Coward's *Charley's Aunt* at the Palace Court Theatre in Bournemouth, taking on the small role of the college scout in the play and understudying the three male leads, valuable work experience so early in his nascent career as an actor. In early 1940, Ian began his last term at RADA, eventually bidding farewell to his student days in productions of *Henry V* and *Twelfth Night*. On 29 February 1940, he received his first ever mention in the *Stage*, the weekly newspaper of the theatrical profession, when it reported that he had been successfully awarded his diploma.

Ian wasn't out of work for long after leaving RADA. Following more assistant stage manager duties, this time on the Phillip King comedy *Without the Prince* at the Whitehall Theatre in the West End (his first experience of working in London's theatreland), Ian took the initiative and contacted the theatrical renaissance man Herbert Farjeon (born in 1887), a respected critic, librettist, theatre manager, playwright and researcher. Ian had always admired revue's combination of separate sketches, songs and dance routines, and in 1940 when Ian boldly approached him, Farjeon was preparing a touring revue called *Nine Sharp*. Securing an audition at London's Little Theatre a week after he first approached Farjeon, Ian chose a popular song from another revue running at Webber Douglas and, careful to make sure of his material's suitability, tried it out on an older, more experienced actor with whom Geoffrey had become friendly, one John Le Mesurier.

After Ian had finished singing, Le Mesurier said in his endearingly languid manner:

'Very nice, but why are you singing it in that *dreadful* American accent?'

'I wasn't aware that I was,' Ian replied, rather taken aback.

'You are,' Le Mesurier affirmed calmly but firmly, 'and it's dreadful. It's a Bobby Howes-type number and it's English. Sing it in English.'

The future film and TV comedy genius's advice did the trick and Ian passed the audition for *Nine Sharp* with flying colours.

Contracted on the incredibly generous salary of £4 10s. per week as both a performer and assistant stage manager, Ian's feet barely touched the ground as he ran most of the way home. Turning the corner from the Old Brompton Road into Roland Gardens, he saw most of his friends sitting on the steps of the house, enjoying some unusually warm sunshine. As he ran up to their jubilant, welcoming embrace, he kept bellowing one statement over and over again: 'I've got it! I've got it! I'VE GOT IT!'

> To a man (and woman) they belted down the pavement towards me in wild, abandoned enthusiasm, and I was kissed and embraced in a manner usually only accorded to a striker who has just rammed home a perfectly poised centre from Kevin Keegan. In those early days the unconfined joys experienced by any one of us when getting a job were shared by all. It was a wonderful camaraderie; the exuberance of youth is incomparable.[14]

Nine Sharp's ten-week tour opened at the Arts Theatre in Cambridge in June, and Ian's personal nirvana was complete when the play's six-day residency was blessed with the most glorious summer sunshine which he and the rest of the cast and crew duly made the most of, bathing in the sun's warm, invigorating glow from the bottom of punts on the river Cam.

The *Nine Sharp* tour was also emotionally significant for Ian as he experienced the deep, uninhibited joys and pain of first love, falling for a young soprano and actress called Dilys Rees:

> I had been very attracted to her during rehearsals. She was of medium height, as pretty as a picture with a trim little figure and had a head of dark tumbling locks. She was kind. She was friendly,

always an attraction to a newcomer who feels a bit shy and out of things, and she had an engaging sense of humour. Very soon indeed I fell in love with Dilys hook, line and sinker. This was a love much more complete and overwhelming than anything I had ever experienced before, and it exploded inside me bringing an ecstasy of happiness. A few months later it was to bring a despair and pain that was almost disembowelling ... The fact that she was seven years my senior meant nothing; the fact that she was happily married to a young doctor was earth-shattering.[15]

While Ian wrestled with the rawness of first love, Britain's security was becoming more and more precarious. Belgium and Holland and, unbelievably, France had fallen to the Nazis by June 1940 – the month of Ian's twentieth birthday – while the British Expeditionary Force had been routed on the beaches of Dunkirk and only saved by the heroism of an ad hoc fleet of small English and French boats, nearly all unarmed. For Ian, the time had come for him to join the army. Although he could have deferred his training because *Nine Sharp* had transferred to the West End under the new title of *In Town Again*, he chose to do his duty for king and country instead, and said an emotionally fraught goodbye to Dilys at the same time:

I was to spend my last night (and penny) buying orchids for my love and escorting her to the Café de Paris where we dined and danced to Ken 'Snakehips' Johnson, the West Indian band-leader who was later to die in a direct hit on the building. I clung to her so tightly on the dance floor and sang 'I can't love you any more, Any more than I do,' into her ear. Around one in the morning, at the table, the conversation finally ground to a halt, held tight in the vicelike grip of emotion. I could hardly see through eyes that were awash with tears.[16]

Arriving for training in a haze of depression at Catterick Camp, North Yorkshire, on 12 September 1940 as part of the 51st Training Regiment felt like starting again for Ian. His comfortable, upper-middle-class home life, wild RADA adolescence and the 'blissfully care-free life of the professional theatre'[17] were gone, replaced by the serried ranks of a battered army the War Office was slowly but surely starting to rebuild after the debacle of Dunkirk. Ian found the monotony and fatigue of basic training a welcome distraction from his turbulent personal feelings and, for the first time, discovered he had the ability to relate convivially to people from all walks of life, regardless of class.

For the first month of training, Ian and the rest of the recruits were confined to camp until, after repeated marching exercises – the infamous 'square bashing' – he knew how to carry himself as a soldier. For this formative stage of his army life Ian was under the command of two fiercely authoritarian non-commissioned officers: 'If Sergeant Slade was our father during that period, Lance-Corporal Bottomley was our mother, and both were ramrod straight in deportment and discipline.'[18]

Even with military obedience being drilled into him every hour of every day, Ian's yearning for the theatre never left him. After a few weeks he joined the regimental concert party, but the rather ramshackle (to his eyes) ensemble only put on one show during his stay at Catterick.

After ten weeks, Ian moved up the army class structure by being posted to the Royal Military College at Sandhurst to begin training as an officer. Here, the cadets were allowed the luxury of sleeping two to a room and were waited on by civilian batmen (servants). A major eye-opener for Ian in this more rarefied military atmosphere was the colourful, if always deferential, language of the Brigade of Guards drill sergeants who conducted the officer cadets through yet more square bashing: 'MISTER Carmichael – you 'orrible little man! You aren't in the fuckin' *Desert Song* now! Put yer 'at on straight and try to look like a fuckin' soldier, SIR!'[19]

As well as the omnipresent drill exercises, the officer cadets learned driving and maintenance, gunnery, how to use and repair a wireless set, and map reading. Ian also had to grit his teeth for a return to the classroom to learn army law and the King's Regulations. Keen to follow his father into a regiment comparable with the East Riding Royal Garrison Artillery, his father's unit,

Ian was posted to the 22nd Dragoons on completion of his training. He emerged from Sandhurst in March 1941 as 2nd Lieutenant I.G. Carmichael, Royal Armoured Corps.

The Dragoons' hometown was Whitby, which sat at the mouth of the River Esk, with Teeside to the west, Scarborough to the east and York to the south-west. The sleepy town's principal distinguishing features were and are two defunct lighthouses built on pier extensions at the mouth of the harbour and the ruin of the sixth-century abbey high above the town on a cliff edge, made world-famous by its inclusion in Bram Stoker's classic vampire novel *Dracula*. Ian's new posting felt like coming home: 'For me, from the moment of my arrival, Whitby and its people have always spelt pure enchantment.'[20]

The 22nd Dragoons' commanding officer came across to the young, newly qualified officer as a pompous Colonel Blimp-like figure:

> Lieutenant-Colonel G.L. Craig ... was in his early forties, of medium height, dapper, possessed sandy hair which was slightly receding, walked with a suggestion of a limp and he sported a spruce little cavalry moustache ... In wartime, when everyone wore battledress throughout the daytime hours, he was, except on military exercises, always seen in service dress. He was, by his own admission, lazy. He always had a lie down on his bed after lunch – but he was also astute enough to realise that if he didn't work too hard, to retain his rank and regiment, someone else was going to have to. Consequently he developed decentralisation into an art form ... 'Cragie' and I had nothing whatever in common; yet for some quite unaccountable reason he took to me. He also bullied me, derided me, belittled and, at times, humiliated me – though to give him the benefit of the doubt, he may not have realised he was humiliating me – but one thing he never did was ignore me.[21]

With 'Craigie' unsure of what duties would suit Ian best, to begin with he was allocated to 'C' Squadron, one of the regiment's three fighting units.

The wry, humorous undertone present in army life manifested itself during Ian's time at Whitby in the friendship he struck up with one Second Lieutenant Haddock, 'known fairly obviously as "Fish".'[22] Together they attended the Spa dance hall in Whitby, which hosted all-ranks parties, and during one evening Ian met 'a sensationally pretty'[23] blonde local girl named Pym McClean wearing a startling salmon-pink dress, while Fish dallied with her friend who, it transpired, was her cousin:

> 'An interesting evening,' Fish said as we had a final nightcap. 'What was yours like?' And with an arrogance that has embarrassed me throughout every one of the thirty-eight years since, I replied, 'I intend to marry mine.'
> And I did.[24]

After that first momentous date, Ian spent all of his off-duty hours with Pym. Putting the heartbreak of his relationship with Dilys firmly behind him, Ian had taken to his new amour 'immediately. She was young and fresh, blue-eyed ... [and] was born and bred in the Yorkshire area ... She was warm, she was "game", she was genuine. There was an innocence about her, an unsophistication that disarmed even the most worldly ... She was also patient, considerate, tolerant, totally unselfish and, fortunately for me, a good listener.'[25] As well as having found his soul-mate in Pym, Ian had also found his ideal home: 'The area was peppered with innumerable little country pubs where one could go into the back room and have the most delicious ham-and-eggs with real Yorkshire ham. Where it all came from in 1941 heaven knows, but there it was. That summer I fell in love, not only with Pym, but with the whole area.'[26]

Later in 1941, the time came when the 22nd Dragoons had to move on to the Helmsley training area for more advanced, battle-ready manoeuvres. With an impressive display of emotional discipline, Ian and Pym agreed that after saying their tearful goodbyes the night before, she wouldn't come to see him off at the allotted time of noon the following day. Come the day itself, however, even though Ian noticed Pym continually driving around the meeting point where the Dragoons' vehicles were assembled in her mother's Morris Eight, he was too much of a gentleman to let on that he ever knew.

Helmsley is a small market town and just around the corner from its market place is Duncombe Park. In 1941 its eighteenth-century mansion had been leased to a girls' school that was now deserted due to the evacuation of the pupils. Instead of occupying the vacant and inviting stately home, the 22nd Dragoons were billeted in a camp of new Nissen huts, flimsy structures that did little to keep out the cold of the bitter winter of 1941–42. On the plus side, Pym had an uncle in Helmsley whom she could stay with on her evening or weekend trips to see Ian, so the freezing Lieutenant Carmichael took as much warm comfort as he could from her visits.

Ian's army career continued in the ascendant: he was appointed (unofficially) assistant adjutant, the leader of the HQ troop of four tanks. At the same time, an incident occurred that, however much he protested to the contrary, proved that Ian possessed the mettle that real soldiers were made of. In the second week of the Dragoons' stay at Duncombe Park, after some routine maintenance, Ian and his troops were 'sheeting up' – covering the vehicles with tarpaulin – when, while he was on top of his tank and trying to close the hatch of the turret, the heavy metal lid suddenly snapped shut with unexpected force and severed the top of the second finger on Ian's left hand. The picture of calm and control in a crisis, Ian simply said '*Christ!* I've lost a finger' and confidently brushed off the concern of his men:

> 'Come on,' I said, with an air of command and authority that had always escaped me before, 'I'm all right. Get them sheeted up.' I stuck my wounded fist into the top of my overalls and looking for all the world like the traditional pictures of Naploeon, as solicitous as a mother hen, I ensured that every last detail was completed before finally dismissing the troop.
>
> Then my sergeant suggested that he should walk me back to the mess. 'I'm perfectly all right,' I lied. 'Don't worry, I can manage.'

However, he insisted. We walked the half-mile or so back. He wanted to hand me over personally to the [medical officer] but I refused his offer graciously, bade him goodnight, opened the front door, closed the door behind me and fainted on the mat.[27]

The intense cold of the winter gave way to an equally extreme heatwave and drought in the summer of 1942, and Ian and his men found themselves fighting brush fires, as well as the boredom of inaction at the indecisiveness of the high command on what the role of the 22nd Dragoon's motorised units would be in the invasion of Europe. In May it was finally decided that Ian's HQ squadron would be a Recce (reconnaissance) Troop at the same time as Pym decided that she and her beau should become engaged, which was duly and happily announced by the couple on 30 May.

Meeting Captain Nigel Patrick of the King's Royal Rifle Corps, the brigade entertainments officer, inspired Ian to mount a theatrical production to help relieve the tedium of the 22nd's posting and, hopefully, raise the spirits of the men. A new garrison theatre had just been built in Duncombe Park, and with the support of Craigie, Ben Levy's comedy *Springtime for Henry* was granted four performances which played to capacity houses. The actresses Anne Bibby and Benita Booth joined Ian and Nigel in the four-role cast, an unexpected bonus for the all-male audiences. The opportunity to host another production was denied Ian when at the end of February 1943 the regiment was moved again, this time further south, to Warminster in Wiltshire. This relocation and more subsequent inaction gave Ian the opportunity he'd been denied at Duncombe Park, and he put on the revue *Acting Unpaid*, which proved to be another high point on his growing CV as a proactive army entertainments organiser.

'We were married in Sleighs village church on 6 October [1943],'[28] Ian remembered later in life, proudly and affectionately recalling the day that he said 'I do' to Pym McClean, the love of his life. 'It was a white wedding, sparsely attended on a very grey day that had austerity stamped all over it. All clothing at that time was rationed and our respective mothers and various aunts rallied round, unselfishly sacrificial, to equip the bride and her three bridesmaids.'[29]

Ian returned from a brief honeymoon spent in Scarborough and London to discover that in the regiment's new home in Banbury, action was at last imminent. In 1943 the tide of the Second World War had indeed been slowly turned: the German army in Russia had been beaten back outside the city of Stalingrad and in Africa, thanks to the innovative command decisions of General 'Monty' Montgomery, the Afrika Korps was on the point of destruction and surrender. The planning of the attack on Hitler's 'Fortress Europe' was well under way and the 22nd were to join a new, secret armoured division nicknamed 'Hobart's Funnies' after its commander Major-General Percy 'Hobo' Hobart. The 9th Armoured Division, directly under the overall control of the legendary Montgomery himself, was charged with the use of experimental equipment that would be instrumental in establishing a bridgehead during the allied invasion. Its member regiments were stationed as far apart as Cumberland, Suffolk, the Kyles of Bute in Scotland and Stokes Bay near Gosport in Hampshire.

The secret weapons of the 9th Armoured used a variety of innovative and extraordinary vehicles: DD tanks, amphibious Sherman tanks that could be launched at sea; CDL tanks, which were mobile searchlights; AVREs, multi-purpose Churchill tanks equipped with an assortment of accessories for filling in or spanning anti-tank obstacles and destroying concrete barricades; CROCODILES, flame-throwing Churchill tanks; KANGAROOS and BUFFALOS, amphibious, tracked troop carriers, and CRABS, which destroyed minefields. The latter machines were Sherman tanks fitted with a projecting boom that held a revolving drum that rotated at high speed, beating the ground in front of the vehicle with heavy chains to explode all the mines in its path. Ian's brigade was to be equipped with CRABS.

By spring 1944, the whole of the Allied invasion force gradually moved south in preparation for the commencement of Operation

Overlord, the assault on strategically selected Normandy beaches in France. Ian's Brigade HQ moved to a large house called Corbie Wood in Weybridge and, with training now complete, had little left to do but wait. Pym was able to secure another compassionate posting in her role as a driver for the army and was now billeted in London and, as trains ran from Corbie Wood every half an hour into Waterloo, the couple 'grabbed as many days and nights together as we could, each one of which we imagined would be our last.'[30]

On D-Day – 6 June 1944 – Ian heard about the landings of the 22nd Dragoons and Westminster Dragoons in Normandy 'on a magnificent midsummer morning'[31] over breakfast at Corbie Wood. The commanding brigadier immediately briefed his officers about a battle plan that had been so secret that only he, and possibly his chief of staff, knew the exact details. As part of the command structure of the 9th Armoured, Ian, among several others of his fellow officers, was required as a liaison between units of the attacking forces that required squadrons of 'Funnies' to assist in their assault.

Ian's first sight of a foreign country was when his own country was invading it. On 16 June – D + 10 – Tactical Brigade HQ crossed the English channel in an American landing craft, its two huge doors crashing into the surf as the troop carrier delivered a Humber scout car onto the shores of France, a vehicle that was to be Ian's personal transport throughout the remainder of the European campaign. As the Humber negotiated the battle-scarred landscape around Courseulles-sur-Mer, Ian was two days short of his twenty-fourth birthday. By his own admission inclined to be idle, the invasion inspired Lieutenant Carmichael to previously untapped levels of endeavour as the 'Funnies' were constantly in action. 'Our specialist machines, techniques and knowledge were immediately required for a new offensive elsewhere. And so it was to be throughout the entire campaign in north-west Europe.'[32]

One unofficial duty Ian took part in during the initial assault was curbing the enthusiasm of his commanding brigadier for suicidally close visits to the front line. This involved the collusion of his fellow liaison officers at Brigade HQ in marking the position of the German front line on the operations room maps a good three-quarters of a mile nearer to Allied territory than was actually the case, a daring piece of subterfuge that protected the lives of both the reckless brigadier and his secretly relieved fellow officers.

Ian's most harrowing experience of the war occurred on a visit to a part of the British sector where a new 'push' was being prepared with the aid of Ian's old nemesis Craigie, now promoted to a full colonel. As heavy artillery shelled the German positions ahead and they retaliated by sending over aerial bombers at night, Ian and his colonel dug in as best they could:

> On our third sleepless night one of the German bombers was hit by ack-ack fire and crashed but twenty yards from our temporary accommodation. The approaching hysterical scream of its twin engines as it hurtled earthwards had, I was convinced, my number written all over it. It erupted with a mighty roar as it hit the ground, bursting into a raging inferno which lit up the entire area, thus providing a king-sized flare for the following waves [of bombers]. It wasn't long before a remaining stick of bombs still housed in its belly exploded and the small-arms ammunition destined for its machine guns started to go off like firecrackers on 5 November. My bed-roll, barely dried out after torrential rain during our first day, was, by the time the last flame flickered out from that burning aircraft, sopping wet again. The following morning two charred corpses were removed from the machine and buried respectfully slap next door to our 'bedrooms'.[33]

Dealing with such experiences was a fact of every day life for the young British soldier and Ian, like so many of his countrymen, dealt with them in a matter-of-fact, level-headed way, a remarkably calm and mature state of mind for men in their early twenties.

The relentless Allied assault continued until the Germans had been pushed back to Holland and northern Belgium, where the retreating *Wehrmacht*'s position became temporarily entrenched.

In this brief lull in hostilities, for the first time since the Second
World War began, Ian had time to consider his future.

> Until I had joined the army I had spent my entire life day-dreaming
> about a successful future for myself somewhere in the realm of show
> business. From the age of about seventeen this had crystallised itself
> into an unwavering resolution to become an actor, and never, since
> then, had I considered any other career. Between the ages of eighteen
> and twenty I had had practical experience of the life which confirmed
> that my decision had been the right one. I could conceive of no other
> way of earning my living. I adored it. I lived and breathed 'theatre'.[34]

However, Ian's success in rising through the ranks in the army to
a commanding and responsible position, not to mention the
prospect of a regular, if not overly generous wage now he was
married, made him question, as the bitter Dutch winter of 1944
began to bite, whether his future now lay with the British army
instead of its antithesis, the British theatre.

In 1945, Ian's military star continued in the ascendant as he was
promoted to the rank of captain, with the ominous prospect that by
the end of the war in Europe – which by now the Germans were
clearly losing – he would be posted to Burma in the Far East to
continue the fight against the Japanese. On 4 May, acting as duty
officer at Brigade HQ, Ian sent out the communiqué to all the units
he was responsible for that the German forces' surrender was
confirmed. 'It is difficult to describe to anyone who has not lived
through six years of total war the immediate feelings of euphoria
that burst when the news arrives that the final whistle has been
blown,'[35] Ian observed with his characteristic understatement.

> A tight cork exploding from a bottle of champagne would produce
> nothing in comparison with such effervescence. For six long years the
> people of Europe had never seen a light of any sort or description in
> the streets after dusk unless it had been either a blue one, the slim
> pencil-light of a masked-down torch carried by a pedestrian, or the
> narrow – extremely narrow – letter-box slits to which the lights on all
> vehicles had been reduced. The fact that the maiming and killing had

stopped; the fact that one had come through unscathed; the fact that that night every light in the [nearby] town could be put on and the curtains left open, were all causes for unconfined ecstasy.'[36]

Ian saw a way out of being posted to the Far East, and a way out of his dilemma over his professional future, when General Brian Horrocks, the senior welfare officer of 30 Corps, arrived one day at Brigade HQ and announced that now the fighting was over, the welfare and entertainment of the occupying forces was to be a priority. A corps repertory company was to be auditioned and assembled who would mount concert parties for the troops. 'A little over a week later,'[37] Ian was summoned to an audition at the garrison theatre at Nienburg, thirty miles north-west of Hanover. As Ian prepared to sing 'Moonlight on the Waterfall', he realised with a start that he knew the major in charge of auditions. Richard Stone had been a fellow student at RADA.

'Richard was a driving force,'[38] Ian recalled with evident admiration.

> That was and always has been his forte. The whole '30 Corps Theatrical Pool' project, as it eventually came to be known, was his. He was a human dynamo. Though good company, he was at times exhausting to be with. He lived and breathed his job and consequently assumed that all his minions did the same. He never relaxed; he was on the go the whole time. His plan was always the grand one, the broad strategy, and like so many other men with similar abilities he found it difficult to consider detail; that was for someone else to take care of – and for another year that someone was destined to be me. There and then he told me ... that he would definitely give me a job in the Pool and that eventually a posting order would be sent out for me, which in ten days it was.[39]

One of the first auditions Ian sat in was from 'a doleful-looking corporal'[40] who was an aspiring comedian:

> He came back after lunch and sang 'A-Tisket, A-Tasket, I've Lost My Yellow Basket', did a few intervening jokes and smoked a fag

which he kept laying down on the end of a chair … and I thought he was *death-defyingly* unfunny. And my chum Richard Stone said, 'You're quite wrong, you're quite wrong, I'm going to book him into such-and-such concert party as principal comedian,' and indeed that's what we did.[41]

The melancholy looking corporal was Frankie Howerd. For the rest of his life, Ian claimed that his initial dismissal of Howerd's show business potential was 'the cross I have to bear.'[42] However, the two men became friends to the point where the unconventional funny man sought out Ian's advice:

He gave me a terrible job to do just before I was demobbed. By that time I was his CO and he came up and said, 'Look, I've been playing these shows now for a year, and I want to continue with this in Civvy Street when I get out. I'm really in a quandary about what to do, because I've no money really, apart from what I got as a soldier; I have an invalid mother dependent on me; I have no experience; I just don't know what to do. Should I get out and try and shine in the big parts of Civvy Street, or should I stay on for a few more months in the army and get more experience here?' He was asking *me* – I was only about 25 myself at this time – but I did say, 'I think you should go out, because you'd get more experience out in the big world than you will staying in the army.'[43]

The rest, as the cliché goes, is history.

Ian's initial duties involved travelling hundreds of miles across Germany seeking out indigenous civilian entertainers to complement those being assembled from the Allied forces. At the beginning of his third week with the Pool, Stone asked Ian to become his staff captain, an immediate vacancy that needed to be filled. Although Ian had initially wanted to perform as part of one of the touring companies, the twin attractions of more money and a chance to develop the organisational skills he had first shown at Duncombe Park won him over.

In July 1945, Pym Carmichael was demobilised 'on the grounds that she was pregnant.'[44] With the soon-to-be-parents having no home of their own, Pym went to stay with her mother while Ian planned his return to the stage with Stone in a new production of *Springtime for Henry* at Nienburg. Ian delighted in his return to the spotlight, and a few months later his enthusiasm for the profession he loved was fully restored when he played Romeo in *Romeo and Juliet* 'in a powder-blue ensemble which had perhaps better be forgotten.'[45]

The following April, Ian was promoted to major, the highest rank he would achieve in the British army. On 8 July, he was back in England being demobbed in Leeds. He was given a cardboard box containing a demob suit, a hat, a mackintosh, a pair of brown shoes and one shirt with three detachable collars. As he sat on the train bound for Brough and a reunion with his wife and first child, Lee, who had been born on 2 April and whom he had yet to see in the flesh, Ian reflected on the five years and ten months he had spent away from England:

> Like thousands of others – I make no claim to being unique – I have never known what it is like to be between twenty and twenty-six years of age in a normal peacetime atmosphere. Have I missed anything? I don't know – I think, perhaps, I became a man quicker. But now the test was to come. It was a great feeling to be out – there was no denying that; but I was frightened. In fact, I think I was very frightened indeed.'[46]

CHAPTER 5

Happy to Be with You

A return to theatreland and life on the breadline in London

FOR THE SECOND time in nearly seven years, Ian felt like he was starting his life all over again. With 'no job, no home, no car and precious little money'[1], after two weeks spent enjoying his new family at Elloughton Garth, the former Major I.G. Carmichael departed for London, the only place he would be able to make his name as a professional actor. Some good fortune was on his side, as following his own demob, Richard Stone had established a theatrical management agency with his partner Felix de Wolfe and, as promised, immediately put Ian on his books. This first act of kindness was comforting in a city littered with bomb damage and in some cases unexploded bombs, and plagued, like the rest of Britain, by the rationing of everything from eggs to razor blades. With an austere diet and a limited income, it would be some considerable time before Ian was able to fill out his one-size-fits-all demob suit.

Along with future acting and entertainment luminaries who had been demobbed from the forces such as Jon Pertwee, Richard Todd, Patrick Macnee and Spike Milligan, Ian used any help he could to restart his career. His first course of action was to offer his services for free to the Sunday Services Society, an organisation that had been formed with the express aim of showcasing the talents of performers returning from the war, in the hope that any production they put on would be offered commercial management and a West End run.

Ian was lucky: *Between Ourselves*, the new revue he performed in as a member of the 'Wines and Spirits' contingent of the cast – performers who are not given any special or featured billing – was taken up for the West End, but the interminable negotiations that took place once an offer had been made to stage it were not good news: his money was running out.

Just as Ian's personal circumstances were reaching crisis point, help came via his old room-mate Geoffrey Hibbert's father Arnold. Totally unknown to Ian and at his son's urging, the senior Hibbert had written to his old theatrical entrepreneur friend A.R. Whatmore on Ian's behalf. Following an interview in his office on St Martin's Lane for a touring play Whatmore was staging, at which he had to wait a very long time to be seen due to the sheer number of out-of-work actors up for the parts on offer, Ian was offered the staggering amount of £12 a week – 'an increase of not much under 200%'[2] on his last acting wages – in a provincial tour of the light comedy *She Wanted a Cream Front Door*, opposite the comic actors Robertson 'Bunny' Hare and Peter Haddon.

When the play opened at the Apollo Theatre on Shaftesbury Avenue where, despite mixed reviews, it ran for four months, Ian was able to spend his downtime searching for a home in the capital for his family. With taking out a mortgage simply not an option, and after several depressing weeks looking at wholly unsuitable rented flats, he eventually found an appealing, unfurnished apartment in a converted Victorian house at 12 Cranley Gardens, just off the Fulham Road. At £5 a week and with the added blessing of the landlord not requiring a deposit, Ian secured the property and, thanks to the generosity of R.P. Carmichael's in Hull, was able to furnish Cranley Gardens relatively comfortably. Within weeks, the Carmichaels were a settled London family, giving Ian's fluctuating morale a huge boost.

When out of work, as was frequently the case at this stage of his career, extra, paying work was provided by the Players Theatre, in

1947 based under the arches below Charing Cross Station. Specialists in staging nostalgic Victorian music-hall shows, complete with a loquacious chairman played by the extrovert actor Leonard Sachs who also managed the Players, the theatre was very generous in the amount of work it offered new performers. 'They were wonderful to us up-and-coming young people,'[3] Ian remembered fondly. 'They did a different bill every fortnight, and if you were gonna be out of work for a bit, you only had to ring them up and say, "Look, I'm very out of work, can you possibly put me into your bill next week or the week after?" and they always bent over backwards so to do.'[4] During his time at the Players Theatre, for a very welcome £8 per week, Ian lent his not inconsiderable vocal talents to performing the songs 'Put Me Among the Girls', 'There are Nice Girls Everywhere', 'I Do Like To Be Beside the Seaside' and 'At Home Tonight'. (In 1953, the BBC turned the Players' Victorian entertainment experience into the TV show *The Good Old Days*, with Sachs playing the same role he still did in his own theatre.)

On Thursday 6 December, Ian opened in the American comedy *Out of the Frying Pan* by Frances Swann at the 'Q' Theatre, 'a stone's throw'[5] from Kew Bridge. It appealed to Ian because it concerned the fortunes of six student actors who shared an apartment in New York, a scenario that resonated with Ian's own personal circumstances as he recognised in the play 'a transatlantic Cranley Gardens'[6], peopled as it now was by other acting friends like Donald Houston, Patrick Macnee and their respective wives. With three of the original American cast in the production, the play opened to an enthusiastic review in the *Stage*, with its reviewer commending 'some excellent fun and comedy situations'[7] as well as praising 'the other two of the male section [who are] well played by Ian Carmichael and Peter Boyne,' a gratifying notice in only Ian's third West End show. During one rehearsal, however, Ian and Alexander Archdale, another graduate of the Players Theatre, demonstrated to their American colleagues the singular British actor's penchant for 'corpsing' – that is, laughing uncontrollably, usually at some apparently innocuous line in the script. Completely bemused by this hysterical display, the American director took his fellow countrymen to one side and explained: 'You've gotta be patient, understanding and sympathetic. It's not their fault. There is still rationing in this country, you know, and it's all caused by a lack of red meat.'[8]

Outwardly, 1947 continued to improve for Ian with a four-week run of Rodney Ackland's comedy *Cupid and Mars* at the Arts Theatre, the *Stage* again giving a Carmichael-featured production a favourable assessment, describing the play as 'uproariously funny'[9] and 'exquisitely witty'[10]. At home, however, things weren't good: 'At the end of the last quarter of 1947 I had to pocket my pride and beg a loan from my father to pay the landlord, otherwise we would have been out on the street,'[11] Ian recalled of this austere period. 'The following year Pym had to sell a family heirloom – a three-stone diamond ring that was left to her by her great aunt – to enable us to make ends meet. It was a worrying and disheartening two years. We had no car, no fridge, no TV and only a hired radio.'[12]

Despite this hardship, Ian clung doggedly to his belief in a career as an entertainer, sentiments echoed by his contemporary Nicholas Parsons, who was experiencing similarly financially severe times. 'Then, we were still treated like rogues and vagabonds and strolling players, an estranged breed of individuals,' he says today. 'Nowadays actors and actresses are all trying to look like the person next door. Somebody of [mine and Ian's] generation would never dream of doing anything like that.'[13]

CHAPTER 6

Hollywood, England

*Ian becomes a star of the London stage and arrives on British
television and celluloid*

O N 21 MAY 1947, a few weeks before Ian's twenty-sixth
birthday, he was delighted and slightly nervous to receive
an invitation to an audition from the hallowed halls of the
British Broadcasting Corporation. Then, as now, an institution
that dominated the media in the United Kingdom, the BBC was
known chiefly for its quality radio network, which included the
Light Programme and the World Service, but in the late 1940s had
revived its nascent television service that had been curtailed by the
outbreak of the Second World War. Based at Alexandra Palace,
television's importance could be easily gauged from the pages of
the BBC's listings magazine the *Radio Times*, which presented
detailed information about the Corporation's radio output
throughout the bulk of the periodical but relegated its condensed
TV information to a few pages at the back. Nevertheless, with a
monopoly on broadcasting in the UK, the BBC was the only place
to be for a young actor wanting to face the challenges inherent in
the development of a new, exciting communications medium.

The standard letter from the BBC's Television bookings
manager to Ian via Richard Stone was fascinating in its detail and
precise formality:

Dear [Mr Carmichael,]

We have pleasure in inviting you to a preliminary audition at [Besant Hall, Rodmarton Mews, Baker St] at [11.15 a.m.] on [2 June 1947.]

This audition will not be held under full television studio conditions, and make-up is therefore not essential. Dressing-room accommodation will be available, however, should you prefer to change and/or make-up; if so, you should attend not less than 30 minutes earlier than the time stated above.

Your performance should not exceed ten minutes in length.

An accompanist will be available, but you are at liberty to bring your own accompanist if you so desire.

In the event of your performance being considered of prospective interest for our Television programmes, you will be informed in due course of any engagement we are able to offer, or may be asked to attend a further audition, under normal Television studio conditions, at Alexandra Palace.

We wish to make it clear that the BBC does not accept liability for travelling or other expenses which you may incur in connection with any audition(s).

Please state by return if you accept the above invitation; in the absence of a reply within reasonable time your place at the audition will be given to another applicant.

In the event of attendance, please bring this letter with you to facilitate admittance to the studio.

Yours faithfully,

for Television Booking Manager[1]

Every inch the keen and committed tyro actor, Ian replied:

Dear Sir

Reference your 03/PC/HB dated 21st May.

I shall have much pleasure in attending audition at Besant Hall at 11.15am on 2nd June 1947.

I remain, yours faithfully,

Ian Carmichael[2]

At its TV auditions in the 1940s, the BBC operated a simple card system that succinctly detailed the appealing qualities of the prospective artist. Ian's read as follows:

DESCRIPTION:	Personable young man.
DATE OF AUDITION:	2.6.47
PERFORMANCE:	Victorian comedy number.
TIME:	4 mins.
EXPERIENCE:	Farjeon Revues. *Cream Front Door* etc & Players Theatre. Really legitimate actor, & should prove very useful in Television Revue or production.
	[MARKS OUT OF TEN] 9[3]

Nervously pacing the floor at 12 Cranley Gardens as he awaited a reply from the still anonymous television booking manager in July, Ian must have been disappointed when the reply eventually arrived and informed him,

> With reference to your audition on 2 June 1947, we regret to inform you that we see no immediate prospect of offering you an engagement in our Television Variety Programmes as at present planned. We have taken the liberty, however, of adding your name to our list of artists in the event of being able to place you in [a] production. We should like to thank you for giving us the opportunity of hearing your work.[4]

Ian's disappointment was short-lived; by the middle of August he was appearing in the variety show *New Faces* and being paid eighteen guineas for a single performance, an incredible fee for an actor who only nine years previously had been spending all the earnings from his first professional engagement on a single knickerbocker glory in the Strand Corner House. In those early productions for the BBC in the hot, small and cramped confines of the studios at Alexandra Palace, Ian also met someone who would completely change his life.

Michael Mills, a light entertainment producer for BBC Television and slightly older than Ian, was the exact opposite to the dashing young actor he first employed on three half-hour TV revues called *The Passing Show*. Whereas Ian, even in the straitened circumstances of early and fragile self-employment, was always immaculately attired – a constant throughout his life – Mills, despite his senior position in BBC management, was considered by his favourite artiste to be 'a bit of a scruff'[5], a state of affairs Ian attributed to Mills being a single man who lived on his own (even if he was always busy romantically).

Despite their contrasting approaches to gentlemanly dress, the two men were both extremely well read, shared a love of vintage musical theatre and were articulate and consumed with nervous energy when they committed to a production, a *simpatico* mind set that would subsequently carry them through many years of success with the BBC. Mills would eventually give up his bachelor status in the early 1970s when he married Valerie Leon, a shapely actress many years his junior, who was most famous at the time for a series of adverts in which she violently pursued a young man who risked his life by wearing Hai Karate aftershave. 'Michael was bombastic and an eccentric,'[6] Valerie recalls today. 'There was a twenty-five year age difference between us, which is a lot and I suppose he was a father figure. At that time in my life I was incredibly neurotic and he sort of looked after me. When I was in the theatre at night and he was being a TV director/producer, he was a great cook and I would come home and a meal would be laid out; he'd make some fish soup or something like that.' Commenting on a marriage that would produce two happy and healthy children, Valerie adds with a smile, 'He always said we were his best production.'[7]

During rehearsals for *The Passing Show*, Mills invited Ian to a 'greasy spoon' café across the road from the large hall they were rehearsing in at the back of the Cumberland Hotel. On the table between them was the book of *Tell Her the Truth*, a pre-war musical comedy that had been a successful vehicle for the light comedian Peter Haddon. Without any preamble, Mills asked Ian if he would consider playing the lead in the adaptation he was preparing for the BBC. Ian seized the opportunity without a second thought: 'It was a zonking great light comedian's role complete with a love interest and musical numbers – in every way the sort of part I had always dreamed about playing; the sort I felt in my bones I should be playing, and which, so far, nobody but Michael had ever offered me. I was over the moon.'[8]

The three performances of *The Passing Show* earned Ian a satisfying thirty-five guineas. Apart from the gratifying financial rewards from that production, he considered the TV version of *Tell Her the Truth* a step in the right direction as far as the development of his career was concerned, even if on a personal level all of his work at Alexandra Palace was a bittersweet experience. 'The extraordinary thing was, because my parents lived up in Hull, they couldn't see any of it at all,'[9] Ian remembered. 'At that time you could only get television in the London area of the Home Counties. I *believe* they could get it with a bit of luck in Brighton, but that was as far as it could go. So all that early work of mine, nobody saw, really.'[10] Nevertheless, Ian gained valuable experience working on Mills's innovative productions, and by the time of 1949's *Jill Darling* he was being paid forty guineas, his most substantial professional fee to date. He recalled that the conditions the shows were produced under were very intense for the performers: 'We used to do them in these *very* small studios, and [once] you got your artists in there, the dancing girls, you got [in an] orchestra, and it was *all live* … you never saw a camera until about 6.30 in the morning when you were going out, live, at 8 o'clock in the evening. It was breathtaking stuff.'[11]

At the same time as he was making his name as an actor, Ian was supplementing his income by organising military concert parties for Richard Stone and his new business partner Felix de Wolff. One particular show was lacking a comedian. As luck would have it, on a boozy night out with friends to celebrate Donald Houston securing the lead role in *Blue Lagoon* (1949), Ian and his entourage stumbled upon a striking entertainer in a club on Regent Street. Dressed in a dinner suit, the top-heavy ex-Guardsman with the Easter Island-statue head made even more incongruous by the addition of a red fez, had Ian and his friends in hysterics with his carefully rehearsed shambolic act:

'You all know Tommy Cooper; everything went wrong. He was *hysterical*. So I rang my boss and I said, 'You needn't look any further, go and get Tommy Cooper.' And he got him, which is as far as it goes as discovering is concerned, but there was a bit of a problem with him, actually, because he was so good at his own act he wasn't a production comedian: you couldn't put him into other sketches or anything like that. That's as far as my discovering him goes.'[12]

Stone and Wolff were also making demands on Ian in the theatre. Building on his personal success in playing the lead in *Tell Her the Truth* for the BBC, they secured for him the part of Norman, the foil to an elder principal comedian called Prosper, in a 24-week touring production of Charles Culliver's operetta *The Lilac Domino*. The two characters were together on stage for the whole evening and the casting was a major breakthrough in Ian's stage career. 'My nagging doubts as to my future finally vanished and the optimism that replaced them was also, I am delighted to say, shared by my hitherto anxious bank manager,'[13] Ian wrote with evident relief. 'It was to be the emergence of Ian Carmichael, light comedian, for the very first time in full-sized commercial theatres and the credit goes in its entirety to the training, coaxing and encouragement of one man – Leo Franklyn.'[14]

The 52-year-old Franklyn had starred in the same role in the pre-war production of *The Lilac Domino* at Her Majesty's Theatre and was the main draw in the touring production. 'We played theatres all over the country and he really taught me my A, B, C of comedy,'[15] Ian recalled. 'He taught me all the ground work, all the tricks of the trade, all the things to avoid, all the things to pick up. He was wonderful, absolutely *wonderful*, one of the most *unselfish* comedians, most unselfish. He helped me tremendously. He was a big peg in my life.'[16] There was a good reason for the Carmichael-Franklyn double-act being so slick and memorable. Right from the beginning of their working relationship, Franklyn insisted, 'From now on until we open you and I have got to live in each other's pockets. We've got to learn everything we can about each other – what makes us tick, what makes us laugh, what makes us cry, our individual quirks and foibles – we've got to learn to think as one man.'[17] Prosper and Norman were a popular hit nationwide, with the *Stage* noting approvingly, 'Leo Franklyn works hard with Ian Carmichael to instil topical humour with happy results.'[18]

The ninth of September, the end of *The Lilac Domino* tour, was a day of mixed emotions for Ian. The same day in Chubb Hill nursing home in Whitby Pym had given birth to the couple's second daughter, Sally. While ecstatic about his family news, which, like the testmatch scores, Franklyn had mischievously worked into the operetta's final performances, Ian was sad about having to take his leave of a mentor he now regarded as a dear friend after six months together on the road. Although the two men would sadly never work together again, the bond they forged in 1949 would be strong and life-long.

A sign of Ian's success in *The Lilac Domino* was that during its final weeks he was being courted by Prince Littler, one of the most powerful men in British show business, chairman of both the Stoll Theatre Corporation, Moss Empires Ltd and a director of Howard and Wyndhams Ltd, to appear in a revival of the 1932 Drury Lane musical *Wild Violets*, scored by Robert Stoltz. Billed as 'A Musical Comedy of Romance and Youth,' the lavish show concerned the amorous adventures of three boys and three girls in Switzerland in 1902. For the first time in Ian's career, money wasn't a problem, which proved to be a double-edged sword. 'I didn't want to do [it], because there wasn't the part there, it was a miserable part,'[19] he recalled. 'I'd done terribly well with *The Lilac Domino* and, in my eyes, this was inferior. I think they offered me 25 quid a week to do [it], and I said, 'Look, I don't want to do it, that's all there is to it.' So they came back and said, 'All right, we'll make it 30 quid,' so I said, 'It's not [the money], I don't want to do it, I'm not trying to push my salary up,' and [they] said, 'Alright, 35.' It went up as far as 40 and then I felt I couldn't say no. I had to bring up these two daughters of mine, so I had to earn the money.'[20] Ian opened in *Wild Violets* at the Bristol Hippodrome on 25 October, slightly chastened by the knowledge that 'everyone has his price,'[21] but in his defence £40 a week was an astonishingly good wage in 1949 when the UK was still deep in the grip of post-war rationing and thrifty reconstruction. Ian consoled himself that the new addition to his family was well cared for financially, and stayed with *Wild Violets* until its final performance on 27 May.

While he was working intensively in the theatre and for the BBC, in a testament to his stamina, Ian also began to make inroads into the British film industry. In 1947 he had received the call he had always wanted, namely a booking to appear in a feature film. Arriving for work on the director Gordon Parry's *Bond Street* after getting up at 4.30 a.m. to get the train from King's Cross to be on set at Welwyn Studios to start work at 8.30 a.m., he was immediately struck by the difference in atmosphere between British film and BBC Television:

> My first experience of working in a film studio ... was the complete antithesis. Whereas at Alexandra Palace everything had been go, go, go, a feverish, frenetic few hours devoted to getting through [a] show as many times as possible before it went on the air that very evening, at Welwyn, where my talent was to be immortalised on 35mm film for the first time, there appeared, by comparison, to be an inertia usually associated with mausoleums – much more, I am bound to say, my pace of working. Deadlines have always scared the life out of me. They are stimulating to those who find them necessary, but to me they are apt to produce panic and are, consequently, counter-productive. The film studio, therefore, immediately held more appeal for me than its television counterpart.[22]

Given a dressing room key, Ian changed into his costume of tailed jacket and striped trousers and, on set at 8.30 a.m. sharp, was able to take his time in absorbing the unique atmosphere of a film studio:

It was a large set, and also lounging around on it at the same inappropriate hour were about sixty extras all in full evening dress … It is at moments like these that I have always admired the film actor. Next time you're at the cinema, or watching an old [film] at home on the box for that matter, stop for a moment to consider that passionate embrace between the leading man, in immaculate dinner jacket, and his leading lady, who, in the most revealing of Givenchy creations, stands with him on a moonlit terrace outside the Villa Bianco on the Italian Riviera. More like than not it was performed in a freezing studio at 8.30 on a Monday morning in midwinter when both of them were half asleep; but don't let me spoil it for you.[23]

Ian's work on *Bond Street* took two days. Parry changed the shooting schedule, concentrating on scenes between the principal actors Derek Farr, Roland Culver and Paula Valenska and, in the event, Ian wasn't called at all. Returning the following day, he shot the first dialogue he ever spoke on film – the unprepossessing 'Good morning, General' – and his work was done. As he began 'the long haul'[24] back into central London from Welwyn he was a bona fide film actor and £40 richer because of it. When the film was released in 1948, Ian could be seen making the most of a small part as the receptionist at the plush Majestic restaurant, playing a man who, judging by his affronted reaction to General Chester-Barrett's arrival with the much younger, gorgeous Elsa (Paula Valenska), was both a snob and a prude. The way Ian looks her up and down *very* disapprovingly gave an early glimpse of his comic potential.

In his next movie, Ian made it onto the film's title credits, and his character even had a name – if only a Christian one – 'Bill', the postman. In only his second film, Ian was working in the thrilling medium of Technicolor, still very much a novelty in British film. In *Trottie True* (1948), the story of a music hall actress who became one of the famous 'Gaiety Girls', the chorus girls in Edwardian musical comedies at London's Gaiety Theatre, directed by Brian Desmond Huff, Ian had a brief but engaging part as the jovial cockney Bill, collecting the mail from a post box and flirting with the maid Martha (Gretchen Franklin) just before a hot-air balloon crash-lands on Trottie's house. Although brief, his performance was an appealing one, and he was given a particularly memorable line with the broad cockney, 'Blimey, look at 'im!' as the balloon plummeted towards Trottie's abode.

Trottie True was swiftly followed by *Dear Mr Prohack* (1949) and a move back into monochrome. In a step down from the film work he had done up until now, Ian had no dialogue, but the film would be significant for him as it was his first experience of working with the genial character actor Cecil Parker (in the title role), a performer who would figure significantly in Ian's later career. In his single, silent scene as an uncredited assistant in a hat shop, he presents Prohack with a new hat at which he nods approvingly, looking rather disgruntled when his customer leaves him to dispose of his old headwear.

In *Time, Gentlemen, Please!* (1952), Ian had the honour of being (only) in the first scene of the film and speaking the first lines of dialogue. His role as an unnamed government Public Relations Officer is fascinating with the benefit of hindsight, as Ian's character was a harassed, three-piece-suit-and-old-school-tie-wearing, well-mannered chap who now looks like the blueprint for all the similar roles he would play in later life. More interesting still in that regard was his part as Bernard (no surname this time) in the B-movie horror story *Ghost Ship*, also released in 1952. Bernard really is a 'silly ass', a guest on Guy Thornton's (Dermot Walsh) cruiser who brays drunkenly at him 'Here, here!' and 'And so say all of us!' Intriguingly, Ian's scene is written and acted in such a way that it's as if the audience was expected to recognise him, and by the time the scene was shot he had indeed become a noted star of the London revue scene. His double act with the pianist Henry (Anthony Hayes) looks like a scene lifted straight from a sketch show as Bernard asks him to play a hornpipe so that he can demonstrate a nautical jig. The scene, with the most dialogue Ian had yet spoken on the cinema screen, impressed as it showed how effortlessly good his drunken acting was, culminating in a very funny mangling of what Bernard was attempting to do:

You just said there wasn't a hornpipe at this party who knows as much about me as I do!

By *Meet Mr Lucifer* (1953) starring Stanley Holloway in the first British film, courtesy of Ealing Studios, to attack television – then a serious threat to cinema's existence – Ian had received his first positive review in the press, although he wasn't mentioned by name. Perhaps because of the obvious musical talent he showed in *Ghost Ship*, he was unrecognisable as a blacked-up Man Friday in a shabby *Robinson Crusoe* pantomime who suddenly breaks out into inappropriate song. Writing in the *Star*, Ray Nash found the four stories in the film 'never as funny as the incidentals ... demon Holloway's remarkably authentic-looking pantomime ... with its buxom Robinson Crusoe and a Man Friday who sings "Maybe It's Because I'm a Londoner".'[25]

In *Miss Robin Hood* starring Margaret Rutherford and Richard Hearne and also released in 1953, a sweet story of how people-power saved the job of popular serial writer Henry Wrigley (Hearne) on a national newspaper, Ian was back to background acting as a decent chap, this time in the office where Wrigley worked. His, admittedly small, part in the film was a direct result of his collaboration with Hearne on the latter's BBC TV series *Mr Pastry's Progress* in 1951. This had come about because in December 1950 Michael Mills had advised the BBC's Head of Light Entertainment Ronald Waldman of Ian's interest in television production as, in the more flexible working environment in the early days of BBC Television when performers could easily cross the studio to become production personnel, Mills had encouraged Ian to direct an edition of the variety show *Starlight* (1948–59) featuring the singer Petula Clark, which he had successfully done on 11 August 1950. He commended the young soloist highly, saying, 'I could have wished for no one else with whom to share my baptism of fire. Whether she felt similarly disposed towards me, I doubt if I shall ever know.'[26]

Mills duly contacted Ian regarding an interview with Waldman and suggested he write to the executive directly. The flattered actor wrote to Waldman on 5 November 1950 from the Theatre Royal in Bolton, one of the dates on the tour of the musical *Wild Violets* he was starring in:

> I received a letter from Michael Mills towards the end of last week, with regard to the possibilities of my returning to TV at the end of the year to do some production work. He said that you appeared to be prepared to let me 'have a go' – and also mentioned the possibility of my coming to work on your staff for a limited period.
>
> When discussing this with Michael a few weeks ago, I had visualised purely freelance production work in order that it would not interfere with my work as a performer.
>
> However I really am most interested in the idea, [and] would very much welcome a chat with you on the subject – if that were possible.
>
> I shall be returning to town next weekend – I shall be available all Sunday, [and] all Monday morning. Is there any chance of seeing you at all? If next weekend is not suitable, I shall also be returning to town the weekend after next [and] the weekend after that as well.
>
> I finish work with this show on Dec 9 – from which time I am *very* free (as things are at the moment anyway).
>
> Hoping to be able to see you on this matter soon, [and] at your earliest convenience.[27]

Ian's meeting with Waldman was a fruitful one because by June 1951 he was working with Hearne on four fifteen-minute editions of *Mr Pastry's Progress*, 'a weekly glimpse into the fortunes and follies of television's favourite handyman,'[28] following a trial run on the 31 December 1950 edition. Characteristically, Ian would claim, 'it was the Corporal teaching the General, really. He was a big star before I happened along. I just sort of presented his sketches on the television.'[29] Credited as 'Produced by Ian Carmichael', the apprentice's duties extended to writing a workable script for each fifteen-minute instalment with Hearne, which gave the comedian a workable structure for his slapstick routines and gave Ian a through grounding in television production.

Ian's performance in the director's chair on *Mr Pastry's Progress* went so well that in July he was offered the chance to reformat the current affairs panel show *We Beg to Differ*. Beginning on the radio, it had switched to television in 1949 and featured celebrity panellists – principally Gilbert Harding – debating issues of the day such as 'If the team were appointed as a Joint Chancellor of the Exchequer, what new tax would they impose to bring in about ten million pounds a year?' and, a lot more frivolously, 'While there are dozens of female leg shows on the stage, why is there no masculine equivalent of the beauty chorus?' Up until Ian's appointment as producer (replacing Richard Afton), *We Beg to Differ*'s format had been the traditional panel show set-up of the participants facing the host as they rather formally sat side by side. Ian had grander ideas; he reconfigured the programme's presentation as a 'smart drawing room set'[30] and was very specific in his requirements:

> 1 small sitting room suite
> 1 Georgian armchair
> 1 comfortable straight-backed armchair
> 1 pouffe
> 1 low rectangular coffee table
> 1 round occasional table about 2' in diameter. Not too low – standing
>   about 2'6"
> 2 additional small round occasional tables about 1' – 1'6" in diameter.
> 2 pairs of brown velour drapes[31]

His intention was to create a more intimate, convivial atmosphere between *We Beg to Differ*'s participants and, by extension, between the series and the viewing audience. Unfortunately, the relaunch was a misfire: following a negative press reaction to the changes Ian made, the series was promptly cancelled after two editions (although it would be revived on radio and latterly on television again in 1965). Keeping faith with Ian's proven abilities as a TV professional, Waldman offered him the directorship of the one-off special *It's a Small World*, a puppet show written by Ted Kavanagh with additional dialogue by David Croft, an old army friend of Ian's. Transmitted on 23 March 1952, the fifteen-minute extravaganza featured voice work by Bill Fraser, Graham Stark, Kenneth Connor and Deryck Guyler, a conscious effort by Ian to 'offer employment to several of my out-of-work actor chums.'[32] Interestingly, the programme listings in the *Radio Times* for *It's a Small World* informed the reader that 'Ian Carmichael [was] currently appearing in *The Lyric Revue* at the Globe Theatre,' testament to how successful his new West End production had become.

1951 was the year of the Festival of Britain, the year that the country made a concerted effort to shake off post-war austerity and celebrate the best in English innovation, craftsmanship and industry. At the same time, a novel theatrical experience was attracting attention, a development of the nineteenth-century American tradition most commonly called 'revue' (Ian had already performed in what was regarded as the first modern revue, *The Passing Show*, for the BBC). Best known for their visual spectacle such as large-scale choreographed dance numbers, these productions also included sketches that satirised contemporary personalities, current affairs or literature. (As such, they were the distant ancestors of *Beyond the Fringe*, the sketch show that would trigger the 1960s satire boom). Richard Stone had persuaded John Perry (one of Noël Coward's circle) who was putting together *The Lyric Revue* in Hammersmith, to see Ian – despite Perry believing Ian to be 'quite dreadful'[33] after witnessing his desperate overacting in *Wild Violets* – and, following a persuasive audition, he was hired.

The distinctive thing about the London revues of the early 1950s was that while the writers and composers were established names – Coward, the musical double act Michael Flanders and Donald Swann, Richard Addinsell, conductor Norman Hackforth and Kay Thompson, among others – the performers were predominantly newcomers. Apart from Ian, future luminaries such as Myles Eason, Jeremy Hawk, Tommy Linden, Dora Bryan, Joan

Heal, Pamela Marmont, Hilary Allen and Roberta Huby were
entrusted with the revues' combination of cutting-edge sketch
comedy, dramatic presentations and diverting musical interludes.
When Eason became ill, the understudy who stepped into the
breach was one Nicholas Parsons. 'I joined *The Lyric Revue* for
about a month and that's where I first got to know Ian,' he recalls
today. 'I remember I used to have a little car – not many actors at
that time had cars – but I always wanted a car and I used to drive
him back [home] every night. I got to know him very well and
realised what a delightful and engaging chap he was, as well as
being extraordinarily talented.'[34]

An unspoken rule of revue was that each performer had their
own, signature routine in which they could make their mark, and
Ian was very fortunate in being awarded 'The Hangman's Son' or,
as it became more commonly known, 'Darling Boy'. Living up to
revue's reputation for pushing the boundaries of good taste, the
rather macabre sketch dealt with a small boy whose father was a
hangman at a time when capital punishment was still on the statute
books in the United Kingdom as a punishment for serious crimes,
primarily murder. In a quaint, deliberately old-fashioned lyrical
style, the first verse and chorus established the 'darling boy's'
singular character:

> He loved to swing on the garden gate,
> Play for hours with the neighbour's cat,
> He loved to read: but more than that
> Out in the garden, early or late
> He'd bowl his hoop along the paving
> Good as gold 'til day was done,
> He'd not be found misbehaving ...
> He was the Hangman's small son.
>
> He *was* a darling boy!
> Obedient, quiet and charming –
> Never was rude or alarming,
> He would smile and say 'Yes, Papa':

As fair as Fauntleroy,
Oh, how could you find any harm in
Someone so kind and disarming?
He would smile and say, 'Yes, Papa'.[35]

Dressed in a small boy's Victorian 'knickerbocker' suit of Lovat tweed and oversized cloth cap, Ian skilfully negotiated 'an intricate, busy and exacting routine'[36] that culminated with the darling boy strangling his father with his skipping rope and blithely carrying on bowling his hoop. Presumably, the point being made was that a family member's involvement in violence contaminated everyone around him, but, even if the satirical point was slightly obscure, it was still daring subject matter to put on the London stage in 1951.

Because the performers in revue were relatively unknown, the routines and sketches could play with and subvert the audience's expectations. In 'Sweet Belinda', Ian and Joan Heal, in a sedan chair, took to the stage directly before the finale in King James I period costume and began singing what looked like an engaging duet. However, as the song progressed, Joan became trapped inside the chair and Ian embarked on increasingly desperate efforts to get her out, the couple all the while continuing manfully with the song until Joan's head became stuck in the window in the door of the sedan chair. Innovative at the time, the routine's success can be judged by how many times it has been copied down the years, particularly by Morecambe and Wise, whose BBC TV shows often featured a musical number that went hilariously wrong. To make 'Sweet Belinda' look spontaneous and convincing, Ian practised and practised. 'I am a meticulous performer,'[37] he admitted.

> It is the only way I know how to work – the extempore is not for me. I knew exactly on what note of music and on what word in the line the window had to be opened or the door-knob had to come off. Joan worked the same way which made for a harmonious relationship and, I like to think, a well-honed and highly polished end-product. A year or so later when Joan had a baby daughter, she christened her Belinda.[38]

The audiences certainly agreed with Ian – they could still be heard laughing as the finale began.

Despite being a product of the Lyric Theatre in Hammersmith – as the show's name indicated – *The Lyric Revue* began its professional life with a provincial tour. On the opening night in Cardiff, however, the omens weren't good. 'Revue is slick and sophisticated, and it is not every theatre-goer's cup of tea,'[39] Dora Bryan recalled in her autobiography. 'Certainly it didn't go down at all well in Cardiff, where we opened. We were a dreadful flop, and the management very nearly decided not to take it into London, but thank goodness they took the risk. The London audiences appreciated it, and we were a tremendous hit. On the opening night we took fourteen curtain calls, and we ran in the West End for two years [sic].'[40] The *Lyric Revue* period was an exciting time for Ian. As well as contending with headlines like 'Brighter Than Coward' and 'This is Brilliant', the hottest ticket in town had royalty, cabinet ministers, international VIPs and visiting American film stars in its audience every night, sometimes all at once. The show played for eighteen sold-out weeks at the Lyric before being promoted to a West End venue in the Globe Theatre on Shaftesbury Avenue for a further nine months.

The Lyric Revue was such a success that towards the end of its run, the management team decided to christen a new production *The Globe Revue* and keep the same cast together (with the exception of Roberta Huby, who was amicably replaced by Diana Decker). This re-titling made a virtue of the production's location at the Globe Theatre, as when it had been called *The Lyric Revue* (referencing the theatre in Hammersmith), some confusion had arisen over the booking of tickets. Once again, Ian was fortunate enough to secure one of the show's best routines. 'It was a bit of a mime, really,' he would recall modestly:

> It was a little insignificant gentleman in a bowler hat, trying to undress with decorum under a mackintosh on a crowded beach, to go for a swim. In revues, you always had to have a 'number' of your

own if you wanted to make a mark. Yes, you were in sketches, you were in this, that, and the other, but if you wanted to make a mark you *really* had to have a number of your own. And when they came to do *The Globe* ... there wasn't one for me and Billy Chappell, the director, [came up] to me one day and said, 'Look, I've been given this idea. What do you think?' So I said, 'It sounds like an awful lot of work. I'd like a few nice lines with some jokes,' and he said, 'I think we can have fun with this. I think we can do it well.' So I put myself in his hands and he had Donald Swann write some music, and we did it. And it was, I'm delighted to say, successful ... It was like hard work, I can't tell you. In the heat of the summer, all the clothes underneath your mackintosh stuck to you and you couldn't get them off.[41]

The sketch, titled 'Bank Holiday', made the biggest impression on Ian's career so far. The weekend after its debut, the famous *Sunday Express* cartoonist Giles devoted eight separate frames of his weekly cartoon to an illustrated version of Ian's complex routine with the heading, 'Undressing on the beach. Bold new satirist reinterprets classic English custom.' Two months later in the magazine *Theatre World*, the reviewer commented, 'Though Mr Carmichael appeared in *The Globe Revue*'s predecessor, none of the items gave him the chance to make such a deep and favourable impression. Now he has set the seal of success upon his career and for years hence the mere mention of his name will be the cue for someone to ask, "Do you remember him undressing under his raincoat in that revue at the Globe?"'[42] In later years, the original artwork of the Giles cartoon and Loudon Sainthill's design for the 'Bank Holiday' backcloth, both gratifyingly signed by their creators, would be cherished mementoes that hung in Ian's home.

The *Globe Revue* closed in November 1952, bringing the curtain down on a young but by now seasoned cast who had been together for a year and ten months. Although more revue work would follow for Ian with *High Spirits*, *At the Lyric*, *Going to Town* and *In Picture* (as director), he considered his time spent with his fellow performers from the *Lyric* and *Globe* revues to be very special.

Speaking in 1979, he commented that 'even today, though we have all gone our separate ways and may not see each other for years on end, between those of us that are still left there remains a deep-rooted friendship and loyalty.'[43]

As Ian, Pym and the girls enjoyed a much-needed holiday in mid-1953 on the banks of the River Esk in Ian's beloved Yorkshire, Ian received a call from Richard Stone that would turn the three-week vacation into a major celebration. The agent nonchalantly told his client, 'Look I know you don't want disturbing, old boy, but the juvenile lead in a new MGM movie that starts shooting with four weeks' location in Holland in a month's time is on offer and the director wants to see you right away. The stars of the picture are Clark Gable, Lana Turner and Victor Mature.'[44] Even though Ian was extremely tired after the punishing schedule of performances for *High Spirits*, he pulled himself together enough for a fifteen-minute meeting with the director Gottfried Reinhart at Claridge's in London. Ian was even more shattered the day after – he'd arrived back in Yorkshire at 9 p.m. on the train to be met by a concerned Pym – but Richard Stone made his day by telephoning to confirm that he'd got the part of Captain Jackie Lawson, an officer in Military Intelligence. Ian Gillett Carmichael would be appearing in a film with American stars who, not so very long ago, he had been watching wide-eyed from the stalls of his local cinema.

Arriving the designated three weeks later for location filming near Arnhem in Holland, Ian was in equal parts impressed and overawed by Clark Gable, the first Hollywood star he met face to face. 'He was a very, very professional gentleman,'[45] he recalled. 'He was always first on the set in the morning. He always knew every line of his part. He was a very taciturn gentleman, really; I mean, he was such a big star, everyone wanted to go and touch him and talk to him so he had to be a little bit aloof when he was around, and I understood why he was aloof. But that didn't mean he was an unpleasant man, he was a very pleasant fellow. I was *terrified* of working with him – *terrified*.'[46] Ian's nervousness diminished over the following weeks, as the novice film actor became a confident film star in the making.

Once the location filming had been completed, production moved back to England at Borehamwood Studios. One night, Gable's co-star Victor Mature, playing the oddly-monikered 'The Scarf', head of the Danish resistance, invited Ian and Pym for dinner and drinks with him and his wife in the Grill Room at the Savoy Hotel where they were staying. Neither Ian nor Victor were working the next day, so by 10 p.m. they had both tucked more than a few dry martinis under their respective belts. During coffee, a waiter arrived at their table with a written message:

'Blast,' said Mature. 'They've switched things. I'm on call at 7.30 in the morning.'

'Oh, look,' I said, 'it's already getting late. Pym and I will down this and leave you.'

'What the hell for?' said our host.

'Well, you'll want to get to bed, and you've got your lines to learn for tomorrow's scenes.'

'In the first place, I'm not tired,' he said, 'and in the second, I know my lines.'

'You know them?' I said. 'How come? You've only just had your call?'

'I learned the whole film before I left Los Angeles,' he said.

I felt and no doubt looked incredulous.

'That's amazing,' I said.

'What's amazing?' he replied. 'What other way is there of doing it?'[47]

The press weren't kind to *Betrayed*. The bizarre decision to allow Gable, Turner and Mature to use their (very) American accents not only implied that the Bronx and Brooklyn were Dutch principalities but completely undermined any historical authenticity the film may have been striving for. *Betrayed* was also seen as a stepping stone in the fall of Gable's once illustrious career, a decline that made the reviewer in the *Daily Express* 'feel sad.'[48] The *Star*'s verdict was sterner: 'When will Hollywood realise that strip cartoon heroics and [the] real battle of the last war, with all the memories it evokes, simply will not mix?'[49] The magazine *Time and Tide*, meanwhile, highlighted the anachronisms: '[Gable, Turner and Mature] seemed singularly unDutch. Their conduct and sense of security on the other hand seemed almost double Dutch.'[50]

When the film premiered at the Empire Leicester Square on 19 August 1954, Ian experienced a betrayal of his own. He was astonished to see the actor Louis Calhern given co-star billing – even though he hadn't been on the Arnhem shoot or anywhere near the interiors filmed at the MGM studios in Borehamwood – and most of his own scenes consigned to the cutting-room floor. US executives had decided to introduce a new character once they saw a rough cut of *Betrayed* in Hollywood, and Captain Jackie Wilson's appearances had been ruthlessly cut down. After the initial shock, Ian philosophically accepted that this was clearly the way the film business worked. Despite his disappointment with *Betrayed*, 'I liked the hours, I liked the less claustrophobic atmosphere as compared with the theatre, I liked the work itself, and I liked the pay.'[51]

The British film industry's preoccupation with wars old and new in the 1950s came calling on Ian's time again when he was offered a role in the director Zoltan Korda's shot-for-shot Cinemascope remake of *The Four Feathers* (1939). This time Ian was impressively credited under 'With ...' on the film titles and played Thomas Willoughby, one of a group of four officer friends serving in the Royal North Surrey Regiment, sent to the Sudan to avenge General Gordon's death at Khartoum. Three of them take a dim view of Harry Faversham's (Anthony Steele) desire to resign his commission and he's branded a coward by being given three white feathers by his friends. Faversham then spends the rest of the film earning his contemporaries' forgiveness and respect by rescuing them all from the Arabs.

Ian, having been a soldier and an officer in the Second World

War, made perfect fictional officer material, straight backed and with stiff upper lip firmly set:

C.O.:	The general idea is to look stupid and make as much noise as possible. That shouldn't be very difficult for you, Willoughby.
Willoughby:	Oh, thank you!

And, about to be sent on a dangerous mission:

Willoughby:	Is it true you asked for me for this little job?
C.O.:	Yes, Tom.
Willoughby:	(*Sardonically*) Thank you so much.

Ian also acquitted himself well in the action sequences, convincingly using a rifle in a prison breakout. One critic was presciently the first to note that he provided 'the silly ass motif'[52], a phrase that would return to haunt Ian on more occasions than he cared to remember.

Full of gung-ho attitude and the feeling that 'there's no place in England for a coward', *Storm Over the Nile* was handicapped by its origins in a pre-Second World War film which predated the 'total war' of the 1939–45 conflict, and by being released during the chilly ambiguities of the Cold War between the United States and the Soviet Union, a point that wasn't lost on reviewers. 'What will the younger generation … make of these old fashioned heroics?'[53] the *Star* wondered, while the *Sunday Times* optimistically summed the film up as 'good colour photography: schoolboy sentiments: handsome battles.'[54]

Even at this early stage in his film career and in a supporting role Ian discreetly shone, and his admirably stoic performance (which looked tailor-made for the nineteenth century) was praised along with his three co-stars as 'impeccable'.[55]

By 1955, British cinema needed more than the *Boy's Own* heroics of *Betrayed* and *Storm Over the Nile* or the repressed, suffering-for-the-good-of-all Englishmen in *The Cruel Sea* (1952) and *The Dam*

Busters (1954) that contorted 'the stiff upper lip into something like a deathly grimace.'[56] The narrative of the former film was constructed like a history lesson, designed to educate the audience that 'war is hell' but was, dammit, necessary. Ian's next film *The Colditz Story* left behind the rigid stereotypes. Taken directly from the pages of Major Patrick Reid's wartime memoir of the same name, away from John Mills's and Eric Portman's serious central performances were insouciant, clever Englishmen flippantly taunting the Germans as they faced a grim incarceration in the Third Reich's supposedly escape-proof prison. Part of the formula of war films of the time was that the Germans were uniformly dour, and in *The Colditz Story*, one of them, a fat and jovial man, even commented on how the British thought that Germans were supposed to have no sense of humour, showing how much the clichés of the genre had been subverted. *The Colditz Story* was also a very funny film, mainly because of Ian and Richard Wattis's double act as the Grenadier Guards officers Robin Cartwright and Richard Gordon, confounding their Nazi oppressors with impromptu wit. Ian impressed from the moment the determinedly nonchalant Cartwright appeared, telling a brusque guard not to shout and to stop being such 'a self-inflated little man.' As the main comic relief in the film, Ian and Wattis provided the humour and comedy routines, which included tricking the Germans into shooting at a dummy called 'Agatha' hanging from a high window.

If their on-screen partnership succeeded by looking so natural, it was because Ian and Richard had quickly formed a bond during the making of *The Colditz Story*. They had both been to school at Bromsgrove and, during shared hire-car journeys to Shepperton Studios where the film was being made, Ian warmed more and more to the balding man with owlish spectacles and a haughty voice. He recalled, 'Once again in my life, a friendship was established on the solid and, to me, infallible foundation of concordant senses of humour.'[57] His early-morning and evening rides with 'Dickie'[58] made bearable the experience of having to get up at 6.30 a.m. and go to bed at midnight after performing in *Going to Town*.

In his ninth film role, Ian had progressed to being listed as sixth in the credits after the two main stars John Mills and Eric Portman, rapid progress for a performer only five years into his film career. *The Colditz Story* also showed – much more than *Betrayed* – how accomplished he was as a dramatic actor. There was a real tension in Ian's performance as the prisoners mounted 'Colditz Capers', a concert designed to conceal an escape attempt. In a piece of bravura directing by Guy Hamilton, the camera cuts in shot by shot to a close-up of Ian's eye staring intently through a gap in the curtain, as he checks that all the German officers are present in the audience so they won't detect the prison break being prepared under the stage. Director of Photography Gordon Dines's bleached, almost expressionistic black and white photography added immeasurably to the suspense of the scene and the film as a whole, emphasising the harshness of being a prisoner of war.

With the escape going according to plan, Ian and Wattis slip easily into their Flanagan and Allen tribute act, performing a relaxed, synchronised dance routine as they sing 'Underneath the Arches' with some vintage jokes dropped in, including one that the comedian Eric Morecambe would later make famous:

Gordon:	What's that on your shoulder?
Cartwright:	What this?
Gordon:	Yes.
Cartwright:	It's a Greek urn.
Gordon:	What's a Greek urn?
Cartwright:	Oh, I don't know, about thirty bob a week, I think

Reflecting on his success in revue in the 18 February 1954 issue of the *Stage*, Ian said, 'I'm afraid that managers and directors may think of me only as a revue artist, and much as I enjoy acting in sketches I feel there must be a limit to the number of characters one is able to create. What I would like now is to be offered a part in light comedy or a farce.'[59] Thanks to the generosity of the legendary theatrical impresario Hugh 'Binkie' Beaumont, who had subsequently taken an interest in Ian's career, his wish was granted when Beaumont offered him the part of TV producer David Prentice in Alan Melville's new comedy *Simon and Laura*, playing opposite Dora Bryan as Joan, a television scriptwriter.

There was a sense of Ian biting the hand that had helped feed him and his family by appearing in Melville's play as it was a wickedly funny topical satire on BBC Television, an institution that had been growing in popularity throughout the early 1950s, reaching an early peak in the sales of TV sets for Queen Elizabeth II's Coronation in 1953. Of course, Ian had actually been a BBC TV producer, which made his casting even more apposite. The play concerned the troubled marriage of Simon and Laura Foster, two out-of-work actors who are offered the chance to star in a daily, fictionalised version of their relationship. Putting on a brave face for the sake of the cash possibilities, complications arise from romantic misunderstandings with Prentice and Joan until television, a medium that is repeatedly shown throughout the play as artificial, inadvertently transmits the truth about Simon and David's feelings for Laura and Joan. (Perhaps there was hope for the new medium after all).

Starring as the raffish Simon and the flirtatious Laura were the theatrical veterans Roland Culver and Coral Browne. Despite being a refined and stylish actress, Coral occasionally let the more earthy side of her Australian nature show. One evening, a sure-fire laugh from the audience on one of her lines of dialogue fell flat because the mature actor who was playing Simon and Laura's butler Wilson distracted the audience with the more elaborate than normal manner in which he was laying a table for dinner. After the curtain fell and on the way back to their dressing rooms, Coral suddenly wished Ian well in getting on with her understudy who would be deputising for the following week's performances:

I was dumbfounded. 'Understudy?' I said. 'Why? What's happening to you?'

'I'm going into hospital to have an operation,' she replied.

I was even more dumbfounded. 'I had no idea,' I said. 'I am sorry. What are you going to have done?' – and, half turning to the elderly character actor who was following behind us, she said, 'I'm going to have eyes put in the back of my fucking head.'[60]

Ian's sense of achievement in making it into, as he saw it, legitimate theatre was heightened when in the spring of 1955 the Rank Organisation contacted de Wolffe and Stone to offer him the part of David Prentice in the film version of *Simon and Laura*. Even more excitingly, the movie was going to be made in colour, a sure sign of how well Rank expected the film to perform. As initial filming and the final performances of the play overlapped, Ian felt some awkwardness, as he was the only actor from the original stage production who had been asked to appear in the film. However, his sensitivity soon evaporated under the welcoming *bonhomie* of Peter Finch, playing Simon, the effervescent Kay Kendall (Laura) and the gamine Muriel Pavlow (Joan).

Director Muriel Box's translation of *Simon and Laura* into a movie made the story into a remarkably modern, still relevant comment on the artificial nature of television and the vacuity of fame. The title of the film also being the title of the TV series in the film added an extra layer of self-awareness to a playful satire that, among other things, poked fun at the BBC's reputation for being tight-fisted with money, the pedestrian nature of television professionals – Joan, *Simon and Laura*'s scriptwriter, was a graduate of *Insect Life in British Ponds* – and how the class system dominated the BBC; Simon and Laura's agent Bertie (Hubert Gregg) happily informed his clients that the head of BBC Contracts 'used to be my fag at Eton.'

In retrospect, it's fascinating to watch the emergence of Ian's popular screen persona before it hardened into an archetype. Prentice may have had a tendency to take his jacket off and execute a bizarre, loping walk when he was thinking things through, but he was no fool. There is none of the later stumbling foppery in his courtship of Joan – he just asks her out and she accepts, recognising Prentice as a relaxed, sensible and engaging young man. The TV producer is not above losing his temper and throwing his fists around either, giving Simon a black eye during a row on the Christmas Day Special after simmering resentments among the four principal characters come to a head.

The major achievement of Ian's characterisation of David Prentice is that it doesn't look like an actor giving a performance, a criticism that could be made of Kay Kendall and Peter Finch's more grandstanding turns as the eponymous Simon and Laura, entertaining though they undoubtedly are. With effortless ease, Ian delivered a fully rounded, three-dimensional character whose humour arose from his personality, beliefs and opinions rather than a reliance solely on one-liners or physical comedy routines, perhaps explaining why he had been the only cast member of the original stage play retained for the film version. In an unassuming way, Ian's characterisation of Prentice was an important step forward for British screen comedy and its significance wasn't lost on the reviewers of the time, even though he actually had very few funny lines. The *Evening News* praised the 'life-like portrait of a little BBC Caesar from Ian Carmichael,'[61] the *Daily Sketch* proclaimed that 'Carmichael's study of an earnest young TV producer walks off with the film'[62] and the *Daily Mail* considered his performance to be 'a masterpiece of comedy.'[63] Elsewhere, the *Daily Herald* advised its readers to 'watch out ... for the imminent rise to stardom of Ian Carmichael, who plays the producer with wit and gusto'[64] while the *The Times* boldly stated 'Mr Ian Carmichael, as the BBC producer, comes close to stealing the film from [Peter Finch and Kay Kendal].'[65]

His time had come.

CHAPTER 7

Lucky Ian

The Boulting brothers and film stardom

I AN'S SUCCESS IN landing an 'also starring' role in the film version of *Simon and Laura* was quickly overshadowed by a phone call he received from his agent. The unflappable Richard Stone calmly told his client that the Boulting brothers, a talented film partnership of identical twins, had come calling. 'They rang up my agent one day with, I think, a banal statement that "We want to make him a film star"[1],' Ian would later recall with typical understatement.

The Boultings had built up a considerable reputation by the spring of 1955 when they approached Ian. Forming their company Charter Films in 1937, Roy Alfred Clarence and John Edward Boulting (born on 21 December 1913) stood out in the British film industry as independent film-makers with a social conscience. Both were committed to the Liberal Party – John had fought with the Communists against fascism during the Spanish Civil War – and while they would take it in turns to produce, direct and sometimes write, most of their films dealt with socially and politically relevant issues. Their movies educated and informed, but they also entertained.

During the previous decade, the Boultings had made *Pastor Hall* (1940), the first British film openly to condemn Nazism, and the first of their productions to be well received by both audiences and critics. During the Second World War, the brothers eagerly played their part, Roy making documentaries for the Army Film Unit while John went one step further, producing a dramatised documentary about a bomber crew for the Royal Air Force in 1945's *Journey Together*. (It starred a young actor called Richard Attenborough, who would remain a committed Boulting collaborator.) From there, the twins fashioned an even more impressive body of work. Among their later achievements was *Fame is the Spur* (1947), starring Michael Redgrave as a socialist firebrand whose principles are gradually eroded by the Establishment, a contentious subject in a country then under a Labour government. 1948 saw their adaptation of the Graham Greene novel *Brighton Rock*, which brought the seediness of seaside crime vividly to life, and had a mesmerising central performance by Attenborough as the psychotic Pinkie. 1950 offered *Seven Days to Noon*, an edgy contemporary thriller about the threat of nuclear terrorism in London that, typically for the Boultings, was equivocal in its portrayal of the bomber and the authorities desperately trying to track him down.

It's easy to see why Ian, an ex-serviceman and avid cinema-goer, was flattered and rather stunned by the Boultings' attention. After his agent's phone call, he went downstairs to tell Pym. Her reaction to her husband's unexpected good fortune was, perhaps, quite understandable: 'she looked at me as if it were forenoon on 1st April'[2].

As Ian reeled at the offer of working with two of the country's most innovative film-makers, the national mood in Britain, which had always been of interest to the Boultings, was subtly changing. Food rationing had ended in July 1954, and its abolition coincided with the economy picking up, leaving behind post-war austerity and entering a consumer-driven boom. For the first time, many households were affluent enough to enjoy the benefits of appliances like fridges, washing machines and, particularly, televisions. At the same time, there was the waning of respect for the Establishment, symbolised by the fragmentation of the Empire – something which the United Kingdom could no longer afford – which would reach its nadir with Britain's humiliating failure to control the Suez Canal with France in 1956. This move away from traditional values such as respect for one's elders and 'betters', and the beginnings of a more materialistic culture could also be seen in the emergence of the teenager: a new, economically independent young person able to enjoy a liberating lifestyle of fun, fashion and modern music. (The teenagers' preferred music of choice, rock and roll, arrived in late 1956, and was immediately seen as the end of civilisation as it was then known.)

The undercurrent of irreverence stirring in the nation had first manifested itself on the cinema screen in the 1954 comedy *The Belles of St Trinian's*, an anarchic live-action cartoon in which nearly everyone, from the very un-ladylike St Trinian's public school girls to their near-bankrupt headmistress, is a criminal, a drunk or a gambler or out for themselves. Similarly inspired to spotlight changes in modern Britain that weren't necessarily for the best, the Boulting brothers offered Ian the chance to be the central figure in their new series of film satires. Like the St Trinian's films, the twins' movies would be strikingly different to the staple 1950s British cinema diet of stiff-upper-lipped Second World War heroes and sometimes twee Ealing Studios comedies that Lindsay Anderson, who would become the *enfant terrible* of British cinema in the 1960s, bemoaned as 'snobbish, emotionally inhibited, wilfully blind to the conditions of the present, dedicated to an out-of-date, exhausted national idea'[3].

In sympathy with Anderson's viewpoint, the twins' new target was the Establishment itself, and shortly after contacting Ian, on 2 April 1955 they sent him two new novels of which they wanted to make film adaptations with him as the lead. They were *Private's Progress* by Alan Hackney and *Brothers in Law* by Henry Cecil – gleefully irreverent satires on army life during the Second World War and the legal profession respectively, bastions of the British state that hadn't previously known such open criticism. Delighted, Ian considered the roles 'tailor made for me,'[4] and, with a spring in his step, walked into the Boultings' office in London's Grosvenor Street to discuss the firm offer of starring in two films, with the further promise of being 'under contract to do a certain number of films at pre-arranged prices'.[5]

The young actor bonded with the twins immediately, an empathy that was helped by them being as fanatical about cricket as Ian was (John even had an oil painting of W.G. Grace, the legendary England and Gloucestershire cricketer, above his desk). Their temperaments and ways of working were very much in accord; calm and thoughtful, the bespectacled John and the chain-smoking Roy would always carefully consider Ian's views on a role or particular scene and either agree graciously, or articulately and convincingly tell him why he was wrong. The atmosphere on their studio sets was tranquil, a quiet air of calm concentration in which voices were never raised. 'If one was directing, the other was producing,' Ian recalled unequivocally. 'If they had any disagreement, it was in the office afterwards, it never came on the stage. But I think they were just in so much accord.'[6] Sometimes, if there was a piano on the set and the studio was on a break, John would relax the mood further by attempting to accompany Ian's singing of 'Home Again', the song that closed the *Globe* and *Lyric* revues. In such a relaxed, productive and creative atmosphere, it was no wonder that he felt his work for the Boultings 'gave me more pleasure than anything I had done before.'[7]

Speculating about which of the creative pair he enjoyed working with the most, Ian remarked:

> I found that people who had worked for John and Roy, when they were asked that question, they nearly always answered by naming the first one who had directed them. They were both absolutely *ace* – they were very, very good, one was not better than the other. But I worked first with John and I was terribly inexperienced in the film industry, and John was my guru. He was absolutely superb and took me through with great tenderness and care and sensitivity, and so John was my favourite, always. But that is not to decry Roy.'[8]

If Ian was content during the twelve-week shoot for *Private's Progress*, his route to a starring film role had been anything but. He had vigorously fought against what he saw as the prejudices of the entertainment industry in order to gain his current position, although when he eventually learned how the Boultings had chosen him, Ian would exasperatedly wonder if all his angst and hard work had been worth it after all:

> I'd done all these revues, and in those days casting directors were a little bit bigoted in their approach. If you were a revue artist, they considered you a revue artist but [not] an actor, whereas all intimate revue, really, was not done by singers and dancers, it was largely actors and actresses who could sing a bit and dance a bit. But as far as film and play casting directors were concerned, you were a revue artist. So I thought 'I've got to fight like blazes to get out of revue and into a play.' Eventually I succeeded in doing it thanks to Binkie Beaumont, who I worked for a lot in revue, and he gave me this play *Simon and Laura*, and the moment I'd done this the Boultings rang up and offered me [a] contract.
>
> It was much later on that I said to John Boulting, 'It is extraordinary, you know, once I got into a play you immediately saw me as an actor' and he said 'Absolute nonsense, dear boy, absolute nonsense. We cast you because of that undressing-on-the-beach sketch we saw you do in *The Globe Revue*, and furthermore when we came to try and remember your name, we couldn't.'⁹

Private's Progress opened to the public at the Rialto cinema in London on 17 February 1956, barely three months after the buzz in the press about Ian's potential as a screen actor in *Simon and Laura* had died down. Indeed, the Boultings were so impressed with their new star that Ian appeared in four different poses on the film poster. The critics confirmed the twins' faith by being almost unanimous in their praise for his star turn as the hapless Private Stanley Windrush (a surname that referenced the SS *Empire Windrush*, the ocean liner that had brought Jamaican immigrants to Britain in June 1948). The film became one of the popular hits of the year, not least because it was released when National Service in the armed forces was still compulsory for all young men in Britain, immediately striking a personal chord with a large percentage of the cinema-going public. The success of *Private's Progress* completely vindicated the Boulting brothers' dedication to making films that were 'extremely serious without being solemn'.[10]

The film was a watershed for the twins as, in its critique of British life, it turned away from the sometimes grim subject-matter of their earlier work towards comic observation. Ian's Windrush was a naive innocent, called up to the British army during the Second World War and caught up in the machinations of rank-and-file malingerers, petty criminals, deserters and, at the other end of the scale, senior officers who, to a man, were corrupt and self-interested. Under the Boultings' subversive direction, the film had finally broken the mould of the British war film that *The Colditz Story* had cracked a year before. (Such a departure from the twins' patriotic work wasn't lost on the War Office, which withdrew the promised help with locations, vehicles and weapons once they'd read the script, adding around an extra £5,000 to the film's budget.[11])

The beaming innocence and endearing physical clumsiness of Stanley Windrush, part of a cosseted and eccentric upper-class family, represented a type of Englishman, who, by the mid-1950s, was dwindling in significance in British life due to the decrease in importance of the upper class as a political force. Actor Kenneth Griffith, a close friend of Roy Boulting, recalled that 'Ian Carmichael [personified] the innocent face of England – already disappearing as the last of British ethics disappeared; strangely enough, hand-in-hand with the disappearance of the Old Empire.'[12] The setting for the film might have been the 1940s, but its tone and characters, propelled by an up-tempo, brass-heavy soundtrack, were definitely 1955.

Private's Progress also introduced cinema audiences to a raft of British character actors who, with some additions, formed the core ensemble casts of the Boultings' remaining 1950s and early 1960s films. Kenneth Griffith, John Le Mesurier, Dennis Price, David Lodge, Victor Maddern, Miles Malleson and, in particular, the gap-toothed, grinning presence of Terry-Thomas more than complemented old Boulting hands like the fresh-faced Richard Attenborough and the glowering William Hartnell. Such a collection of talent populated the screen with a memorable rogues' gallery of grotesques, from Thomas's frustrated, boozy Major Hitchcock to Price's suavely criminal Uncle Bertram.

Acting opposite such potentially scene-stealing performers could have been intimidating for a young actor, but as the innocent at large, Ian's characterisation was designed to react against the more scene-stealing performances. The graceful ease with which he makes what could have been an upper-class caricature into a convincing and sympathetic portrayal of an unworldly man led astray is what ultimately makes the whole film work.

The reviewers of the time certainly thought so. As far as they were concerned, a major new talent had arrived, the *Daily Herald* astutely recognising that 'Ian Carmichael's air of bewildered innocence ... is going to make him a star.'[13] 'Whether as satirist or slapstick artist, Mr Carmichael here looks like the best discovery of the kind since the war ended,'[14] proclaimed the *Evening News*, while the *Northern Chronicle* was delighted that Ian was 'now deservedly promoted to stardom ... He is extremely funny throughout – not least when he staggers home last in a Company cross-country run, carrying one shoe and looking more sodden than his own socks.'[15] The *Star* observed that Ian's 'vague, comic innocence confirms the bright promise he showed as the harassed young television producer in *Simon and Laura*'[16], while the *Sunday Express* noted his talent for 'wearing the resigned look of someone who walks into a man-hole on every one of life's corners.'[17] Away from the comedy, *The Times* praised the subtleties in Ian's performance, admiring his 'unfailing tact and sympathy.'[18]

His comic highlights are numerous, but standouts include the sequence in which Windrush arrives back at camp drunk and very disorderly from the local pub, asking for his 'gaspirator' and giving his rank and name as '999 Picklepuss' to a stone-faced David Lodge. In another scene, he does a marvellous double take as he realises Major Hitchcock is watching the same film he and his mates have gone AWOL to see. Elsewhere, memorably confronted by a twitchy army psychiatrist assessing his suitability as an officer played by the formidable John Le Mesurier, Ian acquits himself well with a beguiling combination of keenness and bewilderment:

Psychiatrist:	Right …
Windrush:	Wrong.
Psychiatrist:	No, no, no, I haven't started yet.
Windrush:	Ah.
Psychiatrist:	Beer?
Windrush:	Sheba.
Psychiatrist:	Coffin?
Windrush:	Spitting.
Psychiatrist:	No, no, no! 'Coffin'. C-O double F-I-N.
Windrush:	Oh, um … gravestone.
Psychiatrist:	Mother?
Windrush:	Hubbard.
Psychiatrist:	Father?
Windrush:	Boiled beef and carrots!

Something *Private's Progress* had been criticised for was how the mood changed from military lampooning to a dramatic raid behind enemy lines in the final reel, a change in tone the *Evening News* considered 'a serious weakness of the picture. The Boultings' humour seems to have gone sour midway.'[19] The reviewer missed the point, as the mood change was part of the satire: while audiences had been invited to chuckle at the petty crimes of Windrush and his comrades, Uncle Bertram's raid was on an altogether grander criminal scale – posing as commander of a German platoon to steal art treasures for his own profit – and, consequently, no laughing matter.

In a film that was a showcase for Ian's talents, this shift in emphasis allowed him the opportunity to show how versatile an actor he really was, demonstrating his confidence in playing scenes that were tense and dramatic. In a performance of finely observed detail, his hand visibly shakes as he holds a gun on two German officers (one of whom is an uncredited Christopher Lee) and, after discovering their suicide, he nearly vomits and shakily wipes perspiration from his forehead and the sweat band of his cap. The awkward Windrush from earlier in the film had gone, and been replaced by a believably frightened man clearly out of his depth.

Controversial changes in tone apart, *Private's Progress* was a successful validation of the Boultings' new approach to social and political comment, and six months after its release it had reportedly earned them £150,000 in profit.[20] The left-wing *Tribune* summed up the general consensus of opinion when it said:

> There is nothing the Establishment fears more than the custard-pie, simply because there is no answer to it. Even if you dodge successfully, your top hat still falls off.
>
> I can think of many suitable recipients of custard-pies in the contemporary British scene, and I am hoping that John and Roy Boulting, emboldened by the enthusiastic support the British public has given to *Private's Progress*, are keeping another nice, large, round squishy one carefully concealed behind their backs.[21]

The film was such a departure from the patriotic genre of Second World War films that were a regular feature in British cinemas that a Mr R. Parker, a cinema owner in Exeter, caused a memorable *faux pas* with his local barracks. Without seeing the Boultings' latest offering, and assuming that *Private's Progress* would help the Devonshire Regiment and Wessex Brigades with their recruitment campaigns, Parker arranged with them for uniforms, equipment and sentry boxes to be put on display in his cinema's foyer. On the day the film opened, a party of fifty officers and men, complete with a bugle band, were due to march through Exeter to the cinema before the curtain went up. By the time the inaugural screening day of *Private's Progress* arrived, someone further up the chain of command had clearly taken the trouble to watch the film, resulting in a swift withdrawal of the army's co-operation. 'Nobody has turned up,'[22] Parker told the press, clearly bemused. 'Three army lorries came to the cinema and removed everything, lock, stock and sentry boxes. I had reserved fifty seats for the army party. We were even going to have a recruiting sergeant in the foyer and all my girls were dressed in red tunics and busbies. They had to strip them off and hand them back.'[23] The whole PR debacle was like a scene from *Private's Progress* itself and would, no doubt, have rendered John and Roy Boulting helpless with laughter.

For Ian and Pym, the instant, almost overnight success that Ian's first collaboration with the Boultings brought seemed unreal: suddenly he was a national figure and could see his picture 'featured in those movie magazines that I used to buy and study so avidly as a boy.'[24] The tide of good fortune continued. Following the success of *Simon and Laura*, the Rank Organisation had offered Ian a three-film contract, in what the *Daily Mail* reported as Rank's bid to 'set [him] on a big money career as the new bright hope of British pictures'[25]. Now apparently the darling of both the biggest film company in England as well as an iconoclastic independent, Ian Gillett Carmichael couldn't quite believe his luck. Which was to prove just as well.

The initial signs for Ian's Rank career were good, with his first comedy film for them, *The Big Money*, to be made in the still novel, and expensive, medium of colour, a clear indication of how much faith Rank had in their new signing. Striking blonde actress-of-the-moment Belinda Lee was the love interest, distinctive character actor Robert Helpmann co-starred as a memorable villain disguised as a priest, and the whole enterprise was in the capable hands of the experienced director John Paddy Carstairs, who had helmed the successful Norman Wisdom comedies *Trouble in Store* (1953) and *Man of the Moment* (1955) for Rank.

Encouragingly, Ian's character was a marked departure from the upper-class Windrush, offering him the chance to broaden his repertoire in only his second starring film role. Willie Frith is an inept, working-class pick pocket with a Teddy Boy quiff, one of a family of petty crooks who inadvertently acquire a case full of counterfeit notes, 'the big money' of the title. Intrigue and chaos then ensue as Helpmann's gang try to reclaim their ill-gotten gains while Willie attempts to impress Belinda Lee's barmaid with the stolen money.

What happened next in the production of the film starkly brought home to Ian the difference between the Boultings' relaxed, democratic approach to film-making, which meant they had worked with him almost as an equal partner, and how a large organisation like Rank expected its stars to behave. Coming from *Private's Progress*, a film on which he felt 'everything was superb and beautiful and well directed,'[26] Ian was confident enough to be very blunt about the shortcomings of his new script: '[*The Big Money*] was appalling; it really was the most *awful* farce I'd ever read ... I loathed it'.[27] He urged Joseph Janni, the producer, to rewrite a screenplay that he felt, after a promising beginning, deteriorated into 'the broadest comedy clichés.'[28] Even though Janni and Carstairs apparently didn't share their leading man's reservations, on the Thursday before filming began at Pinewood Studios, Ian received a phone call from Bryan Forbes, a fellow actor he had worked with on *The Colditz Story*, who was now developing a second career as a staff writer and script doctor on problem screenplays. It came as something of a surprise to Ian to learn that Forbes had been instructed to tighten up the script for *The Big Money* before shooting started. Ian quickly realised that in Rank pictures if a leading actor had a valid criticism of the script, that insight would be publicly ignored, even if it was privately acted on: a clear case of 'actors act and writers write'.

Undeterred by having caught out his new employers, or perhaps spurred on because of it, Ian accepted Forbes's offer to help with the script changes and, in particular, rewrite the part of Willie to suit Ian's acting style. Easily slipping back into the writing skills he had honed at the BBC, Rank's star-in-waiting 'spent the weekend with [Forbes] and we knocked out something that was really very much of an improvement.'[29] However, Ian's well-meaning, extra-curricular work met with short shrift from Rank's management: 'Earl St John, the executive producer at Rank, rang [Forbes] the next day and said, "I gather you've been speaking to Ian Carmichael over the weekend." Bryan said, "Yes, it's a film for him," so [St John said] "Right, I'm taking you off it, kid, send the script back." So, the script went back and I had ... to shoot it [as originally written], we did it, and I wasn't happy with it *at all*.'[30]

The attitude of Rank's management was hard to fathom. From recognising that their new star had been right about the script needing work – even if they didn't agree openly – they judged Ian's extramural, if arguably naïve, input into rewrites to be completely unacceptable within their studio structure, even if he *had* improved the quality of what they were about to spend a lot of money making. The curious saga of *The Big Money* took an even more dramatic turn when, after the film had finally been shot, edited and shown to Rank boss John Davis, he decided that, having spent some £175,000 on the movie, he wouldn't release it because 'it wasn't funny enough.'[31]

Somehow, the situation was leaked to the press, and on 23 July 1956 the *Daily Mail* ran a story about the film's shelving. At the time riding high on the success of *Private's Progress*, very much in the public eye and therefore newsworthy, Ian was sought out for a quote. He was understandably diplomatic, declining to mention the back-stage politics he'd been involved in but pointedly distancing himself from the *The Big Money*'s perceived failure: 'All I can say is that if the powers that be think it unfunny, I'm relieved they are not going to show it. I applaud the courage of Mr Davis's decision, but I can take no responsibility for the unfunniness of the film.'[32] On the same day that the story appeared in the *Mail*, the Boulting brothers took the unprecedented step of sending a telegram to the *Daily Sketch* defending their new leading man. Published the next day, it went a step further than Ian's tactful remarks, stating in a comment designed to infuriate those Rank insiders in the know, 'Carmichael warned ... executives last year that the script was not good and urged comprehensive rewriting.'[33]

It was no surprise that following the troubled production of *The Big Money* Ian's contract with Rank was terminated by mutual agreement in mid 1955. It had been a hard lesson – a secondary film career with the biggest film studio in England was stillborn but, in a sign of Ian's evident integrity, he had shown that he couldn't stand by while bad decisions were made, even if his commitment to artistic improvements went beyond what the powers that be considered appropriate territory for an actor. It also wouldn't be the last time in his career that Ian would be at loggerheads with his creative collaborators.

With some relief, then, Ian returned to the Boulting fold, visiting London's Law Courts in preparation for his role as Roger Thursby, the tyro barrister at the centre of *Brothers in Law*. On the day shooting commenced at the British National Studios in Borehamwood, it was Ian's thirty-sixth birthday and director Roy Boulting wished him 'many happy returns' before the camera started rolling, clearly a good sign for the actor after the previous stressful four months. Typically for the Boultings' well-drilled production machine, the shoot was a smooth one, even if the twins were refused permission to film in the main lobby of the Law Courts and the dining hall of Bencher's in Gray's Inn. However, the canny brothers turned this setback into an asset, speculating on the reasons for the refusal in the press release for the film in early 1957:

> To date this legal mystery remains unsolved. The Boultings wonder – was the script too funny? Was there too little pomp and too much humerus [sic] circumstance? Was the script too true to be good – for the legal johnnies? Or perhaps those irate brass hats in Whitehall gave a sharp warning to the white wigs?
>
> Nevertheless, the team that made *Private's Progress* carried on with their now much more expansive task, and completed yet another – FILM THAT <u>THEY</u> DIDN'T WANT MADE![34]

Ian was by now a bona fide celebrity, and journalists were keen to interview him in as much detail as he would allow. In late

November, *Picturegoer* magazine was exceptionally excited that he might be departing for Hollywood in view of the positive press he had received there for *Private's Progress*, praising 'a rare comic performance'[35] and 'perhaps the most brilliant young comedian in British films.'[36] A firm offer that *had* recently been put to Ian was the chance of starring on Broadway, but he was in two minds about leaving behind his beloved England once more: 'It would mean uprooting the whole family ... Besides, when I came back it might mean building up my career all over again.'[37]

Interviewed in a two-part article by Margaret Hinxman entitled 'Britain's Conquering Clown', it was the first time Ian had talked at length about his life and career in the press. He was refreshingly and disarmingly honest, discussing everything from his parents to his insecurities about his chosen profession. '[My parents] were quite wonderful,'[38] he revealed. 'They never tried to dissuade me. When they saw I'd made up my mind [to act] they gave me all the help they could.'[39] Ian went on to talk about how he was at a difficult personal crossroads in his life when he was demobbed from the army. 'I was in an agony of indecision. I went into the army as a boy. I'd already done a year of show business. Yet it was the life I wanted to live and I loved it. But after the war I was a man. I had responsibilities – a wife and a child. And I was getting nowhere.

'I felt like someone driving a car and knowing that he's headed for disaster, but not being able to take his foot off the accelerator,' he admitted. 'For two pins I'd have chucked it all. It was a desperate, horrible feeling. Why didn't I give up? Because of cowardice. Not pride or courage or anything noble like that. But cowardice. I just kept hanging on and hanging on, hoping and waiting.'[40]

In the second part of Hinxman's interview, Ian discussed his attitude to money, a philosophy that may go some way to explaining the reputation for being less than charitable that he was already acquiring among his colleagues. 'I want comfort for my children and I want them to have the leisurely, contented childhood that I had,' he explained. 'I don't mind about myself. I don't even mind so much about my wife – though I love her dearly. But I mind about them. That's why I don't throw my money around. I don't go to nightclubs or lavish money on unnecessary things. Partly because I don't want to, but also because I want to give the children a good, solid background that money can help to provide.'[41]

Released at the beginning of March, *Brothers in Law* followed the same template as *Private's Progress*, with an innocent everyman figure – Carmichael's Thursby – conducted through the rituals and pitfalls of another Establishment institution, with a second Richard Attenborough character, Henry Marshall, as his guide. If the humour is more genteel in nature than that of *Private's Progress*, it's because the British legal system as depicted here appears to be trapped in the nineteenth century. It's surely no coincidence that the portly figure of the absent-minded and eccentric Grimes (Miles Malleson), rushing from one case to the next through the cloisters of the court with Thursby trailing behind, suggests the eccentric characters of Charles Dickens. Another Dickensian character, the amiable cockney crook Archie Green (Terry-Thomas, playing against his usual persona of the 'bang-on' upper-class rogue), almost steals the film in a scene where he enlightens Thursby on how to have the case against him dismissed:

> **Thursby:** In almost every respect, I'd say you were utterly and deplorably wrong.
>
> **Green:** Eh?
>
> **Thursby:** But on this single point of law, I'm reluctantly obliged to agree that you're right. On a technicality they must discharge you.
>
> **Green:** Well, of course they must. I've given you the ammunition, all you've got to do is fire the gun and come out of court another satisfied client of Alfie Green. So do me a favour, will you? Go and do it.

Although over forty years of widely reported legal blunders and corruption have blunted the film's point, *Brothers in Law* was cutting-edge satire in 1957. The suggestion that the legal profession was an exclusive clique that contained almost-senile bumblers who entrusted cases to inexperienced barristers and was full of criminals who knew how to exploit the system, was as ground-breaking in its day as G.F. Newman's raw exposé of police sleaze, the BBC drama series *Law and Order*, would be in 1978. Perhaps mindful of its daring, *Brothers in Law* backed away from the satire in the final reel to show Thursby winning his first major court case fair and square, in a cosy, Ealing Studios-style ending that has his legal triumph witnessed by family and friends.

The Boultings did, however, reserve some bite for the final scenes: Thursby and Marshall are shown dressed identically and walking in step together, brothers in law, effectively legal 'twins'. The point is a little clumsily reinforced at their lodgings, when two attractive identical female twins they are clearly attracted to arrive to stay.

With two films in a similar vein now released, it was possible to discern the differences between the Boultings' approach to comedy and that of Ealing Studios, the film company that had made an equally impressive name for itself with witty critiques of English culture such as *Passport to Pimlico* (1949) and *The Man in the White Suit* (1951). Shortly after *Brothers in Law*'s release, one commentator observed of the Boultings, 'like the men of Ealing they choose a British institution or some genuine aspect of British life for their scene, but their treatment of it is satirical rather than laudatory, fantastic rather than down-to-earth, urbane and sophisticated rather than proletarian. They have the sort of blissful imagination that can see the elaborately comic possibilities in ordinary material.'[42]

Ian appeared more relaxed in his second Boultings outing, totally at ease and believable playing a character a lot younger than his thirty-six years, and confident enough to underplay the humour as the more restrained tone of the film demanded. As ever, he was adept and accomplished at the physical comedy, making it believably gauche. Gems included his stumbling over a golf bag and fumbling with the clubs in an important 'social' match with a moody judge played by his *Private's Progress* sparring partner John Le Mesurier. With hands shaking and eyes closed as he takes the swing, the scene is funny because the inept Thursby is taking it so seriously. Also priceless is the barrister's baptism of fire in court as the judge feeds him the legal terms he doesn't know, Ian running through facial expressions ranging from terror to gratitude to incredulity; it's made even funnier by the judge continually getting his name wrong.

Ian remained a hit with the critics. Indeed, the critics were almost falling over themselves to praise him. The *Daily Sketch* applauded 'Carmichael's triumph in his best performance yet, and the Boultings' skill that the blundering hero never loses our sympathy amid the laughter.'[43] The *Evening Standard* went further, singling Ian out as 'our best light comedian'[44], while the *Daily Herald* was taken with his 'startled, double-take face'[45] and the *Manchester Guardian* described him as 'a natural, irrepressibly funny in his well-bred, well-intentioned, bewildered ineptitude.'[46] In the *News Chronicle*, there was a timely assessment of how Ian had perfected his comic gifts:

> I foresee the day when we shall have no better screen comedian in Britain. Vaudeville, of course, runs in his blood; and he has learnt not only to work for his effects but [also] to tone them to a hair's breadth in the hard school of West End revue. He will slave for hours to perfect one stumble on a stairway and, having got it, will make it seem effortless thereafter.[47]

The film was conclusive proof that Ian wasn't a one-film wonder, another achievement for the Boultings which was, if anything, more palatable than their previous offering, as it '[substituted] warmth and humanity for the sour cynicism of *Private's Progress*.'[48]

Ian may have appeared more comfortable in *Brothers in Law* because in March 1956 he had been awarded a prestigious Silver Heart by the Royal Variety Club of Great Britain, engraved with the encouraging endorsement: 'The Actor Who Made the Most Progress in 1955'. By the time shooting started on his second movie for the Boultings, he was also socialising with his employers. The trio's shared love of cricket had resulted in a complete set of cricket paraphernalia accompanying the film unit on location. This would be assembled next to the film set, and the moment shooting stopped due to lack of sun, the whole crew would pick up bails, ball and bat and start playing. For Ian, it must have been the quintessential English way to make movies.

As well as playing during filming breaks, the brothers enticed Ian into the charity games they organised every year, as they did with all of their principal actors. Such was the twins' overwhelming enthusiasm for the game that Ian credited them with getting him playing cricket again, not least because during the summer their favourite pastime was to relax on the sun deck below the Father Time Stand at Lord's cricket ground, a venue to which they would frequently invite him. Those long summer days led to Ian being a regular visitor to John Boulting's house in Acacia Road, St John's Wood, a short distance from where Ian lived and, conveniently, no distance from Lord's. John's daughter Lucy remembered the singular impression the visiting actor made on her: 'As a child, I was really fascinated by his voice and mildness. He always seemed gentle, courteous and sincere.'[49]

During October 1956, with, as he saw it, only two films of any note released, Ian was typically surprised to be invited to the Royal Command Film Performance on 29 October at the Empire Theatre on Leicester Square. While Pym eagerly indulged herself with a new strawberry-coloured evening gown, accompanying long white gloves and a white fox fur, Ian understandably panicked when he was asked by the organisers to act as the stage compère, introducing a cavalcade of screen luminaries such as Joan Crawford, Laurence Harvey and Marilyn Monroe after the royal presentation. His panic increased when he found out that the first part of the ceremony required him to stand alone on the stage and give the Loyal Address on behalf of the British film industry to the Queen, a state of affairs that he thought clearly indicated 'somebody had undoubtedly had a rush of blood to the head.'[50] As the new leading man of the moment, however, Ian was flattered into the task although, in another example of his high artistic standards, he found the speech written for him substandard and promptly went round to see John Boulting to get him to rewrite it.

Armed with an excellent script written by John Boulting, Ian's first presenting role was a great success. The redoubtable Joan Crawford, worried about falling over as she was presented to the Queen, even allowed him to walk over to her as she entered and take her hand as she curtsied, a favour that the Hollywood siren rewarded two days later with a delightful letter of thanks. As the fresh, stylish public face of such a prestigious event, it really looked as if Ian had arrived as an immaculately brilliantined new leading light in entertainment.

The good omens for his career continued with the film Ian started working on at the beginning of November 1956, the movie adaptation of the 1954 novel *Lucky Jim*. As the self-proclaimed critics of post-war Albion, it seemed like the screen adaptation the Boultings had been waiting for, as the book was written by Kingsley Amis, one of the so-called 'new wave' of British writers which included John Osborne, author of the ground-breaking play *Look Back in Anger* which premiered in the same year as *Lucky Jim* went into production. While Osborne's play firmly established in the public consciousness the idea of the 'angry young man' – a new, controversial figure in British literature whose principal cause was attacking established moral conventions as well as the Establishment itself – Amis had been there first with his disaffected protagonist Jim Dixon.

No young man was more angry than Dixon, a frustrated scholarship lecturer at a provincial university who couldn't stand the tedious and out-of-touch syllabus of Mediaeval History he had been contracted to teach. Chief among his distractions from his dull university duties were pulling faces at the people he disliked, women and boozing, characteristics which led the *New Statesman* to brand Amis, himself a university lecturer, as 'brashly, vulgarly, aggressively insensitive ... a literary Teddy Boy'.[51] Indeed, the old guard of the literary establishment were up in arms at the horror, as Evelyn Waugh perceived it, of 'this new wave of philistinism [with] these grim young people coming off the assembly lines and finding employment as critics, even as poets and novelists',[52] while Somerset Maugham deplored the idea of the new white-collar academics, 'whose idea of a celebration is to go to a public house and drink six beers', and was glad that he would 'not live to see'[53] the mess these people would undoubtedly make of his beloved United Kingdom.

With *Lucky Jim* a bestseller, controversial *and* forged from the *Zeitgeist*, the Boultings had, Ian observed, 'longed to secure the rights to [the] book and were desperate to make the film'[54]; after all, here was their chance to make the definitive statement about 1950s Britain. For Ian, too, there was a prize opportunity to demonstrate his acting range in a part completely different from the avuncular gentlemen Windrush and Thursby. However, he would later disarmingly admit, 'I'm ashamed to say I had never read the book when I was offered [the] part, so I didn't realise what a plum I was being offered.'[55]

Ironically, however, the initial filming of *Lucky Jim* the movie would prove as controversial as the book it was based on. Although the Boultings were acting as executive producers, as directors of British Lion, the company bankrolling the film, *Lucky Jim* would be made by a trio who had optioned the adaptation rights: Vivienne Knight, a former film publicist now acting as producer, the distinguished writer Patrick Campbell and the director Charles Crichton, veteran of several Ealing comedies including *The Lavender Hill Mob* (1951). From the minute filming started at the MGM Studios in Borehamwood Ian wasn't happy, feeling there was a lack of empathy between himself and Crichton and finding the director bad-tempered; at the same time, the Boultings were far from content with what they were seeing in the 'rushes' (film sequences shot each day). After two weeks' filming, as Ian recalled, 'we finished with Charlie Crichton on a Friday night and we opened on a Monday with John Boulting. [Knight, Campbell and

Crichton] just vanished and John took over.'⁵⁶ At first, this situation didn't improve the relationship between Ian and his co-star Hugh Griffith, playing Dixon's boss Professor Welch. 'It wasn't a happy company,' Ian recalled. 'Hugh ... who liked a drink or two, thought that I had insisted on the sackings and, as he was a close friend of Crichton's, was rather annoyed by it all.'⁵⁷

Although Crichton kept a dignified silence, a clearly upset Knight had no qualms about speaking to the press, with both the *Daily Mail* and *Daily Express* picking up on the story on 3 December. 'It is not a question of withdrawing,' Knight told the *Express*. 'We were just asked to go and we had no alternative. In the few days before this, Mr Crichton had shot a key scene for the film which I considered excellent in every way.'⁵⁸ Elaborating on the situation further in the *Mail*, she said, 'Mr Crichton and I wanted to make it a comedy of character and observation. [The Boultings] saw it as a comedy of situation and had some "gimmicks" about it with which we could not agree.'⁵⁹ Mindful that an unwelcome spotlight was being turned on one of the most eagerly anticipated British films of recent years, Roy issued a succinct statement designed to bury the controversy: 'There were artistic and creative differences of opinion between us and the other producer and director. They have now withdrawn from the picture. I cannot discuss the two weeks' filming they did.'⁶⁰ The announcement seemed to do the trick, with no one more pleased than Ian to have John back in the director's chair. Once the studio had recovered from the production upheavals, Ian would feel that 'a funny film'⁶¹ resulted from what had been an initially fraught atmosphere.

More than their previous two films, *Lucky Jim* symbolised the contradictions particular to the Boultings' approach to comedy: on the one hand they were modern, iconoclastic satirists, on the other they practised a cosy fondness for old-fashioned, even hackneyed, slapstick. The latter is evident in set pieces such as Dixon getting drunk on cherry brandy and setting fire to his professor's spare bed, the chaotic college procession through a quad packed with flowers and, in particular, Ian's virtuoso performance as Dixon, high on drink and pep pills, delivering a lecture in which he deplores the 'the self-centred slop about the good old days' before collapsing on stage, to the hilarity of the watching students. At the other extreme, the film uses the acid, modern wit suggestive of Amis' novel in dialogue like Dixon's exchange with Terry-Thomas' literary poseur Bertrand Welch:

Welch: He's considering my book for publication.
Dixon: That shouldn't take him very long, should it?

Elsewhere, there was a jab at commerce as Sir Hector-Gore Urquhart (Clive Morton) commented, 'in business I have to suffer four hours of boredom every day' and a daring attempt at some of Amis' coarseness, as Dixon advises Bertrand to 'f–all down the stairs,' censor-tempting dialogue for the time. Overall, though, the *Daily Telegraph*'s assessment was very perceptive: 'the pace was always being rushed and farcical episodes introduced. To end a potentially original subject with such a hackneyed device as a car chase was a sign of weak invention and mixed style.'[62] Even the eccentric musical score, which consisted of several male vocalists singing in harmony and commenting on Jim's trials and tribulations throughout the film, seemed clumsy, obvious and misplaced.

Not unexpectedly, *Lucky Jim* elicited the most press coverage of all Ian's films so far, and while the movie itself was criticised for its erratic tone, his performance again met with almost universal praise. Shabbily dressed, with a floppy fringe, Northern accent, inclination to gurn, liking for a drink and with a tendency to look at the girls' legs in a tutorial session, Ian's Jim Dixon was a convincing malcontent, a world apart from his previous good-mannered screen characterisations, even if he didn't capture the seething bile of the Dixon in Amis's novel. The critics were again impressed. 'Carmichael … proves how hilariously a resourceful comedian can turn the wrong part into the right one,' noted the *Daily Mail*, going on to say, 'He has found an unsuspected new aggressive streak in his make-up, and expresses Jim's awkward cussedness in a harsh, flat new accent several drawers from the top.'⁶³ The *Telegraph*, despite its brickbats about the film itself, was even more complimentary: '[Carmichael's] Jim, complete with North-Country accent and the ability to pull comic faces, might so easily have been the author's creation brought to life off the page.'⁶⁴ In the *News Chronicle*, the reviewer simply said that Ian gave 'a performance of pure gold.'⁶⁵

There was a notable exception among the press compliments. Writing in the *New Statesman*, Lindsay Anderson, previously on-side with the Boultings in their challenging approach to British cinema, lashed out at the film and, in particular, Ian's portrayal of Dixon, unfairly dismissing his sophisticated acting as a variety act: 'Jim Dixon ... has been stripped of personality, and turned into a farcical lay-figure. He emerges as our old favourite, the College Idiot, who does everything wrong but gets the girl in the end ... Ian Carmichael does not *act* Jim; he does him as a turn, with comic grimaces and an intermittent accent.'⁶⁶

Reflecting on *Lucky Jim* much later in life, Ian suggested that the reasons for its shortcomings were the combination of a turbulent production process and, typically for such a self-effacing man, perhaps his unsuitability for the title role:

> John did a jolly good job, but I think he started off with a script that he wasn't totally happy with [from Campbell]. He'd liked to have done the script himself and there were certain things he didn't agree with. I knew Kingsley Amis well, but I was always told, never to my face, that Kingsley wasn't really happy with the way *Lucky Jim* had been performed and presented ... Looking back, analysing, being self critical, I think *possibly* I was miscast. I think someone like John Alderton, who wasn't around at the time, would have been better casting.⁶⁷

In the final analysis, *Lucky Jim* was a qualified success, a film that Ian would later admit 'certainly didn't feel like a classic when we were making it.'⁶⁸ After its release in America, the *New York Times* came closest to capturing the thoughts of those cinema-goers who had enjoyed the Boultings' previous impeccable work: 'Let's fervently hope this stale attempt at mirth, the sliding back and forth from leaden coyness to plain custard-pie confusion, does not mean the end of all the sly civilised fun we have come to expect from the British specialists.'[69]

While the twins would return to, and indeed perfect, their state-of-the-nation satire in 1959 with *I'm All Right Jack*, for their next project for Ian they offered him a vehicle that appealed directly to his distinctly 'olde worlde' sensibilities, a film he considered 'a little domestic trifle of timeless charm.'[70]

1958's *Happy is the Bride* was a remake of the 1941 film *Quiet Wedding* directed by Anthony Asquith, starring Margaret Lockwood and Derek Farr, itself an adaptation of Esther McCraken's 1938 stage play. In the lightweight story of the trials and tribulations about the nuptials between David Chaytor (Ian) and Janet Royd (perfect English rose Janette Scott), can be found the answer to why the Boultings decided to follow up three ground-breaking satires with the remake of a twenty-year-old comedy of manners. The film opened on the village green with a game of cricket – the twins' favourite hobby – and meandered through a gentle farce involving the local philanthropic gentry and concerned, supportive locals in a rural, idealised England that appealed to the twins' liberal nostalgia. Ian and Janette emerged as creditable romantic leads, even if the film itself was judged to be deficient, as, in the words of one reviewer, it tried 'to bring an old play up-to-date by changing superficial details, without realising that the whole structure of society on which it was based has altered.'[71] Ian was again rewarded with some approving notices, the *Daily Mail* commending his act of 'swallowing hard, perpetually apologising, and never finding the right word for anything, [staggering] blithely from blunder to blunder and [sealing] the whole shambles with his dishevelled and diffident charm.'[72] Less eloquently but more directly, the *News of the World* claimed Ian was 'just about the best light comedian in the business.'[73] However, for the *Daily Telegraph* the Boultings' idyllic rendering of a cosy pastoral England was just too much, its reviewer sourly if amusingly commenting, 'This is the sort of thing that makes foreigners look at each other and decide that the United Nations is a mistake.'[74] Despite being an inconsequential addition to the Boultings' canon, *Happy is the Bride* is nonetheless extremely engaging because of the likeability of the characters.

In what was by now becoming a recurring motif in the Boultings' films, Ian was afforded another run-in with Terry-Thomas, this time facing off against his nemesis in the guise of a dour and petty-minded country policeman (sounding suspiciously like he had been revoiced by another actor) who arrested Ian's David Chaytor for dangerous driving. In *Happy is the Bride*'s funniest sequences, Chaytor had to suffer the indignity of Thomas questioning whether he was a British subject, and sniffing his breath for signs of intoxication, while he methodically wrote down the driver's bewildered statements before the constable entertainingly repeated them in court, word for faltering word, in a ponderous drawl.

By now used to working with a man who was as an established part of the Boultings' screen repertory company as he was – in the same year as *Happy is the Bride*, Terry-Thomas would star as *Carlton Browne of the F.O.* for the twins – Ian was again witness to a wayward habit of Terry's that offended his own sense of perfectionism in learning the script:

> The one major problem with Terry was his inability to get his dialogue right in a couple of takes. I believe one of our scenes together for *Happy is the Bride* went to something like thirty-three takes and that, believe me, was by no means the record for Terry. He would fiendishly whittle words away until he felt comfortable. Terry was notorious for that. He would say to the Boultings, 'I can't quite get my teeth round this word, can I change it to so-and-so?' For example, say he was reciting 'Mary Had a Little Lamb': he would say, 'can't I just say small or, even better, just "Mary Had a Lamb"? I mean, everybody *knows* the thing is little, don't they?' The Boultings were very tolerant and would allow Terry his leeway in playing the part. Terry was never

aggressive or demanding; he would always ask in the most charming of ways. Of course, the Boultings knew that it didn't pay to aggravate any performer, and if the new lines or missed word worked it was accepted with a cheery smile.'[75]

Ian's main *Happy is the Bride* co-star Janette Scott had made her first film at the age of five (uncredited) with her mother Thora Hird in Alberto Cavalcanti's *Went the Day Well?* (1942), a propaganda piece that imagined the wartime nightmare of the infiltration of England by German forces. Since then, Janette had worked steadily as a supporting actress in films such as the Boultings' 1952 biographical movie *The Magic Box* (about the inventor of the movie camera, William Friese-Green), and the historical melodrama *Helen of Troy* (1956) with Stanley Baker and Brigitte Bardot. *Happy is the Bride* initiated a screen partnership between her and Ian that would endure for a further two films and a TV play, not least because the evident on-screen chemistry between them reflected how they related off it:

> Ian was delightful, we got on very well and we would have lunch together every day. He was, as I was, a big music fan and I do remember I'd just got a new LP, as they were in those days, of the Hi-Lo's and so we would listen to them during lunch. I was quite musical and Ian was fairly musical and he would sing the melody and I would do some of the harmonies. We did enjoy that sort of camaraderie.[76]

In particular, the couple bonded over their approach to working: 'He was as word-perfect as I was,' Janette says. 'I was brought up – my mother being Thora Hird – from a professional acting family, to always be early and dead letter-perfect and our comedy timing together just gelled.'[77] Forming such a close bond with the Boultings' favourite star also enabled Janette to discern Ian's appeal to audiences. 'Although he wasn't conventionally handsome, he was attractive to women and not threatening to men,' she muses, 'interestingly enough, like the men he admired – Fred Astaire and

Jack Buchanan – neither of whom were, in the conventional sense, handsome in any way, shape or form.'[78]

As well as the pleasure she drew from working with Ian, Janette found working on *Happy is the Bride* an all-round rewarding experience. At the time contracted to ABPC films at Elstree Studios, she was invited to join the Boultings' repertory company and was immediately struck by Charter Films' family atmosphere. 'Roy [the director] took me out to lunch before the film started to break the ice a bit, just so that we wouldn't meet on the first day of the film. He was lovely. I absolutely adored him and a couple of years later, I could really understand why Hayley Mills fell in love with him and found him so attractive. He was very attractive as a person.'[79] There was, however, one peculiarity that arose during filming, symptomatic of Roy's eccentric approach to film-making:

> He had a thing about the fact that my ears stuck out, which no one had ever mentioned to me before. He would come up to me and be talking to me and looking at my ears! It was very distracting. He would stick my ears back if he wanted to do a full-on close-up scene of me! God knows what the make-up people used! It would be the cause of great hilarity when Ian and I would be playing a scene together and suddenly one of my ears would ping off the side of my head! We laughed about it because my ears don't stick out – they're very normal.'[80]

Perhaps because of its deliberately nostalgic English feel, Janette remembers '*Happy is the Bride* was quite an amazing success worldwide, particularly in the Commonwealth countries – Canada, Australia and so forth. There were loads of competitions connected with it which, in those days, didn't happen that often.'[81]

During early 1957, the BBC approached Ian with the chance to star in his own half-hour comedy special. This offer saw the Corporation rewarding a performer who had to a large extent learned his craft in the entertainment business with them, a point that was openly recognised in the programme's title, *Carmichael's Night Out*. Transmitted on 14 March 1957, the special was a spoof of a well-known 1956 BBC series called *Saturday Night Out*, in which spectacular live events such as circuses and, memorably, a train crash were presented each week. As well as starring as 'the man taking the mike', Ian was also one of the scriptwriters, a clear indication of how much professional clout he now carried with his old employers.

Directly after *Happy is the Bride* finished production the BBC came calling again, offering Ian the principal role in the TV comedy play *The Girl at the Next Table*, written by the gifted Philip Mackie and overseen by the highly regarded director Stuart Burge. Building on his recent graduation to the status of romantic lead, the play offered him the opportunity to play a young man constantly tempted away from commitment to matrimony by a variety of other girls. Impressed by both Janette and Virginia Maskell (who had also appeared in *Happy is the Bride*), he persuaded them to take on the slightly daunting challenge of recorded-as-live-television. 'Ian very much wanted to do it,'[82] Janette remembers. 'It was an extremely good part for him. He called me up and asked me if I would, as a favour, be in it, but I felt that I had moved on from television and I was doing so well in films. Of course, with a chum like Ian asking me to do it, I did it and we had a good time.'[83] Also in the cast was William Franklyn, a delightful piece of casting for Ian as he was the son of Leo, the stage comedian who had taken him under his wing all those years ago in the early stages of his career. The only slight downside to the enterprise was Ian's dispute with the BBC over top billing, an incident that led the head of Light Entertainment to inform a colleague, 'we have recently had great difficulty in dealing with him'[84] and that 'his head seems to have been a little turned by his success'.[85]

An actor working at the time, who wishes to remain anonymous, corroborates this view. 'Ian got a terrible name for himself in the 1950s,' he says. 'He became a very selfish actor and was *very* unpopular. Whatever it was – film, television or theatre – he would always try to upstage, pull focus and block his co-stars' light. It got so bad that a phrase started doing the rounds in the business:

"doing a Carmichael". Derek Nimmo, who worked with Ian in the film of *The Amorous Prawn* [1962] so he should know, had to put up with an actor repeatedly stepping into his light one night on stage, and afterwards he took him aside and said, "My God, you were doing a bloody Carmichael!"' Ian's meteoric rise to fame perhaps explains why he got such a bad reputation. Going from supporting roles to being a fully fledged film star within the space of a year must have been difficult to handle even in the more refined entertainment industry of the 1950s.

The gala premiere of *Lucky Jim* took place at the Edinburgh Film Festival on the 19 August 1957, but due to Ian's commitment to *The Girl at the Next Table*, transmitted the previous evening, he was unable to attend, an absence the *News Chronicle* regretted as it felt he would have been delighted by 'an almost endless ripple of comfortable laughter.'[86] Ian wasn't too worried; by the middle of 1957 he was a national celebrity and able to afford a rare and coveted Mercedes Benz 300, which he proudly drove to Yorkshire with Pym and the girls aboard to visit his parents and in-laws. As he arrived back in his hometown of Hull in August, he was every inch the famous and successful film star.

CHAPTER 8

'Blow You, Jack, I'm *All Right!*'

Continued theatrical success, a new home and an iconic British film

D
URING HIS MUCH-NEEDED holiday in Hull in August 1957, Ian was sent the script for a New York comedy called *The Tunnel of Love* that was then being performed on Broadway. He perused the script while indulging in his favourite pastime on the sunny pitches of the Scarborough Cricket Festival, and was struck by the pedigree of the partners behind the play's management team. One of them was the portly actor Robert Morley. Twenty-two years senior to Ian, he was a fellow graduate of RADA who had made a name for himself in films like *The African Queen* (1952) and *Beau Brummel* (1954) playing larger-than-life Englishmen, characters who were extensions of a real-life personality who was 'garrulous, witty and [adored] holding court.'[1] Morley's business partner was his manager Robin Fox, a suave, charming gentleman who was the father of the actors James and Edward. Morley and his manager's track record in the theatre dated back to 1947, when the former had co-written and performed in *Edward, My Son,* an intense family drama staged at Her Majesty's Theatre in London. Fox impressed Ian with his offer to come to Yorkshire to discuss Ian taking on *The Tunnel of Love* – momentously, his first starring role in the West End – and he was further won over when Fox arrived with the gift of a cigarette lighter mounted in a cricket ball. Fox's attentiveness was a clear sign that Ian was now moving in exalted

theatrical circles, and he confessed that his visitor 'was two-thirds of the way home before we had gone into lunch.'[2]

However, Ian had reservations about the play. Written by Joseph Fields and Peter De Vries, it was a lively comedy that told the story of the cartoonist Augie Poole and his wife Isolde's attempts to raise a family, which mainly consisted of Augie's wife dragging him off to bed whenever she reached the optimum temperature for conception. The situation was complicated by Poole's seduction by Estelle Novick, an attractive worker from an adoption agency, who became pregnant with his child. Nine months later, Poole was alarmed that the baby offered to him and his wife for adoption would be his own. Ian's doubts about the play, its obvious comedy appeal aside, revolved around *The Tunnel of Love*'s unambiguous preoccupation with sex. John Osborne's 1956 play *Look Back in Anger* had been the first to lift the lid on what the critic Kenneth Tynan called the 'casual promiscuity'[3] of the post-war British generation, but its staging at the innovative Royal Court defined it as a piece of experimental theatre, rather than Ian's usual province of a mainstream West End farce with a predominantly conservative, middle-class audience. Understandably, as a performer associated with humorous material that was at the opposite extreme to scandalous, Ian was worried that audiences would find the permissive *The Tunnel of Love* offensive. (It would be the following year before theatrical taboos on sex were well and truly broken by Shelagh Delaney's *A Taste of Honey*, which had the unmarried heroine Jo, who shared a flat with a young homosexual man, left pregnant by a black seaman). Although his misgivings weren't completely dispelled by his lunch meeting with Fox, Ian finally agreed to step into Augie's shoes. Rehearsals began on 30 September 1957 at the Apollo Theatre in London, with the rest of the cast consisting of Barbara Murray, Charlotte Mills, Ian's *High Spirits* co-star and old friend Dilys Laye and, once again, Bill Franklyn, playing 'a fertile wolf whose wife only had to look at his trousers to become pregnant.'[4]

The affable Morley himself was directing the play and favoured working straight through from 9.30 a.m. to finish around 3.30 p.m.

The charitable actor's offer to his cast of '[peeling] off into the wings for a cup of coffee and a sandwich'[5] during working hours was interpreted by his assistant Ros Chatto as meaning she should provide a full Ascot-class buffet lunch and several bottles of red wine. After five days of such disruptive generosity, Ian was elected by the cast to suggest tactfully to Morley that in the interests of getting the play ready for its Liverpool premiere in three weeks time, the standard working day of 10.30 a.m. to 5.30 p.m. with an hour for lunch should be adhered to. Even though Ian won this concession on behalf of his fellow performers, he had to address another eccentricity of Morley's, which was continually to change the staging of a scene after it had been rehearsed the day before: 'Not happy about it at all, my darlings. We can't possibly have the bar that far up-stage, you're lost up there, all of you – can't see your beautiful eyes, Barbara dear. I'm going to bring it down to the front and that will necessitate moving the sofa to the side of the stage and that chair over into the corner.'[6] As *The Tunnel of Love* was ten days into rehearsals and Morley had not yet 'set' Act 1, the director had to concede that Ian had a very good point.

Despite the leading actor's anxieties about the subject matter, the play opened to responsive audiences on tour. At one venue, however, Ian had to do some on-the-spot improvisation that would prove memorable for all the wrong reasons:

> In Leeds we were doing a 2.30 matinee. Bill and I were on the stage alone together and two girls had to come on, Barbara and Charlotte, and they didn't turn up. They were discussing their children three floors up or something. Anyway, we ad-libbed and ad-libbed and ad-libbed for what seemed like years – *generations!* – and we eventually ran out of anything one could say pertaining to the play, so we dried up stone dead. And then I thought, 'Gosh, I've got an idea!' I invented an entirely fictitious character and thought 'This'll go on forever', so I said to Bill, 'Have you heard anything of George Warburton recently?' And he said 'Yes, he's dead.' ... It killed it *stone dead!* I suppose in retrospect I could have asked Bill what he died of, but it didn't immediately come to mind, y'know.'[7]

After the five-week provincial tour, *The Tunnel of Love* had a West End opening in December at Her Majesty's Theatre (scene of one of Morley's earlier theatrical successes) on the Haymarket. The out-of-town critics, while acknowledging that the play was flagrantly about sex, had praised 'a delicacy of touch in the writing, and particularly in the playing, that disarms, and a subject that might have been offensive, vulgar and coarse, becomes a medley of sophisticated, frank conversation and outrageous situation,'[8] and recognised that 'this spicy revel is acted with such high spirits, good taste and sophistication that however near the bone it gets, it seldom chills the marrow.'[9] The reception was more mixed in London, ranging from unanimous endorsements to notices from the less liberal critics that the play was 'tasteless'[10] or 'a joke in bad taste.'[11] Happily, none of the adverse criticism made any difference to the box-office returns, with *The Tunnel of Love* going on to run for a year in London, indicating that audiences were clearly ready for a change in the theatre's attitude to sexual relations. Ian himself continued to impress the critics with his development as a theatre performer, the *Stage* noting that 'he has advanced remarkably in technical resourcefulness and comedy invention since his days in revue … In a long part, he proves himself to be a comedian who can act as well as amuse.'[12] In a sign of the snobbish critical divide between theatre and film/television that was prevalent throughout the 1950s, the *Stage*'s reviewer had clearly been absent from the cinema when Ian had been busy proving himself as an actor over the previous three years.

During the run of *The Tunnel of Love*, an interview with Ian was published in the theatrical paper that found him in an expansive, contented and grateful mood. He had clearly impressed the article's writer, R.B. Marriott, with his 'slightly crazy, wonderfully ridiculous comedy, which no-one else on our stage can do so well'[13] in a play that also gave him an 'excellent opportunity for *acting*.'[14] The feature was illustrated by a picture of the leading man in a relaxed pose, fixing the photographer with a confident, level stare as he offered a revealing insight into his attitude to work. The Ian

Carmichael of December 1957 was completely at home in comedy and, unlike some of his peers, showed no inclination to move beyond it into drama, 'not even Ibsen,'[15] and clearly wasn't a man concerned about theatrical trends. 'I do not believe there is a dearth of English comedies,' he reflected. 'This section of the theatre seems to me to be doing very nicely. It may appear otherwise, simply because as a rule the attention of the Press is given to new writers such as John Osborne and to "serious" plays ... it just happened that [a comedy] from America seemed best for me at this time.' Ian also plainly saw his early success in revue as part of an ongoing process: 'the confidence and quickness required in [it] to put over a sketch or character in a few moments, taught me a great deal which I now find useful in a straight play. High comedy also frequently demands that rapid impressions are made, and it is very important to establish a comedy character as soon as possible.'[16] He also gave his most enlightening ever insight into how he was able to sustain the energy of a role during a long theatrical engagement, revealing that after a character had become 'fixed'[17],

> I know just what I shall do, how I shall do it, and the exact timing and positions. This method, I think, helps me to keep up a standard of performance. Because every move and expression has been strictly planned and set to a pattern, it is possible to give the impression of a completely spontaneous performance even on an 'off' night – and we all have our 'off' nights.[18]

Despite his evident enjoyment of his good fortune, Ian's characteristic self-effacement shone through in the interview, particularly when he attributed some of his success to the influence of Robertson Hare, Peter Haddon and Leo Franklyn, concluding disarmingly, 'these great artists also gave a little more confidence to a fellow who, perhaps, still has not enough confidence in himself.'[19]

In early 1958 Ian found time to continue his association with the BBC, happily accepting the great honour of appearing on Radio 4's *Desert Island Discs* with Roy Plomley on 7 April, to discuss his life and ever-developing career, and to play some of his favourite music. Keen to retain the services of a performer who was by now nationally famous as well as popular, the BBC was in a generous mood, allowing one of their producers, Leslie Bridgemont, to wine and dine Ian on the 16th and offer him the starring role in a new radio series. It was early May before the busy actor replied:

> I have thought this over at length Leslie during the last fortnight. The moment I come out of *The Tunnel* I have two films to make, one after the other – and quite honestly, under the circumstances I would prefer to have my weekends free to relax. It was most kind of you to offer me the series, [and] I am most grateful to you. Thank you for such a splendid lunch.[20]

Securing Ian's commitment to a full series for the BBC eluded them for the moment, although the Corporation would keep on trying.

In Spring 1958, with Ian's financial fortunes in the ascendant, the opportunity arose for him and Pym to buy their first home. A combination of being offered the freehold on their second rented home at Eton Villas and their daughters Sally and Lee growing up, prompted the couple to put into action a long-cherished plan to move to an area of London with closer access to the countryside. With Ian's offer of £2,500 for the freehold accepted on Eton Villas, the Carmichaels suddenly had property behind them. The day the letter of confirmation arrived, they drove straight to the district they had in mind, Mill Hill Village in the Totteridge Manor green-belt area of north London.

Mill Hill Village remains one of the most desirable locations in the capital. A quiet oasis with the central feature of a pond, and composed mainly of well-built Victorian dwellings set among tall trees, through some quirk of its geography the area has always given the impression of being located further into the countryside than it actually is. After visiting some local estate agents, by 3 o'clock that same day, incredibly, Ian and Pym had found the house that would be their family home for the next nineteen years.

Situated at the end of a cul-de-sac just off the Mill Hill end of Totteridge Lane, Moat Lodge was a large, rambling house, composed of an old 'study wing' at least a hundred years old which had been built on in the 1930s to transform it into a generously proportioned family home. The privacy of the house's location was almost total, the back garden surrounded by a chest-high hedge, with a large field at the front which was shared between crop rotation and the film producer Sydney Box's dairy herd from his adjacent farm. Box was the vendor behind Moat Lodge, and by some coincidence his wife Muriel had directed Ian in his breakthrough film *Simon and Laura*. There was a curious sense of destiny in the Carmichaels now being wealthy enough to purchase their dream home from one half of a couple who had arguably been responsible for the lucrative path Ian's career had taken.

Moat Lodge was like an extension of Ian's personality. Comfortable, classy and unpretentious, it was like a corner of the very best of rural England preserved from the nineteenth century. Not too far away, Mill Hill School offered a well-appointed cricket field that Ian would often visit, and the secluded, tree-lined locality would be a haven for him after the frantic hustle of film and theatre work elsewhere in London. Returning home and almost immediately relaxing in the country atmosphere, he would often find Sally and Lee, aged nine and twelve respectively in 1958, tending to their animals – among them, rabbits, ducks and ponies – on a piece of land rented from Box at a generously small fee. Ian's feeling about his ideal home was, for once, not tempered by his tendency for understatement: 'It was a magnificent spot.'[21]

Ian's sense of general well-being, enhanced by the purchase of a home for his family at long last, had been slightly marred when the troubled *The Big Money* finally saw the light of day at the end of May, nearly three years after it had been made. Ian remembered that the film's release was initiated by an enthusiastic Rank employee: 'Hugh Stewart, who did the Norman Wisdom films, went to [the head of the studio] and said, "Look, I've got a scene with Norman in the current film set at Ascot and I don't want to go there. I know there's some scenes set at Ascot shot in the studio in *The Big Money*. Can I see it?" He saw it and came back and said to the powers that be, "It's not all that bad. Give me a budget and I'll put some music on it and it can go out."' [22]

Ironically the only film with Ian as a leading man that was made in colour, *The Big Money*'s opening scenes reflected the promise he must have seen in it when he read the script. The early shots of a Technicolor London were very striking, focusing in on a suburban street where Ian's fashionably Teddy Boy-coiffured Willie Frith returns to a neatly kept upper-working-class household for a family meeting with his parents, sister and younger brother. The film takes an imaginative, subversive turn when the family deposit on the table a horde of stolen goods they've acquired during the day, including wallets, watches and a first edition book. The empty-handed Willie is an incompetent thief in a family of thieves, and the Friths' outward suburban respectability was funded by a life of petty crime.

The originality of the opening quickly evaporated once Willie's would-be girlfriend Gloria (Belinda Lee), the barmaid at the local pub the Red Dragon, entered the story. Although a sexy and seductive actress, Lee was constrained by a part that required her to do little more than be intoxicated by money and glamour. The old adage that 'love is blind' aside, after a while Gloria's persistent shallowness made you wonder what Willie saw in her, undermining his credibility as a character. At a time when post-war consumerism was well into its stride, Gloria's topical (if annoying) materialism was, however, the engine that drove the narrative, leading Willie to steal a case full of counterfeit money from Robert Helpmann's gang boss 'The Reverend' so he could lavish the proceeds on her.

As if the portrayal of the working class as either criminal or acquisitive and disloyal wasn't questionable enough – at one point

Gloria's friend Bobbie (Renée Houston) persuaded her to steal all
the money from Willie – there was also the condescending subtext
that people should know their place in society. Willie took Gloria
to the upmarket Royalty Club, initiating the old comedy standard
of the social interloper out of his depth in more cultured company,
which peaked with Willie's attempt to suppress his hiccups
resulting in a strangulated belch that interrupted a refined female
singer, embarrassing Gloria in front of her would-be peers. Add to
this broad comedy The Reverend's gang being characterised by all
the clichés of American gangster films – typical dialogue: 'you
scummy bunch of punks!' – and *The Big Money* painted a picture
of a cartoon London underworld where the characters were too
one-dimensional to make the contrived farce believable, something
that had been clearly apparent to Ian after he'd finished reading the
screenplay. The disorientating sense of things not being as they
first appeared in the opening scenes of the Frith home was continued
in the film's only other original touch: disguising a violent gangster
as a church minister.

The final scene, with Willie in prison, his Teddy Boy quiff
symbolically cropped, promising to serve his sentence and change
his criminal ways, felt like the film-makers were wagging a
patronising 'crime doesn't pay'/'money is the root of all evil'
finger at the audience, as if such obvious moralising was necessary
by the mid 1950s. It was a vaguely unpalatable ending to a film that
was a curious combination of borderline-offensive stereotypes and
knockabout slapstick.

Throughout *The Big Money*, it was obvious that Ian was
working relentlessly hard to make the film work, his youthful,
innocent looks enabling him to portray convincingly a rather
gauche man of twenty-four when he was already ten years older.
The decision to put him in a Teddy Boy wig was a boldly modern
one, accurately equating the working-class fashion cult of
'extravagant sideburns and long greased hair, swept up in a quiff'[23]
with crime, infamously illustrated in April 1954 by a violent fight
between two gangs of Teddy Boys on St Mary Cray station in

Kent. Although he didn't come across as conspicuously working class, Ian was allowed to drop his h's to roughen his accent, and his awkward, yearning looks at Gloria and propensity to stutter whenever he was with her were particularly well acted, fleshing out Willie's sketchy personality. When he and Gloria booked a hotel room together (a potentially provocative scene in 1955, given that they were unmarried), Ian showed his flair for romantic humour when the couple were wound together in an amorous embrace:

> **Gloria:** Willie, there's someone at the door.
>
> **Willie:** I can't hear 'em (*carries on kissing her*).

The love scene was memorable as it allowed Ian to demonstrate his true strength in comedy, that of underplaying: the more restrained his delivery, the funnier the end result always was. It was a brief, isolated moment in a film in which, on the whole, Ian's performance was required to be anything but subtle. The amount of purely physical comedy involved approached almost silent-movie proportions as, among other routines, he dropped things, spilt a drink down Gloria's dress, sneezed at the feathers in a woman's hat, dropped handfuls of money from his pockets, knocked over a champagne bucket and fell down the stairs in the Royalty Club. The film's ending certainly wouldn't have been out of place as the climax of a Charlie Chaplin or Harold Lloyd film farce, as various characters fought it out for possession of the money in a hotel, a mêlée that involved Willie, two rival gangs of crooks, some Arabs and a bell-boy who is punched in the face twice then knocked out with a champagne bottle. Perceptively, one reviewer noted that Ian had been 'forced into a style better suited to Norman Wisdom.'[24]

The Big Money was the first Ian Carmichael film to which the critics reacted unfavourably, not surprising when the discerning star had already disowned it before he shot a single scene. The *Sunday Dispatch* felt that the film '[staggered] dismally in the wake of better and faster jokes'[25], with the *Manchester Guardian* accurately observing, 'the film's one comic idea is funny enough, but it is done to death.'[26] More worryingly as far as Ian was concerned, for the first time there was a backlash against his performance, which must have come as something of a shock when he had only starred in four movies. Reviewers variously felt that *The Big Money* showed 'Ian Carmichael, who has grown much more famous since the film was made, as a sort of caricature of Ian Carmichael',[27] 'cringing beneath a red wig'[28] and, rather unkindly, wondered 'couldn't [he] add another facial expression to the two he's already got?'[29] Most damningly, the *Sunday Times* was the first to call time on Ian's brand of film comedy, declaring, 'The weakness is the playing of Ian Carmichael, whose assumption of butterfingers desperation is rapidly losing for me the novelty it once held.'[30] With such a negative reaction from the press to a film he knew would be a failure from the outset, it's no wonder that Ian fervently wished that Hugh Stewart had left *The Big Money* 'at the end of the corridor where he found it!'[31] More than any other film, with its numerous scenes of pratfalling and physical comedy business, *The Big Money* would reinforce Ian's popular stereotype as a 'silly ass', ironic considering that it was the least representative of him as a comedy actor.

Ian completed his commitment to *The Tunnel of Love* after nine happy months on a Friday in August 1958. At his leaving party, he was presented with a particularly special gift from the cast and stage crew. During the play, he used a large Windsor chair in a comedy routine that concealed how physically aroused Augie was, first using the cushion on the seat then the supporting rungs for the chair's arms and back. Embellished over the weeks the play had run, the sequence by now halted *The Tunnel of Love*'s forward momentum as Ian was prone to 'milk' the scene for all it was worth. Once he had unwrapped his huge leaving present, tied up with red ribbon, he was speechless to find the Windsor chair confronting him. A brass plate had been fixed to the headrest that read: "*From those left in The Tunnel"*, while at Bill Franklyn's instigation, a smaller plate fixed to the front of the seat had been inscribed with the cheeky pun *"The Milking Stool"*. Very touched by the company's generosity, the chair became one of Ian's 'most treasured possessions.'[32] As the drink and good cheer flowed around him, however, Ian was the only one who knew that, just before his farewell party had begun, Pym had telephoned him to say that during that afternoon, his father had died.

The following day, Ian and his family made the journey to his parents' home in Ferriby in Yorkshire (the house where Ian grew up having been sold in 1948). Meeting up with some in-laws at York railway station, the sad family group then continued on to comfort Ian's mother and make funeral arrangements. Arthur Carmichael had been suffering from angina attacks for nearly a year; a dignified and self-reliant man throughout his sixty-four years, he had made the decision to keep the declining state of his health from Ian and his sisters. If Ian's mother Kate knew, she too had kept her own counsel. However, three days before his death, Arthur was diagnosed with terminal lung cancer. His doctor and Kate decided that he should be told in order to prepare himself emotionally, and as a meticulously tidy man throughout his life, he spent the next few days putting his estate in order.

During the last week of Arthur's life, his eldest brother Robert had telephoned Ian with the news that the situation was serious and that his place was at his father's bedside in Ferriby. Robert's response to Ian's reply isn't recorded, but it's likely he would have been extremely taken aback by his nephew's decision to honour his commitments to *The Tunnel of Love* and travel to Yorkshire at the weekend – by which time it was too late. Even though Ian insisted that his father 'would, I know, have understood',[33] for a man who was normally so generous and had a reputation to be envied in putting others first, it was, perhaps, a sign of the contradictory and rarely glimpsed selfish side of Ian's nature; at best, he had acted out of a misplaced sense of loyalty to his theatrical colleagues. Either way, if ever there was an occasion when the old theatrical cliché of 'the show must go on' should be ignored, it was the death of a parent.

With his father's funeral behind him, Ian began work on his next film, exercising his release clause from his Boultings' contract to make the political comedy *Left, Right and Centre* for another production team. This new venture came under the auspices of producer/directors Frank Launder and Sidney Gilliat, the partnership behind the risqué *St Trinian's* movies, which were also funded by British Lion. Launder and Gilliat's new film had more in common with the satirical social commentary of the Boultings (which is possibly what attracted Ian to the movie) than stocking-flashing school girls and cross-dressing leading men, although the experienced comic actor Alistair Sim, who had played the St Trinian's buxom headmistress Miss Amelia Fritton, along with other stalwarts of the series Eric Barker and Ian's old friend Richard Wattis, were retained for the new project.

Prefaced by a quote from Shakespeare – 'a plague on both your houses' – *Left, Right and Centre* concerned the efforts of a TV personality, Robert Wilcot (Ian), to become elected as the Conservative MP in the Earndale by-election. His main opposition was the Labour candidate Stella Stoker (Patricia Bredin), a fishmonger's daughter and graduate of the London School of Economics. Unfortunately for their campaign managers Glimmer (Barker) and Hardy-Pratt (Wattis), the candidates fell in love, defining the film as a farcical political version of *Romeo and Juliet* (as the opening quote suggested), with the Tory and Labour parties substituted for the warring Montagues and Capulets. The situation yielded such wonderfully sardonic dialogue as 'if this obscene cancer spreads it'll make a mockery of the House of Commons', and 'carried through to its logical conclusion this sort of thing would make party divisions utterly meaningless!' Its sharp, humorous dialogue wasn't the only way in which *Left, Right and Centre* was the complete opposite of *The Big Money*: with the exception of Wilcot's old flame Annabel (Moyra Fraser), all the characters – upper- and lower-class – were three-dimensional and well written, the humour arising naturally from the situations and characters rather than artificially inserted comic set-pieces.

The opening, mock-serious Boulting brothers-style voiceover was a sure sign that the twins' recent film satires had influenced Gilliat's screenplay. Although some critics complained that the film didn't go far enough in its critique of the electoral process, *Left, Right and Centre* was ahead of its time, and in some ways ahead of the Boultings' satirical remit, in its appraisal of how politics could be compromised by the mass media, particularly television. British politics has taken its first tentative steps towards embracing the modern communications medium when TV networks had been granted the rights to cover the Rochdale by-election in February 1958, and 1959, the year of the film's release, was to be even more significant for political television coverage as it was a general election year.

Left, Right and Centre was sophisticated in its treatment of the subject, opening with the TV panel game *What On Earth Was That?*, featuring actual game show TV celebrities of the time Eamonn Andrews and Gilbert Harding, in a thinly disguised version of shows of the period like *What's My Line?* and *We Beg to Differ* (which Ian had briefly produced). By giving the audience an instantly familiar frame of reference, Harding's comment that the party that won the by-election would be the one that embraced TV was made both instantly topical and far-sighted. Wilcot, another panellist on *What On Earth Was That?*, then made Harding's opinion one of the main themes of the movie by revealing that he would be standing for the Tories in Earndale, despite having no previous parliamentary experience; his unique selling point to the electorate of simply being well known on TV was an outlook that, if anything, is even more relevant fifty-two years later. That Wilcot had nothing of real substance to say was underlined by an early clip of him as an interviewee new to television, fumbling for the right words, before more recent footage showed him as the adept TV celebrity, practiced in slick repartee that still says nothing. An election banner proclaiming, 'Vote for Wilcot, the man who knows exactly what he's doing', reinforced the absurdity of a vacuous celebrity who knew exactly the opposite. The comic potential of this contradiction between the public media face and the reality behind the scenes was mined in several clever lines of dialogue, including:

Harding-Pratt: I hope our candidate's up to snuff.
Peters: He's smashing on the telly.
Harding-Pratt: That's not necessarily a sign of political genius.

The status of television as an institution that hadn't necessarily been universally welcomed into the nation's sitting rooms was also addressed:

Wilcot: You don't watch TV?
Stella: Not since Dad threw it out of the window.

Following on from the delayed release of *The Big Money*, which showed just how badly Ian's performance could be compromised by the wrong script and unsympathetic direction, *Left, Right and Centre* was a delight for the actor as he was able to play a believable and flawed adult, and in many ways his Wilcot is a career best comedy performance (unjustly overshadowed by the film that followed). Although outwardly charming, when first introduced the TV celebrity isn't a particularly nice man; he's self-important, vain, not a little pompous and in love with his TV image, proclaiming 'my name is familiar in any home'. As well as the chance for Ian to demonstrate how skilled he was in delivering some particularly well-written witty banter, the script allowed him some delightfully cynical scenes with his uncle Lord Wilcot (Alistair Sim), who hoped that his nephew's election would be good news for his bankrupt country seat. Ian also skilfully showed how amusingly juvenile the self-opinionated Wilcot became when under the influence of love, nearly applauding one of Stella's election speeches and, after he's finally kissed her, sporting a rapt, cat-that's-got-the-cream expression as he rocks backwards and forwards on his heels. With Wilcot a more worldly-wise character than Ian's previous screen roles, the actor was also able to act his real age (thirty-eight) for the first time.

The *Financial Times* was quick to spot the similarity with the movies Ian had made earlier in the 1950s, commenting, 'as in the Boultings' films (the presence of Ian Carmichael emphasizes the resemblance) a hallowed institution is merely used as the backcloth for some fairly conventional gag comedy'[34] but recommended *Left, Right and Centre* for 'a good deal of verve'[35]. The *Sunday Times*' Dilys Powell, who had been distinctly unimpressed by *The Big Money*, applauded Ian's latest vehicle as an 'extremely funny film'[36], while the *Daily Herald* drew comparisons between the movie and a real life TV personality making his debut as a political candidate: 'The best satirical point is that Carmichael is cast as a tele-hero turned politician. Mr Robin Day should take a long, cool look at this film before he begins his campaign in Hereford.'[37]

As well as offering one of Ian's finest leading roles, *Left, Right and Centre* was a rich ensemble piece, with a supporting cast of fine performers such as Eric Barker, Alistair Sim and Richard Wattis, that satisfied Ian's preference for working 'with *actors* rather than comedians, because they played the part for what it was worth; reality came into the piece, and they weren't going out just to get laughs. I wasn't jealous of laughs,'[38] he explained, 'I wanted them to get laughs when they were there in the script. You wanted someone who was going to give a true performance of that man, and if there were laughs in the script he would get them.'[39]

As Ian rightly pointed out, there were many incidental joys in *Left, Right and Centre*, from Sim's dissolute and greedy Lord Wilcot, turning his insolvent stately home into an amusement park, complete with fruit machines fixed so they won't pay out jackpots and 'Lord Wilcot's Own Parsnip Wine', to the double-act of the campaign managers Barker and Wattis, acting almost as a

Greek chorus as they commented on events. Barker in particular was given a memorably funny rant about Robert Wilcot's romantic nature: 'I'll teach the Tories to nominate a sex maniac for a respectable seat like Earndale. No wonder they had to send him to the Antarctic! Heaven knows what he'd be like in a heatwave!'

One brief scene, showing facsimiles of the heads of real politicians like Harold Macmillan and Hugh Gaitskill as targets in Lord Wilcot's coconut shy, was a notable first, predating the person-specific satire boom of the early 1960s by five years. It also looked forward to Ian's next project for the Boulting brothers, which would be one of the finest examples of British film satire ever made.

The starting point for the twins' new venture *I'm All Right Jack* was Britain's trade unions, the bodies that represented the interests of workers throughout industry. Up to 1958, there were approaching nine million trade unionists in the United Kingdom, with all but half a million affiliated to the Trade Union Congress, the movement's governing body. By 1953, the unions already had a significant influence on the country's economy. Since that year, their relationship with the ruling Tory government had been steadily deteriorating, and the rise in the number of industrial stoppages – an average of 1,791 per year between 1945 and 1954, thereafter rising to an average of 2,521 every twelve months – was increasingly motivated by the trade unions' curious combination of social responsibility for their members, left-wing politics and self-interest. From the mid-1950s, it had also become clear that a rift was developing between the well-paid, complacent union leadership élite and the members on the lowest rung of the union ladder. Disillusioned with their management, the union rank and file had more faith in their committed, unpaid representatives, the shop stewards. These men collected trade union dues in factories, recruited new members and enforced legislation agreed between the unions and factory management. In Britain's car industry, the shop stewards' individual popularity on the factory floor had enabled them to build up influential personal followings.

This situation resulted in the late 1950s in a rash of unauthorised local strikes, instigated by the shop stewards rather than their union leaders, mostly without any discussion or negotiation, and usually provoked by internal union disagreements or tensions between skilled and unskilled workers. Ominously, an investigation by a court of enquiry into the stoppages at Ford's Dagenham plant accused the shop stewards of controlling 'a private union within a union, enjoying immediate and continuous contact with the men in the shop, answerable to no superiors, and in no way officially or constitutionally linked with the union hierarchy.'[40] As far as the Boultings were concerned, such volatile organisations were ripe for lampooning. 'We enjoy making fun of the Establishment', Roy explained, '[and] the trade unions are part of the Establishment.'[41]

The new economic bogeyman of the chief shop steward, together with a dash of Frank Cousins, the militant head of the Transport and General Workers Union since 1956 who had no time for compromise in bargaining for higher wages, became the lynchpin of the twins' latest satire in the guise of the severe Fred Kite (Peter Sellers). Glowering at all and sundry above a clipped moustache, at the first opportunity he would reveal his sympathies for Soviet Russia and 'all them cornfields and ballet in the evening'. Kite was a new addition to a roll-call of characters that reunited most of the major and minor players from *Private's Progress* including, among others, Stanley Windrush (Ian), Bertram Tracepurcel (Dennis Price), Sidney De Vere Cox (Richard Attenborough) and Major Hitchcock (Terry-Thomas). Keen to film a sequel with the same strong cast, the Boultings had specifically asked Alan Hackney, the author of *Private's Progress*, to write a follow-up novel that traced the original characters' fortunes in 'Civvy Street'. The obliging Hackney duly delivered *Private Life* in the same year that the film of his book went into production, working on the script at the same time. The new story followed Windrush's misadventures at his Uncle Bertram's Missiles Ltd factory, where he became a pawn in the latter's plan to pull off a massive financial fraud after unwittingly bringing about a strike that was called by the aggressive Kite.

The Boultings' decision to change the logical title of Hackney's sequel to *I'm All Right Jack* signified the seriousness of the twins' satirical attack from the outset, paraphrasing the rather less polite working-class saying of the time, 'Fuck you, Jack, I'm all right'. With their new movie, the brothers would finally deliver their definitive statement on 1950s' Britain, targeting not just self-interested organised labour but corrupt employers, frivolous consumerism and an ambivalent media; as in *Left, Right and Centre*, a parody TV panel show with a real presenter, in this case *Argument* with Malcolm Muggeridge, was an important part of the narrative. Perhaps inspired by the topicality of their material, the Boultings also made *I'm All Right Jack* their most complete and well-structured film satire to date. It scored over *Private's Progress* in sustaining the comic tone throughout, over *Brothers in Law* in not softening the lampooning in favour of a feel-good ending and over *Lucky Jim* in avoiding a fudged compromise between slapstick and contemporary sardonic bite.

A further mark of the film's qaulity is that almost every scene is crammed with detail that illustrates the Boultings' vision of an England receding ever further from a land of fair play and social responsibility and into a modern world of amorality, triviality and selfishness. At the beginning of the film, one of the last bastions of the secure established order, peer of the realm 'old Sir John' (Sellers in a cameo role) is shown being woken in his London club on VE Day. The by now customary voiceover knowingly informed the audience 'there goes Sir John – on his way out' and that the post-war society would be 'a new age, and with that new age [would come] a new spirit,' a solemn statement that is immediately followed by Private Knowles (Victor Maddern), perched on a lamp post, turning his V-for-Victory sign into a two-fingered insult directed straight at the viewing audience.

Following Windrush's odyssey through various prospective offers of employment, the increasingly sarcastic narrator notes his desire to supply the 'vital needs for which the people had hungered for so long' – in this case the hardly essential Detto washing powder, the appearance of which is followed by an inane advertising jingle. The jokes keep on coming: Windrush's next employment opportunity is a sweet factory where the machines are designed to look as if they have faces vomiting forth an unpalatable goo, there are flatulent noises in the background and people sneeze on the chocolate. Once he reaches Uncle Bertram's factory, a 'No Smoking' sign is being flagrantly ignored by happily puffing workers, and hidden in a stack of crates are three men playing cards who should have been dismissed because of over-manning but have been kept on the payroll by the machinations of the union. Later, upsetting a stuttering union rep (Sam Kydd) with his over-enthusiastic working practices, it looks like Windrush is going to be on the receiving end of a taboo-busting reprimand for 1959: 'You silly c-c-c-clot.' *I'm All Right Jack* was full of such pleasures, including the swaggering, upbeat theme song performed by Al Saxon, a popular singer who had two Top Ten hits in 1959 which openly celebrated the every-man-for-himself culture of the film:

> I'm all right, Jack, I'm okay,
> That is the message for today.
> So, count up your lolly, feather your nest,
> Let someone else worry, boy, I couldn't care less.
> You scratch my back; I'll do the same for you, Jack,
> That is the message for today.

As well as the abundance of classic humorous moments, *I'm All Right Jack* stood out in the Boultings' 1950s comedies as it allowed the three main characters at the centre of the story to develop beyond their initial satirical functions, adding some genuine humanity to the film. Sellers' Kite starts off as a pompous, pretentious and obtuse union firebrand – 'We do not and cannot accept the principle that incompetence justifies dismissal. That is victimisation.' – but once the strike, in many ways his defining moment, has started, Kite's wife (Irene Handl on fine form) ironically decides to down tools herself and leaves him: 'From what I can see, the only time you ever jolly well do any work is when you're on strike.' Abandoned by both his spouse and daughter Cynthia (Liz Fraser), the heartbroken demagogue is left gazing sadly at a photograph of him and his wife on their wedding day. With most of the country's workers on a sympathy walkout, there is a striking contrast between the national industrial unrest Kite had triggered and the absurd, lonely figure wearing his wife's apron, standing on a dried-up slice of toast in an untidy kitchen.

At this point, at the express request of Tracepurcel (Dennis Price), who fears that the countrywide strike is going to scupper his planned fraud, Terry-Thomas's Major Hitchcock is ordered in to Kite's abode to try and salvage the situation. The personnel manager at the factory, Hitchcock represented the indolent, upper-class snob in the workplace, a man more interested in an out-of-hours 'time-and-motion study of my own' with an attractive redhead than in the staff he considers to be 'an absolute shower' (another outing for Terry-Thomas's *Private's Progress* catchphrase). He harbours particular contempt for Kite, a man he sneers at as the 'sort of chap who sleeps in his vest.' When the two men confront each other amid Kite's domestic disorder, they are finally revealed as not so different; bereft of any industrial clout they are shown for what they are: two isolated, self-opinionated men. Hitchcock tries hard to show compassion – commenting on Kite's 'charming little place', and, poignantly, darning one of his socks for him – as between them they devise a plan to get Windrush dismissed, touchingly demonstrating that the two polar opposites have more in common than they realised.

The other component of the central trio was Ian himself, recreating his career-defining role of Stanley Windrush, who, in the brave new world of 1950s British business found that 'his impeccable breeding and generosity of spirit are not assets but handicaps'.[42] Creatively restless and not one to look back, the actor would feel that his reprise of the character that had made him famous and wealthy wasn't satisfying because 'I was simply repeating the part. I'd liked to have gone on to pastures new.'[43] This was a surprising admission given the calibre of the ensemble cast and the incisiveness of John Boulting, Frank Harvey and Alan Hackney's screenplay, that 'boisterously [distilled] the essence of mid-1959.'[44] Leaving aside Ian's personal reservations, the Windrush of *I'm All Right Jack* is the pinnacle of his embodiment of a disappearing sense of British innocence, good humour and fair play and was far from the 'buffoon'[45] that Ian would dismiss him as in later years. More than Kite and Hitchcock, as the character that the film follows from beginning to end, Windrush developed from the easygoing victim of *Private's Progress*, who had plainly learned nothing from his experiences, to a man righteously enraged by the corruption around him.

As if this transitional journey wasn't enough of a gift for an actor, the Boultings again offered Ian some beguiling comic scenes. In a passionate clinch with the busty Cynthia, a woman so in thrall to consumerism that she asks Windrush if his teeth are his own as 'they're so nice and white I thought they might be dentures', his affronted reaction, which she can't see, is hilarious. Elsewhere, his old wartime adversary the psychiatrist Waters, now an equally twitchy time-and-motion man, fools him into demonstrating that a pile of crates can be moved a lot faster by a forklift truck than the union specified. The scene is made all the more funny because Windrush, with his innate good nature, goes out of his way to be helpful, taking Waters' request for help at face value. Once Stanley's unwitting productivity has triggered a walk out by the workers, Hitchcock confronts his former soldier with a memorable tirade that shows just how much Windrush's good intentions have been misconstrued: 'You were damn bolshy in the army and now you're trying the same thing here! ... Don't come the innocent with me, Windrush! You haven't been here more than five minutes and the whole place is on strike! You're a positive *shower*! A stinker of the first order!' As if to reinforce the Major's opinions of him, Stanley then slams the door of his bubble car on Hitchcock's hand and drives off over his foot.

Ian's funniest set piece came at the beginning of *I'm All Right Jack*, and stands now as one of the finest examples of his talent for physical comedy. Given a guided tour of a sweet factory looking to employ him, Windrush grows steadily more nauseous due to the upsetting aromas and amount of confectionery he eats, his impeccably suited and bowler-hatted city gent becoming progressively more unsteady and ill-looking. The sequence climaxes with Windrush collapsing into one of the machines and being sick as his hat, caught up in the production line, is covered in icing and cherries. The *News Chronicle* applauded the routine as 'the best bit of visual slapstick I have seen since [silent movie comedian] Larry Semon ran silently riot in a sawmill when I was eight.'[46] In other press coverage there was a feeling that *I'm All Right Jack* was a career highlight for Ian, as he gave 'a wonderfully sustained comic performance'[47] in 'the part of his life.'[48] With some remarkable foresight, the US magazine *Time* remarked that Ian's character was 'the sort of friendly Freddie that P.G. Wodehouse likes to write about.'[49]

It was in the film's final scenes, with all the personalities in the Missiles Ltd dispute invited on to a television discussion programme, that Ian took both the film and his film career to another level. Offered a bribe by Cox to keep quiet, it gradually dawns on Stanley how his honesty has been manipulated by both the management and the unions. In a virtuoso performance, and one of the high points of 1950s British cinema, Ian looks convincingly troubled and conflicted, smoking nervously as his indignation and rage slowly build through a speech of dawning, affronted realisation:

> I'm gonna find it pretty difficult to say what I want to say in a few words. In fact I'm now only just beginning to catch on. As my friend Knowlesy would have said, I must have been dead stupid. I've swallowed *everything* they've given me to swallow ... *Everything*! All the phoney, patriotic claptrap of the employers, all the bilge I've heard talked about workers' rights until my head's reeling with the

stink of it all … Trouble is, everyone's got so used to the smell they
no longer notice it. Furthermore they're *deaf* too! So deaf they can't
even hear the fiddles, in fact they don't want to! Wherever you look,
it's a case of '*blow you, Jack, I'm all right*!'

As the Boultings had liberal political sympathies, it's tempting to
think that these sentiments came direct from brother John's mouth.
The fact that Ian knew the man well may have inspired him to
deliver such an impassioned performance, but there's no doubt
that such acerbic, tightly written dialogue contributed to some of
Ian's finest dramatic moments on film. His *tour de force* continued
with assaults on Kite and Uncle Bertram respectively:

Your politics? 'To each according to his needs, from each as little as
he can get away with, and no overtime, except on Sundays at double
the rate!' That's a damned fine way to build a new Jerusalem!

   All your talk of *country*! You're always wearing such a ruddy
great Union Jack no one can see what you're up to behind it!

Just as Windrush had sanitised the well-known working-class
saying in his first outburst, there follows some wonderfully
antiquated name-calling between Stanley and Tracepurcel
indicative of the censorship standards of the time ('Bounder!'
'Cad!' 'Skunk!'), before the panel show ends in pandemonium.
While a virtuous Stanley scatters Cox's money around him, the
studio is wrecked as an unruly mob of I'm-all-right-Jacks –
audience, technicians and panellists – tries to grab the cash. In a
decidedly downbeat ending, Windrush is invalided out of Missiles
Ltd due to mental instability, once again unwittingly falling into
the trap of doing what the conspirators wanted. His retirement
from the rat race to the artificial paradise of a nudist colony with
his father brings him no peace either. Although *I'm All Right Jack*
ended with the comical sequence of a semi-naked Windrush being
chased by an eager group of nude women, the point being made
was a grim one: no matter how much you try to keep life pure,
avarice of some kind will always intrude.

Ian's impressive performance did not go unnoticed by reviewers, with the *Chronicle* praising his 'last impassioned tirade on television against the equal corruption of management and labour, which he utters quite magnificently,'[50] and the *Star* noting how 'he brilliantly busts open the whole crazy set-up.'[51] The more perceptive critics also spotted how this time around the Stanley Windrush character recalled other notable innocents in fiction, with the *Media Guardian* describing him as 'a veritable Candide'[52], the eponymous hero of the French philosopher Voltaire's 1759 satire about a man who becomes a disappointed optimist. Meanwhile, the *Financial Times* spotted the similarity between *I'm All Right Jack* and the American film director Frank Capra's movies *Mr Deeds Goes to Town* (1936) and *Mr Smith Goes to Washington* (1939), as 'the central figure, the innocent young man, disillusioned by the carelessness and greed around him, [was] clearly influenced by Capra's Christian heroes.'[53] The paper also pinpointed the main distinction between the films, with all-conquering American idealism replaced by a peculiarly British cynicism: 'the fervour of Smith and Deeds moved the multitudes. The Boultings' hero is hauled up before the magistrates and bound over to undergo psychiatric treatment. The lampooned Establishment is allowed to win hands down.'[54] Cultural differences aside, it must have been flattering for Ian to be mentioned in the same sentence as characters played by Hollywood giants like Gary Cooper and James Stewart, actors he would have grown up watching from the stalls of his local cinemas such as the Dorchester and the Savoy.

I'm All Right Jack was without a doubt the most successful film Ian was ever involved with. It was the number one film at the British box office in 1959 with over two million people going to see it, more even than Billy Wilder's seminal Hollywood comedy *Some Like It Hot*, which was released in the same year. The *Northern Chronicle* even went so far as to say that it had taken more money in Britain than 'any film ever made.'[55] At the beginning of September, when the Prime Minister Harold Macmillan went to the Queen's Scottish residence at Balmoral to ask for a suspension of Parliament and a general election, in the evening he was treated to a special screening of the film that had been arranged for Her Majesty. *I'm All Right Jack* was also the Boultings' most successful film in America, taking over £4,900 a week at the Guild Theatre in New York, more money than any film previously shown there. At home, it was a critical as well as a popular hit, variously lionised as 'the Boultings' best for some years'[56], a 'fantastically funny farce with savage and serious political satire'[57], and commended as a 'British film [risking] being funny AND controversial at the same time.'[58] Frequently repeated on television over the following years, *I'm All Right Jack* became such a part of the fabric of British popular culture that the title was immortalised in the chorus of the New Wave band the Boomtown Rats' first single in 1977, the aptly titled 'Looking After No. 1'.

Back in 1959, there was some disagreement with the widespread thumbs-up the film received, predictably from the left wing of the British press. A set visit by the *Daily Worker*'s Nina Hibbin in February 1959 found one of the technicians grumbling that 'It's making working-class people out to be fools',[59] and when the same paper reviewed the film it was particularly needled by Sellers' characterisation of Kite, complaining that 'we are no longer invited to laugh *with* working people but to join in jeering at them.'[60] The *Worker* went on to say, 'no one objects to fun being poked at trade unionists – trade unionists themselves would be the last to complain and the first to enjoy [it]. But to be sincere a satire must hold up a mirror to real life. This is what the Boulting Brothers have not done.'[61]

Even when *I'm All Right Jack* was being criticised in the press, journalists couldn't resist praising Sellers's turn as the self-important Fred Kite, and overall the critical response to the film, good and bad, suggested his performance was the tour de force of the movie and one of the main reasons for its success. In what must have been a bitter-sweet moment for Ian, the approving notices he received for one of his best film roles were eclipsed by the amount of plaudits heaped on his co-star, among them 'by far the best thing he has ever done'[62] (*Evening Standard*), 'Sellers gives not the most versatile but certainly the most characterful performance of his career'[63] (the *Star*), 'he emerges as a great actor of comedy as opposed to a great comic'[64] (*Daily Mail*) and 'a creation of Dickensian size, depth and richness'[65] (*Evening News*). Typically, Ian never publicly exhibited any jealousy or acrimony towards his co-star for having his big moment hijacked. Quite the reverse, in fact:

> [Sellers] was very, very good in the role. [The Boultings] had a lot of trouble with him to start off with, 'cos he didn't want to do it. He said, 'Where are the laughs? There are no laughs in this part.' It took a lot of persuading to get him to do it. Now, one is led to believe that he did become a very difficult man later on, but Kite was the first well-directed big part in a movie that he had, and he had a real plum there. He was very good, he was very well behaved and everything, and that's really the part that pumped him right up into the stratosphere.[66]

Sellers had first come to prominence as an alumnus of the 1949 BBC radio *The Goon Show*, with its pioneering brand of anarchic, surreal humour that is still influential in comedy today. Just as the Goons had broken conventions, the critics sensed they were on to something new with Sellers; although he was five years younger than Ian, he had been able to transform himself into a convincing middle-aged man who looked at least fifteen years older than his co-star. Although in drama Sellers' technique would be called 'character acting', it was still relatively new in film comedy, even though the actor was following in the footsteps of his hero Alec Guinness. The Ealing comedy star was equally adept at chameleonic changes in appearance and manner, most notably in the multiple roles of *Kind Hearts and Coronets* (1949). Although Sellers deservedly achieved the accolade of a British Academy award for the best British actor of 1959 for *I'm All Right Jack*, ahead of such heavyweights as Laurence Olivier and Richard Burton, it was unjust and inaccurate of the press to conclude that the 'old professionals' (Ian, Terry-Thomas, Dennis Price et al) were just 'playing for laughs'[67] and that '[the cast] and Ian Carmichael [played] second fiddle to Peter Sellers.'[68]

At the end of the 1950s Ian was in a contradictory position. He was a wealthy man living in a beautiful and luxurious home with a devoted wife and family, and was unquestionably one of the brightest stars in British comedy's firmament, both on the stage and the big screen. Conversely, no matter how good he was in an individual role, in movies he remained limited to the part of the genial blunderer that some critics were already calling 'his usual film self'[69], comments which reinforced the stereotype and ignored the promise he had shown as a dramatic actor in *I'm All Right Jack*'s final scenes. In fact the huge success of the movie ironically worked against Ian's desire to diversify in his film career, the actor feeling 'that [it] set a stamp on what people thought I could do for a very long period of time. I was only offered buffoons, really ... I turned down more than I actually did.'[70]

Nevertheless, *I'm All Right Jack* was still a high point of Ian's years working in British movies, successfully capping a decade he had begun as a supporting artist and ended as a star. In spite of his success, Ian remained a committed film buff at heart, and always made a point of taking a keepsake from the sets of the films he worked on. From the Boultings' definitive national satire he kept the pair of blue dungaree overalls that he had worn while driving a forklift truck. Instead of hoarding them to fetch a ridiculous price at a future auction of cinema memorabilia, Ian wore them for home decorating around Moat Lodge. It said a lot about the man that he had such a relaxed and non-precious approach to cinematic mementoes, even if there was a degree of mischievous vanity involved. Remarking in 1979 on his acquisition from *I'm All Right Jack* he declared, 'It does my ego good to know that after twenty years I can still get into them.'[71]

CHAPTER 9

Carry On Ian

*Two of the finest films in Ian's career, a notable musical
disappointment and how he might have been able to* Carry On.

I N 1959, THE British electorate had returned a Conservative
government who, despite industrial stoppages instigated by
the Fred Kites of the work place, were still riding high on the
tail end of the 1950s economic boom. In America, John F.
Kennedy's new Democratic broom had swept the Republicans
from the White House, and his presidency, characterised by his
dazzling film star good looks and a glamorous family dynasty,
offered the promise of a progressive new leadership for the Western
world. On the eve of his fortieth birthday, Ian, too, had every
reason to believe that his personal boom time would continue.
Straight after *I'm All Right Jack* finished filming (fulfilling his five-
film commitment to the Boulting brothers), he arrived at the
Associated British Studios in Borehamwood to begin work on
another film comedy, *School for Scoundrels or How to Win Without
Actually Cheating*. The film was an adaptation of Stephen Potter's
novels *Oneupmanship*, *Gamesmanship* and *Lifemanship*, spoof 'self-
help' manuals from the fictitious College of Lifemanship in Yeovil,
which instructed the modern gentleman on how to get the better of
his social opponents through a series of sleights of hand and clever
ploys. Potter's books were a new, cynical strand of British humour
that, like the Boultings' satires and the *St Trinian's* movies, were

inspired by the more materialistic and self-serving side to British society that had emerged with the post-war consumer boom.

Reflecting the popularity in Britain of the US under the vibrant Kennedy administration, for the first time Ian found himself working with an American producer, the equally dynamic Hal E. Chester. He had been involved in movies since the 1930s and had produced some diverse material, such as the murder thriller *The Weapon* (1937), a series of gritty dramas about an abused boxer called Joe Palooka and, most outstandingly, the atmospheric horror film *Night of the Demon* (1957), based on the M.R. James story 'Casting the Runes'. Fittingly for a man who had put boxing on the cinema screen, the diminutive Chester was 'possessed [of] a face which, if it hadn't looked so youthful, might have seen several years in a boxing ring.'[1]

As well as the American's colourful appearance, the producer impressed the actor with 'his ability to put it all together. Throughout the time I knew him he always managed to gather around him a package of considerable talent.'[2] On *School for Scoundrels* the talent in question included the Ealing Studios-schooled director Robert Hamer, who had made the 'Haunted Mirror' segment of the supernatural anthology *Dead of Night* (1945) and, demonstrating his directorial flair for both drama and comedy, the classic *Kind Hearts and Coronets* (1949). The author of the script was no less impressive. Peter Ustinov was something of a polymath; as well as writing, producing and directing he had acted to great acclaim as the Roman Emperor Nero in the movie epic *Quo Vadis?* (1951) and in Max Ophuls' stylish film *Lola Montez* (1955), a biography of the nineteenth-century adventuress. The cast was equally notable, assembling a selection of actors who were by now part of an unofficial repertory company in British film comedy and who had all acted with Ian before, including Alistair Sim, Janette Scott, Peter Jones, Irene Handl, Dennis Price (who had also played the murderer Louis Mazzini in *Kind Hearts and Coronets*) John Le Mesurier and, as Ian's rival for the affections of Janette Scott's April Smith, Terry-Thomas.

The casting of the two central roles in *School for Scoundrels* couldn't have been more appropriate. While Ian had been repeatedly cast as variations of the well-meaning, if gullible, everyman of post-war English life, Thomas had gradually evolved a screen persona that was the exact opposite. His plummy voice and aristocratic sneer, often complemented by a penchant for dandified suits and cigarette holders, helped define him as a character that was the yin to Ian's yang: selfish, preening, acquisitive and cowardly. Thomas's amoral screen self also somehow possessed an irresistible, oily charm. By 1960 Thomas had become the quintessential English 'bounder', seen in such portrayals as the bankrupt 'Captain' Romney Carlton Ricketts in *Blue Murder at St Trinian's* (1957) and the 'man of rubble from the nostrils up'³ *Carlton-Browne of the F.O.* (1959). These were upper-class characters like Ian's Windrush, who were adrift in the modern world but, crucially, determined to maintain an easy and indulgent life through often nefarious, 'caddish' behaviour.

Thomas's and Ian's careers also had intriguing parallels. Like a lot of their contemporaries, they had learned the fundamentals of the entertainment business by performing for the British forces during the Second World War, and both had been major contributors to BBC TV in the late 1940s: Thomas masterminded and starred in the ground-breaking comedy series *How Do You View?* while Ian became popular through period musicals and plays. They had both come to prominence in the British film industry at the same time and, significantly, in the same film, the Boulting brothers' *Private's Progress*. It was Ian's and Thomas's association with the gifted twins that cemented the idea of a rivalry between the two men's screen personas, from Windrush versus Hitchcock, to Thursby versus Green, to Dixon versus Welch to David Chaytor versus Humourless Country Policeman. *School for Scoundrels* traded on this rivalry and was the culmination of the two men's partnership both as performers and as the popular film versions of themselves, as the perceptive reviewer in the *Sunday Times* noted: 'The timid failure … is played by Ian Carmichael …

The bristly bounder whose success with waiters, cars, tennis courts and girls drives the hero to such extremes is the one who has been driving Mr Carmichael to extremes on the screen these past four years: the actor is Terry-Thomas.'[4]

Delighted to be working with her *Happy is the Bride* co-star again, Janette Scott was well placed to observe the differences between the two men. 'I didn't ever get the impression that they were that close,'[5] she reflects, perhaps surprisingly. 'They were friendly and they undoubtedly had respect for each other's talent and comedy timing. Ian and I always ate in the studio canteen, while Terry always disappeared off the [studio] lot and would sometimes have lunch with whoever went to the local pub; not necessarily the cast, it could be the technicians. On a Friday evening, Ian and I would look forward to our respective weekends and our respective homes, while Terry would still be keen to hang out at the pub.'[6] Highlighting the major difference between Thomas's and Ian's working methods and lifestyles, Janette mischievously observes, 'providing that Terry was OK and hadn't been to the pub for lunch, the afternoons went as well as the mornings.'[7] More significantly, she remembers: 'Robert Hamer had a really bad drink problem, not helped by liquid lunches with Terry.'[8]

For a film that Ian remembered as having 'a good script and a strong cast [where] everybody knew everybody'[9], *School for Scoundrels'* production was beset by major problems, not least the director's alcoholism, with Janette recalling that Hamer's descent into the bottle was 'really sad for such a very talented man.'[10] To Chester's credit, he had given the director another chance by offering him a major British film with a celebrated cast, and had taken great pains to ensure that Hamer stayed both on the wagon and on schedule. Ultimately his sterling efforts would come to nothing, as Ian ruefully recalled:

Hal Chester, the little volatile producer of *School for Scoundrels*, looked after [Hamer] like a child. He picked him up in the morning and took him to the studio, he looked after him at lunchtime, he took him home at night and everything was hunky dory. He was

OK, he was *compos mentis* and played well. It was in the last fortnight, I think, that it was a night shoot [outside the BBC club] and I got down there and he was stoned out of his mind. He was absolutely rolling around, couldn't do a thing. So, I'm afraid he had to be removed. The producer directed that night, and then after that, for the last few weeks, another director came in who never got credited called Cyril Frankel, who I was in the army with, strangely.[11]

As well as Hamer's behaviour, the film's budget was also in a precarious state. '[Chester] spent a great deal of time running around trying to get enough money to finish it,' Janette remembers. 'At one point he re-mortgaged his house in Hampstead to get *School for Scoundrels* finished. I've no idea why the funding was a problem.' Away from these production complications, Ian and Terry had to contend with Chester's sometimes over-enthusiastic streak, which, perhaps because of the financial pressure and his difficulties with Hamer, had manifested in the producer trying to 'improve' the script. Ian and Thomas were appalled when he brought in an American writer, Patricia Moyes, to try and slant Ustinov's screenplay more towards a US audience, interference that the patriotic Ian admitted was 'guaranteed to make me turn red, white and blue with anger when dealing with an essentially English subject.'[12] In the event, none of the amendments were used, although Chester's intrusion and tendency to take credit for things he hadn't done would continue to rankle with Ian as, criminally, Moyes and Chester would be credited for the screenplay instead of Ustinov: 'Hal did not write a single perishing line! All he did was grumble about Peter and try and bring in American gags for the American market.'[13]

Compared to these problems, Ian's relationship with the hangdog Alistair Sim (playing the *Lifemanship* author Stephen Potter) would be light relief. A respected stage and film actor, Sim was equally at home in serious and comic parts, from the chilling detective in the film version of *An Inspector Calls* to the authentically frumpy headmistress and her crooked twin brother Clarence in *The Belles of St Trinian's* (both released in 1954). As Sim was a very eccentric personality, Ian had been warned during production of *Left, Right and Centre* that the Scottish actor could be 'a very difficult man to get on with,' although, when it came to filming their scenes together, Ian had found his co-star to be '*marvellous, absolutely wonderful*'[14]. Sim's unconventional nature became more apparent during the making of *School for Scoundrels*, much to Ian's consternation:

> The thing was, he never wanted to touch a prop. When I got to the Yeovil school, in one of the early scenes there, he gave me tea and muffins. It was all put in front of him: he was the host. The director said, 'Hand the muffins to Ian' and [Sim] said, 'No, no, no, let him help himself, I don't want to handle anything.' So there was I, the guest, and I had to help myself to the muffins and pour my own tea, practically.[15]

Despite all the trials and tribulations involved in its making, none of the behind-the-scenes tensions were evident in the finished edit of *School for Scoundrels*. The relatively simple story unfolds seamlessly, as Ian's diffident Henry Palfrey tries to steal April Smith (Scott) from under the moustache of Raymond Delauney (Terry-Thomas) by using the techniques of Sim's Stephen Potter, the slippery genius of Lifemanship. This skill involved the socially ruthless attitude of either being 'One up or one down … on your opponents at all times' and this is what gave the script its distinctive, cruel humour in a movie where there were no good guys. Whereas in Ian's previous film confrontations with Terry-Thomas the latter had always played the aggressor, in *School for Scoundrels* all the main characters are self-serving; the honest, if put-upon, Palfrey becomes as predatory as Delauney in order literally to seduce a superficial girl who is dazzled by fast cars, charm and wealth. Watching the film over half a century after it was released, it impresses as one of the earliest examples of the comedy of social cruelty that would be explored by recent series such as *I'm Alan Partridge*, *Curb Your Enthusiasm*, *The Office* and *Extras*, where the audience is invited to laugh at the embarrassment and humiliation of its protagonists. This very modern quality keeps

School for Scoundrels relevant now, and helps to explain why the American director Todd Phillips thought it ripe for a Stateside remake in 2006.

For Ian, *School for Scoundrels* is the film where the worm turns. The script is almost self-aware in the way that it cast the Carmichael and Thomas personas in their usual roles then gradually subverted them to the point where Ian/Palfrey beat Terry-Thomas/ Delauney at his own game by effectively becoming Terry-Thomas. If *I'm All Right Jack* had demonstrated how effective Ian could be as a dramatic actor, *School for Scoundrels* broke the mould completely by allowing him to play the villain. That he was clearly enjoying himself in delivering a performance of such raffish relish as the Lifemanship-literate Palfrey indicated just how much of a delight for him it must have been to break free, however temporarily, from the strait-jacket of the 'innocent buffoon' stereotype. It shouldn't be too much of a surprise to learn that because of this, *School for Scoundrels* narrowly trumps *I'm All Right Jack* as Ian's best film.

The high points are many. As the film begins, the audience immediately sympathises with the usual Carmichael character who is subservient to employees who have no respect for his authority, is replaced in Saturday's football team by a friend who is a better player and is outshone by Delauney's intellect and style when Palfrey takes April out to dinner. Most humiliating of all, he is conned by the wonderfully named Dunstan and Dudley Dorchester (one of whom was originally to have been played by Ustinov) into buying a 'vintage' car which runs on the dubious 'helical friction principle'. Delauney mocks the monstrosity as looking 'like a Polish stomach pump' and sneeringly wonders, 'what sort of an idiot would drive a thing like this?' Palfrey's shame is compounded in a tennis match in which Delauney, taking the side of the court that will keep the sun in his opponent's eyes, delivers a calm and constant barrage of shots as the latter flails all over the court and nearly hits April with one serve. Throughout all these scenes, Ian's nice-guy-taken-for-a-ride act is played at its most natural, and is at its most effective in the scene where Palfrey has no choice but to sit and listen to Delauney's charm offensive on April over dinner. Ian's by turns stern, furious and exasperated expressions again highlight what an effortlessly skilled reactive actor he was.

Later, schooled in Lifemanship and, significantly, dressed as a breezy dandy *à la* Terry-Thomas – with waistcoat, pipe, bow tie, hat and scarf – Palfrey (and by extension Ian) takes great delight in getting the better of his adversaries from earlier in the film. His revenge on the Dorchester brothers is particularly satisfying, as he gets them to take back the embarrassing automobile that they've duped him into buying in exchange for a brand new car and one hundred guineas. Again, it's Ian's sincere underplaying of his dialogue about meeting a car aficionado who'd 'be prepared to pay … *anything*' for the Dorchester's old crock that makes his metamorphosis into a silky rogue so believable. This is shown particularly effectively in the scenes where he gets the better of his accountant Gloatbridge (Edward Chapman), deliberately making the ex-smoker uncomfortable by offering him a cigarette. With Ian exhibiting slyness, manipulation and charm, the sequence climaxes when Palfrey, having further undermined Gloatbridge by doctoring his figures, finally persuades the man to accept a cigarette when he hasn't smoked for ten years.

Predictably, though, it's the scenes where Ian outwits Terry-Thomas that are *School for Scoundrel*'s greatest moments. It was rare to witness the moustachioed *bon vivant* on the back foot, so to see his good-natured adversary finally getting the better of him was a treat. Delauney becomes more and more anxious on his way to collect April for a return tennis match with Palfrey, the latter deliberately delaying him by nonchalantly settling down to read the *Sporting Life* then leading him on a completely unnecessary detour which culminates in the flustered Delauney having an accident. 'Oh, bad luck. And new paint work too,' purrs Palfrey, his innocent inflection infuriating Delauney even further. By the time they arrive at the tennis club, the car's exhaust is damaged, its number plate is hanging off and the unhappy driver faces disgrace through being thirty minutes late, an unforgivable breach of etiquette for which he is entered in the complaints book.

The tennis match that follows, with Thomas and Ian playing each other one on one, is one of the comedic highlights of both men's careers. In a complete reversal of their previous bout, Palfrey is quietly confident and graceful, playing with one relaxed hand in his pocket and his street clothes, as Delauney progressively loses his cool to his opponent's tease of 'You're putting it on a bit, old man' in reference to his waistline and attempts to show him how to play tennis properly. This time, of course, it is also Delauney's turn to squint into the sun. Palfrey's transformation into his opposite number is further signposted when he throws Delauney's 'hard cheese' taunt back at him, enraging him to such an extent that he is reprimanded for the frustrated exclamation 'Oh, nuts!' 'Language, old man, language! Ha-ha!' offers Palfrey in return, mock-innocently making his rival's discomfiture worse.

Both Ian's and Thomas's playing against their usual archetypes in the tennis match is recognised as one of the highlights of post-war film comedy, so much so that it became one of the sequences used in a series of 'One-to-One' TV advertisements for British Telecom in the 1990s, with Ian's part played by the comedian Vic Reeves. For routines that would become such iconic comedy set pieces, Ian remembered that the filming of both matches was rather too relaxed for his own liking:

> The tennis match material was a joy to do, although it personally worried me enormously. I had filmed a golf match scene with John Le Mesurier for *Brothers in Law* which worked brilliantly. The Boultings had insisted that the scene be scripted down to the very last detail and planned, shot by shot, before we filmed it. I felt that this tennis match should be done in the same way but Hal E. Chester disagreed. We were just told to go on playing in-between the scripted lines of dialogue and, if anything funny or unusual happened during the actual play, they would cut it in and use it. It seemed a little bit hit-and-miss to me – quite literally – but Terry and myself went along with it and I think we just about pulled it off.[16]

With Delauney well and truly expelled from April's affections and Palfrey awarded his Lifemanship Diploma because of his caddish behaviour during the tennis match ('passed with honours'), *School for Scoundrels* took a darker and slightly unconvincing turn in its final quarter. Palfrey's entire campaign of Oneupmanship had been building towards getting April back to his flat so he could use the 'Uncle Ploy', a tactic so titled because it implied a platonic relationship 'for trust and confidence', but was really a way of getting the object of one's desire from 'the living room to the bedroom in three easy moves.' For Ian to play a part that required him to make a whisky glass slippery so his female companion would spill its contents over herself, obliging her to change into his dressing gown, which he could dismiss as 'sexless' in his final provocative act of seduction, was a bold departure for Ian at the time, further distancing him from his honest and wholesome image.

As Potter and Delauney burst into Palfrey's flat to save April's virtue, Delauney accuses him of being 'a bounder', a sure sign that the two have by now completely changed places. Ironically, this proves to be the trigger for Ian's old film persona to snap back into place as Palfrey undergoes a last-minute change of mind, despite having exhibited no pangs of conscience in his previous scenes as a Lifeman. With a mortified Potter exclaiming, 'Not sincerity, Palfrey!', the latter confesses all to April and the two collapse into a romantic clinch that looks like an eleventh-hour failure of nerve by the writers and director, going completely against the grain of the film's overall cynical tone. However, the happy ending was knowingly undercut by Potter addressing the audience directly: 'Once sincerity rears its ugly head, Lifemanship is powerless … Stop that music! Orchestra! Stop that infernal din!'

Appropriately, the mocking tone was back in full effect during the end titles, when Delauney could be seen literally following in Palfrey's footsteps to the Lifemanship college in Yeovil.

For a movie that has become one of the most celebrated examples of British film comedy, Janette Scott remembers that '*School for Scoundrels* came out very quietly but word of mouth made it a success. The critics could be sniffy about comedy and sniffy about British output in general.'[17] Looking at the English reviews from the time of the film's release in March 1960, there was certainly the sense that the film was dismissed as an interesting failure. The *Southern Dispatch* judged 'the comedians work resourcefully'[18] but felt overall that the movie was 'a dullish comedy graced, rather than retrieved, by half a dozen funny moments,'[19] while the *Financial Times* went further, claiming that 'the film has not, finally, the wit or the style or the brilliance that such distinguished collaborators owed it.'[20] While there were good notices for the three stars' performances, it took *Time and Tide* to recognise the film's overall merit, its reviewer praising *School for Scoundrels* as 'something precious, individual and extremely rare.'[21] It seems that the movie's ahead-of-its-time social comedy was appreciated everywhere but in its country of origin, ironic considering it was such a characteristically English subject. Reinforcing this view and the short-sightedness of British critics, Janette Scott recalls that the film went on to be 'an amazing success and ran for nearly a year just off the Champs-Élysées in Paris.'[22]

School for Scoundrels was released at the end of an intense five-year period for Ian when, in a testament to his prodigious work ethic, he had made an amazing *ten* films. Unfortunately, the regularity with which one followed the other highlighted the fact that he'd basically been playing a similar kind of role ever since *Simon and Laura* in 1955. Ian did, after all, have the right face for it, as his old friend Patrick Macnee perceptively noted: 'He had a wonderful enquiring look about him, as if he always wanted to know what was coming next'.[23]

Of course, an actor or actress constantly playing the same role tailored to their personality was a mainstay of cinema, from Charlie Chaplin (the funny/sentimental tramp) to John Wayne (the phlegmatic cowboy) to Marilyn Monroe (the sexy, dizzy blonde); if a star was popular, and therefore bankable, in a particular role, they would be offered more of the same as it sold cinema tickets. Ironically, *School for Scoundrels* was the one film that had depended on Ian playing his usual archetype to begin with (just as it depended on Terry-Thomas playing his) before the actors swapped roles and successfully acted out of character. However, the frequency with which Ian's films were released appeared to show that the actor who 'had made a fortune out of misfortune'[24] was confined to a path of diminishing returns. The *Star* decided that 'Ian Carmichael is the protoype of all one-downers: decent, bumbling, happy go-lucky'[25], while the *Sunday Times* noted that the director curbed 'Mr Carmichael's tendency to turn every role into Mr Toots'[26] and, in perhaps the most back-handed compliment Ian received in his entire career, the *Sunday Express* praised his 'splendid incisiveness as a sophisticated villain, compared with the boring familiarity of his act as a witless, hapless stooge.'[27] With critical warnings like these becoming more widespread in the press, something clearly had to change.

British film comedy had undergone a major shift in emphasis in 1959 with the release of *Carry On Sergeant*, the first in producers Peter Rogers' and Gerald Thomas's series of screen comedies which, as its writer Norman Hudis recalled, 'turned out to be one of the funniest and most successful comedies for many, many years.'[28] Like the Boulting brothers' films, the *Carry On* comedies had introduced audiences to a repertory company of comic actors which, with various additions – notably Sid James and Joan Sims – would continue from film to film, and include Kenneth Williams, Charles Hawtrey, Hattie Jacques and Kenneth Connor. Although the *Carry On*s borrowed from the Boultings' template of lampooning pompous authority figures, in a sure sign that popular tastes were changing, Rogers' and Thomas's emphasis was on cartoon characters rather than satire and, increasingly, bawdy humour that centred on beautiful actresses like Shirley Eaton, an early sign that 1960s British cinema was about to considerably relax its attitude to sex. Even if the *Carry On*s were critically vilified, their growing popularity with cinema-goers initiated a shift away from the mature film comedies of the 1950s towards broader and coarser fare. As a result, the home-grown cinematic opportunities for the generation of sophisticated performers like Ian, Terry-Thomas and Janette Scott, whose careers had flourished in the previous decade, began to look limited.

In 1960, though, a situation arose behind the scenes of the *Carry On* films that might have seen Ian's career follow the new trend in British film comedy. Leslie Phillips, an actor only four years younger, had pursued a similar calling to Ian through West End comedies, and his breakthrough film role had been the Hollywood movie *Les Girls* (1958), in which he had taken the role of a 'silly ass' character comparable with those played by Ian at the time. Having made *Carry On Nurse* and *Carry On Teacher* (both 1959) and *Carry On Constable* (1960), Gerald Thomas wanted Phillips to commit to *Regardless* and *Cruising*, the next titles in the series, tempting him with a profit-share deal which he very quickly realised was never going to materialise. Phillips had no intention of becoming identified with an ongoing series that would typecast him all over the world, as he recalled in his autobiography:

> When I told [Thomas] I wasn't going to carry on (so to speak), he greeted the news with an evil glitter in his eye and uttered what he mistakenly thought would be the ultimate threat.
> 'I'll get Ian Carmichael!'
> 'Dear old Ian,' I chortled. 'Do give him my love.'
> And that was the end of *Carry On* for me.[29]

It's easy to see why Thomas thought that Ian and Leslie would be interchangeable. Both were suave, gentlemanly and amusing, ideal casting for a romantic, slightly caddish lead in a comedy. However, even if Ian had briefly speculated that becoming a member of the *Carry On* team was where his cinematic future lay, and Thomas *had* asked him to join, being a very shrewd man Ian would have turned the offer down for similar reasons to Phillips. As the *Carry On* producers were also notorious for holding on very tightly to the purse strings of their budgets, it's unlikely they could have afforded a bona fide British film star like Ian anyway.

Ian with Kay Kendall, Muriel Pavlow and Peter Finch in a break between takes on the film version of *Simon and Laura* (1955). *Getty Images*

The cover of *Picture Show & Film Pictorial* promoting *Lucky Jim*, 2nd November 1957. *Robert Fairclough Collection*

The seminal cast of *I'm All Right Jack* (1959). Left to right: Terry-Thomas, Richard Attenborough, Ian and Peter Sellers. *Getty Images*

Ian with
his four time
co-star
Janette Scot

Alamy

'I'M ALL RIGHT
PETER
SELLERS... JACK'
IAN CARMICHAEL · TERRY-THOMAS
A BOULTING BROTHERS PRODUCTION · A COLUMBIA PICTURES RELEASE

One of Ian's finest acting
moments: the climatic scene
from *I'm All Right Jack* (1959).
Pictorial Press Ltd/Alamy

Ian with John and Roy Boulting.
Rex Features

Raymond Delauney (Terry-Thomas) and Henry Palfrey (Ian) in the classic film comedy *School for Scoundrels*. *AF Archive / Alamy*

The poster for one of the Boulting Brothers' brilliant satires of British life, from 1963. *BFI*

Where "I'M ALL RIGHT JACK" *left off*
...*this takes off*!

THE BOULTING BROTHERS'
SELLERS PARKER JEANS SYKES MILES
HEAVENS ABOVE!
CARMICHAEL HANDL KINNEAR KARLIN PETERS

The cast of *The Amorous Prawn* (1962). Left to right: Liz Fraser, Ian, Derek Nimmo, Cecil Parker, Bridget Armstrong, Joan Greenwood, Roddy McMillan and Harry Locke. *courtesy of Bridget Armstrong*

Ian's last film as a leading man, the bizarre *Case of the '44s* (1965) *Robert Fairclough Collection*

Moira Lister, Ian's favourite leading lady. *Getty Images*

Ian's friend and neighbour Patrick Macnee with Ian during location filming for the *Armchair Theatre* production of *The Importance of Being Earnest* (ITV, 1964). *Freemantle Media Ltd / Rex Features*

Ian at home with his first wife Pym. *Derek Shuff / Rex Features*

Ian with his cricket side from one of the Boulting brothers' charity matches. Included in the first eleven are Eric Sykes (back row, second from left), Terry-Thomas (next to Ian), John Le Mesurier (second row, far right) and Kenneth Griffith (centre).
Courtesy of the Lord's Taverners

Ian at the stumps with *Z Cars* actor James Ellis.
Courtesy of the Lord's Taverners

Ian with his daughters Lee and Sally at home in Mill Hill, North London. *Getty Images*

The Corgi Classics Bentley from the BBC TV series *The World of Wooster* (1965-67), one of the few items of merchandise to feature Ian. *Robert Fairclough Collection*

Ian with the young cast of *Bachelor Father* (BBC, 1970-71), including Ian Johnson (second from left) and Briony McRoberts (second from right). *© BBC*

Ian in the early 1970s on classic detecting form as Lord Peter Wimsey with his manservant Bunter (Glynn Houston).
© BBC

Ian as Sir James Menzies in *Strathblair* (BBC, 1991-92) with his son Andrew (David Robb) and Flora McInnes (Kika Mirylees). *© BBC*

Ian with the regular cast of *The Royal* (ITV, 2004). *ITV/Rex Features*

Ian proudly showing off his OBE on 22nd October 2003. *Rex Features*

Ian with his second wife Kate Fenton at home on the Yorkshire Moors. *Daily Mail/Rex Features*

The ITV tribute to Ian shown at the end of *The Royal* on 5th June 2011. © *ITV 2011*

In memory of Ian Carmichael
18th June 1920 – 5th February 2010

As slightly bluer winds of change blew through British film comedy – and directly after finishing *School for Scoundrels* in early 1959 – Ian concentrated on a return to the London stage in a musical comedy, pursuing his liking for humorous material that was stylish, unusual and clever and, perhaps, to make his mark in a genre that had been increasing in popularity since the end of the war. *The Carefree Heart* had attracted him as it was based (loosely) on the medical plays of the French writer Jean-Baptiste Molière and because the pedigree of its American writers and composers was equally impressive. Robert Wright and George Forrest had become renowned for their adaptations of Edvard Grieg's *The Song of Norway* (1944) and Alexander Borodin's *Kismet* (1953), musicals that had brought them considerable international acclaim. *The Carefree Heart* had fared less well, however, and its tour of the United States came to an abrupt end before it reached Broadway. Considerable rewriting had followed and, undeterred, Wright and Forrest were determined to mount a new production of the play, now re-titled *The Love Doctor*, in the United Kingdom. On hearing the songs and reading the book of the play, however, with some trepidation Ian began to understand why the play had failed in America. Uncharacteristically indecisive about turning down the lead role because of the enthusiasm shown towards him by the production team, Ian and his agent Richard Stone took the play to the management duo of Robin Fox and Robert Morley, with whom Ian had enjoyed such a success with *The Tunnel of Love*. Eventually, the duo decided to produce *The Love Doctor* in tandem with Lynn Loesser, Forrest and Wright's nominated producer, while Albert Marre, the man behind the successful American production of *Kismet*, would direct. The stage was then set for Joan Heal (who had appeared in revue with Ian and Dora Bryan) and Douglas Byrne to join Ian in the lead roles.

Opening at the Opera House, Manchester, on Thursday 27 August 1959, *The Love Doctor* took as its theme mistaken identity, and centred on a tramp, played by Ian, who impersonated a medical specialist called Sganarelle and became involved in matrimonial intrigue in a small village in the nineteenth century. In an indication of the musical's determined originality, the design was as engaging as the subject matter, with the Frenchman Bernard Daydé realising the scenery like the pages of a children's storybook. Despite the ingenuity on show, the critical reaction to the show's initial run was reserved, although there was a positive review in the *Stage* which praised 'the scintillating cross between pantomime and musical farce'[30] and, in particular, delighted in Ian's return to theatre after a year away: '[his] return to the stage is as happy as it is welcome, and with Joan Heal and Douglas Byrne he excels in a sparkling and risqué number, "Anatomy".'[31] Ian himself felt that, even though the critical notices weren't unanimous in their praise, 'the general consensus of opinion was that the show was tuneful, easy on the eye and, though there was still a lot of work to be done, it was full of promise.'[32]

Ominously, Marre's interpretation of 'a lot of work to be done' went considerably further than Ian's. In a period when elaborately staged musicals like *Kiss Me, Kate* and *West Side Story* were in vogue, the director decided that the only way to bring *The Love Doctor* up to the standard of his new musical's competitors was to deploy new songs, new dance routines and new scenes that would be rehearsed and incorporated into the evening performance: if they didn't work, the whole process would begin again the next day, Sundays included. This went on for four weeks. The situation was incredibly wearing on the cast and production team, and morale did not improve when Michael Stewart, the American author behind the musical *Bye, Bye, Birdie* (who would enjoy huge international success five years later with *Hello, Dolly!*) was flown in to do a week's rewriting. Wishing he had trusted his initial reservations about *The Love Doctor*, Ian confessed that his time spent trying to make a moderately lame duck fly 'was one of the most exhausting four weeks of my life.'[33]

The behind-the-scenes situation deteriorated further once the play reached the New Theatre in Oxford. The demanding Marre was finally replaced by Wendy Toye and Robert Morley himself as directors, in an effort to bring some much needed stability to a production whose leading man was so run down that he had developed an abscess on a wisdom tooth and had to play 'one performance in excruciating agony and the following four, after surgery, with two stitches in my jaw.'[34] Wright and Forrest deserting a production that they plainly thought was by now beyond saving hadn't helped Ian's embattled spirits, and neither did Fox's and Morley's decision to put *The Love Doctor* on in the West End after all, despite their shattered leading actor's protests. The production had received a new injection of money to keep it going, and the producers were left with no option but to put it on at the Piccadilly Theatre, beginning on 12 October, to try and recoup some of the new investment. It ran for just two weeks before closing.

If there was one stage production in Ian's career that was a classic case of ambition exceeding preparation, *The Love Doctor* was it. Even though the show might have been moderately improved once it was up and running, the punishing regime Marre had imposed on his cast gradually drained his performers of any enthusiasm they had for the show once it reached its prestige location in the West End. Comparing such a light period fantasy with assured musical successes of the day like *My Fair Lady*, *Guys and Dolls* or *The Boy Friend* was perhaps unfair of the press, but it didn't stop a slew of negative reviews with headlines like 'Musical with a Note Missing' (*Daily Telegraph*)[35] and 'I was Fortunate ... I Fell Asleep' (*Daily Express*)[36]. A balanced appraisal of the show did appear in the *Stage*, with the reviewer noting the production's general lack of confidence: 'Somehow, nothing comes to life. The comedy falls flat and the romance never takes wing ... Ian Carmichael, as a tramp who impersonates Sganarelle and performs a mock operation to cure "dumb" Lucinda [Heal], works furiously as well as delicately to bring the character the fakery and charm it requires. He has his moments, but in the end is defeated.'[37]

Overall, *The Love Doctor* was one of Ian's most disappointing experiences in the theatre. A lot of physical and emotional effort had been expended for virtually no reward, and a high-profile return to musicals, a genre he was eminently qualified for, was stillborn. In later life, he would tersely refer to the play's uncharitable reception by the critics as nothing less than a 'mauling'[38]. As the 1960s progressed, he could only watch ruefully as actors less musically gifted than himself like Richard Burton, Ron Moody and Peter O'Toole won over critics and audiences with their unsuspected talent for singing and dancing in successful musicals, both on the stage and the cinema screen. However, immediately following the early termination of *The Love Doctor* and rather than rest, recuperate and take stock of the experience, Ian's tendency to bury disappointment under more work found him accepting another film role. 'If you fall off a horse,'[39] he reasoned with characteristic optimism, 'theory has it that you should get right up there again.'[40]

After the dictatorial regime he had endured on *The Love Doctor*, a grateful Ian found himself in safe hands with his new film *Light up the Sky!* The sympathetic director was Lewis Gilbert, who had helmed one of the earliest films the actor had appeared in, 1952's *Time, Gentlemen, Please!* As well as being welcomed by a familiar face behind the camera, Ian's new role was made easier because he was able to draw on his wartime experience as an army officer in creating the role of Lieutenant 'Ogie' Ogleby, an upper-class officer in charge of a searchlight battery called Lionheart tasked with locating enemy aircraft in 1942. Ian was by now famous enough to be given top billing but to appear in what was essentially a supporting role, in this case behind the film's two other above-the-title stars Tommy Steele and Benny Hill, an arrangement he was more than happy with as it 'allowed me to lick my wounds'[41] following his traumatic experience in the West End.

Gilbert had been a director since the 1940s when he had made documentary films for the Royal Air Force (a distinction he also shared with John Boulting). During the next decade, Gilbert's first-hand experience and knowledge of the armed forces had seen him develop into a respected chronicler of Britain's involvement in the Second World War. His films *Albert R.N.* (1953) and *The Sea Shall Not Have Them* (1954) explored the valour of the Royal Navy, while *Reach for the Sky* (1956) and *Carve Her Name with Pride* (1958) were, respectively, biographies of the air ace Douglas Bader and allied secret agent Violette Szabo. Gilbert's work was part of a major genre in post-war English film and literature that celebrated Britain's role in the Second World War and which, although earnest and well meaning, tended to be overly respectful in its depiction of rank-and-file personnel. *Private's Progress* had tried to explode the heroic myths about the British armed forces that Gilbert had helped to perpetrate, so there was not a little irony in the director casting Ian, the star of that iconoclastic film, as the commanding officer of an army unit of 'military misfits [and] non-entities' that were clearly inspired by the Boultings' ground-breaking rogues' gallery.

Light Up the Sky! was a development of *Private's Progress* as the cast of characters – a would-be chef, a hackneyed music hall double act and a misanthropic corporal among them – were presented as a group of disparate (but not criminal) individuals united in a common cause who found themselves suffering long periods of banal inactivity, punctuated by short spells of frenetic excitement: in short, the film was a realistic portrayal of modern warfare. The spells of downtime highlighted the trivial rivalries, camaraderie and jealousies in a group of men forced to spend long hours together, such as Sid McCaffey's (Hill) frustration with his philandering brother Eric (Steele). The comic potential of stealing livestock from the local farmer was also exploited, as was the tentative, poignant relationship between the bereaved Ted Green (Sidney Tafler) and his surrogate son 'Smithy' (Johnny Briggs). Such a scenario, mostly confined to the searchlight battery and barracks, was ideal for the theatre, and *Light up the Sky!* had initially premiered as Robert Storey's play *Touch It Light*. Significantly, virtually the same claustrophobic premise, complete with flawed characters, had been the basis of Keith Waterhouse and Willis Hall's 1959 Second World War play *The Long and the Short and the Tall*.

What particularly impressed about *Light Up the Sky!* was the casting of so many comic performers or light entertainers in straight roles. Apart from Ian, there was the established comedian Hill, pop singer Steele (whose very 1950s quiff was the only anachronistic feature of the film), experienced comedy actors Harry Locke and Tafler and an early appearance by the impressionist Dick Emery. While performers with well-developed comic timing undoubtedly enriched the often-amusing dialogue, to a man the searchlight unit came across as credible characters that could be funny rather than comic creations *per se*, the humour making their lived-in, war-weary personalities even more authentic (and most of the actors had either served in the Second World War or had done National Service). As far as Ian was concerned, with little fanfare Gilbert's low-key film had quietly answered those critics who felt that he was just a 'comedy' actor who was beginning to repeat himself. Even if this fact wasn't widely remarked on by the press, there was a lot of truth in the *Guardian*'s comment that Ian was 'not, for once, playing a funny man.'[42]

Put simply, Lieutenant Ogleby, a man not even dignified with a first name, is one of Ian's finest, most enjoyable and refreshingly different roles. A cricket and theatre lover and a slightly pretentious intellectual – calling his men 'legionnaires' – 'Ogie' is nonetheless completely convincing as a leader of men, very wise to his unit's tendency to go poaching and their lax attitude to sentry duty, mild transgressions he allows as long as they don't put the operation of the searchlight at risk. Fair-minded but stern when he had to be, he saw the motley band of brothers almost as errant children, using a wry sense of humour to discipline them when necessary, such as when a missing Eric didn't challenge the approach of his motorbike:

Ogleby: Why didn't you come out to see who it was?
Eric: I knew it was you, sir. Sound of yer bike.

Ogleby:	For all you know, Marshal Goering has had a bike made to sound exactly like mine.
Eric:	But it's Sunday, sir.
Ogleby:	My dear child, if ever this country is invaded, it will be at 3 o'clock on a Sunday afternoon. Will you be ready?
Eric:	Yes, sir.
Ogleby:	Thank you. I'm profoundly relieved.

At the same time, the Lieutenant had to contend with the division between the officer class and lower-ranking personnel – however much the legionnaires fell out between themselves, they presented a united front before their commanding officer. His frustration with this unwritten army etiquette boiled over when Smithy went absent without leave to find his girlfriend, and in the scene where Ogleby reprimanded his men for closing ranks, Ian showed the same assured, dramatic confidence that he had demonstrated a year before in *I'm All Right Jack*: 'For heaven's sake, do you want him hunted down like a criminal? The C.O. has decided to hand the whole matter over to the military police. Smith will be caught and charged with desertion, and you know what that means! But if we can get him back here ourselves, and quick, we can deal with him in our own way.'

Ogleby's innate humanity in helping to reconcile the personal problems of his men was shown to be tragically ironic at the end of the film when, after he personally went to find Smithy and persuaded him to return to the legionnaires, a German aircraft killed the young soldier during an air raid. The wistful, almost unreadable expression Ian affects as his shocked unit returns to their duties is a touching and remarkable display of restrained emotion. The briefest of shots, it is nonetheless a mature piece of serious film acting that made it hard to believe that this was the same actor who had double-taked, pratfalled and stuttered his way through the 1950s.

Earthy, lively, slightly sentimental and sadly underrated, *Light Up the Sky!* deserved to be a bigger success than it was. By 1960, though, the Second World War film genre was an over-familiar one, which may explain why the film's box-office takings were modest. The quality of the film certainly didn't explain its lukewarm reception. As well as featuring one of Ian's most sensitive performances, it was an intimate portrayal of Britain's wartime *esprit de corps*, showing how humour in the face of adversity was a strangely British characteristic and how the most unremarkable of men could rise to the challenge of defending their country. The critical response certainly indicated that the film should have performed better at the cinema, with the *Evening News* describing it as 'a disarming human comedy. It does not look big, but it steals your heart and tickles your ribs hugely.'[43] In the *Daily Worker*, never a huge fan of Ian's work, he received his best ever review from the paper, commending the film's depiction of 'the genuine spirit of the army hut, with its sense of comradeship, its larking about, its surprise inspections, and its petty squabbles.'[44] More pertinently, the *Daily Telegraph* applauded how the 'men are nicely observed, well short of caricature, and their goings-on will provide for many the delights of recognition, perhaps of identification.'[45]

The misfire of *The Love Doctor* aside, 1959 and 1960 hadn't been bad years for Ian. One incredibly successful and one moderately successful film had shown that there was a lot more to him as an actor than those critics who had already written his artistic obituary had predicted. It was not without some revived confidence, then, that Ian looked forward to the rest of the 1960s. As the new decade began, he was completely unaware that the next ten years would be the most professionally and personally turbulent of his whole life.

CHAPTER 10

Take it Easy, Old Feller

A lifelong friendship, Hollywood and a change of priorities

B Y 1960, IAN Carmichael was a name that theatre producers wanted on the marquees above their productions, preferably in London's West End. Having Ian attached to a show now guaranteed superior funding, a generous amount of publicity and, depending on the quality of the production, healthy box office returns. The high-profile failure of *The Love Doctor* hadn't affected the enviable position Ian had reached, following his rapid rise to film stardom, of being able to cherry-pick the theatre productions he wished to appear in. There were no more soul-destroying auditions; he just waited for a call from Richard Stone to tell him that a new script was on the way. It was the kind of illustrious professional standing every aspiring actor dreamed of attaining.

For the second time in two years, Ian found himself in the company of an energetic, diminutive producer, a situation that moved him to remark amusingly that 'around that period my life was becoming peopled by dynamic little men.'[1] Harold Fielding, possessor of sandy-coloured hair, an infectious grin and a curious, high-pitched voice, was blessed with a determination and zeal for putting on the best shows humanly possible that impressed Ian to the point that he considered the small powerhouse of a man 'our most outstanding theatrical producer'. Rather than succumb to tantrums like Hal Chester, Fielding thrived on stress, once declaring 'I'm always at my best in a crisis.'² Inspired by the optimism and positive attitude of the new producer who wanted to work with him, Ian eagerly turned to page one of *The Gazebo*.

He enjoyed it so much that the morning he started reading it in bed, he stayed there for three solid hours until he'd finished. The third American play Ian had been offered in a row, Alec Coppel's play was a comedy with darker undertones than the actor had dealt with before, a sign that while he was being offered increasingly stereotyped roles in film, theatre producers were, refreshingly, more than willing to take risks with Ian's stage roles, as long as he continued to make people laugh. In *The Gazebo*, which revolves around the murder of a blackmailer by television scriptwriter Elliott Nash, lurked something of Alfred Hitchcock's stylishly twisted cinema thrillers like *Rear Window* (1954) and *The Trouble with Harry* (1955). This is particularly evident when Nash decides that the best way to dispose of the corpse is to bury it in the foundations of an eighteenth-century gazebo that his wife Nell has just bought for their home. Elliott's frantic attempts to keep his crime secret, together with Nell's continued bemusement at his seemingly inexplicable state of agitation, offered Ian and a female partner the opportunity for an impressive double act. His theatrical clout now enabled him to get the colleagues he wanted: director Anthony Sharp, designer Reece Pemberton, who had worked on *The Tunnel of Love* and, most importantly, his leading lady from the same production, Barbara Murray.

However, Ian's increasing influence in London's theatre community was of little use when, two weeks before rehearsals were due to start, a subdued Barbara phoned him to apologise for being pregnant and informed him that she would, sadly, have to withdraw from *The Gazebo*. This was a distressing blow for Ian, as he and Barbara 'got on famously together'³ and 'the thought of having to find someone new with whom I could dovetail so amicably filled me with trepidation.'⁴ After a whole day's consideration of other actresses who could fill the requirements of a slim figure, bright blue eyes, blonde hair and immaculate, light comedy timing, Ian and Sharp decided that there was only one actress who fitted the bill: Moira Lister.

Born in Cape Town in 1923, the daughter of an army major, after several years appearing in South African productions the ambitious Moira had come to London, making her English stage debut on 12 April 1937 in *Post Road* at the Golders Green Hippodrome. More distinguished work followed at the Shakespeare Memorial Theatre in Stratford-upon-Avon and with John Gielgud's company in the 1950s, where she played her favourite roles Juliet and Desdemona, also delivering striking performances in 1956 as Margaret in *Much Ado About Nothing* and Regan in a Japanese version of *King Lear*. Away from Shakespeare, her sophistication and delicate, upper-class voice had appealed to Noël Coward when he cast her in his period comedy *Present Laughter* in 1947. This production gave Moira the popular image of an actress who, as well as being beautiful and glamorous, could also be a witty commentator on life's dramas and idiosyncrasies. On film and television she was equally captivating, playing Denholm Elliot's adulterous wife in *The Cruel Sea* (1952) and deceitful but alluring women in episodes of the fashionable ITV spy series *Danger Man* and *The Avengers*. An enterprising actress, in 1958 and 1959, shortly before Ian approached her to star in *The Gazebo*, she had taken her one-woman show *People in Love* on tour around Africa and Australia.

Fittingly for an actress under consideration for a comedy, an element of farce entered the interview Moira granted Ian and Sharp at her plush Belgravia flat. Ian was concerned, in equal measure, that his female co-star should be both blonde and not taller than he was: "'What are we going to say to her?' I said. "We can't just go up to an actress of Moira's standing and say "Excuse me, we've just called to see if you are smaller than Ian."'"[5]

The leading actor's wish to see the colour of Moira's hair was also frustrated by the actress sweeping in to see them dressed in a headscarf; viewing of the Lister locks was quietly abandoned as it could only have been achieved with the rather odd request for her to remove her headwear. Any potential embarrassment and sensitivity over height on Ian's part immediately evaporated when he sensed a 'chemistry [that] mingled on sight. Sparks crackled and the rapport was instantaneous: and no wonder – she is, I was to find out later, a Leo. Once again an identical sense of humour was to prove the foundation for a successful partnership.'⁶

In later life, Ian would openly and enthusiastically state, 'I got on very, very, *very* well indeed with Moira,'⁷ and their relationship certainly seemed to go beyond the usual boundaries of professional colleagues, with an identical approach to comedy that inspired both actors to higher standards. The two had an empathic bond, evident from their habit of finishing each other's sentences to being able to guess what the other was thinking, that can only be found in the most intimate of friendships. Their backgrounds were also similar. Moira came from a prosperous middle-class *milieu*, just as Ian did, and had aspired to an even grander lifestyle, at twenty-nine marrying the Vicomte Jacques Henry Guy d'Orthez, a French cavalry officer and champagne producer. While Ian enjoyed a tranquil life with Pym and his girls out at his 'country house' Moat Lodge, Moira made the most of her opulent Belgravia residence, carrying on her career even though she was, by marriage, French royalty. The two actors also looked like they belonged together: Ian was suave and relaxed, while Moira exhibited a Grace Kelly-style cool that was softened by her playful humour, an attractive pairing which meant they would often be cast as a couple. Despite their evident closeness, Ian, as ever, behaved like a perfect gentleman and the relationship stayed platonic, Moira joining a long line of women, Dora Bryan and Janette Scott among them, whom Ian counted among his good friends.

Following a four-week tour of the provinces that had garnered a positive reaction, *The Gazebo* opened at London's Savoy Theatre on 29 March. Despite Ian's delight at his 'professional marriage of kindred spirits'⁸ with Moira, the critical reaction to the play in the West End was decidedly mixed. One of the more generous reviews appeared in the *Stage*, with the reviewer commenting, 'it takes time to get going, and the final revelation about the alleged murder with which the writer is involved takes some of the bite out of the drama.'⁹ Once again, it was Ian's star turn that elicited most praise from the paper: 'Mr Carmichael plays Elliott with a light, easy going touch, even in his most alarmed or dangerous moments managing to be amusing. For my taste, he overdoes his double-take technique and prances about too much. Otherwise the performance has something of a virtuoso portrayal which, now I come to look closer, is what really keeps the play moving and holds one's interest.'¹⁰ The lukewarm critical judgement elsewhere made little difference to *The Gazebo*'s popularity with theatregoers and it went on to run for over a year, firmly consolidating Ian and Moira's working relationship.

The Gazebo was a happy production. Content in another West End hit, Ian could afford to be generous, presenting Sharp with a cigarette box inscribed with the heartfelt sentiment, 'Thanks to your expert guidance and wise counsel, I got away with murder.' As well as enjoying a jovial working relationship with his director, Ian became acquainted with Moira's varied, and somewhat eccentric, circle of friends. He was particularly fond of one story she told him about 'one of the chinless set'¹¹ who had taken her to dinner at the Savoy Grill after coming to see the play:

> 'Tell me,' he said. 'This chap Carmichael; does he enjoy actin'?'
> 'I presume so,' replied Moira, 'otherwise I doubt if he'd do it.'
> 'Well, I hope so,' said her friend, ''cos it must take up an awful lot of his time.'¹²

On 19 September 1961, well into *The Gazebo*'s run, Ian began work on another movie, *Double Bunk*. If ever there was a film that symbolised how tastes in British film comedy were diverging in the early 1960s, director and writer Pennington Richards' nautical comedy was the one. The casting spoke volumes. Once again paired with the twinkling Janette Scott (as Peggy), Ian played Jack Goddard, a plucky and honest new husband who takes on the run-down houseboat *Jasmine-Gray* and triumphs against marina owner and upper-class cad Leonard Watson (Dennis Price deputising in a part clearly written for Terry-Thomas). This strand of the film plainly belonged to the same lineage as *Happy is the Bride* and *School for Scoundrels*, while Goddard's co-skipper, the roguish Sid, was a new element. Played by the crinkle-faced Sid James, the actor was part of a new generation of performers who had established themselves mainly on radio and television, in his case *Hancock's Half Hour* and *Citizen James*, but had latterly become a fixture of the *Carry On* films. Together with his stripper girlfriend Sandra (Liz Fraser, another *Carry On* alumnus), the mischievous Sid could have stepped straight off the set of the most recent *Carry On* movie. Despite *Double Bunk*'s pre-publicity stressing Ian and Janette as the star names, the film's theme song, perhaps in acknowledgement of the *Carry On*s' growing popularity, was sung by James and Fraser in a saucy double act, which even ended with Sid's trademark innuendo-laden laugh. In *Double Bunk* he even shared the same first name as his character, just as he would in many of the *Carry On* films.

Double Bunk's two main stars were happy to see each other once more. 'Ian and I were delighted to be working together again,' Janette Scott remembers with a smile. 'I don't think we ever had a cross word.'[13] The chemistry between the two stars, by now on their third film together, had been noticed by the press, and a resourceful photographer had persuaded them to appear in some photographs that teased the public by showing the duo acting very much like a couple – one notable shot had them cuddling together in the stalls of a cinema. However much the press may have wished for more, any supposed romantic liaison was purely in the interests of publicity. 'There are no stories,'[14] Janette says categorically. 'Ian was very happily married. Our outside lives never really involved each other because we had happy lives away from the studio.'[15]

The enjoyment of a week's filming by the Thames in the Indian summer of September 1960 was slightly marred for Janette by an incident that could have come straight out of the script of any of her films with Ian:

> I had a lovely new Alpine Sunbeam sports car in moonstone white with a black leather interior. I had only had it a couple of days. I parked my car where I was told to park it along with many others, which happened to be in front of the river. Once again, Ian and I were co-starring for the first scenes of the film in another old car and this old car had to go down a hill, turn left and go along by the river. So, we got in the car and Pennington Richards yelled 'Action!' and off we went, but Ian couldn't turn or stop the car and it went straight into the side of my new one! There I was, sitting in the car that had nearly demolished mine and I was practically in tears, but there was nothing Ian could have done.'[16]

Unfortunate automobile accidents aside, *Double Bunk* was completed on time and released at the end of March 1961. The film is an entertaining hybrid: part romantic comedy, part caper movie and part unofficial *Carry On* film. There is an undeniable *frisson* in seeing the educated Ian paired with the cockney Sid, although it can't have been apparent at the time that the leading man of 1950s British film comedy was handing over to his 1960s successor. The humour, ribald for the time – revolving around Peggy and Jim's need to buy a home so they can consummate their marriage, and Sandra's striptease act – now looks charmingly dated rather than daring. But the evocative location filming on the Thames, that includes landmarks such as the Houses of Parliament and Tower Bridge, as well as the whiff of lighthearted class war between Goddard, Sid and Watson, is enough to put a new spin on the established Carmichael formula of the decent-but-luckless chap in trouble.

Unfortunately, the critical reaction was symptomatic of how resistant the British press was to the simple pleasures of broad humour. For such an innocuous film, *Double Bunk* generated some scathing reviews. 'The names Ian Carmichael and Janette Scott, though belonging respectively to a couple of pleasant people, are apt to strike dread into a critic's heart when they appear above a film title,'[17] the *Daily Mail* announced, going on to point out rather inaccurately, 'Together they have been in some stinkers. *Double Bunk* is no exception.'[18] An affronted *Evening News* felt that 'Ian Carmichael lets down himself and his fans by appearing in this sort of drivel'[19], while the *Sunday Telegraph* declared 'this feeble, witless, lifeless affair achieves nothing whatever – excepting the utter waste of that delectable comedian, Ian Carmichael.'[20] Although it seemed that some sterner critics weren't prepared to accept Ian in anything that they judged fell below the standards of his impeccable 1950s film comedies, the more populist papers found his venture into more risqué waters a pleasant diversion. 'It's a hilarious piece of malarkey and I laughed throughout, just as though I had been at a happy party,'[21] applauded the satisfied reviewer in the *News of the World*, while Ian also notched up another surprisingly positive review from the *Daily Worker* (perhaps inspired by Sid's line 'Makes you wonder that there isn't something in this socialism after all.'): 'A modest comedy, this, but a very pleasant one, with plenty of good-humoured fun.'[22] Unfortunately, the nagging criticism that Ian was stuck in a creative rut was becoming more frequent, with the *Observer* noting, in its appraisal of *Double Bunk*'s archetypal characters, 'an unnerved, eternal-bachelor husband, played of course by Ian Carmichael.'[23]

'It was a very exhausting and a very tiring period,'[24] Ian recalled about the early 1960s. Although he felt himself still to be a young man at forty-one during the run of *The Gazebo*, that was very much middle age at the time. 'In those days,'[25] Ian explained, 'actors could do theatre in the West End and they could do their films in the daytime, because nearly all the films were made in the studios around London. If you really wanted, [film companies] would book you, and your agent would say, "Look, I'm sorry, he must be away at half past 5, because his curtain goes up at 7 o'clock at St Martin's" or whatever. So, I made lots of those movies while I was appearing in leading roles in the West End. And that was a bit tiring.'[26]

That was something of an understatement. *The Gazebo* was a very demanding show and Ian never left the stage for the duration of each performance. His intense emotional and physical commitment to the play, as well as the filming for *Double Bunk* during the day, was to prove the trigger that set off a nervous breakdown, a tragedy that had been building through fifteen years of constant touring, theatre roles, film-making, television production and personal appearances ever since he had left the army in 1946. By his own admission, Ian had never learned to relax, and holidays were rare; the three weeks he had spent with Pym, Sally and Lee on the River Esk in Yorkshire was a rarity, and that had been back in 1953. Ian vividly remembered the day he finally lost control:

> The moment *Double Bunk* finished I had a number of post-production chores to attend to and a long-playing record to make, all of which dragged my debility down further. No sooner had I completed this schedule than Pym announced that she had promised to go away and stay with my mother, who was also feeling a bit down, for a few days. I became difficult and on the day of her departure; having most reluctantly taken her to King's Cross Station, I returned home angry and sorry for myself. At lunchtime I went to my local to have a couple of pints to drown my sorrows. I had nothing that in normal circumstances I could not have coped with at mid-day and still given a performance in the evening. The circumstances, however, were not normal and I arrived at the theatre frightened, shaken, demoralised and feeling as weak as a kitten. I went straight into Moira's room, poured out my woes, and told her that I was terrified I wasn't going to be able to get through the first ten minutes, then, realising I was going to black out, I left the sofa where I was sitting with my dear leading lady, walked into the wings and collapsed.[27]

Although after he had been revived, Ian had tried to perform, after a couple of pages of dialogue he left the stage, finally admitting that he was too ill to continue. The next morning Harold Fielding called and, despite Ian's protestations, insisted that the Carmichaels should immediately select a holiday destination that he would pay for, flights and all. Ian and Pym had never been out of England together in their lives before, so a vacation was long overdue. They settled on St Moritz in Switzerland and, with Lee and Sally in the safe hands of relatives, enjoyed an idyllic two-week break from the stresses and strains of London. Ian returned to *The Gazebo* on 23 December, laden down with presents for 'the tolerant cast who had been so inconvenienced by my sudden departure two weeks previously'.[28] Despite feeling rejuvenated, in the matinee performance the day after Boxing Day, Ian's voice failed him completely and he was only able to perform the first act. On his doctor's advice, he left *The Gazebo* permanently on 28 January 1962.

With the prospect of no new employment on the horizon, Ian had some space to reflect on what had happened to him. He was considerably shaken.

> Hitherto I had always thrived on work. It had, I think, helped me to retain a youthful appearance that in fact belied my age. I now decided that I must pause for a deep breath and reassessment of my lifestyle, and in doing so I didn't very much like what I saw. I had a beautiful home, a loving and dutiful wife and two gorgeous daughters whom I worshipped and who were, by now, fast approaching the ages of fifteen and twelve, and yet we had never all been away together alone on a proper family holiday. In a few years' time the girls would be young ladies and, in the natural way of things, leaving the nest for good. I was horrified – it was rapidly becoming later than I thought.[29]

Taking the advice of Eric Barker that he should put them before his work, Ian and his family departed on 30 March for a small, quiet village called Villefranche on the Cote d'Azur in France, Ian having booked them into a small hotel overlooking the harbour full of fishing boats. On the Friday before they left England, however, Ian had received a telephone call from an excited Stone, telling him that an offer had been received from Hollywood for Ian to star in a feature film comedy called *Bachelor Flat* with Tuesday Weld. If Ian accepted the job, he would have to depart for Los

Angeles on 1 April; bearing in mind Barker's advice, the Carmichaels had left for Villefranche anyway, Ian having decided that he would wait to see the complete script of *Bachelor Flat* before committing himself. At the end of a first week of blissful relaxation, the second half of the screenplay arrived and Ian decided that, faced with the choice of making a below-par Hollywood comedy or continuing to lie in the sun with his attentive family on the first real holiday of their lives, he would rather stay where he was.

'I didn't go,'[30] he recalled simply. 'Another actor, an old friend, went in my place and as a result established himself firmly in the Hollywood studios. I don't believe I ever saw the film when it eventually came out, but, as I remember, it didn't set the world on fire. What would have happened to me had I gone? A question impossible to answer. Do I regret not going? Never. I completed a holiday with the three girls who are dearest to me and we all enjoyed every minute of it; I wouldn't hesitate to make the same decision again, even with hindsight.'[31]

Ian was being discreet, but the old friend in question was Terry-Thomas. After the lukewarm reception accorded *Bachelor Flat*, his Hollywood career really took off with *It's a Mad, Mad, Mad, Mad World* (1962), the first of the 1960s' big-budget caper movies that put Thomas alongside such legends as Spencer Tracy, Sid Caesar, Phil Silvers, Ethel Merman and Buddy Hackett. From this point on, Thomas never looked back, enjoying considerable financial rewards for *How to Murder Your Wife* (1964), *Those Magnificent Men in Their Flying Machines or How I Flew from London to Paris in 25 Hours and 11 Minutes* (1965) and *Monte Carlo or Bust!* (1969). Peter Sellers would follow him to Hollywood to work first with Stanley Kubrick on *Lolita* (1963) and *Dr Strangelove or How I Learned to Stop Worrying and Love the Bomb* (1964), before he became an international comedy star as the hapless Inspector Clouseau in *The Pink Panther* (1964).

That both of Ian's Boultings contemporaries became global stars via Hollywood suggested that, had he taken the lead role in *Bachelor Flat*, his career might have taken a similar lucrative path.

Thomas succeeded because he presented a stylised, caddish Englishness that some Americans imagined was how their transatlantic cousins really were, while Sellers flourished behind a succession of brilliant comedy avatars, Clouseau being his most celebrated after Fred Kite. Ian would have offered the kind of pleasant, decent and gauchely endearing Englishman who would have had a place in the US alongside all the bounders that became Thomas's stock in trade, Ian following in the traditions of Hollywood gentlemen like the Davids Niven and Tomlinson, Jack Buchanan and Nigel Bruce. It's notable that while Sellers and Thomas both died young, Ian, content with his domestic home life and position as an exclusively British entertainer, lived until he was eighty-nine.

During the run of *The Gazebo,* one of the daytime assignments Ian took on was a new TV play, his first for ITV. *Gilt and Gingerbread* told the story of the stockbroker Charles Yeyder, who was left with £200,000 worth of valueless shares and faced financial ruin. Mortimer Wilmot – played by fellow Yorkshireman Terence Alexander, looking like a streamlined Terry-Thomas – proposed to Yeyder a face-saving deal that would have 'startling repercussions on his domestic life.'[32] The denouement of *Gilt and Gingerbread* concentrated on showing how Yeyder outwitted Wilmot, who had caddish designs on the stockbroker's wife Louise (another duet for Ian with Moira Lister).

The introduction to the article in the *TV Times* promoting Lionel Hale's play pulled no punches in its description of Ian's career in 1961: 'For several years Ian Carmichael has not had much acting variety. He has achieved fame and fortune as a film star it is true, but he has been typed in "young clot" roles. Now, with [the ITV network] Associated-Rediffusion's *Gilt and Gingerbread,* Carmichael has a change from this kind of part.'[33] Speaking about his return to television, Ian offered an insight into his prejudices concerning contemporary drama. '[The play] has style, which is rare these days. It is not kitchen sink drama. It is not about the lower orders. It is not about landed gentry who won't do anything. And I play not a clot but a middle-aged stockbroker who lives elegantly.'[34] As ever, Ian spoke highly of his glamorous co-star: '[Moira and I] have been appearing together on the stage as man and wife for more than a year in *The Gazebo* ... I am thrilled to be back acting with Moira in *Gilt and Gingerbread*.'[35] While it was not hailed on its transmission as a classic by reviewers, the play helped to remind the television audience that Ian was an actor who could play varied roles with aplomb.

Following the rave reviews he received for *I'm All Right Jack*, Peter Sellers had become the Boultings' new leading man of choice. There was no resentment on Ian's part, as his contract with the brothers had expired and he remained friends with all three of them. During the summer of 1961 the brothers had begun work on *Heavens Above!*, a satire that was designed to attack the most sacred cow of them all – religion. Their new film cast Sellers as the Reverend John Smallwood, fielding a fashionable regional accent (Birmingham) that suited the more democratic 1960s. If the film had been made a few years before, Ian would undoubtedly have been in the starring role and speaking in Received Pronunciation.

Roy Boulting was producing *Heavens Above!* and had been using Richard Stone's agency to arrange some of the casting. Ever loyal to the man they had made a star, Roy remarked to Stone how he regretted not being able to find a part for Ian. A few days later Stone's phone rang again and, after some consideration, Roy told Ian's agent that if his client was amenable, the part of 'The other Rev. Smallwood' (the film was a mistaken-identity comedy) was his. Two weeks after Roy's initial call, Ian joined him at Shepperton Studios and, equipped with 'a top jaw full of protruding teeth and a pair of ears that stood directly out from the sides of my head like those of a dormouse, I committed my performance to celluloid'.[36]

The 'other' John Smallwood should have got the job of vicar in the village of Orbiston Parva instead of Peter Sellers' character. Farcically, Ian was mistaken by Miles Malleson's psychiatrist for

Sellers' Smallwood and the latter concluded, thanks to Ian talking about 'the other Smallwood', that the man was a paranoid schizophrenic. This developed into a mildly amusing scene that ended with the incorrectly diagnosed Smallwood being locked in a library. At the end of the film, with Sellers's Smallwood now orbiting the Earth in a space capsule, Ian's Smallwood finally took over the parish, only to be drenched in the pulpit as the absence of lead on the roof (stolen by Eric Sykes' character Harry Smith) let in a rainstorm. Strikingly, though Ian only had a few minutes of screen time, he still got star billing above actors such as William Hartnell and Sykes, who were on screen for a lot longer. He's reasonably entertaining, but is only there as part of the 'Oh look, it's ——' cameo factor and because his old friends the Boultings gave him a job.

During the latter part of 1961, Ian had high hopes for *Critic's Choice*, another American play, this time by Ira Levin, which in New York had starred Henry Fonda. It deals with a Manhattan theatre critic called Parker Ballantine in the unenviable position of having to review his second wife's play that, if he does so honestly, could cost him his second marriage. Ian was excited by a character 'with infinitely greater depth than anything I had played before. It was well within my range and I wanted to stretch myself further than I had been called upon to do to date.'[37] Although Moira had agreed to appear as Ballantine's first wife, rehearsals in October were thrown into disarray when she announced she was pregnant. 'This, I reflected, was becoming a habit,'[38] Ian noted ruefully.

Critic's Choice began its provincial tour in Oxford with Moira's understudy Anne Berry taking her role, a move that proved popular with the cast, crew and, most importantly, audiences. The play itself wasn't so popular and Ian put its mixed reaction from the critics, when it began its West End run at the Vaudeville Theatre on 6 December, down to several jibes Levin made in the play at the expense of the professional critics. Although he had chosen the part of Ballantine to refute criticism that he only ever accepted the role of 'the dithering buffoon,'[39] it was frustrating for Ian to read reviews that claimed he was appearing in a part that 'has few opportunities to display the talents that won him a large personal following.'[40] Despite the play's six-month London run being a qualified success, Ian himself 'never had a single regret about choosing the part. I enjoyed every moment of every performance.'[41]

While he was appearing in *Critic's Choice*, Ian made his return to BBC Television at the beginning of January 1962 in the first episode of *Compact*, a soap opera set in the offices of a fashion magazine that had been commissioned because of the success of Granada Television's Northern 'kitchen sink' soap *Coronation Street*, which had debuted at the start of the decade. *Compact* was rather more cosmopolitan in its outlook as it was set in the 1960s' burgeoning media culture, and part of its up-to-the minute remit was to include an interview at regular intervals with a real-life media personality. Watching the 6 January episode with a considerably jaundiced eye, the reviewer in *The Times* wrote:

> The climax of unreality is reached when the staff assemble for their weekly celebrity interview, and there, lo and behold, is Mr Ian Carmichael on a piece of low-slung furniture, smiling for the photographer and insisting on a plug for his current West End show which he proceeds to name and to quote the times of performance. The celebrity interview, it appears, is to be a fixture of the programme.[42]

Ian's cameo as himself made little difference to the success of *Compact*; at its height, the series attracted an astounding thirteen million viewers.

Throughout 1962, a new four-piece rock and roll band signed to EMI records constantly toured England while Ian alternatively played himself on television and worked on his next film *The Amorous Prawn*, easing himself back into the business with a light workload that the four young musicians from Liverpool would scarcely have believed. The band was called The Beatles and their first single 'Love Me Do' was released on 5 October, a month before *The Amorous Prawn* opened in UK cinemas.

Ian's new film was a military farce concerning the exploits of a rogue unit of Highland infantry who, to help out their impecunious commanding officer (and, needless to say, line their own pockets) in his absence and in cahoots with his wife, turn the family home into a hotel and pretend to be domestic staff. Anthony Kimmins' play had run in the West End for two successful years, even though its traditional, farcical structure had not been popular with the critics. Early in 1962, Ian had been offered a part in the film version, to be directed by Kimmins himself.

The New Zealand-born actress Bridget Armstrong, one of Ian's co-stars in *The Amorous Prawn*, remembers seeing him perform on stage before getting to work with him. 'In the early '60s, I saw Rex Harrison and Ian performing a musical number terrifically – very Fred Astaire – at the *Charity Midnight Matinee* at the [London] Palladium. Such style and line!'[43] Bridget had impressed *The Amorous Prawn*'s writer and director Kimmins 'because he saw me in the play *The Marriage Game* on the last night of a tour ending at the Theatre Royal in Brighton, when I got lots of laughs. Because of that, he wrote a part in the film especially for me.'[44]

During the making of the film, Bridget was able to observe some of Ian's eccentricities at first hand. 'He was legendarily tight,'[45] she says with a smile. 'Dennis Price and Cecil Parker had a sixpenny bet with me to ask [Ian] for a penny so I could phone my nanny and see how my baby boy Mikey was doing. So I asked him and he said, "I'm sorry, but I don't have any money on me." But I got my sixpence! Ian [also] brought in a bottle of wine every day and he used to have a tiny glass with his lunch. And he would always mark the level on the bottle! And there was a scene in the film where we were getting changed and Liz Fraser suddenly said, "Look at Ian!" He was putting a uniform jacket on over one he was already wearing. He must have thought he looked a bit puny so was bulking himself up!' The movie saw a mixture of comedy talent old and new, with Fraser (*Carry On*), Ian (the Boulting brothers) and Joan Greenwood, the husky-voiced diminutive actress who had starred in some of the best Ealing comedies. 'Jean

Greenwood was *wonderful*,' Bridget enthuses. 'She was so small she was like a delicate little bird. She'd recently had a baby with Andre Morell, quite late in life.'

Play the game of swapping the cast for members of the *Carry On* team, and you can see Charles Hawtrey in Derek Nimmo's part, Sid James as the amorous Prawn himself, Barbara Windsor in Bridget Armstrong's shoes and Leslie Phillips or Terence Longdon standing in for Ian. The similarity to the *Carry On* films wasn't lost on the reviewer in America's *Time*, who observed, 'If the film were called *Carry On Farce*, it would probably represent both the hope of the film makers and the wishes of a few million cinema goers.'[46]

The general critical reaction was mixed. The *Guardian* was generous in its appraisal, commenting, 'This is the sort of work which, whether on stage or screen, will appeal to those who like to see Mr Ian Carmichael playing the suave, comic butler, Mr Cecil Parker demonstrating exasperated bewilderment, Miss Joan Greenwood displaying the deep-toned charm which is so much at odds with her diminutive stature and, finally, Miss Liz Fraser displaying brief and fancy underwear. In fact it belongs, whether on stage or screen, to a harmless immutable tradition.'[47] The *Observer* wasn't so charitable, caustically dismissing 'a moribund farce with Ian Carmichael, Cecil Parker, Joan Greenwood and Dennis Price. If you would fall about hysterically at the sound of these indomitably mannered comedians reading passages from the telephone directory, you'll enjoy the film – the lines are hardly funnier.'[48] Ian himself was a critical hit with film reviewers once more. The *Evening News* reckoned 'the slender fun [was] held together by Ian Carmichael, whose raucous, get-fell-in-style corporal becomes, in a moment, an obsequious, grotesquely refined *maître d'hôtel*', while *The Times* said 'Mr Ian Carmichael manages to infuse a certain relish into his quick-change from corporal to *maître d'hôtel* and back again.'

In fact, the most surprising thing about *The Amorous Prawn* was that Irene Handl wasn't in it anywhere.

CHAPTER 11

Profession Recession

*A troubled two years which witness the end of Ian's career
as a film star*

THE LANDSCAPE OF British films had undergone a sea change
by the early 1960s. Building on the ideas of writers like John
Osborne and directors such as Lindsay Anderson in the Free
Cinema movement, a new, edgy realism had arrived. Uncompro-
mising social dramas like *Saturday Night and Sunday Morning* (1960),
The Loneliness of the Long Distance Runner (1962) and *This Sporting
Life* (1963) explored the dilemmas of working-class life in a provincial
setting. With this 'new wave' had arrived a new school of film actors
– Albert Finney, Tom Courtenay and Richard Harris, among others
– who broke the mould of film stars speaking with Received
Pronunciation, putting regional accents to the fore. Their movies
were symptomatic of wider changes in British culture, from the
relaxation of the ban on D.H. Lawrence's controversial novel *Lady
Chatterley's Lover* in 1960 to the rise of The Beatles, which saw the
United Kingdom finally shaking off post-war austerity and
conformity, and the gradual softening of class barriers, largely due to
an improved state education system. Perhaps most significantly, the
arrival of the contraceptive pill for women in 1961 revolutionised
sexual relations in Britain, and the earthy appeal of Courtenay,
Finney, Harris and other actors in a rougher mould seemed to
symbolise the country's new mood on celluloid. Even though they

appeared in more commercial fare, the most successful rising stars of the day, the working-class Michael Caine and Sean Connery – masculine, charismatic leading men who typified the new 'upwardly mobile' archetype, making his own way in the world without the benefit of a privileged background – provided the glamour.

While this was all good news for the British film industry, it wasn't particularly good news for Ian. Public and commercial taste in films, moving on to a fresh generation of more 'gritty' actors who embodied the *Zeitgeist* of 1960s Britain, only compounded the problems he was facing in his own career: 'For several years I had been trying to find a new sort of film role. All I was being offered (by the trunkload) were variations on the same old bumbling, accident-prone clot ... I was getting tired of them and so were the critics; it was only, I figured, a matter of time before the public did too.'[1] In trying to redefine the way he was perceived in the film industry, Ian had perhaps been inspired by the way his contemporary Dirk Bogarde, who had been saddled with the role of a charming matinee idol ever since *Doctor in the House* (1954), had successfully made the transition into adult fare. *Victim* (1961) had cast Bogarde against type as a blackmailed gay man and at a stroke completely changed the kind of work he was offered, leading to equally mature roles in *The Servant* (1963), *King and Country* (1964) and more.

Ian's ambitions were more modest than Bogarde's. As he'd said during the publicity for *Double Bunk*, what he yearned for was the chance to show his mettle as a romantic lead in the kind of sophisticated thrillers that one of his heroes had made so successful: 'The sort of pictures I'd like to make more of in the future would be in the category of the Cary Grant–Ingrid Bergman film *Indiscreet*.'[2] The actor felt that the Alfred Hitchcock template of the innocent bystander caught up in a suspenseful mystery would be ideal as a vehicle both for broadening his acting ability and exploiting his already established comedic talents. And he wasn't alone in this wish within the entertainment world: 'If you speak to any light comedian, Leslie Phillips or whoever, they'll all say they'd like to do a Cary Grant film.'[3]

Ironically, Ian's aspiration to turn his film career around was helped by one of the stars of the British 'new wave'. In 1962, Eon Films had released *Dr No* starring the up-and-coming Sean Connery. It was the first of their film adaptations of Ian Fleming's espionage novels about James Bond, a gentleman secret agent who inhabited a vivid world of exotic locations, beautiful women and bizarre villains. Although far from an accurate portrayal of a spy's life, Fleming's novels emphasised the excitement of the Cold War, in which spies were the front-line troops in the covert struggle between East and West. With spy scandals like the defection of MI6's Kim Philby and the Profumo affair front-page news, spies were becoming exciting if shadowy figures in the public imagination. Although box office returns for *Dr No* were slow to build and despite some negative reviews, the public eventually took to 007 as a potent reflection of the times, and a second Bond thriller, *From Russia with Love,* was commissioned for 1963. Bond had lit the fuse for a new pop-cultural phenomenon and it wasn't long before the cinematic potential of Fleming's literary cocktails began to appeal to other film-makers.

With the spy craze about to roll like a juggernaut to the end of the 1960s, the timing couldn't have been better when Hal E. Chester, the producer of *School for Scoundrels,* offered Ian the very role he had been waiting for, in a comedy thriller called *Hide and Seek.* The ingredients were quintessential Hitchcock: Cambridge maths professor David Garrett (Ian) becomes entangled with an alluring, mysterious young woman called Maggie (the gamine Janet Munro), in a frantic pursuit all over England headed by a Communist master-spy, Hubert Marek (the flint-eyed Curt Jurgens.) In a contemporary touch, the plot riffed on *From Russia with Love,* with the kidnapping of Garrett's friend plotted via chess moves, just as a chess grand master had orchestrated the assassination of 007 in Fleming's spy story. The cast was peppered with quality character actors of the period like Hugh Griffith, Kieron Moore, George Pravda and Kynaston Reeves.

The quality of the writer and director particularly excited Ian: the screenplay had 'the most original twists and turns in the plot'⁴ and, delightedly, he thought, 'this is my *North by Northwest*: this is absolutely wonderful!'⁵ The scriptwriter, a young novelist and another rising star called David Stone, would contribute to the authentic espionage TV series *Danger Man* (relaunched in 1964 on ITV) and Roman Polanski's psychological thriller *Repulsion* (1965). The director Cy Enfield was a more seasoned but no less impressive pair of hands: he had made the tough road drama *Hell Drivers* in 1957 and, directly before starting work on *Hide and Seek*, had overseen the acclaimed historical epic *Zulu*, starring Stanley Baker and Michael Caine. With such a distinguished pedigree among the cast and production crew, Ian didn't see how the film could fail, believing that he had at last found 'the gear change that I so badly needed to get me out of the Stanley Windrush mould.'⁶ (In a *frisson* between the real and fictional worlds of espionage, the film even included Mandy Rice-Davies as an extra under the pseudonym 'Mandy Moray'. Together with Christine Keeler, she had been one of the 'good time girls' at the centre of the Profumo scandal that had nearly brought down Harold Macmillan's Tory government.)

Unfortunately, Ian had reckoned without the intrusive tendencies of his colourful producer. Always a man with a propensity to 'add his own talents to those of his extremely capable lieutenants,'⁷ Chester's interference in *Hide and Seek* for some reason went way beyond his previous meddling of inserting of jokes aimed at the American market into *School for Scoundrels* (and which in any case had been rejected). Ian was also as powerless to salvage the situation as he had been ten years before on *The Big Money*:

> Hal E. Chester kept interfering and interfering and interfering, and we got way behind on the schedule. We were warned [by the studio], we got further behind, and one day they said, 'Look, you finish at the end of this week,' and we had three weeks left to shoot. So, for the last two days, [Chester] put bits of set all around the studio and we just shot bits like that so he could stick them together, and of course it was absolutely no good.⁸

Ian was extremely disappointed with the way *Hide and Seek* turned out, consoling himself with the thought that 'I don't think anybody ever saw it.'[9] His chance to reorient his career and, indeed, jump aboard the lucrative spy bandwagon was gone. 'That I'm *very* sad about, because [it] was a lovely story and a lovely script and just the sort of stuff I wanted to do.'[10]

Ian's conviction that *Hide and Seek* was rarely, if ever, seen is borne out by my researches. After extensive enquiries, the only film print to be found is the negative held by the British Film Institute, who unfortunately don't possess a viewing copy. All that is left in the public domain appears to be two tantalisingly modish posters and a handful of photographs.

However, despite what Ian believed, *Hide and Seek* did have a public showing. It opened in the ABC cinemas on the Fulham and Harrow roads in mid July 1964, ironically two months ahead of the release of the third James Bond film *Goldfinger*, which would see the enthusiasm for all things 'spy' explode globally. In a sign of the distributors' evident lack of faith in the film, it was part of a double bill with the catch-all pop anthology *Just for You* which, coincidentally, featured the *I'm All Right Jack* balladeer Al Saxon. With one eye clearly on the commercial success of 007, the designer of one of *Hide and Seek*'s two promotional posters had delivered a design that was very similar to one of *From Russia with Love*'s billboards. Aping the strap-lines '[Bond's] new incredible women ... His new incredible enemies ... His new incredible adventures ...', similarly tinted black and white photographs of Ian accompanied the equally sensational slogans, 'The Dangerous Game That Two Can Play!!! ... played with your wits ... played with your lips ... played with your life!!!' While this graphic pastiche of Bond's marketing offered the intriguing sight of Ian involved in unarmed combat, something he had not been seen doing on film before, the other poster took a different approach, referencing fashionable 'Mod' graphics: black and white photographic cut-outs of the main cast were poised between the letters of the film's title. It clearly wasn't a good sign when the publicity for a movie looked like it was aimed at two different audiences.

That the film disappeared almost without trace following its (brief) London opening is very likely attributable to the dreadful reviews it received. For a project that had initially held such promise for Ian, they would have been doubly wounding because *Hide and Seek*'s critical notices were, without a doubt, the worst of his entire career. Despite the *Sunday Times* gamely suggesting 'Ian Carmichael gives his best screen performance for some time,'[11] elsewhere the broadsheet and tabloid press were unanimous in their condemnation of both Ian's acting and the film itself. The *Daily Herald* weighed in with '[the movie] looks as if it had been scooped up from the cutting-room floor and tacked together by someone in a hurry,'[12] a pretty accurate assessment of Hal E. Chester's film-making skills, which the *Daily Worker* found 'so excruciatingly inept that for the first 20 minutes or so (before our senses mercifully become numbed) it is almost physically painful to watch.'[13] The *Evening Standard* derided a 'style [that] veers widely between the belly-laughs of the *Carry On* series and the sophisticated larks of the Cary Grant vehicle',[14] while the *Evening News* delivered the body blow, finding *Hide and Seek*, 'pitifully short of invention, thrills or even the most basic elements of commercial film-making.'[15]

The critics had Ian in their sights like never before, even if some of their criticism questioned why a performer of his stature had become involved with such a disaster, clearly not aware of the exceptional script that had first enchanted him or the gifted director who had given him such confidence in the film. 'What we care about is that a light comedy actor of Ian Carmichael's quality should be wasted on such a string of unfunny non-thrills'[16], opined the *Daily Mail*, but elsewhere patience with Ian's film persona was wearing thin. 'I wish he would learn to keep his trousers on and his facial expressions under control,'[17] the *Daily Herald* demanded bluntly (if amusingly), with the *Sunday Telegraph* despairing of 'the glazed performance of Ian Carmichael'[18] and *The Times* castigating his apparent inability to 'decide whether he is meant to be the hero or the buffoon.'[19] Most tellingly, the *Daily Express*, while informing its readers that in his latest film Ian presented 'his familiar impression of the eternal idiot,'[20] offered an accurate but worrying capsule overview of his film career to date: 'Ian Carmichael was 44 on Thursday. Time has ravaged that look of vacant, wide-eyed, open-mouthed astonishment which he showed us first in *Private's Progress*, nearly a decade ago. Mr Carmichael is now a little too senior for the sort of thing which requires him to fall into ponds. He is also much too good an actor.'[21]

Even though there was concern for the path Ian's career was taking in the comments of the *Express*, there was also the clear implication that his film career as a light comedian had run its course. Taken in the context of the more critical comments in the press, there was the more ominous subtext that, because of being typecast, Ian had worn out his welcome as a film star full stop, which, ironically, had concerned him just before he began work on *Hide and Seek*. Even though Hal Chester had seriously damaged the actor's opportunity to reorient his career, and arguably put his whole livelihood at risk as a result, Ian was so good natured he couldn't bring himself to bear a grudge: '[Chester could be] the most infuriating man to work for and yet one could never actually dislike him – I couldn't, anyway.'[22]

However, Ian's comment in the press release for *Hide and Seek*, that 'It's tough getting to the top, and it's tougher to stay there,'[23] took on a very gloomy undertone in the light of the film's unmitigated commercial and critical failure. Alarmingly, his next movie, *Case of the 44's* – incredibly, his last as a leading man – would be even more of a comedown.

Case of the 44's is just as obscure today as *Hide and Seek*, released in March 1964. Significantly, it earned only a passing mention in Ian's autobiography, when he recalled 'a strange and abortive feature film that contained no dialogue in Copenhagen.'[24] Like his aborted Cary Grant-style thriller, a viewing copy is virtually impossible to find.

After working with such a talented group of collaborators on *Hide and Seek*, Ian's choices of partners on his new cinematic venture were mixed to say the least. Approached by the small company Compton-Cameo films, he was perhaps persuaded into assuming the role of the moustachioed Scotland Yard detective Jim Pond (which sounded suspiciously like a paraphrase of James Bond) by the film's producer Jon Pennington, who had taken a creditable path through the British film industry up to 1964; he had produced the successful Cliff Richard vehicle *Expresso Bongo*, the Peter Sellers satire *The Mouse that Roared* (both in 1959) and the Second World War drama *The Valiant* (1962). Tom McGowan, the director, had a rather more erratic track record in film-making. His career veered from 'The Hound that Thought He was a Raccoon' for the colourful TV series *The Wonderful World of Disney* in 1960 to, completely at the other extreme, the sex-exploitation films *Cherry and Harry and Raquel* – for the infamous master of celluloid sleaze Russ Meyer – and *Wilbur and the Baby Factory*, both released in 1970.

Compton-Cameo films were an Anglo-Danish production company at a time when Denmark was one of Europe's main producers of pornographic movies. Ian's co-stars and the supporting cast of *Case of the 44's* were *all* Danes – the most prominent among them being Lotte Tarp, playing Miss 44, and Bent Christiansen. Even though the film was given an 'A' certificate on its release (a '12' today), a look at the film's luridly written press release made it clear that, somehow, the distinguished, charming man of British films had become caught up in a soft-core Danish sex romp:

> Pond soon finds it to be no ordinary case. After much meditation and calculation he comes up with the figure 44 ... large ... from this he knows he is on to something BIG.
>
> We wouldn't try to fool you – all comes out well in the end, but on the way, there are murders, mad scientists, dreams, drugs, drinks, and oh, so many girls ... well, you see the film.[25]

A glance at the cast list also indicated that the production might not have been up to the usual professional high standards that Ian was used to: 'THE DOG – just a dog we picked up.'

From the sound of it and the few photographs available – Ian with a ridiculous handle-bar moustache, seated in a boat accompanied by a pipe, bicycle and union flag – *Case of the 44's* (*Agent bh 44* in Danish) was one of those strange movies typical of the mid-to-late1960s in which a bemused, established star was adrift in a mash-up of surreal imagery, soft-core sex, risqué humour and a hip contemporary soundtrack – see David Niven in *Casino Royale* (1967), Victor Mature in *Head* (1968), Laurence Harvey in *The Magic Christian* (1969) and Peter Sellers in anything between 1964 and the end of the decade.

Why Ian lowered himself to be involved in an exploitation film is a complete mystery. One modern commentator speculated that he 'must have needed a new suit'; on the other hand, it may simply have been that he 'had to bring up these two daughters of mine, so I had to earn the money.'[26] With the benefit of forty-six years of hindsight, it's unlikely that Ian knew at the time what he was becoming involved in. *Case of the 44's* appears to be the forerunner of those 1970s film sex comedies in which recognised (if rather embarrassed) character actors featured, such as Ian's contemporaries Richard Wattis and John Le Mesurier, but with little or no input into the bawdier scenes. Had Ian known of the vulgarity on display elsewhere in the movie, it's unlikely that he would have agreed to take part.

One of the few reviews that appeared in the press – in the American entertainment journal *Variety* – believed that Ian more than retained his professional integrity, even if the film as a whole wasn't worthy of his talents: 'Often humour falls flat and the goings [on] get pretty silly and predictable, but there's enough to keep it going, including the intermittent appearance of a cast of pretty girls. Ian Carmichael is at ease in his tailor-made role as the would-be investigator, playing it in the traditional tut-tut British key.' *Screen International*, however, was less than complimentary about both the film and Ian's performance: 'Making disappointingly little use of the Danish capital in which it is irrelevantly set, this would-be parody of British-type detection falls very flat (especially if one assumes, as one really must, that it's aspiring to send up the Bond films). Filmed without dialogue, thus incidentally demonstrating that Ian Carmichael would hardly have made the grade as a silent comedian, its feeblest feature is a commentary incorporating most of the familiar types of schoolboy wit. Unfortunately, the entertainment is reserved for adults.'[27]

That his last film as an above-the-title leading man vanished without trace is a sad reflection of how much Ian felt his film career had declined during the early 1960s. Only ten years on from *Private's Progress*, to end his starring roles as the dumb straight man in a hardly seen Danish sex caper, promoted by the tawdriest poster imaginable, which crassly emphasised the physical attributes of Ian's co-stars, was nothing short of ignominious. Furthermore, his appearance in *Case of the 44's*, with exaggerated, Victorian officer-class moustache and tweedy three-piece suit, underlined how out of step with the Swinging Sixties the Ian Carmichael persona now was.

On 17 August 1964, the following short letter from Ian landed on the desk of Robin Whitworth, the BBC's Drama booking manager: 'Will you please note that as from this date, my accredited agents are London Management, of 8 Upper Brook Street, W1, who are authorised to undertake all professional negotiations on my behalf and to whom all contracts and cheques should be sent and whose receipt is a full and valid discharge thereof.'[28]

Brief and to the point, the letter was the most significant change Ian ever made in the business side of his career. Since he had left the army, he had been represented by his wartime friend and colleague Richard Stone through the latter's agency De Wolfe and Stone, an association that, in its early days, had seen Richard personally lobby the BBC to see the potential in a client who was struggling to make his mark in the entertainment industry. Even when Ian's star was in the ascendant in British movies and the theatre, Stone had always kept various producers and department heads at the BBC aware of his client's availability, as the agent considered him 'one of the stalwarts of television.'[29] Usually a very loyal man, for Ian to sever professional links with Stone after nineteen successful years (even if the two men remained friendly personally), showed just how much faith he had lost in his agent's guidance and advice, and the debacles of *Hide and Seek* and *Case of the 44's* seem to have been the last straw. However, one of the last potential projects Stone discussed with Ian in an attempt to revive the actor's professional fortunes was a TV series based on P.G. Wodehouse's Jeeves and Wooster stories, an idea that, in the long term – and rather ironically given Ian's decision to change his management team soon after – would have significant implications for the actor's career.

By the early 1960s, there was no doubt that cinema was being surpassed by television as the nation's primary source of leisure. From 1,101 million cinema admissions in 1956 (Ian's first year as a bona fide movie star), only seven years later the figure had fallen to a meagre 357 million, and from 4,500 operating cinemas in 1950, ten years later there were only 2,950 still open. This decline in cinema-going fed back into the British film industry with the result that fewer films were made, and consequently fewer risks were taken with established stars, something from which Ian's own career had suffered.

For many former film actors and professionals it was becoming clear that television was the way forward. Commercial television had arrived in 1955, and with it the opportunities afforded by the Incorporated Television Company Ltd (ITC) for making American-style film series. These productions attracted a raft of former movie people, from actors Roger Moore, Jack Hawkins, Patrick McGoohan and John Gregson to directors such as Charles Frend, Don Chaffey and Charles Crichton, among many others. Elsewhere among the eleven regional networks that made up ITV, ABC was proving particularly appealing as a forum for fresh, innovative work. *Armchair Theatre* had arrived in 1956, premiering plays solely written for television that took in everything from 'kitchen sink' realism to risqué comedy, romance, thrillers and conceptual science fiction. By 1964, *Armchair Theatre* was such a celebrated fixture of the TV schedules that as many as twenty million viewers were watching. Finding the combination of a huge British audience and new, challenging work irresistible, film actors as diverse as Joan Greenwood, Kenneth More, Tyrone Power, Donald Pleasance and Constance Cummings had taken part in *Armchair Theatre*'s many and varied productions; significantly, Ian's close friend Moira Lister had also added her name to the series' impressive cast list. With this in mind, it's likely that if Ian considered re-orientating his career completely towards the domestic medium that was rapidly supplanting cinema, *Armchair Theatre* would be the ideal place to start.

Leonard White, an avuncular, cultured but forthright man, was *Armchair Theatre*'s producer by the time Ian's attention was drawn to it. His artistic pedigree was considerable: he had been an actor and theatre director throughout Britain and in New York and Canada, learning the craft of TV directing at the Canadian Broadcasting Corporation. While there, he became friends with Patrick Macnee, one of Ian's friends who had left England to pursue other career opportunities when home-grown employment had dried up. While in Canada, Macnee, like Ian, had gone into TV production, subsequently seeing that as his future vocation rather than acting. Both White and Macnee were back in England at the beginning of the 1960s, the latter producing a documentary series called *The Valiant Years* based on Sir Winston Churchill's memoirs and the former setting up a new, off-beat thriller series called *The Avengers*, inspired by Ian Fleming's James Bond novels and Hitchcock's film thrillers. Perhaps surprisingly given Macnee's current line of work, ABC's flamboyant Head of Drama, Sydney Newman, suggested that the actor-turned-producer might like to consider the role in *The Avengers* of John Steed, an amoral government agent who was 'a sort of George Sanders type.'[30] Much to Macnee's astonishment, Newman accepted the exorbitantly high fee he asked for.

By mid 1964, *The Avengers* was a Saturday night must-see. The replacement of original, dour co-lead Ian Hendry with Honor

Blackman's liberated, leather-attired judo expert Cathy Gale had made the series as much a part of so-called Swinging London as Biba and The Beatles. Ironically, Steed's wardrobe of bowler hat, three-piece suits and umbrella made his old-fashioned Establishment Englishness cool when paired with the hip Gale, something Ian's roles as an equally respectable and similarly attired Englishman in recent film comedies had failed to do. By the latter half of 1964, though, both Macnee and Ian were in accord about doing something new on television, if for different reasons: the former to show that there was more to him as an actor than the debonair Steed, the latter to show that Ian Carmichael the TV star could be equally as appealing to audiences as Ian Carmichael the film star.

Curiously, however, Ian's *Armchair Theatre* play, the first by a 'classic' writer, would be very different to those that had preceded it, as Leonard White remembers:

> It came about, like so much of my career, almost accidentally, because we weren't doing that sort of play at all. We were trying to make it all new writing and were commissioning like mad, so it was very different. It came about through Brian Tesler, who had become the Programme Controller at Teddington [ABC's studio base]. Brian was brought in to look after light entertainment originally, but he came up one day and said, 'I wonder whether you'd think of the possibility of doing this. I'm suggesting it as something we do as a special for a holiday weekend. You're in theatre, you'll know this one, it's *The Importance of Being Earnest.*' And I thought, is he serious? He didn't really interfere with us in what I call the '*Armchair* Department' hardly at all. He was very keen on how we scheduled, that was different, but it was only rarely that he would cross the line and give us orders. And so he said, 'I'm asking you to think about it because I know who wants to play in it.' It was Ian Carmichael. Now, once one's going down that path, dear old Patrick Macnee was very well aware that he was only getting known for *The Avengers* and nothing else at all. So I said, 'Patrick Macnee would make a good double act with Ian in that.' And so that's how it went and we cast it well. It was a hell of a cast![31]

First performed in 1895, Oscar Wilde's droll satire on Victorian conventions and morality that suggested 'we should treat all trivial things in life very seriously, and all sincere things in life with serious and studied triviality',[32] had become the Irish wit and raconteur's most performed play, previously attracting actors of the quality of John Gielgud. So it proved with *Armchair Theatre*'s production – increased to ninety minutes rather than the usual hour in recognition of its special status – with some of the best-known contemporary faces recruited to do justice to Wilde's stylish and arch dialogue. As well as Ian as John Worthing and Patrick as Algernon Moncrieff, Ian's old Boulting brothers colleague Irene Handl featured as the governess-with-a-secret Miss Prism, while Wilfred Brambell, best known as the 'dirty old' rag-and-bone man Albert Steptoe since 1962 in *Steptoe and Son*, cut a refined dash as Canon Chasuble who pined for Miss Prism. In the crucial roles of Jack's ward Cicely and his intended Gwendolyn, White respectively cast Susannah York, who at only twenty-five was internationally famous through her recent film roles, and the velvet-voiced Fenella Fielding, an experienced movie and theatre performer whose diverse credits included the voice of a cow in Anthony Newley's surreal 1960 TV series *The Strange World of Gurney Slade* and guest-starring with Macnee in *The Avengers* episode 'The Charmers', appropriately enough as 'a dizzy actress.'[33]

Ian's two main female co-stars in *The Importance of Being Earnest* represented how much tastes in acting had changed around two leading men who had both begun their acting careers back in the late 1930s. Fenella had begun acting in 1954, when Ian was the feted artist of the moment in London thanks to his appearances in *At the Lyric* and *The Globe Revues*, and, impressed by him, she had quite literally followed in his creative footsteps. 'I met Ian when I was almost a beginner,' she recalls in her distinctive sensual drawl. 'He was directing a late-night revue [called *In Picture*] at a fringe theatre in Leicester Square called The Irving, just on the corner of Irving Street, in fact. It had Joan Plowright, who was unknown then, and Rosalind Haddon. I was on it as an ASM [Assistant Stage

Manager] because they knew I could [sing and dance]. Rosalind Haddon was in a play where she had to do [the] second performance on a Thursday night which finished late, and she couldn't get to The Irving until the revue had done two or three numbers, so I went on those nights when she couldn't make it on time. The reason I terribly wanted to do it was that I *adored* Ian Carmichael,' Fenella continues, her seductive voice dropping an octave lower, 'and after the customarily few days as sort of the lowest animal in the chain, I would suddenly, instead of calling him "Mr Carmichael", be able to call him "Ian". I thought he was *lovely* and I admired him so much I could hardly *breathe*! I was a beginner; you know what they're like, they're like these mad raving fans. If Ian spoke to me I practically *fainted*! I think everyone thought he was a rather marvellous director.'[34] Thereafter simpatico with Ian's artistic temperament that she defined as 'very quick'[35] and recognising that he possessed 'a wonderful gift for mime',[36] Fenella was delighted to be working with him again on *Armchair Theatre*.

Graduating from RADA in 1958 after winning the Ronson Award for 'Most Promising Student', Susannah York came from the same generation of actors that had produced the new 'realist' school of performers that included Albert Finney, Tom Courtenay and Alan Bates. Remarkably, she had become an established film face at only twenty-one in *Tunes of Glory* (1960), swiftly moving on to a major role written for her in the adult drama *The Greengage Summer* (1961). In 1963, Susannah starred in director Tony Richardson's and John Osborne's iconoclastic reworking of Henry Fielding's eighteenth-century novel *Tom Jones* with Finney in the title role. Coming from an acting background very different to Ian's, and one that was markedly unlike Fenella's formative experiences in the profession, Susannah's assessment of Ian Carmichael the performer was more critical than that of her *Earnest* co-star. 'Ian wasn't someone I really took to, I must say, although he was a very talented actor,'[37] she confided honestly. 'He wasn't my kind of actor ... I always felt he was trying to prove something in some way [although he was a] very slick and a very efficient actor. He was funny and deft, and perhaps had more potential than he was given leave for. Wilde has a lot of artifice and he was very good at that.[38]

'I was very young at the time and I suppose Ian already seemed a bit old-fashioned to me,' Susannah reflected. 'In my experience of him, he didn't seem to be much of a naturalistic actor. He was definitely an actor on stilts, and there were a lot of those in the 1960s. My leaning is much more towards naturalism. He wasn't very tall, and I always felt he was trying to make himself look taller. He didn't really have "leading man" good looks or charisma; for my money, he didn't, anyway. Albert [Finney], in his funny way, obviously did and has continued to remain so – whether he's got fat or thin he still has that kind of leading man stature. A lot of actors did, but I never really thought that about Ian Carmichael. I thought he was a good ensemble actor and he did well at that, but for me he lacked charisma, which Pat [Macnee] certainly had.'[39]

Susannah was very astute in noting that Ian had something to prove, if only to himself. By his own admission, the years 1963 and 1964 had been 'a recession in my professional life.'[40] Notwithstanding changing tastes in cinema acting styles, two feature films had either failed or been misjudged; a musical version of his BBC success *The Girl at the Next Table* had also fallen through, and while he had no shortage of offers to appear in the theatre, Ian had only found two productions to his liking: *Sunday in New York*, which was staged at the Ashcroft Theatre in Croydon, and Ronald Harwood's surrealistic comedy *March Hares*, which Ian toured in for four weeks. Also in 1964, he and Moira Lister appeared in a BBC production of *Simon and Laura*, and even though the two experienced thespians now occupied the lead roles (Ian's original part was played by Richard Briers), Ian must have felt more than a slight sense of retreading old ground. This sense of artistic *déjà vu* wasn't lost on *Television Today*'s reviewer, who, while admitting it was good to see plays such as *Simon and Laura* remounted for television, suggested that 'it would be even better to see *new* ones of the same ilk.'[41] With *The Importance of Being Earnest* widely promoted as *Armchair Theatre*'s first feature-length production of a theatre classic – and, at that time, one of only two plays in the series to feature location recording, at Maer Hall in Staffordshire – Ian's return to television drama (and his second production for ITV) represented if not a make-or-break point in his career, something pretty close to it. His concerns about his professional life darkened further when his mother, who had missed Ian's father dreadfully in the years since his death, herself passed away in 1963.

None of the tension Susannah York had spotted in him is evident in the finished production, despite behind-the-scenes problems beyond the control of the actors. Fenella remembers, 'There was a strike during rehearsals so it was all extended to six weeks, so what would normally take two or three weeks took *ages*. I cast Pamela Brown. She replaced Katherine Nesbitt [as Lady Bracknell]; because of the strike it meant Katherine couldn't do it so they had to get someone else, I suggested Pamela and they said "yes". I knew Pamela, had admired her for yonks and we had done something together before.'[42]

In spite of the recasting of the formidable matriarch and Ian's worries about his career, he comes across as the most accomplished purveyor of Wilde's wit in a uniformly excellent cast who are clearly relishing the sparkling dialogue. Ian's John Worthing was also a refreshing change from the long line of 'accident-prone clots' he had been saddled with, a sophisticated and clever Victorian gentleman who outwits the redoubtable Lady Bracknell. Recognising Wilde's words are inherently funny and that the best way to deliver them is by underplaying, Ian provides several laugh-out-loud gems, including 'a passionate celibacy is all any of us can look forward to' and 'he also stayed to tea and devoured every single muffin'. Getting the better of Lady Bracknell in her attempt to bar his friend Algy's marriage to his ward Cicely, Worthing/Ian casually mentions that she has '£130,000 in the funds, that's all. Goodbye, Lady Bracknell, so nice to have seen you,' a line thrown off with the effortless aplomb that could only come from years of valuable experience as a seasoned stage comedian.

Susannah York remembered that *The Importance of Being Earnest* was 'a joy to be in. I got on fine with the cast and we all enjoyed it,'[43] a mood that was obviously communicated to the viewing audience, as despite producer Leonard White's reservations, its transmission on 15 November 1964 saw it placed as the twelfth most-watched television programme in the top twenty for that week. Ian was a hit on TV, Patrick was more than happy, having conclusively shown that he had more to offer than starring in *The Avengers*, and, encouragingly, the critics had praised *Earnest*'s 'stylish production'[44] and 'the most enticing band of players that ever swapped lines in a television studio.'[45] As well as significantly raising Ian's television profile, the play was also a vindication for the methodology of the older generation of actors, as White astutely observed: 'Ian and Patrick were of the same ilk, they had the same sort of theatre background. [They both] had that lightness, that class. They both had class without any doubt.'[46]

During the making of *The Importance of Being Earnest*, Ian once again showed how caring and considerate he could be. Macnee's concern over whether or not *The Avengers* would be cancelled after Honor Blackman left was so acute that he'd begun drinking, to the point where it was affecting Ian's friend's ability to concentrate on the script:

> My old chum Ian Carmichael ... quickly realised my lines were giving me trouble, and helped solve the problem with tact and kindness. Ian lived just up the road from me in Mill Hill, and he asked whether I could give him a lift to rehearsals, as his car had gone down with a mystery virus. Delighted to oblige, I looked forward to a few early mornings of theatrical gossip with Ian. I found myself instead being coached by him in my role. Later I discovered that Ian had only pretended his car was disabled, thus creating a relaxed opportunity, when the two of us would be alone, to help me out. I'm not sure I could express my thanks adequately, but such an act speaks for itself.[47]

That Ian had eschewed the opportunity *Armchair Theatre* offered to appear in contemporary and challenging work by new writers in favour of a television adaptation of a classic, would be a significant pointer towards his professional future.

On 30 November 1964 it was the ninetieth birthday of Sir Winston Churchill, the man who, as prime minister, had courageously and successfully led Great Britain through the Second World War. On the same day, the BBC celebrated his near-century with a lavish ninety-minute extravaganza in his honour. *Ninety Years On* showcased songs and excerpts from shows that the great man would have been familiar with during his long and eventful life.

Ian recalled that the production had twenty well-known names that encompassed 'the ridiculous to the sublime'[48] of entertainment stars, with acts as diverse as Dame Margot Fonteyn, Alma Cogan, Cicely Courtneidge, Arthur Askey – and him. A script from Terence Rattigan and a narration spoken by Noël Coward completed *Ninety Years On*'s prestigious status in an elegant production put together by Ian's old champion, Michael Mills. After the disappointments and frustrations of the preceding two years, Ian was delighted to be back on familiar ground for a musical number staged by Freddie Carpenter, who had choreographed so many of his early performances at Alexandra Palace. After breaking relatively new ground with *The Importance of Being Earnest*, Ian's performance of 'Yip-Aye-Addy' in the guise of the Edwardian actor-producer-manager George Grossmith Junior (whom he strikingly resembled) from the musical *Our Miss Gibbs* – with him singing and dancing, resplendent in morning suit, top hat and silver-topped walking cane, backed by an attractive female chorus – emphasised all the qualities that had originally singled Ian out as a talent to watch.

Although Ian was given creditable notices for his performance in most of the following day's papers, he also received a most unexpected review two days after the broadcast in the form of a telegram sent to his home:

SO UPSET THAT SILLY OLD AUNTIE TIMES NEVER MENTIONED YOU MUST TELL YOU THOUGHT YOU WERE PERFECT WARMEST CONGRATULATIONS AND KINDEST REGARDS – LARRY OLIVIER[49]

At the time, Ian hadn't even met the man who was widely considered the greatest living actor in the English theatre. That he should take the trouble to applaud the work of someone he didn't know was particularly gratifying for Ian at a time when he felt his professional standing, if not his enthusiasm and abilities, had been at a low ebb. 'That wire I treasure more than any review I have ever received,'[50] he touchingly recalled.

Away from television and film in late 1964, Ian had been courted by the American impresario John Gale, who was preparing a Broadway staging of the French farce *Boeing-Boeing* by Marc Carmoletti, which had been running successfully in London since 1962 and had been packing in audiences in Paris since 1960. A hectic charade that concerned the raffish Bernard Lawrence's attempts to stop three air stewardesses he is dating from meeting, Gale wanted Ian for the part of Robert Reed, Bernard's old schoolfriend who added to the domestic chaos. In the actor's view, 'it was a play that was all situation; there isn't a funny line in it from beginning to end and in addition I had never been able to find any character whatsoever in the leading role.'[51] However, with no other professional engagements on the horizon, perhaps against his better judgement Ian was weakening towards accepting Gale's offer. This wasn't the first time that Gale had approached the star, seeing in him the same qualities present in David Tomlinson's endearing turn in *Boeing-Boeing* on the London stage, but Ian remained unconvinced about the play's New York transfer for two main reasons: first, he felt that Broadway audiences would be more attuned to the sharp, Neil Simon-style of comedy and, more importantly, if the play was a success he would have to commit to the production for as long as a year, something that he, Pym and his daughters Lee and Sally did not relish in the slightest.

On the first point, a compromise was reached: in consultation with Gale, Ian firmly believed that he had been given permission to create his own interpretation of the role, rather than a reproduction of the 'Robert' that could currently be seen in the West End (now being played by Leslie Phillips and partnered with Ian's friend

Patrick Cargill as Bernard). At least, that's what Ian thought; he later admitted, 'because of the cigarette that was a permanent fixture in Jack's face it wasn't always easy to understand what he said'.[52] Nevertheless, Ian was sufficiently encouraged by Gale's apparent agreement to ask Beverley Cross, the translator, to write some new dialogue that would give Robert's character more depth, something the play's director, Jack Minster, appeared to be happy with. There was no easy answer to the second of Ian's reservations; on Friday 18 December, a few days before Christmas, he said a heartbreaking, tearful goodbye to his family at London Airport (now Heathrow) and departed with actress Maureen Pryor and his young co-star Gerald Harper for what was potentially a year living in America.

Ian's doubts about staying in New York long term were not helped by several incidents that occurred soon after his arrival at JFK airport. An unsympathetic customs official ransacked his carefully packed trunk, and the chauffeur of the limousine that collected him locked all the doors on the inside as it was 'the safest way to travel'. After a night dining at Sardis restaurant with Jack Minster, Ian received a sinister phone call from an unknown man wanting to meet the actor for lunch, insisting they'd been enjoying each other's company well into the early hours at the Blackamore Club, a request he quickly and firmly refused. After such an unsettling introduction to the bustling, frenetic pace of life in Manhattan, Ian's assessment of the city was very blunt: 'I *hated* New York. I *loathed* it.'[53] Clearly, for him an Englishman abroad meant a fish out of water.

This wasn't the case for Ian's co-star, the suave but equally charming Gerald Harper. 'I was a young, single man,'[54] he remembers wryly, 'and, you know, some nights I had other fish to fry.' Although only nine years younger than Ian, in 1964 Harper was very much in the category of actors marked 'up and coming'. After studying to be a doctor, he had changed direction completely to pursue acting as his profession. He had been part of the Old Vic's touring company in both England and the United States, featured in the comic shipwreck movie *The Admirable Crichton*

(1957) and made guest appearances in the TV series *The Planemakers* and *The Avengers*. Despite Ian's recent misgivings about his chosen profession, Harper had no doubt that he was sharing the stage with a major talent: 'He was a film star when I met him. His was a very considerable career and quite right, as he was very talented. Ian was *enormous* fun to work with.'[55]

Given Ian's immediate antipathy towards New York, it wasn't surprising that Harper couldn't tempt his co-star out to share the delights of the city that never sleeps. 'On several nights I'd be suited up, ready to head off towards Times Square to make a night of it and I'd bump into Ian before I went out,' the actor remembers. "Where are you off to, old lad?" he'd say, a cup of coffee in one hand and a sandwich in the other. "Dinner," I'd say. "Fancy coming?" "No thanks, old son," he'd say, and wander off to his room. I was surprised how very shy he was. He was *so* shy, certainly not a starry person and certainly not pushy or aggressive. He was very quiet and relaxed.'[56]

Although Harper has happy memories of his working relationship with Ian and remembers a cool and contemplative man, the leading man's own experience of *Boeing-Boeing* became a frustrating one almost as soon as rehearsals – with three American actresses joining the cast as Bernard's girlfriends – started at the Cort Theatre on 48th Street near Times Square. Robert's new dialogue was discarded and, as Ian had feared, he was in no uncertain terms directed to give a performance identical to the one currently playing in London, a tense situation that resulted in 'numerous heated and time-wasting arguments'[57] with Minster. Harper remembers the situation more diplomatically:

> '[Ian] was a very serious actor, a serious character actor. The director and the management were not absolutely pleased as I think they wanted another David Tomlinson, who was superb I must say. Ian was very different; he really delved into the character. David Tomlinson just turned up in any old suit he had for the play, the older the suit the better; he didn't give a damn what he looked like, but Ian took enormous care. He went to enormous lengths and had

a rather marvellous thick tweed 'galumphing country' sort of suit, which I thought was absolutely wonderful, but the management weren't too keen on it. But he stuck to his guns, which was utterly remarkable.[58]

Although Ian was very despondent at the end of the three-week rehearsal period, feeling that, costume aside, his performance had become an unhappy compromise, to begin with he was encouraged by the response the play had on tour. 'On the tour it was triumphant,'[59] Harper recalls. 'We opened in Newhaven, took it to Boston, had a little tour and then came on to Broadway.'[60] Ian's cheer at the success of the provincial dates was cut short on a matinee day in Boston when it was announced that Sir Winston Churchill had died. Only two months before, Ian had been part of the birthday celebrations for the world-famous statesman; now, thousands of miles from home, he had no option but to stay in his hotel room alone, watching the television coverage of Churchill's London funeral on 30 January 1965. Harper had first-hand experience of the remarkable strength of feeling that the Americans showed towards their British compatriots on that depressing day:

> Everybody was filming the funeral and they were flying it over reel by reel to America and then they were putting it out. It went out during the morning and I was watching it on the television as each film reel was unrolled and [the commentators] would discuss it. We were watching it all morning and then at about noon I thought I'd better get ready for the matinee. So I went downstairs to the coffee shop and said to the waitress, 'I'd like two eggs, sunny side up, some hash browns, toast and coffee' and she said, 'Oh my God, you're English' and she burst into tears. She was standing there sobbing! The reaction in America was incredible.[61]

As Ian, the most English and patriotic of actors, sadly reflected, 'It was not the moment to have been on foreign soil.'[62]

Boeing-Boeing finally opened in New York on Tuesday 2 February. On the day of the show's premiere, Ian was cheered up considerably when, arriving at his hotel – the Algonquin – for what he thought was an appointment with John Gale, he was delighted to find Pym instead. His wife's surprise visit helped the star through the first night, which was greeted by an enthusiastic Broadway audience. The next day, however, Ian's misgivings about the play were confirmed with universally bad reviews. The French farce that would run for nearly twenty years in Paris would run for only three weeks in America. It was left to the film version of *Boeing-Boeing* starring Tony Curtis and Jerry Lewis, released later in 1965, to acquaint the United States with the joys of Carmoletti's play.

In the wake of such an expensive flop, *Boeing-Boeing*'s US management looked for someone to hold responsible, not without some acrimony. Ian was the obvious target because of the friction between him and Minster. Harper feels this is unfair:

> The trouble was, because [Ian] had been so serious about it, when it came off, the management, who always need somebody to blame, tended to blame Ian, which I thought was deeply, *deeply* unfair. I was the blue-eyed boy because I was young and not famous and I did whatever anybody asked me to, whereas Ian was very stubborn and wouldn't. He said, 'No, this is a country boy and I must play it like a country boy.' Stubborn in the right sense; I admire actors who cause a scene at a rehearsal if they are only doing it to get it right, and I thought that was wholly admirable.[63]

The lingering resentment Minster felt about Ian even communicated itself to Nicholas Parsons – an established comic actor who had been the straight foil in the popular, long-running *The Arthur Haynes Show* on ITV from 1957 – who took over from Leslie Phillips as Robert in London once the director was back in England. The story he told *Boeing-Boeing*'s new London leading man about Ian was very much at odds with the scrupulous professional Parsons knew:

> Jack Minster told me that ... for some reason, when Ian played it on Broadway he reinterpreted the role. [He] blamed Ian to some extent for its failure. [He] said, 'Ian didn't want to play it in the broad farcical way that you, David Tomlinson and Leslie Phillips played it. He wanted to treat it more like a sophisticated comedy and prove

that he was more of a Cary Grant-type actor than a farce actor.' I don't know whether that's true or not, but that's what Jack Minster said. I can't believe this, because Ian was brilliant in whatever he did and I thought he was ideal for that role, though I never saw it so I can't comment. Poor Jack Minster; it seemed completely out of character [for Ian]. Jack said he despaired, because Ian suddenly wanted to reinterpret the role rather than play it the way it was written. You can take a character and, according to your delivery and style and your interpretation of the words and the lines, you *can* make it different. According to Minster, that's what Ian tried to do on Broadway and that's one of the reasons the show flopped. It may have been sour grapes on Minster's part ... [Ian] could have been going through a funny phase at the time. Maybe he wanted to re-establish himself as a more serious comedy actor rather than a farcical comedy actor.[64]

There may be some truth in Minster's assertion that the actor was trying to establish himself as a 'Cary Grant-type [performer]' (particularly after the failure of *Hide and Seek*, a specifically Grant-inspired vehicle). Although it's unlikely that such an accomplished professional as Ian would deliberately sabotage the success of a play to do that, his behaviour in *Boeing-Boeing* may have been a rare professional instance of his selfish streak getting the better of him as he was stuck in a play he didn't like. In any case, Gale plainly bore Ian no ill will, inviting him and Harper to a succession of parties that celebrated *Boeing-Boeing*'s continuing success worldwide, repeated invitations that the two men found hilarious for an obvious reason:

The play had run in London for five years, it ran in Paris for [eighteen] years, it ran in Scandinavia for four years, it ran in Australia for two years and Ian and I were the only two people who ever did this bloody play and it came off after three weeks! John Gale, who made his fortune with it – because he put it on for nothing and it ran forever – kept throwing parties to celebrate the 500th performance, the 600th performance, the 700th performance ... About four people had played it in London, there would be hundreds of people there who had played these two parts all over the world, and Ian and I would say, 'We don't know what we're doing at this bloody party as we were the only ones who had had a total failure with it!'[65]

Back in February 1965, Ian had been relieved when after the first week of performances in New York, the regulation fortnight's notice was given to *Boeing-Boeing*'s cast and crew, advising them that they would be out of work before March. He believed that a year in the Big Apple 'would have driven me out of my mind'[66], and delighted in telling the visiting Pym that within two weeks he would be back at home. The early cancellation of *Boeing-Boeing* was beneficial for Harper's career, freeing him up to find early TV fame as a Victorian adventurer resurrected in Swinging London in the BBC series *Adam Adamant Lives!* And for Ian, after too many disillusioning setbacks, a career renaissance courtesy of his old employers would be just around the corner.

CHAPTER 12

Jeeves and the TV Series

*Small-screen stardom arrives thanks to the
venerable P.G. Wodehouse*

IAN'S CELEBRATED INTERPRETATION of P.G. Wodehouse's character Bertie Wooster, the misadventuring, 1920s upper-class loafer who was regularly extricated from trouble by his cool manservant Jeeves, was the coincidental creation of like minds. During 1964, Ian had been discussing with his former agent Richard Stone potential projects, and the most promising idea had been a TV series based around Wodehouse's definitive 'silly ass'. 'Suddenly there was a dearth of good film scripts,' Ian recalled. 'I thought of the Jeeves stories and was once on the point of sending them to the BBC and suggesting a series, when I thought they might seem *passé*. I also felt that I might be *passé*, too, having to go back to the '20s for material.'[1] The actor also worried that he might become even more 'typecast as a featherbrained character,'[2] if such a thing was possible. The idea was dropped. Ironically, and unknown to Ian, five years earlier the BBC had considered the Jeeves stories would be an ideal television vehicle for him. With remarkable foresight, the Head of Light Entertainment Television Eric Maschwitz had predicted, 'Carmichael might be an excellent "Bertie Wooster".'[3]

In a meeting with Michael Mills in the BBC Club during the making of *Ninety Years On*, Ian was astonished to learn that his friend was planning a series based on the Jeeves and Wooster short stories, and had been looking into the idea since 1963, when he had asked the producer Dennis Main Wilson to enquire about securing the TV rights. 'I gather that throughout the English-speaking world all film companies and most television companies have tried to interpret Wodehouse to no effect at all,' Main Wilson reported back in July of the same year, 'and have given up trying, finding obviously that the literary style was too difficult to translate into the visual medium. It is possible, therefore, that the [estate] might be only too pleased to earn themselves some period English currency in return for the use of what looks like a lame duck.'[4] This indeed had proved to be the case, and by November 1964 the BBC had optioned the adaptation rights.

At the time, and despite the failure of the feature film *Hide and Seek*, Ian's ambition was to become a romantic leading man which, he somewhat ruefully commented, was 'hard to achieve when people expect you to be funny all the time.'[5] However, Mills' enthusiasm for Ian to take on the mantle of Wooster 'sort of relieved me of responsibility for the decision. Although it's a silly-ass part it's such a classic one that my inhibitions about playing a clot again just vanished.'[6]

Even though he had been won over, Ian was still committed to the Broadway run of *Boeing-Boeing*. Generously, the producer offered to keep the casting open as the production team for *The World of Wooster* wouldn't be in a position to start work until early in 1965. By February, the fate of the play was clear and Ian immediately wrote to his loyal BBC colleague: '*Boeing-Boeing* has failed on Broadway – we come off next Saturday night, [and] I shall be returning home next week. There are one or two offers waiting for me, but I am not at all sure of [them] until I get home. I wondered if you were in a position to get cracking on that Woodhouse (sic) pilot fairly soon. I will call you as soon as I hit town.'[7]

Just over a week later, he received the following positive and encouraging response:

MANY THANKS YOUR LETTER WOODHOUSE (SIC) PILOT OR SERIES READY
TO GO ONE SCRIPT DONE SECOND READY MIDDLE NEXT WEEK STUDIO
DATES EARMARKED HAVE THIS WEEK COMMUNICATED [THE PLAY'S
PRODUCER] FIRM OFFER YOU PLAY WOOSTER WHICH EARNESTLY HOPE
YOU ACCEPT THINK YOU WOULD BE SUPERB WAITING HEAR FROM YOU
ON RETURN REGARDS — MILLS[8]

Ian returned to England on 22 February eager to don the spats, monocle and Oxford bags of a literary icon.

The ensuing work to get *The World of Wooster* before the cameras was typical of a more innocent television age when, incredibly, it was possible to get a six-part comedy series ready for transmission from a standing start in just over three months (the first episode was aired on 30 May). Michael certainly hadn't been idle in Ian's absence; as producer, he had assigned himself the task of writing three of the adaptations, while Richard Waring, who had been the main writer on the successful BBC sitcom *Marriage Lines* (and, coincidentally, had also contributed scripts to the sitcom *Brothers in Law* inspired by the Boulting brothers film Ian had starred in), was employed to write the others.

In 1965, the demarcations between actor, writer and producer weren't as rigid as they would become at the BBC only a few years later (and which would create difficulties for Ian). As Mills himself had encouraged Ian to pursue a career as a writer and producer in his early days at the Corporation, he completely trusted the instincts of his leading man when he suggested, in discussion with the producer and Waring, that Wooster's first-person narrative, which often contained some of Wodehouse's best humour – choice cuts being 'Aunt is calling to Aunt like mastodons bellowing across primeval swamps'[9] and 'there's no doubt that Jeeves's pick-me-ups will produce immediate results in anything short of an Egyptian mummy'[10] – should be transplanted directly into the dialogue. At a stroke, Ian solved the problem that had stymied many prospective companies interested in adapting the Wooster books.

Right from the start, he was an integral part of the three-man creative team. With the approach to the Wodehouse stories defined, the trio would between them select the stories for adaptation and Waring and Mills would write the scripts. A sign of the high regard in which the producer held his leading actor was that, once written, the screenplays would be sent to Ian to comment on, and many of his suggestions would be included in the final drafts.

With his position as a keystone of *Wooster*'s production office it's no wonder that Ian's fee was confirmed at, for 1965, an incredibly generous 500 guineas per half-hour episode – a staggering £6,400 in today's coinage – plus an additional '£87.10s per programme, which represents one sixth of the additional fees negotiated for the filming sessions and the artist's work in revising and adapting the scripts.'[11] At a time when many former film actors were establishing themselves as TV regulars, Ian's high fee, also reflective of his former standing as a leading man in British movies, set a very helpful precedent within the acting profession.

Of paramount importance once the direction of the series had been decided on was the casting of Jeeves. Top of the wish list had been the revered theatre actor John Gielgud, whose haughty, supercilious manner would have been ideal for the Wooster manservant (and who would prove his suitability seventeen years later as a very similar butler in the Dudley Moore movie *Arthur*). With Gielgud unavailable due to his commitment to a play, by early July the list of performers under consideration read like a *Who's Who* of venerable British character actors. On the very distinguished shortlist was Michael Hordern, Maurice Denham, Leonard Sachs, Herbert Lom, William Mervyn, Clive Morton (who had acted with Ian before), Robert Coote, Cecil Parker (Ian's co-star in *Happy is the Bride* and *The Amorous Prawn*, marked as 'available'), John Le Mesurier and Thorley Walters (Boulting brothers favourites), Hugh Latimer, Frank Thornton, David Langton and Dennis Price, who had locked acting horns with Ian in the films *Private's Progress*, *I'm All Right Jack*, *School for Scoundrels* and *The Amorous Prawn*. The list also included the rather left-field suggestion of the diminutive comedian Charlie Drake.

There was a flurry of activity in early March as Mills, desperate to secure the right actor's services at such short notice, wrote and asked, in quick succession, Price, Parker, Latimer, Thornton, Langton and Coote to audition for the role with Ian. Coote was appearing in a play in America and couldn't attend, but remained the favoured candidate after Price, the new first choice, who proved unavailable. When Price suddenly became free again, Mills was so relieved and tied up with the pressures of production that he neglected to tell Coote's agents Connies Ltd Personal Management that their client had been dropped, an omission that resulted in a severe reprimand from them in early April: 'Mr Coote is much too important an actor to be treated in this manner, and I expect an apology from you personally.' A very aggrieved Connies also expected the BBC to pay 'cable expenses.'[12]

This wasn't the only problem. The distinguished composer Sandy Wilson, who had written the 1920s-set musicals *The Boy Friend* (1953) and its sequel *Divorce Me, Darling!* (1964), and was supplying the authentic period theme and incidental music for the series, was offended when he discovered that Mills had been discussing his score with his own arranger without informing Wilson. 'As you know, I like to be at least consulted over these matters, and I had been waiting to hear from you ever since the music was delivered to you last Wednesday, with instructions to be returned to me – instructions which were disregarded,' he pointedly observed, going on to say, 'a composer has certain rights which ought to be observed, and I would be grateful if you would do so in future, otherwise I shall have to withdraw the entire score from your production.'[13]

In another oversight, Peter Cotes, who was attached to the series as the associate producer on behalf of the Wodehouse estate, wasn't invited to the press launch and, to make matters worse, only learned from the morning papers the day after the launch about the stories selected for the first series. Mills was the recipient of another complaint on 6 April when Cotes's representative warned him in no uncertain terms that 'if Wodehouse, who presumably reads the English papers, infers that Peter is no longer actively concerned with the project, he could very well injunct.'[14] For a series being mounted so quickly, it's not surprising that some glitches occurred in the production process, but with such important contributors being affronted, however unintentionally, it's rather surprising that *The World of Wooster* made it to the transmission of its first episode at all.

Happily such strife didn't extend to the relationship between the two stars. During the auditions for Jeeves, Ian had developed the quavering, stuttering speech patterns that implied Bertie was in a constant state of nervous anxiety – which he had based on an officer he had served with during the final years of the war – and once Dennis Price had been cast, Ian was overjoyed with the patience and dedication his co-star showed in rehearsals. Ian found it difficult learning lines, a problem that grew more pronounced the older he became, and the challenge was compounded by the *Wooster* scripts, in which both he and Dennis were required to give long speeches, in the latter's case the 'explain all' dialogues Jeeves delivered in the closing scene. With very few edits per episode, the stories were recorded 'as live', in other words like a stage play performed before the cameras and a live audience, adding to the pressure on the actors. With both men in accord on the need for constant rehearsal, Ian recalled, 'we both had an understanding of each other's problems and shortcomings which made for harmony and compatibility.'[15] There was no competition between them and Dennis was always the first to acknowledge who was the star of the show. 'I had a totally happy relationship with Dennis,' Ian recalled. 'A lot of two-handed stuff went on with him, and when I was talking to Michael Mills, the director, he'd go and sit down. I'd say, "Come over here, Dennis, because you're in this scene too." He'd reply, "No, no. You arrange it, then tell me what I've got to do."'[16]

Visiting the intense but good-natured rehearsals, the writer Sam Pollock from the *Radio Times* 'admired the way that Mills and Waring, while preserving the plots and the spirit of the author and period, have transformed the stories into modern half-hour farces, which should entertain youngsters who have never heard of Wodehouse, or, if they have, may have thought this stuff was strictly for the old 'uns.'[17]

The sight of Ian dressed in period 1920s clothes – walking along with a silver-topped cane, driving a soft-topped Bentley (at the same time as his old chum Patrick Macnee was driving a soft-topped Bentley in *The Avengers*), playing golf and opening a bottle of champagne while Jeeves calmly took a phone call, against a jaunty, tinkling melody – greeted curious viewers as they watched the title sequence of the first episode of *The World of Wooster*. 'Jeeves and the Dog Mackintosh' aired on Sunday 30 May. The phrase 'overnight success' is much misused, but the series really was an instant critical and popular hit. A typical letter published a few weeks later in the *Radio Times* commented, 'Please convey my congratulations to the casting director for the series of P.G. Wodehouse stories. Ian Carmichael and Dennis Price are excellent in their portrayal of these characters. I have long waited for someone to recognise the potentialities of the Wodehouse comedies.'[18] The dilemmas of Jeeves and Wooster proved an arresting alternative to a viewing public used to a recent BBC diet of earthy and bizarre comedy such as *Steptoe and Son*, *Not Only ... But Also*, *The Likely Lads* and *Till Death Us Do Part*, and delighted some members of the audience who were indeed old enough to remember the 'roaring twenties'.

Sadly, only one and a half of the episodes of *The World of Wooster* survive, thanks to a short-sighted purge of archive recordings carried out by the BBC in the 1960s and 1970s – who would ever have thought that, over forty years later, companies would be crying out to release the BBC's vintage output? In the second series' first episode, 'Jeeves and the Delayed Exit of Claude and Eustace', can be seen all the elements that made the show such an achievement. Although there were some minor additions and changes to make the story work as a half-hour farce, most of the dialogue was lifted directly from Wodehouse with barely a word changed, and it comes across as just as funny as on the page, particularly Bertie's comments that his Uncle Oliver's penchant for alcohol has given him a reputation for 'shifting a bit' and 'mopping the stuff up to some extent.'

Wodehouse's enchanting dialogue aside, it is the performances that make the whole thing work. Even though Ian and Dennis were too old for the lead roles – Jeeves and Wooster were both in their twenties in the original stories – the obvious chemistry between them more than compensated. Appearing to have been born with a monocle, Ian's Wooster is characterised as an over-privileged little boy who's never grown up, constantly nervous and terrified of his formidable Aunt Agatha (Fabia Drake). His attempts to rid himself of his two annoying cousins Claude (Timothy Carlton) and Eustace (Simon Ward), and the farcical situations that ensue, allowed Ian's expressive, reactive acting full reign, as in quick succession he registers surprise, horror, amazement, consternation and finally happiness. Ian also shows himself to be as accomplished as ever at physical comedy, as he relieves Uncle Oliver of the drink the troubled man has being trying to quaff throughout one scene and is blinded by a top hat several sizes too big for him, flailing around comically. Dennis Price complements Ian's hyperactive Wooster perfectly as a suave, calm and educated retainer who clearly knows better than his master but whose composure can be occasionally ruffled: learning that Claude and Eustace are going to be staying in Bertie's flat, he nearly drops his tray. Such an agreeable concoction moved the critic Nancy Banks-Smith to comment in the *Sun*, 'To be paid for watching *Wooster* verges on larceny. I would watch for free. If pushed, I would pay to see *The World of Wooster*' and, tellingly, 'It would be impertinent to praise Ian Carmichael's playing or Dennis Price's under-playing. A beautiful duet.'[19]

The biggest accolade paid to the *Wooster* production team came shortly after the first series ended. A note from Remsenburg, Long Island was short and to the point:

To the producer and cast of the Jeeves sketches.
Thank you all for the perfectly wonderful performances. I am
simply delighted with it. Bertie and Jeeves are just as I have always
imagined them, and every part is played just right.
Bless you!
P.G. Wodehouse[20]

Frank Muir, the BBC Head of Comedy, had flown out to visit
Wodehouse in America and had taken with him film copies of the
first two episodes, as the author was very keen to see how the BBC
had interpreted his stories. To this day, his framed letter still hangs
on the wall of Michael Mills' house.

There were signs of *Wooster* mania everywhere. The respected
writer Joe McGrath, who had worked on the BBC's influential
police series *Z Cars*, dropped a note into Mills' office that read:
'Congratulations, I don't mind staying in on Sunday evenings now
– top hole, spiffing entertainment!';[21] Ian received letters asking
him where a monocle like Bertie's could be bought; teenagers
sought out 1920s-style clothes, and the sales of Wodehouse's books
surged to the point where some had to be reprinted, now adorned
with BBC photographs of Ian and Dennis as the duo. In the best
traditions of the children's toys of the period, like James Bond's
Aston Martin DB5 and the Batmobile, there was even a *World of
Wooster* Corgi Classic car, complete with a miniature Jeeves in the
driver's seat, no doubt on the way somewhere to collect his master.
When Ian was out and about, even though he was initially gratified
by the impression that the series had made, he grew slightly tired
of constant enquiries from the public asking where Jeeves was. To
cap it all, *The World of Wooster* won the Guild of Television
Producers and Directors award for best comedy series production
of 1965. With Jeeves and Bertie having made such an impression
on the viewing public, a second series was a foregone conclusion
and premiered in January 1966, with a third following in 1967.
Both were just as successful as the first.

Capitalising on his breakthrough as a BBC TV star, Ian took time out between the first and second series to return to the West End stage and star with his old friends Patrick Cargill and Dilys Laye in Keith Waterhouse and Willis Hall's comedy of infidelity *Say Who You Are* (Jan Holden completed the play's quartet of characters). The plot revolved around a public telephone box which the participants used to arrange their assignations, and which was part of an ingeniously designed composite set, courtesy of 'Jay' Hutchinson Scott, that incorporated a London street, the façade of a pub called The Hussar, the bottom of a staircase with a lift and the living room of a flat in Kensington. Ian happily recalled that the play was 'a zonking great success from the word go,'[22] and was 'that theatrical rarity – a sparkling, glittering gem of a comedy, complete from the moment it left the typewriter.'[23]

In 1966, the celebratory atmosphere on *The World of Wooster* continued with the BBC and Sandy Wilson's decision to release the song that Ian performed over the closing credits, 'What Would I Do Without Jeeves?', as a single, backed with 'Bertie's Blues'. Now that Ian and Dennis were a partnership with an evident rapport and were happy in each other's company, the recording session also included a part for Price. 'I think it came out really well,' a by now much happier Wilson wrote to Mills. 'Ian was fine, as always, and guided Dennis along very sweetly – rather strange to see Bertie conducting Jeeves!'[24] Ian's nostalgic vocalising of the lyrics amiably sums up the appeal of his lauded characterisation and the series as a whole:

> What would I do without you, Jeeves?
> I'd get in the most frightful stew, Jeeves
> The day couldn't start without you to wake me
> And tenderly shake me
> And proffer that perfect cup of tea you make me.
> Who in the world would I call in
> To winkle me out when I fall in
> Those terrible traps that destiny weaves (and all that sort of rot)
> Oh, what would I do without Jeeves?

Oh, Jeeves? He's indispensable,
What would I do without Jeeves?
He's quite inimitable.
What would I do without Jeeves?[25]

The success of *The World of Wooster* was particularly significant for Ian. With a shortage of any good film or television film scripts in the two years before it went into production, he had felt that his career had been in the professional doldrums. *Wooster* not only made him a nationally recognised figure all over again but also transformed him into a BBC star, a situation he was able to build on productively in the late 1960s and into the 1970s. Ian's identification with Bertie, and the 1920s in particular, would however stay with him, an early sign being that after the TV series, Wodehouse tried to interest Ian in a stage musical version starring him as Wooster, but he turned it down because 'he had always been too old for Bertie and did not want to press his luck any longer.'[26] For Michael Mills, though, his friend's three-year turn as Wodehouse's affable buffoon would be career-defining: 'Bertie Wooster was the best thing he ever did. He is, in appearance, always slightly comic. The clown always wants to play Hamlet – but he was tremendous, working on *Wooster*, and persuaded me to use dialogue instead of a narrator. A lot of people had tried Bertie Wooster before, including [David] Niven, who couldn't do it; but Ian's technique, his control, his straight-down-the-middle performance, were perfect.'[27]

With the arrival of Diana Rigg as Mrs Emma Peel in 1965, *The Avengers* had become more like a sparkling light comedy and, as *the* programme to appear in on British television, would have been an ideal guest-starring vehicle for Ian around the time of his commitment to *The World of Wooster*. Many of his contemporaries, such as John Le Mesurier, Cecil Parker and Peter Bowles, had enjoyed themselves tussling with Patrick Macnee's John Steed and his hip female partners. Moira Lister had memorably vamped it up with an outrageous Russian accent as the master-spy Elena Vazin, complete with garter holster, in 'The See-Through Man'. A part that seemed almost written with Ian in mind in *The Avengers* was Tarquin Ponsonby Fry (a role which in the end went to Terence Alexander) in 'The Correct Way to Kill', an instructor at SNOB (Sociability Nobility Omnipotence Breeding Inc.), a cadre of murderous bounders for hire who operated under the cover of a finishing school for young gentlemen: 'Splendid, splendid! Always correct, even in defeat.' (The reason Ian might not have been asked to appear in the episode, even though he was ideal for it, was because it was directed by Charles Crichton, with whom he'd had a disagreement during the making of *Lucky Jim*.) Ian wasn't averse to guest appearances, so it remains a mystery why he never took up the opportunity for some stylish verbal sparring and pop-art fisticuffs with his old friend Macnee.

He did get his turn in a Swinging London caper, as most actors of his generation did. In the 1967 movie *Smashing Time*, humorist and critic George Melly wrote a lively critique of the 'scene' that, to outsiders, seemed like an endless party for photographers, pop stars and artists who lived in or near Chelsea such as David Bailey, Michael Caine and Mick Jagger. With its social commentary and slapstick, *Smashing Time* in some ways resembled a Technicolor Boultings' film, even though the social commentary was lightweight and the slapstick sequences went on far too long. It starred Rita Tushingham – riding high on the success of the film version of *A Taste of Honey* (1961) – and Vanessa Redgrave, daughter of Michael, as two young Northern girls, Brenda and Yvonne, who go looking for fame and fortune on the streets of London. Ian played Bobby Mome-Rath, a louche, drunken member of the officer class, whose private income enabled him to prey on innocent young women dazzled by the capital's bright lights. Ian's effortless drunk acting was very funny as he seduced Yvonne in a gentleman's club, and, significantly, could have been cut and pasted from *Smashing Time* into any of the colour *Avengers* episodes being made at the time. Although Melly's and director Desmond Davis's depiction of 1960s hedonism was more light-hearted than John Schlesinger's *Darling* (1965) or Lewis Gilbert's *Alfie* (1966), *Smashing Time* followed the trend of all similarly themed films in lampooning the Establishment – those in positions of authority who were completely out of touch with the music, values and lifestyles of the Rolling Stones, Jean Shrimpton, Terence Stamp et al – and presenting its representatives as figures to be ridiculed (a quality shared by *The Avengers*). Ian's Bobby Mome-Rath was part of that trend for Establishment send-up.

Smashing Time, like other Swinging London films, riffed on contemporary trends, and when it went into production in 1966, *The World of Wooster* was an important facet of British popular culture. Ian's persona in the film, with his exquisite three-piece suits and quavering voice, is virtually indistinguishable from Bertie. In a film full of slapstick moments, the scenes of Mome-Rath dealing with his flat being overrun by soapsuds, a grumbling stomach full of laxatives and his old sergeant (David Lodge) falling through the ceiling onto his bed in a hail of rubble, are far and away the funniest in the film, enhanced by Bobby's antiquated language that warms to 'a couple of nice little drinkies' and, alarmingly, 'the games one used to play with Nanny'.

By December 1967, when *Smashing Time* was released, the press had had its fill of Mod culture. 'Show me another film about swinging, trendy, pacy London and I'll show you a clean pair of heels,'[28] wrote Ian Christie in the *Daily Express*, although he did note that 'Ian Carmichael appears effectively as an irritable man about town whose attempts to seduce the big girl are frustrated by the small one.'[29] The *Sun* applauded 'lively if brief support from Ian Carmichael and Irene Handl,'[30] but overall the verdict was, as the *Sunday Times* concisely put it, 'an uneasy blend of farce and satire.'[31]

In *Films and Filming*, however, Robin Bean applauded Melly and Davis for crafting 'a lively, engaging antidote to the more apathetic and deeper analysis of the "swinging city" as seen by [Michelangelo] Antonioni in *Blow-Up*.' He had particular praise for the director, going on to say, 'Davis lets the comedy play for itself, his great strength being in the way he lets his actors develop an individual character based largely on exploiting their own personalities.'[32] Rather touchingly, Bean concluded that, at the end of 1967, perhaps *Smashing Time* showed that 'the hippies [were] the only genuine and emotionally honest people in the country.'[33]

Away from the Carnaby Street crowd, in May 1968 Ian returned to the Lyric Hammersmith for the first time in sixteen years to star in a two-handed musical comedy with Anne Rogers called *I Do! I Do!* by Jan de Hartog. Going against the grain of 1968's permissive tendencies, and first mounted on Broadway, the play was an honest exploration of the fifty-year marriage of 'He' (Ian) and 'She' (Rogers). The *Stage* found the play amusing if slightly unconvincing in its attitude to sex: '[He (Michael) and She (Agnes)] are apparently good and decent, simple and ordinary, except for their cavortings in and around the big double bed that is pitched at the centre of the proceedings. In relation to bed they become not quite what one would expect of such a clean little couple: their luxuriating in sex, expressed of course by arch implication, seems hardly credible. But this aspect of the story and the production is by a long way the most amusing, and reveals Miss Rogers and Mr Carmichael at their most inventive and diverting.'[34] However, critical reaction elsewhere verged on the hostile, and one night when some off-stage knocking was heard at a door, an exasperated audience member cried out, 'For God's sake let them in – whoever it is!'[35] Disappointingly for Ian, *I Do! I Do!* would only run for fourteen weeks.

In October 1968, Ian's sole TV outing was, unusually, for ITV. In an anthology series of plays entitled *The Root of all Evil?* about the corrupting power of wealth, Ian took on a rare contemporary role that was one of his mid-career attempts to change how he was perceived as an actor. In *The Last of the Big Spenders*, shown on 22 October 1968, he could be seen as the irascible Henry Priddis, a minimum-wage shoe-shop assistant who had always dreamed about achieving a life of luxury. The play's write-up in the *TV Times*, ITV's listings magazine, offered an intriguing portrait of how Ian was viewed at this point in his career in some quarters: 'Although Ian Carmichael keeps cropping up in re-runs of his old films, and he had an enormous success with *The World of Wooster*, it's actually nearly four years since he last appeared in a television play. His role as Henry Priddis, in Hugh Whitemore's *The Last of the Big Spenders*, gets him away from what most people think of as "obvious Carmichael casting".'[36]

As the Swinging Sixties gave way to the Cynical Seventies, Ian appeared in the anthology comedy film *The Magnificent Seven Deadly Sins*, produced by Tony Tenser's company Tigon Pictures, whose principal fare up until 1971 had been exploitation horror movies. The overall lewd tone of the film was established from the outset, with slow-motion scenes of a naked model in soft-focus woodland. A cod German voiceover (supplied by Graham Stark, the film's director), informed the audience that while the young lady on the screen wasn't actually in the film, she was 'a close personal friend of the director'.

'Pride', Ian's story, was a rewrite of a BBC *Comedy Playhouse* by Alan Simpson and Ray Galton, the talented duo behind *Hancock's Half Hour* and *Steptoe and Son*. This explains why 'Pride' is a significant cut above the other sketches, which more often than not indulge in not-very-subtle sexual innuendo. (The notable exception is Spike Milligan's 'Sloth', a hysterically funny silent-movie-style trip through a day in the life of an extremely indolent tramp who can't open a gate.) 'Pride' centres on two drivers who each refuse to back down over reversing down a single-track country lane when they meet in the middle. Ian once again took on the persona of a well-to-do upper-class fellow, this time company director Mr Ferris, complete with tailored suit and cut-glass accent. His adversary was the cloth-cap-wearing trade union shop steward Mr Spooner, played by the diminutive Alfie Bass, whose obstinate attitude raised the ghost of *I'm All Right Jack* and resonated with the troubled early 1970s British economy that was increasingly under siege from strikes and industrial disputes. Significantly, while Ferris and Spooner's bickering drew in representatives of the AA and RAC, their wives settled down to a convivial and friendly picnic. Even though Ferris eventually triumphed in forcing Spooner to reverse, in a nicely ironic twist he discovered that he'd gone the wrong way and would have to turn around and drive back the way he'd come. It was Galton and Simpson at their best.

The quality of 'Pride' alone, together with some lively and imaginative animation by Bob Godfrey (who later in the decade would make the seminal children's cartoon series *Roobarb*), wasn't enough to save *The Magnificent Seven Deadly Sins* from a critical drubbing in the press, with most of the critics being standard bearers at the funeral, as they saw it, of British film comedy. *The Times* branded the film unequivocally as 'dire'[37], grudgingly singling out the quality of Ian's story as 'at a pinch, one might make an exception for Ian Carmichael and Alfie Bass, mildly amusing as a couple of motorists who illustrate the sin of pride when they meet bumper-to-bumper in a narrow lane, but it hardly seems worthwhile.'[38] The *Guardian* also noted the 'proper business'[39] of Ian's sketch, but found 'four of the [other] episodes appalling' and felt that 'the eighth deadly sin … is Graham Stark's direction.'[40] By contrast, a lone voice of populist approval was Felix Barker writing in the *Evening News*, who predicted, 'This comedy looks like achieving the eighth magnificent deadly sin – Popularity.'[41] Across the board, however, Fleet Street felt that an audience desiring quality amusement would leave the cinema 'short-changed.'[42]

By 1971, there was no mistaking the sound of the nails being hammered into British film comedy's coffin lid. Luckily, Ian had other fish to fry.

CHAPTER 13

Here Comes the *Bachelor Father*

*The Lord's Taverners, turning foster parent and
a public-school reunion*

I N 1970, AWAY from the worlds of Wooster and theatre and film commitments, Ian continued to enjoy his administrative duties and social life as part of the Lord's Taverners cricket club. It had been founded in 1950 by the actor Martin Boddey for members of the arts who had a fondness for the game and for cricketers who were, in turn, enthusiastic about the arts. The club took its name from a group of actors and broadcasters who used to assemble to watch cricket in front of the original Tavern at Lord's cricket ground, and the primary function of the association was to raise money for the game that gave its members so much enjoyment. Encouraged by the Boulting brothers, Ian had been a member since 1956, and during his time with the association, fellow members included such luminaries as Richard Hearne, David Frost, Roy Castle, Leslie Crowther, Henry Cooper, Mick McManus and Harry Secombe.

The Lord's Taverners inaugural council meeting was held in the Royal Circle bar of the Comedy Theatre on 3 July 1950, a fact commemorated by a bronze plaque now fixed to one of its walls. Its founder member Boddey was its first chairman, while the actor John Mills became the first president. A few weeks prior to this, Captain Jack Broome, who had served in the Royal Navy with Prince Philip, suggested that Mills and Boddey contact His Royal

Highness as it was highly likely that he would be interested in assisting the Lord's Taverners. Recalling the eventual meeting at Clarence House with Prince Phillip that resulted, Ian remembered, 'When it was cautiously put forward that he might consent to become the association's first President, he replied, it is reported, "I couldn't do that. If I became your President I should expect to chair your meetings – indeed, I should insist on doing so – and I really haven't the time. But I will be your Patron if you like." The overjoyed visitors [Boddey and Broome] prepared to take their leave, but before doing so they casually mentioned that the honorary and honourable position of Twelfth Man had hopefully been left vacant. His Royal Highness, perhaps with his tongue in his cheek, enquired the significance of the position. He was told that the traditional duties of that indispensable member of a cricket side are (a) to carry the bag from the station, (b) look after the score book, (c) bring out the drinks, (d) 'sub' in the field, and (e) run for anybody who didn't feel like it after lunch. "Exactly what I thought you meant," said His Royal Highness, and thereupon claimed the right to fill the role.'[1]

The Tavern itself was one of Ian's favourite places. The coterie of in- and out-of-work actors there was a convivial *milieu*, heartening to be in whether you had employment or not. Ian remembered drinking with a distinguished member of the Old Vic theatre company there one Saturday lunchtime:

He was appearing in *Othello,* alternating the title role with that of Iago (generally considered to be the longest role in Shakespeare) with another actor, turn and turn about. We had all downed a considerable number of pints and my turn had come round once more.

'Same again?' I enquired of all concerned. I then said to this actor, 'Shall I skip you this time?'
'Certainly not,' he replied. 'Why?'
'You've got a matinee, haven't you?' I asked
'Yes,' said Richard Burton, 'but it's only Iago this afternoon.'
The Welsh have great constitutions.[2]

'I did a lot for the Lord's Taverners too,' recalls Nicholas Parsons. 'Ian was very much involved in them so I had a lot of contact with him then. Ian had a parting of the ways with the Lord's Taverners [in October 1976]: he thought they were getting too big and commercial and he wanted to keep them small and beautiful. In many ways he was right, because it was a club as well as a charity, and others, including me, wanted to move it forward as we thought if we're going to give our time to raising money for good causes, we might as well try to get as much as we can, and so more business people came in. Once an organisation gets very large it gets more bureaucratic and more impersonal. When Ian moved back to Yorkshire, one didn't see very much of him and I rather lost touch with him until he came to a big charity event at the Lord's Taverners. [The committee] had persuaded Ian to come. It was lovely seeing him again.'³

Readers of the *Radio Times* issue of 12–18 September 1970 were confronted by a cover picture showing a grinning Ian dressed in casual contemporary clothes, astride a child's tricycle. 'Here comes the Bachelor Father!' proclaimed the headline, an intriguing statement that introduced BBC viewers to Ian's new, distinctive venture in TV situation comedy.

By June 1969, Michael Mills had been looking for a new vehicle for Ian, who had been such a success in *The World of Wooster*. Understandably, the actor was wary of anything remotely connected with the 1920s and stressed that his next venture should be contemporary. The project he opted for couldn't have been more current as it was based on the true-life story of one Peter Lloyd Jeffcock, an enterprising single man who was the foster father of six boys and six girls, now in their late teens and early twenties. The commercial potential in his story had already been spotted, but a film based on his life and a stage musical had fallen through; however, Mills, acting for the BBC, had bought the rights to Olga Franklin's book about Jeffcock, *Only Uncle*. He considered the next logical step would be to cast Ian as Jeffcock's fictional counterpart, Peter Lamb, in a part that would present new challenges for him, as he would be the principal comedy actor among a supporting cast of mainly child performers.

Peter Jeffcock was an amazing man. After serving with the RAF during the Second World War, he became an estate manager in the Driffield district of East Yorkshire, a well-paid job that enabled him to develop his ambition: the product of a happy and settled home, Peter wanted to give children less fortunate than himself a comfortable upbringing with him in the role of surrogate father, a radical idea for the 1950s as the majority of foster parents were either couples or single, mature women. Nevertheless, the idea appealed to Peter to such an extent that he committed his pay-off from the air force, his savings and his inheritance to the idea, even though, as he'd suspected, the authorities were initially very resistant to the idea of a bachelor bringing up young children. Eventually they relented, allowing him to foster an unsettled eleven-year-old boy called Ben, who had been moved from one institution to another. When Ben's placement proved a successful one, Peter was asked to take four more children, two brothers and two sisters. The children were always the casualties of broken homes, and if there were more than one child he took both, not wanting to split up the family; Peter would also make his decision based on the case history alone, so his mind was made up before he met any of them.

Before long, he was fostering twelve children, and the family moved to a larger house in Horley, Essex. Entirely on his own, Peter cared for and nurtured the children, ensured they had a successful education and were happy and loved. And, of course, he was acting as their nurse, cook, sock-mender and counsellor, fulfilling the duties of two parents. It was all the more exceptional as Peter was doing this on his own and for so many young people. And in all the time he looked after his family of twelve, his marital status and sexual orientation were never questioned.

There seemed to be a natural affinity between Peter Jeffcock and Ian. They were the same age, Ian had grown up in East Yorkshire where Peter had worked and, every day during the previous twelve years, the actor had driven past the convent in Mill Hill from which the two brothers and two sisters Peter had fostered were from. It's not altogether surprising that Ian became fascinated with Peter's story and, in due course, socialised with him. Briony McRoberts, the feisty Scottish actress who would be cast as Anna Brown, one of the children in Peter Lamb's care, remembers, 'Ian was very friendly with the guy the series was based on and was really keen to do it.'[4]

Won over to Mills' new idea for him, now titled *Bachelor Father*, Ian still exhibited his characteristic wariness, as he was concerned that putting his friend's life experiences into the context of a situation comedy might trivialise Peter Jeffcock's achievements. The man's motivation, Ian felt, was the most fascinating part of the concept and there was a danger it might be sidelined in the pursuit of laughs. His fears were slightly allayed by the employment of his colleague Richard Waring as scriptwriter – a man who had consistently proven his worth to Ian on *The World of Wooster* – but nevertheless he did feel throughout the making of *Bachelor Father* 'there were several occasions when I felt that we were guilty of treating a very sincere man's life's work, his philanthropy and humanity, with levity.'[5] Ian was, perhaps, touchingly over-concerned about his friend's sensitivity: throughout the production of the series, Jeffcock never once complained about the (heavily fictionalised) content.

In modern television terms, what Ian would have favoured would nowadays be called a 'comedy drama', a series that accommodates laughs, action and tragedy, such as *Minder*, *Cold Feet* or *Being Human*. In 1969 the term for this curious TV hybrid didn't exist and with *Bachelor Father* being made under the auspices of the Comedy Department, Richard Waring had to insist that the scripts included 'plenty of moving moments'[6] to offset the comedy and highlight Lamb/Jeffcock's earnest humanity. The writer duly delivered scenes to this effect that Ian was happy with, but had to overcome other, more structural problems. For Lamb's story to have any impact it would have to be built up slowly, as the prospective foster parent won over the powers that be; from a dramatic point of view, it would also be necessary for Lamb to have at least one other adult character to discuss things with, a stipulation which resulted in the creation of his neighbours Harry and Mary and the home-help Mrs Pugsley. For this latter role, the production team were lucky to secure the services of Joan Hickson, the veteran comedy actress.

The casting of the children was of primary importance, none more so than Ben, the first arrival in the Lamb household. The very first actor to audition was one Ian Johnson, around twelve years of age, who impressed Ian to such an extent with his charm, wit and good manners that he was moved to comment to Waring and the director Graeme Muir, 'We'll never do better than him.'[7] Even though dozens of other children were auditioned over the following week, this proved to be the case and Ian was duly hired, becoming the fictional head of the family of five children in *Bachelor Father* and also looking after the young actors and actresses away from the cameras. Ian senior fondly remembered that 'because of his total naturalness and sincerity he was an absolute joy to work with'[8], finding his namesake sympathetic, understanding and helpful concerning the pages of dialogue Ian the elder had to learn and combine with physical comedy routines.

Ian senior was typically good-natured when asked about his experience of working with children, affably commenting, 'I like acting with children ... Provided that they're good kids, as ours are. The hardest work is probably in the rehearsing. The law says that children may only be employed for up to three-and-a-half hours a day, so we spread each episode over ten days instead of the usual week. I learn my lines when the children are at school.'[9] Questioned about children's reputation for scene-stealing, he mischievously remarked, '[I] just stand there and bask in their reflected glory.'[10]

Ian Johnson, together with Briony McRoberts, would be the only two of the original child actors to make it from the first series of thirteen episodes to the second series of nine (the character of her brother, Donald, was kept on but recast). She remembers a rather less relaxed leading actor during working hours, who Theo Richmond, writing the cover story in the *Radio Times* that previewed the first episode of *Bachelor Father*, accurately assessed as a performer who 'has never relied for his laughs on the spontaneous or the improvised. His timing, movements, and entire characterisation are always the result of careful calculation, of painstaking rehearsal,'[11] an intense process not helped by Ian's difficulty in memorising dialogue. 'Ian wasn't that great with kids,' Briony recalls frankly, 'did find it hard learning his lines and was something of a perfectionist, which didn't always make him the easiest person to work with. I'm the same so it wasn't a problem, but some of the kids who came in during the second series were a bit *laissez-faire* and he didn't get on with them.'[12]

Away from the pressure of deadlines and the studio, however, the young actress found Ian an agreeable companion and a perfect gentleman: 'If you'd done something that pleased him he would always put an impeccably written card under your dressing-room door, and that meant a lot to an eleven-year-old.'[13] Briony was also intrigued by the actor's engagingly old-fashioned tastes in clothes and sport. 'Ian used to dress very grandly – he was something of a dandy – and I remember being fascinated as he wore detachable collars and cuffs. I'd never seen that before. He used to have a Rolls-Royce then and would go and sit in it during breaks and listen to the cricket. He even took me to Lord's once. I'm a rugby girl and he took it upon himself to educate me in the ways of cricket!'[14] As relief from the pressures of recording *Bachelor Father*, Ian would always be delighted when old friends would drop by, and Briony remembers one visitor to the studio in particular: 'Moira Lister came on the set one day. I think they'd once had a – shall we say – "flirtation" and it was lovely to see these two legends chatting away about the old days.'[15]

The interview Ian gave in the *Radio Times* to Richmond promoting *Bachelor Father* found him in an upbeat mood. He was enthusiastic about his new series and at pains to distance his performance from what he saw as a completely dissimilar role in *The World of Wooster*:

> Peter Lamb is a very different character … Bertie is the silly ass of all time. Lamb is no ass. I suppose I can best describe him as a fish out of water. He is a man playing the role of mother. The humour springs from this, not the fact he's an idiot … I'm hoping this new series will be a step away from [the 'silly ass']. I still get in a muddle of course – just scrambling an egg produces total chaos and all that, but I still think there's more depth to this character. He's more real, more human, but still, I hope, funny.[16]

Visiting Ian's home Moat Lodge in north London, the journalist was struck by the actor's tranquil domestic situation (a marked contrast to that in *Bachelor Father*), and suggested that his stable family background was the key to both a successful livelihood and a rewarding existence:

> He leads a quiet family life in a comfortable, secluded house on the outskirts of London. Off screen he is far from scatty – like many comedians, he confines the funny stuff to working hours – and his clothes are non-trendy; he calls people 'old fella', and his passions are aroused by few things outside Lord's cricket ground. Looking at his boyish grin, his slim figure, it is impossible to accept he is fifty.[17]

The coverage of *Bachelor Father* also found Ian in reflective mood about his career, and having reached his half-century he was able to look back with an honest perspective. He revealed that he remained as conscientious as ever when he received a prospective script, reading it until the end even if he knew after the first few pages that it wasn't right for him. Ian also acknowledged how much television had increased in importance as an entertainment medium since his star first rose in 1950s British films, conceding, 'The big successes of today are made in television as well as in the cinema.'[18] He confessed to a distrust of early TV production, which he had been intimately involved with in the late 1940s and early 1950s, revealing 'Ten, fifteen years ago I was awfully frightened of television – it didn't seem out of its infancy then and it was still a bit hit-and-miss. Techniques have advanced enormously now and it's possible to be a perfectionist in a TV studio.'[19] On his tendency to be seen solely as a comedy actor, he was philosophical, if notably irked: 'The trouble is, that I can only play parts which the public and the critics and producers allow me to do. I always knew, I suppose, that I had a flair for comedy. I certainly never wanted to play Lear or Hamlet, but I have done serious drama. No one seems to remember it.'[20] At the time of the interview, Ian was in the protracted throes of trying to bring Dorothy L. Sayers' aristocratic detective Lord Peter Wimsey to BBC Television as a drama series, with himself as the lead, a frustrating experience that helped to explain his exasperation at the short-sightedness of his contemporaries in the entertainment business.

The first episode of *Bachelor Father*, 'Family Feeling', transmitted on 17 September 1970, was reflective of the times in which it was made. The fictional Peter, with his chic mews flat in Kensington, private income, succession of trendy girlfriends and habit of offering visitors an alcoholic beverage at the first opportunity, is a playboy figure very recognisable from television and films of the time, be it a fashionable photographer in *Blow-Up*, trendy scientist in *Doomwatch*, suave detective in *Special Branch* or debonair author in *Department S*. But Lamb is a playboy sobering up as the carefree 1960s slowly gave way to the more sombre 1970s; unemployed and living on his inheritance from 'Uncle Reggie', Lamb's girlfriends keep leaving him. Having always loved children, and despite his happy-go-lucky lifestyle, he is envious of his neighbours, harassed parents who live across the mews. In a moment of revelation, Lamb decides to become a foster parent.

Although the idea of a single man fostering children may be nothing out of the ordinary in today's variegated society, in the television schedules of 1970 it was *very* new; in *Bachelor Father*'s new spin on the domestic family comedy, a major plot point could be a man's inability to bake a cake. Forty years ago this was innovative TV, because the majority of the audience watching consisted of a conventional family unit of mother, father and 2.4 children, in which the father was usually the breadwinner and the mother looked after the home (and made the cakes). In being gently pioneering in terms of its subject matter, *Bachelor Father* was part of the tradition of ground-breaking TV comedies that addressed 'taboo' subjects, such as bigotry in *Till Death Us Do Part*, an unmarried mother in *Miss Jones and Son* and homicide in *Murder Most Horrid*.

The first episode of the series was curiously out of sync with the other twelve episodes that followed: Lamb makes some risqué comments about his former girlfriends – possibly to reinforce the idea of him as a reforming hedonist, but still daring for 1970 and rather surprising for an Ian Carmichael vehicle – and during the prospective foster parent's visits to the Children's Officer Mr Gibson (Colin Gordon), Waring's script falls back on Ian's slapstick past, putting him through physical comedy routines based around continually knocking the photograph of Gibson's wife off his desk. Even though Ian performed them immaculately and the pay-off was a laugh-out-loud punch-line from Gibson – 'Have you got something against my wife, Mr Lamb?' – this contrived slapstick seemed forced and, significantly, wasn't present in the other episodes.

Where Waring excelled was in a scene where Lamb, looking to buy a new residence in which to house his adopted family, visits a derelict property where two boys are playing. In one of those 'moving moments' Ian was so keen on in the series, one of the kids smashes a window and Lamb, sympathising with the anarchic impulses the rundown property has brought out in the youngster, throws a brick through another window. The impressed lad cries:

Boy: Cor! I wish I had him for a father!
Lamb: I wish you had too.

Ian's low-key, slightly melancholy emphasis on the dialogue and the idea of an adult behaving like a child symbolised *Bachelor Father*'s appeal: Lamb was an idealised father figure who wasn't so grown-up he couldn't occasionally be juvenile himself, therefore bonding with his foster children but possessing the maturity to offer them guidance. He was never patronising, was always generous, fair and often funny. For a lot of the viewing audience, he was the father they'd always wanted.

Once the extended family were in place, the series settled down into an enjoyably predictable succession of stories that regularly revolved around misunderstandings – a staple element of farce – between Lamb and the children, such as forgotten birthdays and a visiting school friend pretending to be someone else. The gang of juveniles, with Ian Johnson and Briony McRoberts standing out as the rough diamond Ian and sensible Anna, weren't too far removed from the youngsters who could be seen in contemporary shows such as *Here Come the Double Deckers!* and *Freewheelers*: enterprising, well adjusted and well behaved, mostly speaking in perfect BBC English and, in *Bachelor Father* with one exception, noticeably free of any personal issues arising from their troubled backgrounds. Again, the insistence on including material that wouldn't devalue Jeffcock's achievements saved the show from being just another cosy, domestic BBC comedy. In the episode 'Partners in Crime', Lamb took under his wing Christopher Robinson (Kevin Moran); the son of a career criminal, he was a difficult case who stole, lied and hit policemen. When possessions started going missing, Lamb automatically suspected Kevin, insisting, 'honesty is a law in this house', but the responsible adult was later proved wrong when he owned up to misplacing the lost items himself. Lamb's own honesty was shown to be rather questionable when he was pulled over by the police for speeding and unpaid road tax; his sister also delighted in telling his charges that 'he just loved breaking the rules when he was a boy' by stealing apples and hens' eggs. The point that adults don't always practise what they preach was subtly made and wasn't lost on the children (or the audience).

Fundamentally, *Bachelor Father* was a lot like Ian himself: family-centred, conservative, good-natured and charmingly amusing.

This was rather fitting, because it was the closest he ever came to playing himself on screen. In 'House Guests', Lamb was overjoyed that the son of a cricketer he admired was coming to stay the night, a clear allusion to Ian's favourite hobby, and like Ian, Lamb drove a Rolls-Royce. Elsewhere, Waring inserted Ian's speech mannerisms, dropping in 'old lad' and 'splendid fellow', while the clothes Lamb wore looked like they came from the same gentleman's outfitters that Ian himself patronised, judging by publicity photographs of him with his family in the *Radio Times*. With the benefit of hindsight, it's appropriate that *Bachelor Father* saw a fictionalised version of Ian grace the small screen as, amazingly, Peter Lamb would be his last major role as a modern-day character.

In terms of Ian's long relationship with the BBC, the series was a personal high point for him. For performing in a half-hour sitcom, in 1970 Ian was receiving £1,500 per episode, in today's terms a staggering £15,000. By comparison, Tim Brooke-Taylor, the most experienced of the three performers in the BBC comedy series *The Goodies*, was being paid £400 per show. Such a towering fee took Ian beyond being the most highly paid comedy actor at the BBC, to being the most highly paid actor on BBC Television at the beginning of the 1970s.

Ian would later feel that *Bachelor Father* never really won over those critics who had 'a built-in resistance to child actors'[21], a view that wasn't shared by the *Daily Express* in November 1971 when the series ended, the reviewer regretting the show's passing on behalf of his children who 'have been a devoted audience. The appeal has been to Children's Lib – the idea of the lone adult, preferably a bit dim, who is regularly outsmarted each week by a gaggle of school kids,'[22] a formula that the critic noted had taken ITV's more ribald *Please, Sir!*, about a class of older children who usually got the better of their teachers, to the top of the ratings. It wasn't alone there; while *Bachelor Father* might not have got the 'twenty-four million viewers'[23] that Briony McRoberts remembers, it was very popular with the public, Ian defining its appeal as 'frequently funny, occasionally moving, and at its worst, inoffensive.'[24] The main reason it wasn't being renewed for a third series was because Waring was finding it increasingly difficult to devise plots – the same reason the second series was reduced from thirteen episodes to nine.

Nevertheless, Ian would remain very proud of *Bachelor Father*, citing it as 'clean, wholesome, family viewing'[25] in a TV comedy landscape that was increasingly using salacious content in shows like *On the Buses*, *Monty Python's Flying Circus* and ITV's *The Benny Hill Show*. For Briony McRoberts, the best thing about the series was working with such a seasoned and generous leading man: 'I kept in touch with Ian peripherally over the years with cards and so on. You'd know his at once as he had lovely, decorative handwriting. What a gentleman he was.'[26]

'Ian Carmichael has made a corner for himself playing men who are basically Boy Scouts at heart, willing, cheerful and dedicated to upholding the decencies of life,' observed the *Daily Mail* in its coverage of *Play for Today: Alma Mater*, transmitted on 7 January 1971. After the first series of *Bachelor Father*, Ian had been offered the chance to appear in the prestigious drama strand that had been introduced to BBC1 in 1970 to be, as the BBC's Head of Drama Shaun Sutton eloquently put it, 'the main shop window for new and experimental drama.'[27]

Relishing the opportunity to act in a serious drama, Ian took the role of the determinedly upbeat Jimmy Nicholson heading to his school Radbourne for a reunion. Nicholson was a man who had 'applied to life the standards of his horrid public school, the results, of course, being that his wife had left him, his son despised him, his firm fired him and he had become one of the most dreaded bores in the Middle East.'[28] Also starring Max Adrian as the malevolent Headmaster and John Woodvine as the 'howling cad' Chesseman, David Hodson's play was, disappointingly for Ian, considered only a qualified success by the critics. Nancy Banks-Smith in the *Guardian* found that 'the characters were rather over simplified into those with teeth and those with toothmarks' and ultimately found *Alma Mater* 'a simple and slow-moving play.'[29] The *Daily Mail* agreed, finding the production 'too long.'[30]

If *Alma Mater* was considered a dated exposé of the public-school system, it was because Lindsay Anderson had eviscerated it so brilliantly and definitively four years before in his film *If …* Nevertheless, for observers of Ian's career, there was an unintentional continuity in his decent, gradually disillusioned public-school old boy, 'a kind of Bertie Wooster with all the jokes and the private income left out.'[31] His flawed portrayal was the flip-side to his effervescent toff of five years earlier, with Nicholson's dated, patriotic beliefs marooned in the grey, prosaic Britain of the early 1970s.

When Eric Morecambe and Ernie Wise returned to the BBC in 1968, their variety-styled show (now written by Eddie Braben) had become a huge hit and had, over time, replaced *The Avengers* as the most fashionable show to appear in on television (the exploits of Steed and company had ended in 1969, appropriately enough). The young Canadian actress Linda Thorson, who played Steed's last female partner of the 1960s, Tara King, met Ian socially when she was working on *The Avengers*. 'He was a terrible flirt,' she says today, 'but it was all very innocent. It was, "Darling, would you like a glass of champagne?", all very gentlemanly, and you could see immediately why Patrick [Macnee] and he got on so well.'[32]

By 1970, Eric and Ernie were well on their way to becoming Britain's best-loved television comedians, and a guest appearance on *The Morecambe and Wise Show* was considered a great honour; over the 1970s, such leading lights of entertainment as Diana Rigg, Peter Cushing, Glenda Jackson, Edward Woodward, John Thaw, Dennis Waterman, Shirley Bassey and André Previn, among many others, would humbly and delightedly accept the invitation. In June 1971 it was Ian's turn.

After Ian completed his commitments to the second series of *Bachelor Father*, he made one of his rare appearances for ITV, in an episode of Thames Television's sitcom *Father, Dear Father* starring his old friend and colleague Patrick Cargill. Written by Johnnie Mortimer and Brian Cooke, in its style and pacing the series was similar to the slick American comedies like the Mary Tyler Moore and Lucille Ball shows, and like its US counterparts also featured a well-known guest star every week. In 'An Affair to Forget' it was Ian's turn, playing Patrick Glover's (Cargill) dapper accountant Leo Underwood.

Leo was a married man being an absolute bounder, having an affair with his lubricious young secretary, Felicity (Sally James). With his 'old lads' and 'old fellers', suits, polo-neck jumpers and cigar, he could almost have been Peter Lamb in his pre-foster-father days. Ian clearly enjoyed playing the cad, relishing lines like 'You're doing splendidly, Paddy old lad. You're a born liar.'

There was one particularly funny sequence where Leo telephoned Patrick to confirm that he and his wife would be coming over for dinner:

Leo:	I meant to call you yesterday as a matter of fact, but I've, um, (*looks at his secretary's bottom*) got a little behind in the office.
Patrick:	That's all right, old boy. (*To Karen, his daughter*) Can't you leave that alone?
Leo:	(*Startled*) I'm so sorry!

Not subtle, perhaps, but seeing two such masters of light comedy as Ian and Patrick at the height of their powers in a polished and very funny script was a delight. The bubbly Ann Holloway, who played Patrick's daughter Karen, remembers, 'there was a bit of rivalry on [Cargill's] part. He didn't want Ian getting tooooooo many laughs!'[33]

CHAPTER 14

'As My Whimsy Takes Me'

(Motto of the Honourable Wimsey family)

I AN'S INVOLVEMENT IN the BBC Television adaptations of
Dorothy L. Sayers' Lord Peter Wimsey detective novels in
many ways sums up his entire career. Always more of an all-
round creative force than just an actor, from the start he was a
major player in the development of *Lord Peter Wimsey*, just as he
had been with his first BBC series *The World of Wooster* and various
other projects throughout his show-business life. *Wimsey* was set
in the 1920s, a period Ian always had a fondness for, and with
which he was firmly identified in the public mind ever since the
success of his Bertie Wooster characterisation. Ironically, his
triumph as P.G. Wodehouse's 1920s 'silly ass' told against him
during the production of *Wimsey*, as Ian had to overcome resistance
within the BBC to him playing a more serious dramatic character,
a prejudice that would persist, he felt, until the first serial had been
transmitted and proven a success. Ian would candidly sum up his
long and tough slog to get *Wimsey* made as 'possibly the most
frustrating of my professional life.'[1]

Wimsey's route to the screen began when Ian first had the idea
in March 1966, six years before the suave gentleman sleuth found
his first corpse. On the advice of the theatrical agent Herbert Van
Thal, who suggested the part would 'fit you like a glove'[2], Ian
immediately became enthusiastic about the idea, having read some

of the Wimsey books when he was younger, and seen the Hull Repertory Company's stage production of *Busman's Honeymoon*. His sound instincts for a commercial and critical success were immediately engaged and he ordered the fourteen Wimsey books from Harrods, reading them avidly throughout early 1966.

It was clear to Ian that Dorothy L. Sayers's stories were ripe for television adaptation. A graduate of Oxford, and a student of theology and classical literature who had died in 1957, Sayers offered off-beat, often macabre scenarios – from the distribution of hard drugs through coded newspaper advertisements, to a man killed by the deafening clang of church bells – that would make ideal television thriller material. Wimsey's extended family (a rarity for a fictional detective), his faithful manservant Bunter and a vivid array of supporting roles would attract the cream of British character actors. To cap it all, the setting of the series in the 1920s among both the aristocracy and criminal classes would allow the BBC's superlative costume and design departments to demonstrate their talent at recreating authentic historical periods.

Furthermore, to Ian the character was like coming home, as he felt an instant affinity with Lord Peter Death Bredon Wimsey. 'I was mad keen to do [it]', he would later recall, 'because there was a serious side to him, and more depth in the character. He *was* me – or what I would have liked to be me. I admired him, I envied Wimsey his lifestyle, his apparent insouciance, his prowess and intellect.'[3] Particularly appealing to the actor was the way Wimsey concealed his ruthless cleverness beneath a deceptively mild, occasionally oafish exterior, as Sayers had succinctly put it in one of her stories: 'The change in [him] was almost startling – it was as if a steel blade had whipped suddenly out of its velvet scabbard.'[4] In a striking coincidence, as far as Ian was concerned, Sayers even compared Wimsey's physical appearance to that of Bertie Wooster[5] – an initial good omen that would prove to be something of a double-edged sword for him.

It was rare, if not virtually unknown, in the 1960s for actors to approach British TV companies with an idea for a drama series.

However, in the same year as Ian was contemplating filling out Wimsey's bespoke suits, the Irish-American actor Patrick McGoohan, star of the internationally successful spy series *Danger Man*, famously sold the idea for its follow-up, the existential thriller *The Prisoner*, to Lew Grade, the flamboyant head of ITV's Associated Television (ATV) on the strength of an early-morning conversation and a handshake. Overnight, McGoohan's production company Everyman Films had the funding they needed.

Ian didn't have his own production company or the money to buy the TV rights to Wimsey, and in choosing to deal with the hierarchical, compartmentalised BBC took a very different route to working with ITV's Grade, who styled himself on vintage entertainment moguls who acted on hunches for good ideas and made deals directly. Ian's decision to stay with the BBC, and deliberately go against the way they usually commissioned drama, spoke volumes about his sometimes love/hate relationship with the Corporation – namely, loyalty to the institution that had helped make him a star and his tenacious belief in getting a good idea through in spite of sometimes exasperating bureaucratic obstacles.

In general, a producer and writers would develop serials or series at the BBC, with some input from the Head of Department for Drama, Serials, Comedy or Light Entertainment. As Ian had just had a resounding success with *The World of Wooster* for the latter, he made them his first port of call. Perhaps reacting to the unusual situation of an actor pitching a series, their response was not encouraging: Ian was told by letter that there was no risk capital to develop the project, a sale to America was unlikely due to Wimsey being unknown as a character across the Atlantic – as opposed to, say, Sherlock Holmes – and Sayers' period literary style would not fit with the prevailing trend of film series for contemporary spies, playboys and secret agents like *The Man from UNCLE*, *The Avengers* or *The Saint*. Undaunted, Ian unashamedly turned to the 'old boy' network and called Shaun Sutton, a long-time friend and now Head of the BBC Drama Group. Dropping in to see him on his way home from appearing in the play *Say Who*

You Are, and by his own admission 'armed with a large whisky'[6], he began his sales pitch, only to be confronted by every one of the Wimsey books on Sutton's bookshelf and the exciting news that a TV version *was* already being considered.

Unfortunately, this proved to be the first of many disappointments for Ian throughout the late 1960s. The proposed Wimsey series was dropped in favour of another, and Ian's morale suffered a further blow when he discovered that the interested producer, Donald Wilson (who had overseen the BBC's prestigious and acclaimed adaptation of *The Forsyte Saga*, one of the Corporation's first productions to be a success on US network television) did not want him as the lead, an opinion Ian firmly believed was short-sightedly coloured by his reputation as a comedy actor, particularly as Wooster.

With no interest from the BBC, Ian turned resourceful entrepreneur in attempting to sell the idea to commercial television, pitching Wimsey with a professional sales brochure to accompany his business meetings. Sadly, the ITV networks' response was as negative as the BBC's had been: the property was not international enough, the character was too intellectual, the American market would only buy a series, not a serial. Ian and his team encountered further setbacks when they discovered that the Sayers estate would only sell the television rights to all fourteen books. By 1968, the project seemed dead in the water, with the news that a film company had been showing interest and that Sayers' representatives were no longer prepared to consider the option for a television adaptation.

In 1969 Ian was working on *Bachelor Father* when he discovered that the Wimsey film project had fallen through. Approaching the Serials Department again, this time he found them a lot more receptive and, furthermore, prepared to open their chequebook. In April 1970, the BBC agreed to pay £9,100 in two instalments over three years to Anthony Fleming, owner of the rights to the Dorothy Sayers novels, to dramatise twenty-six episodes of the Lord Peter stories in chronological order. Ian's excitement about the BBC's commitment to making a series of Wimsey in colour (the Corporation had gone over to colour transmissions in 1967) was rather deflated by the appointment of Donald Wilson as the producer, 'who had not wanted me in the first place.'[7] To his chagrin, Ian learned that for the lead in *Wimsey* Wilson favoured John Neville, a more serious, dramatic actor with whom the producer had formed a good working relationship on the 1969 series *The First Churchills* (and who, significantly, had been shortlisted to replace Douglas Wilmer as the BBC's Sherlock Holmes). Nevertheless, Ian was confirmed as the star, and with Wilson's stock high at the BBC because of his successful production of *The Forsyte Saga*, work began on *Lord Peter Wimsey* in earnest in early 1970. Wilson was to write as well as produce an adaptation of the first book *Whose Body?* Spreading the workload on the first series, John Wiles was assigned to adapt the next mystery, *The Unpleasantness at the Bellona Club*, and Anthony Steven (who had worked with Wilson on *The Forsyte Saga*) was contracted for the third, *Clouds of Witness*.

Initially, progress was good. By the end of June 1970, John Ecclestone, Head of Programme Planning, was requesting to the Head of Serials, Ronald Marsh, that Ian be booked for eighteen weeks in early 1971, to make thirteen episodes of *Wimsey* for transmission the following year.[8] The relationship between Wilson and Ian also seemed to be developing well: 'Last Thursday I had a long session with Ian Carmichael, which I believe ended in complete accord,' Wilson wrote to Marsh in September 1970.[9] 'He had only one major point at the beginning of the first script, which with some ingenuity I can accommodate (and will, to make him happy, though I don't necessarily agree!) and his other notes were all of very minor importance. We also discussed his characterisation of Lord Peter in considerable detail. All seems to be well.' By October, Ian's preparatory work was sufficiently well advanced for his agent to request an appointment at the theatrical costumier Nathan's, as they 'did him so proud with the clothes of the equivalent period of the [1920s] on the *Wooster* series.'[10]

Shortly after the end of October, however, the production faltered, with Marsh requesting that *Wimsey*'s studio allocation be put back by three weeks.[11] Despite Wilson's upbeat report, Sutton, Marsh and Ian were unhappy with his adaptation, a situation that was quickly becoming a major problem as *Whose Body?* was due to be the first story to be made and transmitted. The novel itself was problematic, as apart from an ingenious premise – the discovery of an unidentified naked body in a bath wearing nothing but a *pince-nez* – character development, incident and plot progression were thin.

At this point, Ian took a decision that illustrated his impulsiveness, perfectionism and intolerance of the occasionally obstructive hierarchy of the BBC. At his own expense, he went outside the stable of the Corporation's contract writers and commissioned the experienced thriller author John Brason – who would go on to score a major success working on the BBC Second World War drama *Colditz* – to write a new version of *Whose Body?*

Despite the best of intentions, Ian's open flouting of Wilson and Marsh's authority was a direct challenge to the way creative decisions were usually made within the BBC. Brason himself was delighted to be involved. In early November, he sent draft scripts of three forty-minute episodes to Ian's home, enthusing that he'd 'burnt the midnight oil on them as I understood there was some urgency', had 'enjoyed doing them, and if nothing comes of it I do not feel I have wasted my time' and felt that his adaptation suited 'your own concept.'[12] Ian was delighted with Brason's approach, but instead of doing the tactful thing and referring the new scripts to Marsh and Wilson, he went over their heads and sent them directly to Shaun Sutton, with a covering note that, considering the situation he was creating, is notable for its amiable suggestion to 'pop down and see you one evening' to discuss the screenplays.[13] It's certainly a striking coincidence that shortly after this, on 23 December, Sutton informed Ian that Wilson would no longer be producing *Lord Peter Wimsey*.[14]

In early January 1971, Sutton found himself in the awkward, and perhaps unique, position of sending a script by a new author

– which a lead actor had commissioned – to his Head of Serials for a series that staff writers had already been contracted to work on, and which no longer had a producer. Sutton diplomatically suggested that Marsh should 'read it and see how it strikes you,'[15] making no further commitment either way. Despite his *faux pas*, which had arguably contributed to the departure of Wilson, Ian remained on speaking terms with Marsh, even though he remained adamant that Brason's approach was the most authentic: '[He] has, throughout, remained very faithful indeed to the original – which Wilson in the first episode we read, certainly had not.'[16]

Despite the success of Brason's script, in Ian's eyes, things went from bad to worse. He was warned in late October 1970 that production on *Wimsey* might have to be postponed for 'possibly as long as six months',[17] although his agent had still not received official notification that this would happen, so Ian had consequently kept his schedule clear in early 1971 for the eighteen weeks of production initially proposed. With filming originally due to start in the last week of January, the actor was promised that the first thirteen scripts would be with him by, at the very latest, the beginning of February. However, with no new producer assigned, the project continued to drift, and when by 27 April scripts still hadn't been delivered, the frustrated actor issued via his agents a stinging rebuke to Shaun Sutton (a man he considered an old friend) detailing the setbacks the project had suffered:

> I think that a perusal of the attached 'developments' (to speak euphemistically under the circumstances) will make only too clear to you the cause of Ian's and my deep dissatisfaction and concern with a situation that has now pertained for precisely ten months to the day.
>
> I don't propose to go into the side issue of the loss of income Ian has already sustained by the postponement. Leave it that it has been considerable.
>
> In spite of this I am sure you will agree that his cooperation, tolerance and forbearance has been, until now, above reproach during a very long period of what appears – on the surface at any

rate – to be a dilatory and inexplicably apathetic attitude on the part of the Corporation.

I would therefore ask you, before total disenchantment engulfs both Ian and me, to let us have at the earliest possible moment not only a full and detailed schedule of proposed dates of the Series, but also (and of paramount importance) the long awaited and long promised scripts.[18]

Things are a lot different in television today. Several TV shows – for instance *Waking the Dead, Inspector Morse, Luther, Wire in the Blood* and *A Touch of Frost* (all crime shows, interestingly enough) – have had their lead actor credited and involved as Executive Producer. In the early 1970s such a position just didn't exist in BBC Television. If it had, the creative no man's land Ian found himself in during early 1971 could certainly have been avoided. Officially acknowledged as a part of the production team, he would have been in a position to arrest the slackening pace of the writing and problems with the scripts; conversely, his well-meaning if misguided decision to involve a new writer over the head of his producer could have been dealt with through the proper channels. However, in his own slightly naïve way, Ian was ahead of his time in TV production, even though he can't have known it then.

The letter of 27 April certainly had the desired effect, and perhaps mindful that they might lose their star asset if the *Wimsey* project wasn't whipped quickly into shape, Marsh requested that the BBC's script unit undertake a study of the screenplays already written to see which was the most suitable as a one-off serial. *Whose Body?*, as ever, remained problematic; on the other hand, *The Unpleasantness at the Bellona Club* and, particularly, *Clouds of Witness* were felt to show 'Wimsey at his detecting best', while the yet-to-be-adapted *Murder Must Advertise* was felt to be 'the best of the lot.'[19] Because of the seemingly insurmountable problems with the first Wimsey novel, Sutton decided on a non-chronological approach to the books, also deciding to proceed with a single adaptation to see how the viewing public took to the aristocratic sleuth. With a meeting scheduled for 19 May with Ian and his agent, the head of the Drama Group was appropriately respectful towards the aggrieved star: 'I don't think we are under any legal obligation to Ian Carmichael, but there could be said to be a sort of moral obligation, in that we have been discussing this for quite a time. I think the single-book idea will satisfy him ... if the project is possible, the earlier it can be started in the New Year the better.'[20]

Ian agreed, and with his acceptance of the revised approach to the Wimsey series there was a marked increase in respect for his opinions from Sutton and Marsh. His rejection of their choice of *Murder Must Advertise* as the first serial was accepted; as a well-informed Sayers aficionado, Ian still insisted that for reasons of character continuity *Whose Body?* should be made first and that *Murder Must Advertise* wasn't suitable for Lord Peter's debut as it showed him undercover and would not allow the audience to get to know the character sufficiently well. However, when Sutton and Marsh insisted that the first novel wouldn't work as the opening mystery, they graciously asked Ian which of the earlier novels he considered the best option. After some consideration he suggested the second novel, *Clouds of Witness*, and it was confirmed as the opening Wimsey case in July 1971. (Brason's adaptation of *Whose Body?* was abandoned, despite Ian's protests).

Quickly assigned as the new producer was Richard Beynon, a go-ahead, talented man who had produced the ground-breaking BBC police series *Z Cars*, was involved in the creation of its spin-off *Softly, Softly* ... and had overseen the BBC2 crime series *Trial*. He was enthusiastic about *Clouds of Witness*, even if he found the denouement 'when it suddenly goes off into Around-the-world-in-eighty days [sic] stuff'[21] disappointing. Ian was delighted with Anthony Steven's revised scripts, remaining as insightful, dedicated and constructive about Wimsey as he had been at the beginning of his quest to get the series off the ground. In September he wrote enthusiastically to Marsh:

Thank you very much indeed for letting me read Anthony Steven's scripts, which I would like to say here and now, I liked enormously. He has done a lot of homework on his subject, and has remained very faithful indeed to the original, which pleases me very much. He has used a great deal of the original dialogue, which was to have been a request of mine to whoever was to do the adaptation, as I think it has character. He has also given the designer a most detailed and accurate description of 110 Piccadilly [Wimsey's flat] straight from the pages of the novel, which may seem a minor point, but to me it shows respect and perhaps affection for the original.'[22]

He went on to say, 'How good to see some real progress at last!'[23] and concluded with the slightly barbed last line, 'I do hope you had a good holiday – I'm still waiting for mine!'[24]

Whatever the setbacks had been, *Lord Peter Wimsey* was about to go into production in a form that, bar the odd caveat, Ian was content with. When the cameras finally began filming *Clouds of Witness* on Howarth Moor in Yorkshire during January 1972, the tenacious actor's six-year commitment to bringing the gentleman sleuth to TV life was finally vindicated.

CHAPTER 15

Lord Ian

Ian becomes a distinguished TV detective in the acclaimed BBC adaptations of Dorothy L. Sayers's books

I N THE WEEK leading up to the transmission of *Cloud of Witness*, the *Radio Times* published a stimulating article about the series, titled 'Whodunnit, Lord Peter?', in which the eminent novelist, crime enthusiast and Ian's sometime friend Kingsley Amis took time to survey the British crime genre and compare Wimsey with other fictional detectives such as Sherlock Holmes and Sexton Blake. Amis praised the longevity of Dorothy L. Sayers's character, remarking that 'he of the eyeglass, primrose silk pyjamas and collection of Sèvres vases, [lives] on in the public mind.' He went on: 'In his later career he had more than his fair share of luck in problem-solving, and perhaps talked a bit too much,' but Amis concluded, 'his best years provide examples of pure deduction that remain unsurpassed.'[1]

As the man taking on the mantle of a sleuth about to take his place in a television landscape awash with imported, slick TV films featuring contemporary crime fighters like *Columbo*, *Banacek* and *McCloud*, Ian was quoted on the singular appeal of the retro Wimsey: '[He] has a great sense of humour and depth of character. He is a highly educated man with a most erudite mind and an encyclopedic knowledge of classical music. Like all detectives in fiction, I suppose, he solves his crimes by brilliance, though he does have a little more background than most.'² Alluding to Wimsey's talent for deception and his own background as a comedy performer, Ian explained: 'I wear the famous eyeglass at times in the serial. It serves a practical purpose when Wimsey wants to look like a complete nincompoop.'³ Although his pivotal role in the development of the series wasn't mentioned, the actor couldn't resist a sly dig in his interview about *Lord Peter Wimsey*'s protracted path to the screen, saying, 'my fear was that I'd be too old for the part before my chance came up.'⁴

To the accompaniment of a sprightly theme tune by Herbert Chappell that really sounded like it was being performed by a jazz quartet in a smoky speakeasy around the corner from Claridge's, His Lordship made his debut on British television screens at 8.15 p.m. on BBC1 on 5 April 1972, just after the American space series *Star Trek* and directly before the *9 O'Clock News*. Ian wasn't the only actor with a background in light entertainment at the BBC in the early 1970s trying to establish himself as a 'serious' actor. Since 1970 Jon Pertwee, a close friend of Leslie Phillips and a veteran of radio comedies like *The Navy Lark* and *The Waterlogged Spa* who, like Phillips, had also appeared in the *Carry On* films, had been playing it straight as the third incarnation of the BBC's favourite time traveller in *Doctor Who*. By 1972, Pertwee – who was the same age as Ian – was into his third year as the velvet-jacketed, Inverness cape-attired Time Lord, proving that so-called 'comedy' actors could pull off dramatic roles. As the Doctor concluded his battle against invading Sea Devils at a naval base, the other dandy on BBC1 that April prepared to investigate the apparent murder of the card cheat Captain Cathcart (Anthony Ainley) at Rydesdale Lodge in Yorkshire.

Unfortunately for the opening story of a new series, *Clouds of Witness* was compromised by the exhausting exposition that dominated the narrative. After a promising start, with scenes that effectively established the upper-class 1920s *milieu* with a grouse shoot and after-dinner chit-chat at the Lodge, the inquest into Cathcart's death took up most of the first episode, delaying Lord

Peter's arrival on the scene – crucial for an opening episode – as its slavish attention to detail tested the patience of the viewer. This is more noticeable in a contemporary era where the *modus operandi* of crimes is explained through flashy film editing in series like *CSI: Crime Scene Investigation* and *Waking the Dead*, but even at the time it must have been noticeably leaden. Regrettably, Wimsey, his manservant Bunter and their police confidant Inspector Parker's investigations followed the same, interminably literal pattern. What kept the audience watching was the central idea of Lord Peter's elder brother the Duke of Denver (David Langton) being on trial for murder, a premise that raised the stakes for the detective by giving him an emotional investment in solving the case. This was beautifully illustrated in a lively exchange between Wimsey and his obstinate sibling, explaining why the sleuth's first televised mystery struck such a chord with viewers in 1972:

> Dammit, man, you're the one who's making a public spectacle of himself! … Do you think that I enjoy seeing my brother and sister dragged through the courts, reporters swarmin' all over the place? Paragraphs and news bills with your name starin' at me from every corner, and the whole ghastly business ending in a great show in the House of Lords with a lot of people togged up in scarlet and ermine and all the rest of the damn fool jiggery pokery?[5]

Happily, the 1920s were brought to life authentically and vibrantly thanks to the BBC's expertise in period drama. Lord Peter's flat, in particular, was a marvellously cluttered evocation of a wealthy aristocrat's hobbies and affectations (as had been detailed in Anthony Steven's meticulous script), including details such as a piano, a well-stocked drinks cabinet, immaculately upholstered antique furniture and Wimsey's prized collection of antiquarian first editions. Elsewhere, vintage cars, starched collars, walking canes, spats and flapper fashions completed the illusion of the Jazz Age, with costume designer Barbara Kronig and production designer Raymond Cusick (at the opposite extreme to his most famous work, the Daleks in *Doctor Who*) plainly making the most of the new colour medium.

The vivid realisation of the characters was what really brought
Clouds of Witness to life, although the almost self-conscious lack of
humour in Lord Peter's dialogue and performance was indicative of
a nervous BBC, concerned that Ian's talent for light comedy might
compromise the credibility of the lead role – absurd, considering
how full of fun Wimsey was in Sayers's novels. The delights among
the supporting roles were many: the solid, dependable and dryly
acerbic Inspector Parker (Mark Eden), the perfect foil to Wimsey's
flamboyance; Rachel Herbert's nervous, naïve but ultimately strong-
willed Lady Mary Wimsey, Peter's sister, and the stubborn,
snobbishly defiant Duke of Denver, Gerald Christian Wimsey,
played with dignified restraint by Langton, who occasionally showed
subtle glimpses of achingly wounded feeling.

Intriguingly, one member of the cast who wishes to remain
anonymous confirmed the BBC's doubts about Ian's suitability for
the title role. 'There are two kinds of comedy. Some of it relies
very much on character and being the person, and some of it is
very much to do with the "lickety-split" delivery of lines and the
character not coming through very much,'[6] he says. 'To be a
leading man in drama you can't do that; you want to meet the
person. It's what Ian could do in his sleep and he fell back on it.
When Wimsey first arrived at Rydesdale Lodge Ian went at such a
rate that I couldn't hear what he was saying. It had a certain air to
it, but you can't do that all the time if you're the leading man. It
makes you very thin. He could have done it if he was doing a Bertie
Wooster thing, but this wasn't Bertie Wooster and it wasn't funny.
There were little clever things that were said, but they weren't
roaringly funny and Wimsey wasn't meant to be a funny man, he
was meant to be attractive. He could have been more attractive if
Ian had been more himself.'[7] In a petulant afterthought, the actor
says, 'Mr Carmichael also had short arms and deep pockets and
never got his round in.'[8]

By contrast, the experienced Rachel Herbert was struck by how
gravely Ian took his commitment to a serious role. 'We never sat
down face to face,'[9] she remembers. 'He was really concerned'

about learning the lines, and was always off in a corner somewhere, either on his own or with the director Hugh David. It really got to Ian, and as soon as the thing finished he was off home. It shows a tremendous amount of tenacity and courage that, as a comedy person, he took on a long-running drama series. I'm used to turning up for a production and finding my character through rehearsals, but Ian knew the script perfectly for day one. He was from the Noël Coward school, who always insisted that his performers should be word-perfect for the first rehearsal.'[10]

The comments of the anonymous actor may betray a certain snobbery about what qualifies as 'legitimate' acting, but there's no doubt that in some scenes Ian hurried the dialogue, and his delivery and movements looked over-rehearsed and not as natural as the other actors. On the other hand, elsewhere he more than held his own against experienced thespians like Georgina Cookson (Gerald's sour wife Helen), Francis de Wolff (the corpulent lawyer Impey Biggs) and acquitted himself surprisingly well in a physical struggle with the odious Grimethorpe (George Colouris, one of Orson Welles's legendary Mercury Theatre players). Significantly, it was where Ian's natural talent for humour had a chance to peep through that he shone most, such as when he nearly drowned in the swamp Peter's Pot, wryly telling Bunter that it nearly 'potted Peter'.

Wimsey's 'man' Bunter – who apparently didn't have a first name – was realised with straight-backed, polite formality by Glyn Houston, an experienced character actor who had featured in television series as diverse as Z Cars, Softly, Softly and films like One Way Pendulum (1964). One of the gratifying pluses of Clouds of Witness is that it deftly elaborated on the relationship between His Lordship and his servant. There was one brilliant scene where Bunter calmly anticipates Wimsey's request for medicine just as he asks for it, illustrating how closely attuned the two men are. Bunter coolly prepares Wimsey's bedroom for breakfast and deals with Lord Peter's waking from a nightmare and shouting for his valet during a bad dream about the Great War spoke volumes about how much Bunter is needed by his master and former commanding officer. Notably, when his master is in danger of drowning in Peter's Pot, Bunter abandons his deferential manner as he tries to prevent Wimsey from going under. The duo have become equals in adversity.

This well-directed and performed scene looks at first sight like filler, but it told the audience a lot about the dynamics between the two men. In the early 1970s, when Wimsey's and Ian's values of patriotism and chivalry were regarded almost with disdain by an anti-privilege *Zeitgeist*, it was refreshing to see representatives of the upper and working classes bound together in a mutually supportive and respectful relationship. Slightly disappointingly, the two left-leaning actors who brought Bunter to life didn't share this view. 'Bunter is completely devoted to [Wimsey], but I find Wimsey unbelievable. I think he was a bloody Fascist,'[11] a frank Glynn Houston apparently told the *Sun*. 'As a poor, Welsh lad, who lived in the pre-war years amid the poverty of the Rhonda Valley – I'm 47 – I think he would rather have died than visit us ... Mind you, Wimsey was a little more understanding than the rest of his kind, but like so many Old Etonians and Old Harrovians today, he believed that "working class" was really another name for hooliganism.'[12] The tough-talking Derek Newark, who took over the role for the next serial *The Unpleasantness at the Bellona Club* because Houston was unavailable, was equally dismissive: 'I think Wimsey is a complete and utter snob. He is arrogant and he regards working class people with contempt. But then, I'm not a great admirer of Miss Sayers's works. Before I took on the role, I read *Clouds of Witness*. I fell asleep a quarter of the way through the book.'[13]

Clouds of Witness succeeded in spite of a script that may have been de-energised by a long period in development, explaining why producer Richard Beynon's reservations about the resolution to the screenplay hadn't been addressed by the time the script entered production. This resulted in an unexpected narrative jump to New York for Peter and two scenes where Wimsey suddenly appeared in the cockpit of a transatlantic aircraft on his way back to England, sitting next to the wonderfully named Lucius Grant (James Walsh) who had never been seen or mentioned before and, after a few lines of dialogue, was never seen again after the journey. Equally, His Lordship's eleventh-hour entrance at his brother's trial, just before evidence revealing that the married Duke had been with his lover Mrs Grimethorpe (Judith Arthy) when Cathcart's death occurred, looked like a cliché in 1972, but at the time Sayers wrote the book (1926) was a legitimate and effective piece of storytelling.

The decision not to play fast and loose with the adaptation, one of Ian's stipulations from the beginning of the series' development, was commendable, following in the traditions of the BBC's faithful version of *The Forsyte Saga*. In the end, the only really significant change was making Grimethorpe disappear from the story in a shooting, rather than under the wheels of a rather convenient tram, a revision that Ian himself thought was 'a great improvement on Sayer's [sic] idea'.[14] Even then, this minor change elicited a stern reproach from one disgruntled Wimsey enthusiast in the letters pages of the *Radio Times*: 'I feel I really must protest at the totally inaccurate conclusion of the otherwise excellent adaptation of *Clouds of Witness*,'[15] Mrs Harriette Middlemiss of Hampshire complained. 'Except for two slight alterations in the first episode, the adaptor had kept strictly to the book until the final instalment; and being an ardent Dorothy Sayers fan I was glad she could not see the way in which her plot had been altered and the excellent "twist" at the end of the story completely ignored ... No one can improve on Dorothy Leigh Sayers by altering her plots. They can only detract.'[16] Defending the adaptation, producer Richard Beynon replied:

We found that dealing with so famous an author as Dorothy L. Sayers was at once both rewarding and demanding. Rewarding because of her splendid characterisation and plots and demanding because their complex nature had not only to be simplified, but made visually satisfying as well. In other words, what succeeds in a novel does not necessarily translate – without adaptation – to the medium of television.

I would like to think that what 'liberties' we took would have been applauded by Miss Sayers herself who, being so fine a professional, must surely have appreciated that what we set out to do from the start was preserve the *spirit* of her work.[17]

This was certainly the case, as in the 8 June issue of the *Radio Times*, Sayers's first cousin Gerald F. Sayers, who knew his famous relative well, wrote in to say:

> What pleasure the BBC's production of *Clouds of Witness* gave me. It was admirably cast and superbly produced, and Dorothy, I know, would have been delighted with it. As you probably know, she viewed with horror the prospect of having her work twisted and mangled in order to suit the requirements of film audiences, and when [Alexander] Korda tried to buy the film rights to *Busman's Honeymoon* he got a dusty answer from her. Lord Peter was a living person to Dorothy and her ideal of what a man should be, and I am sure that she would have approved Ian Carmichael's rendering of the part.[18]

One thing Ian could be very satisfied about was the reaction that *Lord Peter Wimsey* received in the United States. Having been told six years before that an American audience would reject Sayers's creation, he must have been delighted with the influential *Saturday Review*'s enthusiastic preview of *Clouds of Witness* in its 9 October 1973 issue. Commentator Hollis Alpert enthused, 'the [humour] is there throughout, quietly and unobtrusively, for after all, this is a mystery, and the interest and suspense depend on uncovering the facts that lead to the solution. I'd be inclined to say this is old-fashioned detective fiction if it weren't for the fact that, seen after the omnipresent diet of mayhem on commercial television, it seems so refreshing.'[19] Comparing Wimsey's style with his favourite detective series *Columbo*, starring Peter Falk as the scruffy but intellectually brilliant New York police lieutenant, he went on to praise the British series' 'leisure to develop characters and story without flimsy tricks and transparent devices. Columbo ... is a delightful creation. Wimsey, played by Ian Carmichael, is less dependent on the actor's mannerisms; he is, for one thing, to the manner born. His aplomb almost never deserts him, and when it does, the result is very funny. Carmichael is a first-rate actor of light comedy, and his choice for the role is a happy one.'[20] Alpert whetted the appetite of his readers further with his appraisal of the rest of the acting talent involved. 'Some of the players come from British television; others have long distinguished themselves, as in the case of George Colouris, seen as the crusty Mr Grimethorpe. A good deal of care, often loving, has been taken with each of the characters. They may be types – in fact, the intent is to affectionately satirise some British upper-class foibles – but they are caught with precision.'[21] Signing off with the information that the distinguished journalist Alistair Cooke provided a 'hardly necessary'[22] introduction for each Wimsey mystery, Alpert stated unequivocally, 'this is not merely good, or high-minded television; it is superb television.'[23] Alpert's article certainly did the trick, as Ian was happy to recall in later life: 'I always like to think back to that stage when [I was told] the Americans would never go for an effete Englishman, because when [the adaptations] were all finished and shown on American television and everything, the *royalties* that come in! ... They are played on every flippin' station that you could find in America.'[24]

As Ian waited for feedback from the BBC's Audience Research Department to see if another Sayers adaptation would be possible, he accepted a part in the anthology horror film *From Beyond the Grave*. Although his role was mildly comedic, the film was a marked change of pace for him in another attempt 'to get away from the buffoon.'[25] Starring in the segment called 'The Elemental', Ian's silhouette is identical to the figure he presented in 1957's *Brothers in Law*, complete with furled umbrella, bowler hat and briefcase. For a refreshing change, Ian's Reggie Warren is a selfish character, swapping the price tags on a snuffbox so he pays a lower price – even then, he bargains the antique dealer down by another pound. 'I hope you enjoy snuffing it,' Peter Cushing's antique dealer says, straight-faced, clearly knowing what Warren is in for.

'The Elemental' was stolen by Margaret Leighton's comic turn as the eccentric occultist Madam Orlov, who promised to rid Warren and his wife (Nyree Dawn Porter) of an evil spirit that was burrowing into his shoulder. During the exorcism, the comic highlight is Madam Orlov massaging and prodding Warren's face into a variety of bemused expressions.

While the story brought a welcome lighter touch to the film, 'The Elemental' so completely undermined Ian's popular screen image that it looked like the part of Reggie had been written specifically for him. In the cynical early 1970s, his pedigree as a 'decent chap' was turned on its head as Warren is shown to be miserly and selfish, qualities that Ian plays effectively against his usual charming screen persona. His image is subverted even more dramatically when, after the comedy and pyrotechnics of the exorcism, Warren's wife, now possessed by the evil spirit, clubs him to death with a poker. It is an effective, nasty and quite shocking ending. Gratifyingly for Ian, the critics singled out 'The Elemental' as the best of the scary tales, with the *Morning Star* praising the film as 'a soundly constructed thriller [which] has the three Ians – Bannen, Carmichael and Ogilvy.'[26]

If *Clouds of Witness* had established Lord Peter's credentials as a credible TV detective, the follow-up, *The Unpleasantness at the Bellona Club* – commissioned in mid-1972, much to Ian's relief, and transmitted in February 1973 – took the viewer further inside his world of privilege. The cover of the *Radio Times* for the week of the first episode showed His Lordship poised outside a country house with an obedient gundog at his heels, a hint that the new serial would concentrate more than before on Wimsey's own particular social *milieu*. The *Guardian*'s Nancy Banks-Smith found this prospect fascinating, recognising 'a very lavish affair indeed, stuffed with nostalgia. It is the world of Wodehouse's butter-haired young men and, indeed, Wimsey's descent from Wooster is evident.'[27] Referring to the psychologically damaged ex-soldier George Fentiman (John Quentin) in the serial, one of the many thousands of victims of the Great War, Banks-Smith ended her appraisal on a sombre note: 'The war permeates the whole book like mustard gas and visibly burns the survivors still.'[28]

As the title suggested, *The Unpleasantness at the Bellona Club* gave the audience an insider's view behind the closed doors of the upper classes that *Clouds of Witness* had only hinted at, and the catastrophic impact of the Great War on that world was presented uncompromisingly. The members of the Bellona Club were clearly uncomfortable around George Fentiman, the mentally unstable ex-soldier now forced into hard times by his inability to hold down a job. As *Clouds of Witness* had been such a success, there was also a relaxation of the production team's reluctance to feature humour. This change of mind was particularly noticeable in the reactions of Wimsey and his old flame Marjorie Phelps (Phyllida Law) to the drunken journalist Salcombe Hardy (David Morrell) adding a drop of something a bit stronger to his glass of punch at a society party; Ian and Phyllida's alarmed facial expressions are very funny.

The idea of the Bellona Club being an élite society with its own rules is reinforced in the closing scenes when the fraudulent Doctor Penberthy (Donald Pickering) is given a choice of the hangman's noose or the gentleman's way out – being left alone with a loaded revolver. In another of Ian's masterly pieces of understated acting, he retires to the bar and the camera moves slowly in on him as Wimsey nervously waits for the inevitable gunshot. That one of the members complains that Penberthy should have shown more consideration for the members and killed himself elsewhere only adds to the authentic sense of a bygone, privileged and, to modern eyes, slightly insane world. Gratifyingly for Ian, the *Daily Telegraph* commented that as 'the most accomplished actor of his kind, [he] is now Wimsey to the life, dropping his g's as if born to the ducal purple.'[29]

Ian Carmichael was a singular case for the BBC in the 1970s. He had been a highly successful film actor and moved back into television in starring roles due to the support and encouragement of Michael Mills, Shaun Sutton and Ronald Marsh, senior BBC executives. With friends in high places and, as a result, an unprecedented degree of creative input into his BBC projects, there was no other actor working at the Corporation in the 1970s who commanded Carmichael's degree of influence over the productions he or she starred in. It's easy to see how this would have caused friction within a highly regimented organisation. Preparing for *The Unpleasantness at the Bellona Club* in July 1972, Marsh made his feelings plain in a memorandum to *Lord Peter Wimsey* producer Richard Beynon:

> When I told [Ian] we could only obtain facilities in Birmingham[30] I know the only reason he was prepared to consider accepting was his long held wish to play 'Lord Peter'. He immediately asked for the same team from director down [as on *Clouds of Witness*] to work with him. This is not of course possible but in view of the results achieved by Barbara Kronig and his appreciation of her work, not forgetting the importance of continuity of style, can I ask if you would consider moving Heaven and the Television Service so that she could work on the next production sequence.
>
> This may sound light-hearted, it is not. Ian, as you well know, can be extremely difficult. Because of the expensive nature of the show he is working for a considerably lower fee and I think Barbara will support my understanding that he was not difficult over costuming.[31]

As Marsh's memo hinted, the relationship between Ian and Beynon was a fragile one. It didn't improve when, in December, Ian's agents, London Management, issued the producer with a four-point reprimand on their client's behalf, asserting the leading actor's concerns about lack of consultation over the choices of Sayers adaptations, the choice of directors and, the major bugbear, 'the hitherto highly haphazard method of constantly holding himself available for he knows not what or when or for how long',[32] which London Management considered 'impracticable and unacceptable.'[33]

By the end of the following year, the fractious relationship had become public knowledge. A story appeared in the *Sun* in which Ian was uncharacteristically rude about, and critical of, the way the BBC had mishandled *Lord Peter Wimsey*. Reading as if the journalist Chris Greenwood had written his story up from off-the-record comments made by Ian after a few too many clarets in the BBC bar, the infuriated actor bemoaned 'BBC bungling'[34] in failing to dramatise Sayers's books in two thirteen-part series as originally proposed. 'The whole point of these books is that they follow a chronological pattern,'[35] he said bluntly. 'The only way to do them properly is in continuing saga form, like the *Forsyte* stories. Now they've skipped one or two books, to come to *Murder Must Advertise*, missing out all kinds of chronological details. If you ask me, it's bloody madness, picking out novels here and there. It's piecemeal.'[36] Ian's attack was embarrassing enough for Beynon to issue a rebuttal, no doubt through gritted teeth, which Greenwood quoted in the same story: 'I don't agree that the books must be treated in sequence. Each of Dorothy L. Sayers's Wimsey stories are quite self-contained. We've simply chosen those that adapt best for television.'[37] In view of how badly relations had deteriorated between the two men, it was no surprise that after the fourth Wimsey adaptation, *The Nine Tailors*, Bill Sellars replaced Beynon as producer, perhaps because Head of Drama Shaun Sutton considered the whole affair 'an unseemly squabble'[38] which he went on to hope had 'now been resolved in an immaculate manner.'[39]

This was all rather ironic, as *Murder Must Advertise* was the jewel in the five-pointed crown of all the Sayers television productions. As well as the writing, direction, pacing and performances all being a cut above Wimsey's other four cases, the serial immediately engaged because of being set in an environment that up until 1973 was not given much, if any, exposure on television – an advertising agency, Pym's, presented with a believable sense of the *esprit de corps* of office life, from cakes on special occasions to sudden arguments between the staff which were quickly forgotten. The scenario may be familiar now due to the success of the 1960s-set Madison Avenue drama *Mad Men*, but over thirty years ago it was startlingly original, a look inside an exclusive world which beneath the surface wasn't as beguiling as it appeared. There was a good reason for how authentic Pym's looked; Sayers herself had worked as a copywriter at a company called Benson's Advertising in the 1920s. One Stanley Penn had taken over Sayers's job after she left, the success of her Wimsey stories making it possible for her to become self-employed. Interviewed in the *Radio Times* and proudly showing off his signed copy of *Murder Must Advertise*, Penn remembered her as ' a nice old lady with *pince-nez* glasses, a typical auntie, all sorts and beads and things strung round her neck. But she was a tough and determined lady for all that. Always one of the chaps. She had a fantastic wit.'[40]

After Anthony Steven's two respectful adaptations, new writer Bill Craig, who had worked on contemporary thriller series like ITV's *Callan*, brought a shockingly modern edge to Sayers's world. The hedonistic drug culture of the Jazz Age had obvious parallels with the increase in illegal, recreational drug use in the 1970s, with Dian de Momerie (Bridget Armstrong) showing the ill effects of all the good times on her steadily more raddled face. Her cocaine supplier Major Milligan, Peter Bowles, 'cashiered' from the army in disgrace, had turned to dealing drugs for an income, and his relationship with Dian was presented as disturbingly interdependent and emotionally masochistic. Clearly, this was a *Lord Peter Wimsey* that viewers hadn't been expecting. The head of the drugs ring, Cummings (Antony Carrick), looked like a very ordinary shopkeeper but his dead eyes gave him away as a dangerous and violent criminal, the perfect contrast to the glamorous 'de Momerie set'.

Crucially, *Murder Must Advertise* provided final, conclusive proof that Ian was a gifted and subtle straight actor. He portrayed three distinct personalities, a rare opportunity for any performer.

Going undercover at Pym's Publicity to investigate the suspicious death of Victor Dean, one of his two alter egos was Death Bredon (Lord Peter's middle names), which was influenced by a colleague's comment that he resembled Bertie Wooster. This enabled Ian to reprise the ingratiating grins and catchphrases from his famous P.G. Wodehouse interpretation – in effect, Bredon was Bertie in colour. Next up was the enigmatic Harlequin, a masked man in fancy dress making Dian obsessed with him with the eerily whistled tune 'Tom, Tom, the Piper's Son'. Craig's sophisticated script played games with the theme of identity, revealing Harlequin as Death Bredon, the black sheep of the Wimsey family, who was a dissolute cousin physically identical to Lord Peter, and keen to muscle in on Milligan's drugs racket. By flattening his usual sing-song Wimsey cadences and making his voice slightly deeper, Ian cleverly made the second Bredon calmly threatening. In the middle of these two was, of course, Wimsey himself. By now Ian's performance was relaxed and confident, but he was still able to surprise the audience by being strikingly manipulative – encouraging the besotted Dian to attend his mother's drinks party so he can ensnare her further with details of Death Bredon's deplorable reputation and, as the deceptive 'silly ass Bredon', inveigling himself into the confidences of the staff at Pym's.

Ian's tour de force, however, came at the denouement of the case. Like the whole story, the climax is unsettlingly off-kilter, with the arrest of the cocaine gang occurring off screen as Wimsey confronts Tallboy (Paul Darrow), the unwilling coordinator of the dealers' network, who used Pym's newspaper advertisements to transmit a complex code for drugs drops to the gang's pushers. Tallboy is anything but, a weak man sucked into crime due to gambling debts and impending, expensive fatherhood, forced to commit murder because of the threat of blackmail. From the start of a scene that lasts nearly five minutes of screen time, Wimsey is aware that the gang's driver, who has tried to run him down earlier in the day, is parked outside his flat waiting to try again. There is a cold deliberation in how, convinced of Tallboy's honourable intention to give himself up and face the gallows, Wimsey offers the tragic man his own hat so that, in the dark and in silhouette, the driver will kill him thinking him to be Peter (another play on the trope of identity), sparing Tallboy's family disgrace and destitution. After Tallboy has left, the way Ian slowly closes his eyes and collapses on a sideboard, head down, is one of the great, understated moments in the repertoire of a performer never given enough credit for the versatility of his acting. Fortunately Ian had his champions, none more so than the discerning Australian critic Clive James, writing in the *Observer*: 'Carmichael is an extremely clever actor, whose reserves of expressiveness not even a hundred years' hard labour in the salt-mines of British film comedy at its deadliest could completely coarsen. With Wimsey, as with Bertie Wooster, he is turning into one of those thespian efforts which seem easy at the time but which in retrospect are found to have been the ideal embodiment of the written character.'[41]

Paul Darrow, who would achieve fame in the late 1970s as the amoral Avon in the BBC space opera *Blake's 7*, recalls that the climactic, riveting scene of *Murder Must Advertise* wasn't easy to record. 'Candidly, it was tricky. Ian, tired and not getting any younger, fluffed his lines a lot, and I was nervous. Still, we got through it, and the crew and cast applauded us at the end. We were not aware of doing anything other than that which we were required to do. So, it's pleasing that you think we did something special.'[42] Darrow goes on to offer some insightful opinions on Ian's personality and acting style:

> He was, obviously, restricted by his physique, voice and 'class' to certain roles. It would have been difficult to accept him as a hardened villain, for example. Nonetheless, he performed with *élan* and I found him a pleasure to work and socialise with. He could be truculent, but his latent charm soon caused one to overlook any faults. We got on well.
>
> Ian was 'old school', a gentleman actor, such as David Niven et al. Thus, he expected professional behaviour on and off screen. Alas, modern actors, with few exceptions, lack ... I suppose you might call it style, *class*. Ian's generation – Olivier/Richardson/

Gielgud – is gone. Sad, but true. The 'officer' class has been replaced by 'other ranks'. For example, James Bond, according to his creator Ian Fleming, gained a first in Oriental Languages at Oxford, became a Commander in the Royal Navy, was a connoisseur, an excellent card player and so on. Daniel Craig? Both Ians, I guess, would have thought not (good actor though Craig undoubtedly is).

Murder Must Advertise saw Ian acting opposite Bridget Armstrong again, by this time an established and sought-after actress in BBC circles. 'I wouldn't say that Ian was famous for charm,'[43] she says, in contrast with most other performers who worked with him. 'He was very, very focused on making Wimsey a success as it was a very good vehicle for him.'[44] The serial's location work saw some authentic night filming at the country house Cliveden, which had a real-life connection with the decadence of the upper classes. '[It] was notorious for the Profumo scandal. We were told that Stephen Ward had had the use of a cottage in the grounds that he used for costumes and make-up.' The 1920s vehicles held their own problems for the actress: 'The big old car was a nightmare to drive. It was like driving a tank.' Amusingly, Bridget admits that some of her social circle didn't find Dian di Momerie as credible a junkie as she herself did. 'One of my friends said, "You should have come to me. *I* can show you how to snort cocaine convincingly!"'

'It was really cold during the night filming. There I was, running around in a piece of chiffon and one night Ian took pity on me. He said, "Come over to the Rolls for a whisky to keep you warm." I was happy to accept his rare generosity and hospitality while he told me how much he enjoyed performing in South Africa – a forbidden country to performers who were against apartheid.'

New director Rodney Bennett, who had worked on the revived *Z Cars*, *Trial* and *Thirty-Minute Theatre* for the BBC, got to know Ian well during the making of *Murder Must Advertise*. 'He was a very nice man. He was a great theatrical,'[45] he recalls. 'He was not what you would call a modern actor, as I remember seeing him in things like *The Lyric Revue*: absolutely brilliant. He was brought up in a completely different tradition to the one that was pervasive in television in the 1970s, which was far more naturalistic. Also the Boulting films that he did – it would be wrong to say they were mannered; it's cleverer than that. He was so knowledgeable and experienced. He would say, "It's all right throwing a line as long as you know where you're throwing it!" He was full of those sorts of comments.

'On the other hand, he rather disconcerted the lighting director in the studio as the first thing he said was, "Where is my key light?" That was going back to an earlier tradition in filming. Today they wouldn't have key lights in that sense. Ian felt very unsure of himself because he wanted to know how to place himself in front of the camera. He was interesting, *very*, very good and he was immensely helpful to, and liked working with, the young actors. It was just a case of giving him confidence, I think, because he was conscious that he was too old to play Peter Wimsey. I had a sneaky feeling that he had the rights to the books – I may be wrong about that – but I know that he had tried over several years to get the BBC to do it with him in the title role. He was a bit too old but he was wonderfully spry.

'I don't know how adaptable or how versatile he would have been in other roles as Wimsey suited him perfectly,'[46] Bennett concludes. 'There was a disguise element in *Murder Must Advertise*, which he did brilliantly; you know, the "silly ass" part. The comedic side of it he was superb at, it suited him perfectly, but I can't see him in Shakespeare or Chekhov. I don't think he was bothered about that.'[47]

On 21 December 1973, the night that the last episode of *Murder Must Advertise* was transmitted on BBC1, the first instalment of the Radio 4 series of adaptations of Sayers's books starring Ian as Lord Peter was broadcast. It was a common practise in the 1970s for the BBC to remake TV successes for radio with the original actors, a policy that had seen the casts of *Dad's Army*, *Steptoe and Son* and *Till Death Us Do Part*, among others, recreate their roles for the airwaves. After the compromises involved in getting Wimsey onto television, Ian was delighted when Radio 4 offered him the opportunity to serialise *all* the books, just as he had originally wanted to do in the 1960s. He was particularly thrilled that this approach enabled him, as an actor, to explore Wimsey's relationship with his wife Harriet Vane, played on radio by Maria Aitken. 'I've done it in every [medium] now, Wimsey,' Ian would later recall. 'We did the television series first, and when it was successful sound got on to it and they wanted to do a dramatised version for radio. I've also recorded every single book, unabridged, on audio tapes, so I've pretty well broken the back of him, I think.'[48] The success of *Lord Peter Wimsey* on BBC radio also enabled Ian to demonstrate another talent, that of music aficionado and broadcaster. Throughout the 1970s he wrote and presented a variety of shows in which he was able to share his enthusiasm for vintage music, including *My Kind of Music* (1974), *Jack Buchanan – The Complete Entertainer* (1978) and four series of *Ian Carmichael's Music Night* for Radio 2 between 1975 and 1978. In the 1970s, it seemed there was no stopping the man.

The third Wimsey serial *The Nine Tailors* began transmission on 22 April 1974. However, in the first episode something was amiss. The pre- and post-wedding scenes Wimsey attended on behalf of his brother seemed forced and stilted – not altogether surprising, as Anthony Steven had no Sayers source material to draw on and invented all the sequences up to where Wimsey's Bentley crashed near the East Anglian village of Fenchurch St Paul. This deficiency was picked up on in the press, with the *Daily Mail* noting critically that the first part of the opening instalment 'seemed shaky in social tone and sureness of touch.'[49] *The Nine Tailors* was also the only serial where Ian's advancing years became problematic. The wedding was set just before the Great War, ten years before *Clouds of Witness* and sixteen years before *The Nine Tailors*, so it was completely ridiculous for Sir Hector Goffe (Anthony Roye) to call a clearly middle-aged Ian 'young Wimsey'. The addition of a gung-ho moustache to Ian's make-up in an attempt to make the officer Wimsey look different to his civilian self, ironically made him look

even older. Although regular viewers must have been thrilled to see
the flashback to the artillery attack which had seen Wimsey
invalided out of the army because of a breakdown, and the
development of his relationship with the former Sergeant Bunter,
who becomes his valet and then his partner in crime-solving, they
must have surely wondered why all this biographical detail hadn't
come at the beginning of *Clouds of Witness* in 1972. The answer to
that was simple: there wasn't enough easily adaptable material in
The Nine Tailors to make four episodes.

Happily, once the Sayers-derived narrative got into its stride, *The
Nine Tailors* became just as engaging as Lord Peter's previous two
cases, the odd shaky Suffolk accent aside. The climax was particularly
effective and lyrical, the distant sound of rain during Wimsey and
Parker's interrogations creating an unsettling atmosphere, while in
Fenchurch St Paul the villagers prepared to face a violent flood if
their protective sluice gate failed. The bells were used as an early-
warning system to alert the villagers to take refuge in the church,
and when Lord Peter was trapped in the church tower by the
deafening volume of the Nine Tailors, blood pouring from his nose
and mouth, he had his answer to how the jewel thief Deacon (Keith
Drinkel) was killed. In a marked contrast to *Murder Must Advertise*,
the narrative was driven not by conventional criminals but the
elemental forces of iron, steel and Mother Nature.

'How refreshing it is in a world of expense-account thugs from
government agencies to lounge back and watch a gent do his stuff
on the small screen,'[50] wrote Stanley Reynolds in *The Times*,
reflecting on *The Nine Tailors*. 'The other week on the BBC's *The
Lotus Eaters* the British Secret [Service] threatened to have Mrs
Shepherd committed to an insane asylum for life if she did not do
their bidding. Last week on ITV's *Special Branch* the good guys
gassed a couple who were selling British secrets. Is it simply
nostalgia, one wonders, which draws us to the world of Wimsey,
or could it be a more basic desire to see our side playing the game
again? Maybe that is nostalgia.'[51]

On 4 June 1974 on ITV, the *Armchair Cinema* strand of TV films screened *Regan*, introducing an unsuspecting British public to Detective Inspector John Albert 'Jack' Regan (John Thaw) of London's Flying Squad, who would dictate the direction of British TV crime drama for the rest of the decade: violent, foul-mouthed, misogynistic and often drunk, he and Sergeant George Carter (Dennis Waterman) introduced two flawed, earthy and dynamic new crime fighters to UK screens, free with their fists but never corrupt, who made Lord Peter's polite enquiries in Fenchurch St Paul seem further away from reality than ever. More and more, Ian as a performer was receding from contemporary relevance into a comfortable, idealised view of England that his social background, looks and personal tastes made him ideal to represent.

In August 1974, London Management had complained to the BBC again, this time concerning Ian's 'prolonged [and] *complete* absence from home for over *three months* rather than the previous short 2–3-day periodic absences'[52] for the fifth Wimsey serial *Five Red Herrings*, which was due to have all its location filming done in Scotland as the original story dictated. With Bill Sellars now in the producer's chair, there was no compromising and the production schedule went ahead as planned, although the situation remained a source of irritation for Ian.

A sign of how popular *Lord Peter Wimsey* had become by 1974 was the request by Russell Twisk of the *Radio Times* office on 20 June for the production team to consider a *Radio Times Special*, an accolade which was only accorded to the BBC's most prestigious productions. Recent editions of these special publications had been the *Radio Times Doctor Who Special*, released to celebrate the programme's tenth anniversary in 1973, and the *Radio Times Generation Game Special*, published to ride the wave of popularity for Bruce Forsyth's family game show. Although the prospect of a lavish *Radio Times Lord Peter Wimsey Special*, complete with specially commissioned photography and exclusive interviews was an exciting one, inexplicably the *Wimsey* production office didn't follow up the idea.

Away from the reassuring, time-locked stability of *Lord Peter*

Wimsey, television continued to change. By the beginning of 1975, Jon Pertwee's gentleman Doctor Who was gone and had been replaced by Tom Baker's bohemian eccentric, a change that anticipated the equally unconventional, seismic punk rock explosion just around the corner in 1976. In January, *The Sweeney*, the follow-on series from the previous year's *Regan* had begun transmission, changing the fictional representation of the British police on UK television for ever. In tune with the anti-privilege *Zeitgeist* of punk, the members of Ian's officer class in *The Sweeney* – spineless, disloyal and easily corruptible – were always found wanting.

Imperturbably, Lord Peter continued to carry on with his business. Fifth time around in *Five Red Herrings*, Wimsey, on holiday in Scotland, is inveigled into investigating the murder of a misanthropic painter called Sandy Galloway – a magnificently bad-tempered performance by Ian Ireland – who many of the local community have good reason to want dead. While his enquiries proceed at a leisurely, untroubled pace, what makes *Five Red Herrings* special is the varied array of supporting characters: the fastidious Inspector MacPherson (Michael Sheard) keen to show off his pristine incident room to His Lordship as he's never investigated a murder before; the teenage would-be flapper Helen McGregor (Elaine Collins) asking for a Horse's Neck cocktail, much to Wimsey's consternation, and the two sisters intent on convincing Lord Peter that they *could* have committed the murder. Scottish-born actor Russell Hunter's cantankerous Mathew Gowan – his very unconvincing black wig and false beard notwithstanding – completes the memorable ensemble.

In many ways, *Lord Peter Wimsey* was the culmination of Ian's career. With its international success, he no longer had anything to prove either to himself or to those critical voices who doubted his abilities as a dramatic actor. However, even late in life he retained some residual bitterness about what he saw as the BBC's cavalier treatment of him during the production of a series that had been his idea in the first place. Speaking at his celebratory on-stage interview at the National Film Theatre in December 2002, he revealed,

'When I finished one [serial], I never, *ever* knew whether I was going to do another.'[53]

In 1976, Ian was reunited with the actress Phyllida Law, who had played Wimsey's on-off girlfriend Marjorie Phelps in *The Unpleasantness at the Bellona Club*, in the West End play *Out On a Limb* by Joyce Rayburn. 'I can remember Ian in the days when they did revue. I was a big fan of his when I was a gel. I thought he was terribly clever and funny … On *Out On a Limb*, he used to turn up and we'd have the most dreadful rows on stage. He'd clap his hands wildly saying, "Come on, come on, come on folks, *come on!*" because we weren't quick enough.

'I think he was the sort of personality who was always under pressure to get it right,' Phyllida continues. 'He was very much of his period. Funny actors like him and Leslie Phillips have got a very strong metronome inside them, their rhythm and timing is very particular. You used to jolly well know if you were getting it wrong or not doing it the way they wanted!

'Ian didn't live very far from me – I'm West Hampstead and he was Mill Hill – so he used to drive me into work when we were rehearsing *Out On a Limb*. He drove an open-top white Rolls-Royce and he taught me the game you play when you're driving along: you've got to marry somebody you see on the street, you had three choices and if you don't get it right you had to marry the third one whatever. We used to yell with laughter when you told someone they had to marry that incredibly resistible person! God knows what people on the street thought of us.'[54]

'I'd liked to have known him a bit better,'[55] Phyllida says, slightly wistfully. 'I enjoyed working with him very much, I mean, we *shrieked* together! He was very generous and good fun. I didn't know him at all well; I didn't work with him early on enough or closely enough. He was terribly easy to work with. You'd think with *me* turning up to play opposite him he would have been scared but he wasn't – he was very easy.'[56]

*

In 1978, an opportunity arose for Ian to take part in a glossy remake of Alfred Hitchcock's 1938 thriller *The Lady Vanishes*, a production that would turn out to be the last for many years by Hammer Films. In the style of starry ensemble films of the time like *Murder on the Orient Express* and *The Towering Inferno* (both released in 1974), Ian joined a cast that featured Elliott Gould, Cybill Shepherd, Angela Lansbury, Herbert Lom and Gerald Harper, playing opposite *Dad's Army*'s portly Arthur Lowe in recreating the double act of Charters and Caldicott (whose dialogue was retained almost word for word from the original film), originally portrayed by Basil Radford and Naunton Wayne. George Axelrod, the distinguished scriptwriter charged with recreating Hitchcock's seminal mystery, was amusingly acerbic about modern Hollywood's attitude to film history. 'Before the Rank Organisation backed the film, two eleven-year-old Hollywood TV producers with beards asked me to write something set on a train. All Hollywood TV producers are eleven-years-old and have beards,'[57] he told the *Daily Mail*. 'I said to them, "Why not remake *The Lady Vanishes* – that's got a train." They hadn't heard of it.

'When they saw the original they clapped their hands. They asked could they get the young man who played the lead to act the same part? I said they could – but he was now Vanessa Redgrave's father. Could I write the new version in colour – because the original was in black and white? I said "Certainly – I'll make the wine red."'[58]

The shoot was apparently a troubled one. In November 1978 the *Daily Mail* reported that the film was behind schedule, 'well over its £2 million budget'[59] and that scenes were being rewritten on a daily basis by Axelrod, Shepherd was being a prima donna and 'fake punk' Jenny Runacre (who had played Britannia in Derek Jarman's 1978 punk celebration *Jubilee*) hated being stuck in an Alpine village with 'those great acting pros Arthur Lowe, Ian Carmichael and Gerald Harper.'[60] Reunited with Ian fourteen years on from their partnership in *Boeing-Boeing*, Harper remembers things rather differently. '*The Lady Vanishes* was enormous fun to do. Ian and Arthur Lowe took it hugely seriously and they were the success of the film, really. They were a tremendous team,'[61] he says today. 'I remember a scene when we were all sitting in the train. Arthur Lowe suffers from narcolepsy. There was a tracking shot through the train, and when they said "Action", I was sitting near Arthur who went to sleep, only for half a minute or so, but just as the camera was coming down he woke up and did the scene beautifully.'[62]

Throughout 1978 and early 1979, the *Mail* remained fascinated by Ian and Arthur's reinterpretation of Charters and Caldicott. Donovan reported that their double act was so successful that 'Those who have seen the "rushes" of Lowe and Carmichael at work predict that they could easily "steal" the film with their comic teaming. Already several television executives are intrigued by the possibility of starring the two as Caldicott and Charters in their own TV series. That would really give the silly-ass Englishman the last laugh.' Although the mooted TV spin-off never materialised, it was easy to see why Ian and Arthur's attention to detail impressed both journalists and TV management. When the year the film was set in was switched from 1938 to 1939, the duo were worried about the accuracy of the cricketing facts:

Lowe:	This is very serious. Are you sure? Because if it is 1939 it would make it the West Indies we are playing …
Carmichael:	And, in any case, it would be the Oval not Lord's and the English team would be different.
Lowe:	The script will have to be changed. I'll phone Lord's and check with Wisden.[63]

The Lady Vanishes was released in May 1979, premiering at the Odeon in Leicester Square, just after the infamous 'Winter of Discontent' in which railwaymen, power, health and council workers all went on strike, leaving London's famous square piled high with sacks of rubbish. In such a volatile climate, contemporary pop music conveyed a mood of class war, urban meltdown and paranoia in four popular songs of the year – 'The Eton Rifles' by

The Jam, 'I Don't Like Mondays' (Boomtown Rats), 'London Calling' (The Clash) and 'Babylon's Burning' by The Ruts. Britain in 1979 was a long, long way from the upright values of Charters and Caldicott but, as Ian noted, perhaps a beleaguered England now needed men like them more than ever. Talking about his character to Paul Donovan of the *Daily Mail*, he remarked, 'He was the kind of man who may have made people laugh, but he was what the British – or rather the English – race was all about. Whether there is any of that quality he had left about today, I don't know. But if there was a bit more of it I don't think we would be a second-class nation.'[64] Lowe agreed, commenting, 'Hitler thought this sort of man from the well-heeled and well-educated upper-middle classes was effete. But when it came to the test these were the sort of people who saved England.'[65] Donovan respected the actors' views but was pessimistic about the gentleman's place in an England where the National Front was allowed party political broadcasts on television: 'In today's social climate, the silly-ass Englishman – he may have been eccentric but his sense of what was, and what was not, correct was impeccable – appears as redundant as the Dodo.'[66]

The new version of *The Lady Vanishes* was agreeable enough, even if Shepherd and Gould's romantic double act, central to the success of the movie, completely lacked any chemistry. As the diligent *Daily Mail* reporters had noted, Arthur and Ian's double act was far and away the best thing in it. 'The most joyous performance comes from Arthur Lowe as Charters, English cricket enthusiast, very stiff-upper-lip and mind-your-own-business, but a hero when put to the test,'[67] the *Daily Express* reported approvingly. 'As his friend, Caldicott, Ian Carmichael has a less showy part. But it is a splendid and memorable teaming.'[68] In the *Guardian*, Derek Malcolm praised 'Arthur Lowe and Ian Carmichael as the two cricket-obsessed English tourists, desperately trying to get to a Lord's Test Match ... almost as cherishable as Basil Radford and Naunton Wayne.'[69] While giving *The Lady Vanishes* a cautious thumbs-up, the *Financial Times* reserved judgement on what the success of the film might mean for the moribund British film industry: 'The film is fractionally sprightlier than *Agatha* [the story of Agatha Christie's ten-day disappearance in 1926] ... but it is still odd and sad to find the British cinema stuck in this nostalgic time-warp, pre-Second World War. One wonders if the trend-setting success of period extravaganzas like *Murder on the Orient Express* and *Death on the Nile*, rather than raising the pulse of the British film industry, hasn't begun to harden its arteries beyond recall.'[70]

With the release of Ian's autobiography *Will the Real Ian Carmichael ...* in the summer of 1979, an event that, in many ways, signalled Ian bidding a fond farewell to his entertainment career, the *Sunday Telegraph*'s Dina Winsor paid a visit to his new home in Grosmont, North Yorkshire to interview him for a promotional cover feature for the *Sunday Telegraph Magazine*. Ian's 'typically serene and unmoved wife Pym'[71] immediately impressed Winsor as 'a capable, attractive woman: straightforward, serene and tolerant, a calm foil for [Ian's] volatile personality.'[72] However, his wife's demeanour had not always been quite so placid, as Ian revealed:

A lot of things contributed to the move [back to Yorkshire]. Pym was distraught at having to leave the girls – they're both married and live in London – and we did keep on a small flat to use in London when we're there. But I've developed a kind of philosophy. I think there are two ways a man can live after 50: one is for the fellow who wants to die with his boots on, and the other is for the man who realises that it's later than you think and wants to get out and enjoy himself. That's me.[73]

His singular attitude to bringing up his daughters Lee and Sally also received a candid airing:

I didn't subscribe to the Hollywood romanticism of nappies festooning dressing rooms. I liked living two separate lives, work and private life. My acting friends are dear, dear people and I love them, but I've never lived in their pockets – I wanted my children to have a good, stable home like mine. Someone once asked Pym what her daughters thought of their celebrity father and she said calmly they didn't know he was a celebrity.[74]

Winsor was shown the comfortable study where Ian spent many happy hours during the day. 'I just love being at my desk,'[75] he told her. 'I'm a compulsive letter writer and I loved writing my book; but sometimes I just find things to do, like paying bills. I just like sitting there with a pen in my hand surrounded by dictionaries and books of synonyms and antonyms and *Roget's Thesaurus*.'[76]

Winsor did, however, detect a nagging unease in a man who was more than happy to go to the local pub because the villagers 'never talk shop', was a member of the Wine Society and occasionally treated himself to a collectible painting. 'Sometimes I do feel cut off'[77], Ian admitted. 'Can't do voice-overs for commercials up here, and there's a good living to be made that way ... If I was in London I could initiate things more, worry out ideas. But then I always worry. Classic Gemini: heights of elation to the depths of despair. I'm a perfectionist, and I've never learned to relax – I have once or twice bitten my nails with that old frustration even up here.'[78]

Before Ian could get too introspective, the interview was brought to a close when 'Pym [put] her head round the door. "Your bath, Ian. And it's partridges for dinner." "Ah – marvellous."' Winsor observed as Ian '[skipped] up the stairs, Martini in hand: the record player is wired through to the bathroom and you can faintly hear Mozart. Pym gives a gentle smile. Jeeves was quite right to leave. He wouldn't have stood a chance.'[79]

If, on one of his visits to London in 1980, Ian had been walking past one of the less salubrious cinemas there, his eye might have been caught by the poster for the Sex Pistols film *The Great Rock and Roll Swindle*, as it featured two of his Boultings co-stars, Liz Fraser (spelt 'Frazer' on the poster) and Irene Handl. The movie was the final full stop to England's fading film comedies, whose days had been numbered ever since the craze for filmed sex comedy took hold in the mid 1970s. Although these films had made a lot of money at a time when the British film industry was very depressed, in a still sexually repressed country they were only getting audiences because of the promise of titillation. Fused with the story of the UK's most infamous punk band, *The Great Rock and Roll Swindle* was the last gasp of a tradition that had produced some of the finest British films ever made, and found Liz and Irene making a living between the scenes of Sid Vicious massacring the song 'My Way' and Pistols manager Malcolm McLaren plotting to fleece the music industry. As the titles rolled over some animated shenanigans aboard a sinking pirate ship to the accompaniment of the profane song 'Frigging in the Rigging', *The Great Rock and Roll Swindle* emerged as a sad, strange but somehow fitting coda to the long-established tradition of post-war British film comedy.

Ian had clearly got out at the right time.

CHAPTER 16

The Elder Statesman

Bereavement, blacklisting and a creative rebirth

T THE BEGINNING of the 1980s, Ian and Pym were all set to enjoy their semi-retirement. Ian now had the best of both worlds, living the majority of the time in the beautiful Esk valley in Yorkshire while still making some trips to London and staying at his 'pied-à-terre' for theatre work, broadcasting appointments or to resume the starring role in BBC radio's wry domestic comedy *The Small, Intricate Life of Gerald C. Potter* by Basil Boothroyd. Concerning the exploits of a crime writer and his long-suffering wife Diana (Charlotte Mitchell), the series was one of the few contemporary roles Ian took on in the latter days of his career, and it enjoyed a long run, from March 1976 to June 1981.

At the same time as the last series of *The Small, Intricate Life of Gerald C. Potter* was being transmitted, Ian returned to the theatre in *Overheard* by Peter Ustinov, an altogether happier collaboration than their previous experience of working together under the volatile producership of Hal E. Chester on *School for Scoundrels*. The production was a huge coup for the producers, as they had managed to secure the services of a bona fide Hollywood legend to play opposite Ian – Deborah Kerr. Born in Scotland in 1921, Deborah had established herself in British film with some quality roles in the 1940s, primarily in *The Life and Death of Colonel Blimp* (1943) with Roger Livesey in which she played the parts of all three women in Candy VC's life, and *Black Narcissus* (1947), an intense drama of religion, madness and sexual repression. Moving to Hollywood, she was Oscar-nominated six times, most notably for the war drama *From Here to Eternity* (1953), set just before the Japanese attack on Pearl Harbor. Returning to England, Deborah starred as the protective governess Miss Giddens in Jack Clayton's suspenseful horror film *The Innocents* (1961). Her pairing with Ian was a logical step, as she had spent the 1970s doing a variety of stage work in America and Britain, notably *Candida*.

Overheard was another light comedy thriller, centring on the married couple Christopher Caulker (Ian) and his wife Iris (Deborah). Caulker is the British ambassador to a 'Communist Arab Balkan state'[1] where 'the mills of bureaucracy grind small and exceedingly slowly'[2]. Mrs Caulker is bored with the country and frustrated with her husband, and when an incredibly handsome and virile poet (Aharon Ipale) seeks political asylum in the British Embassy, the scene is set for an entertaining romantic triangle, which impressed the reviewer in the *Stage* when the play began its run at the Richmond Theatre:

> Positions are reversed and she discovers in her stolid partner a man who loves her deeply enough to accept the reawakening of her sexual passions by the poet as a stage in the development of their relationship as husband and wife. This is played out delightfully by Deborah Kerr and Ian Carmichael; she has never looked more beautiful or played comedy with more delicacy, while he suggests underlying affection with the utmost subtlety.[3]

When *Overheard* transferred to the West End, opening at the Haymarket Theatre, the *Stage* was again in attendance, reporting, 'Ian Carmichael earns a big welcome back to the London stage with his excellent portrayal of the breezy but shrewd ambassador.'[4] With star names in the cast and respectable and positive notices, the play enjoyed some healthy box office.

'We never got on!'[5] roars the garrulous, rangy Robert Putt in jest. Putt played the embassy security guard who frequently appears to exasperate Caulker. 'Ian was a kind of upper-middle-class kind of chap and I'm sort of middle-working-class, so we had a kind of banter about our different sorts of Englishness. He was very much an Englishman; he was very pro-British. He worked very hard with Deborah Kerr on stage. He was about sixty at the time. During matinee days he was on the old Pro Plus – I think they both were! His costume was very dapper but it was very Ian, based on his own sort of dapper turn out. The costumes all got stolen one day so he came in and wore his own clothes, which didn't look very different.' Speaking about Ian's famous co-star, Putt says, 'Ian and Deborah Kerr got on very well. They had no opportunity not to get on, as they had so much to do. Deborah was always incredibly nice, sweet, charming and gracious to everyone.'

Ian quickly formed an unlikely bond with the left-wing Putt and the latter, like many before him, was able to observe in detail the leading actor's technique.

> During dress rehearsals he was very meticulous, and he had a lot of business fixing drinks in this play. He would say, 'As you see, with Carmichael, nothing is left to chance.' He was perfectly rehearsed and if anything went wrong he wasn't very good at getting out of it. I remember once in the Haymarket while I was on stage, the lights completely fused and the whole place went to black. You know, I'm an actor that came from a workshop background, so I ran off stage and said to the stage manager, 'What the bloody hell …?' Then I heard Ian say to the audience, 'I'm terribly sorry about this, ladies and gentlemen …', then the lights came back on again, so I rushed out and, ad libbing, said to Ian, 'It's OK, sir, we've fixed it, it was a bad fuse,' and he was looking at me, shaking his head, so we just carried on. Quite often he would come up to my dressing room and say, 'Thank you so much, dear boy, thank you so much,' as I was a kind of comic security officer in this particular piece, so I would come on to do a bit of a comic turn which would help to get him out of trouble if he was in any.
> I think he was talking about his first wife, and I've never heard this expression before, apart from in sort of upper-class movies like

Brief Encounter, and he said, 'You know, there was no money in the family.' He was the last kind of bastion of that way of life. Later on he said, 'When I was something in the film business, Robert, I used to accept the offers to do anything as long as my name was up on the screen – direct, produce, *anything*.' He just wanted his name up there.

Ian had a great sense of comedy but it was not left to chance, and when he got it right it was spot on. I think he made the – what's the word? – sop, cad, chinless wonder or 'silly ass'. He was the first actor to make that a credible character. Before then they were just silly, but he had some depth to what he was doing. I think he probably, without knowing it, understood. He wasn't doing any research, they were mainly an extension of himself.[6]

The time Ian now had to devote to Pym should have been satisfying, rewarding and blissful. But with cruel irony Pym was diagnosed with cancer and passed away in 1983, only five years into Ian's semi-retirement. Married in 1943 when Ian was on leave from the army, the rock-solid Carmichaels had survived a world war, Civvy Street penury, the birth of two lively and pretty daughters, the waxing and waning of Ian's career and his distressing breakdown, the stress and strain on a relationship that came with early-morning and late-night filming and television recording, not to mention the punishing treadmill of repeated theatre performances. Put simply, her death just wasn't bloody fair.

Ian had always been strict about keeping his work and home life separate. Now suddenly living on his own he had nothing but an empty home life to ruminate on. As Lee and Sally were based in London with their families, they could only visit Ian's home in Grosmont infrequently, so he was often alone for weeks at a time. Surrounded by the wide-open green spaces of his beloved Yorkshire, he acted as he did in most other situations: faced forward and got on with things without any undue fuss.

Just when Ian was at his most vulnerable, the radio plays he had made in Johannesburg on a working holiday with Moira Lister in the early 1970s came back to haunt him. Feeling against the South

African apartheid regime was hardening in Britain in the early 1980s. There had been a high profile anti-apartheid concert the year of Pym's death and in 1984, the rallying cry 'Free Nelson Mandela' became a hit single for The Special AKA.

Ian wasn't a racist, and didn't endorse apartheid in any way, shape or form. He had, after all, fought against fascism in the Second World War and his generation of actors were, in general, tolerant and liberal people. His attitude to South Africa, though, was that it was such a lovely country that he couldn't understand why more people didn't visit. Like a lot of privileged and upper-class people he was rather naïve about politics. The militant English acting community didn't see that as any kind of defence, however, and, with a whisper here and a whisper there, Ian was quietly and unofficially blacklisted throughout England.

Other entertainers and some sportsmen went to work in South Africa, including the singer Elton John, the rock group Queen and the cricketer Geoffrey Boycott. In 1977, Roger Moore and the Richards Burton and Harris made the action film *The Wild Geese* in the country. However, they were all international stars; the success of *I'm All Right Jack* and *Lord Peter Wimsey* in America aside, Ian had always been a singularly British performer with no constituency outside the United Kingdom. His *Murder Must Advertise* co-star Bridget Armstrong, who was a committed member of the pressure group Artists Against Apartheid, believed that because of his South African fraternisation, Ian became a marked man. Notably, his old Boultings colleague Richard Attenborough was a keen campaigner for human rights and spent a lot of time in South Africa in the early 1980s, researching the suspicious death in police custody of the black activist Steve Biko for his 1987 film *Cry Freedom*. In his autobiography, Attenborough spoke of 'the seductive, laid-back, luxury lifestyle enjoyed by so many of the white population'[7] where it was possible to ignore the Bantustans, harsh internment camps where vast numbers of the native population were kept. Equally significantly, Attenborough would hardly discuss Ian in later life and he would earn only a one-line mention in the actor/director's autobiography, despite the two men having worked together closely on the three films they made for the Boulting brothers.

Just when Ian needed to be working because of his painful bereavement, he now couldn't, at least not as much as he wanted to. Ian had always been very canny with money, to the point where he was ribbed about it by his fellow actors, and was more than comfortably off, so in that respect being blacklisted didn't affect him; it was the frustration of not being able to channel his energies into a substantial creative project to distract him from the deeply painful loss of Pym that he felt most keenly. The man whose name on a West End hoarding could pack out a theatre, had entertained millions in the Boulting brothers' films, had starred in three highly successful flagship BBC Television series and, only months before, had been sharing a stage with Hollywood royalty, suddenly found himself a pariah.

The employment Ian did manage to get in this bleak period was restricted mainly to voice work that kept him off the screen, almost as if by being out of sight he was out of mind. He lent his vocal talents to a prestigious new version of Kenneth Grahame's *The Wind in the Willows*, produced by Cosgrove Hall Productions, a subsidiary of Thames Television run by the gifted animators Brian Cosgrove and Martin Hall who, early in their careers, had designed the introductory titles for *Coronation Street*. In the words of the *Daily Express*, *The Wind in the Willows* puppets were 'so expressive they put a lot of humans to shame – I particularly loved the weasels and stoats with jaws like crafty sharks.'[8]

The models of Toad, Ratty, Badger and Mole, the plucky quartet at the heart of Grahame's stories, were endearingly old-fashioned, their slightly jerky movements complemented by the rich tones of Ian, Michael Hordern, Richard Pearson, Peter Sallis (the genial actor who would later find even greater vocal fame as the voice of the inventor Wallace in the *Wallace and Gromit* films) and, as Toad, a young actor called David Jason, then on the brink of television immortality as Del Trotter in the BBC wide-boy comedy *Only Fools and Horses*. Playing the voice of Ratty in the pilot film, Ian stepped aside for Sallis in the series that followed and moved to vocal duties as the narrator, his inviting, convivial and intimate tones suggesting a changing seasonal landscape where 'the secret woodland paths disappear in drifts of cold white snow' and where 'winter is a time for keeping warm and snug in cosy rooms and being glad you've no need to stir outside'. Ian skilfully created an atmosphere that the *Times Educational Supplement* believed '[took] us back to the hot summers of our youth, the days we believe we can remember "messing about in boats", happy in the knowledge that the British Empire would last for ever and the servants were preparing dinner. Were they tall enough to see over the hedges, Ratty, Mole, Badger and Toad would know that the old clock at Granchester stood still at ten to three.'[9]

This wistful ambience was in stark contrast to Ian's reduced financial circumstances, brought about by the harsh intrusion of international politics into his relatively carefree vocation. It was some consolation then, that Ian would work on 32 episodes of *The Wind in the Willows* and 13 instalments of its sequel, *Oh! Mr Toad!* (1990).

Also in 1983, Ian provided the narration for the BBC documentary *Three More Men in a Boat*, in which Benny Green, Tim Rice, Christopher Matthew and a dog named Bonzo recreated the fictional journey of Jerome K. Jerome's characters 'J', George, Carl and their dog Montmorency down the River Thames. Once again, Ian's distinctive voice, by now developing into the very embodiment of a bygone age, was the ideal accompaniment to a nostalgic English odyssey. One in-front-of-the-cameras job that Ian did manage to attain was a guest appearance in the ITV drama series *All for Love* that starred Jean Simmons (Deborah Kerr's co-star in *Black Narcissus*). Finding the star to be 'a darling woman – a darling girl'[10], Ian took the part of Colonel Hunt. 'That was lovely,'[11] he recalled. 'I had just been widowed at the time, and I played the part of a man who had just been widowed, so it was a very touching and moving thing for me.'[12]

In 1987, Ian was offered the chance to step before audiences again, this time in York in a radically reworked theatre production of Jane Austen's most popular novel *Pride and Prejudice*, first published in 1813. Rightly praised as a critique of the greed, snobbery and vanity of Georgian England, it was equally well known for the romantic intrigue between the simmering Mr Darcy and the prim but lively Elizabeth Bennet. Ian took on the role of Elizabeth's father while Ann Reid assumed the mantle of the 'fussy, gabby'[13] Mrs Bennet, a performance the *Stage* considered so good that it 'was straight out of the book.'[14] In a moribund period for Ian, one of the major compensations was that he struck up another life-long friendship, this time with the sparkling Ann.

With a limited number of offers coming in, author David Pownall's take on *Pride and Prejudice* perhaps wasn't the best of choices for Ian. The *Stage*'s reviewer tartly observed:

> When the star spends half his time on stage having a nap, the effect on his audience can be most surprising. All around me people were nodding off with Ian Carmichael as Mr Bennet, in his cosy fireside chair, surrounded by his clutter of books.
>
> Was it really auto-suggestion of the kind that brought the ban on cigarette advertising on TV? Or had someone turned the heating system up too high?
>
> Certainly air conditioning would be a treat for York audiences, but there is a simple diagnosis for this outbreak of theatrical sleeping sickness. In short: a shallow treatment of a lovely classic through long set-piece dialogues and dull characters.
>
> A yawning American lady tourist said it all with: 'Jeez ... this ain't the story I remember. What the hell have they gone and done with it?'[15]

Happily, an upturn in Ian's professional fortunes wouldn't be far away. In the late 1980s, a young film director named Nick Broomfield was doing the groundwork for his first feature film. His accomplishments are many today, among them the documentary film *Kurt & Courtney* (1998), dealing with the troubled relationship between Nirvana guitarist and singer Kurt Cobain and his wife and muse Courtney Love, and the controversial Iraq War drama *Battle For Haditha* (2007), a fictional account of the alleged massacre of Iraqi civilians by American marines. In 1988, Broomfield was preparing *Diamond Skulls* (neé *Dark Obsession*), written by Tim Rose Price from an idea by the director, an exposé of skulduggery in the British upper classes. Needing an elderly actor to play the part of the avuncular butler Exeter, there was only one man to turn to.

'I didn't really feel that I used Ian well in the film,'[16] Broomfield confesses.

> I'm quite critical of *Diamond Skulls*. The film I intended to make was very much based on the life of Lord Lucan [who vanished without a trace in 1974 after the murder of his children's nanny, Sandra Rivett]. If I had been clearer about that, there would have been more leeway to take some liberties with it, to have had more comedy and a more light-hearted element in it and to have used the talents of Ian properly. I realised it was his last film and I feel *terribly* embarrassed about that as I don't think that I, or the film, were worthy of him. He was always a great hero of mine growing up. I always thought he was wonderful in those [Boulting] comedies and I remember being incredibly thrilled when he agreed to do *Diamond Skulls*. The film was a disappointment for me and, I felt, a double disappointment because of not using Ian's talents more fully.
>
> I had pretty much come from the world of documentaries, so my knowledge of casting was not the greatest and it was obviously guided by Lucy [Boulting, John's daughter], who was the casting director on *Diamond Skulls*. I certainly jumped at the chance of using Ian Carmichael: he was one of the actors I had certainly heard of and I was very enthusiastic about using him.[17]

Lucy Boulting elaborates:

> We wanted to cast an actor that was suggestive of the English Establishment. Nick was thrilled to work with Ian. We just sent him the script and he agreed to do the film. His first day of shooting was

very special; Nick had got the opportunity of working with this
wonderful actor who knew just what was required. I was *so* pleased
to see Ian again. It had been nearly twenty years since he had been a
regular visitor at [my father's] home.[18]

Some younger members of the British entertainment industry were
clearly not as judgmental as some of their supposed elders and
betters. Broomfield continues:

I was very upset about the tone of the film. I very much wanted to
make the film about that world of Lord Lucan, and my mistake was
being persuaded to make more of a fictionalised film, based vaguely
on that world but not *specifically* on that world. I don't think I knew
where I was. In that world there are a lot of larger-than-life
characters, rather like in an Evelyn Waugh book, and Ian would
have been fantastic in that way, but I think you need to be on a very
secure footing so you know exactly what film you're making and to
know how far you can go with the comedy. I wasn't in that position.
It would have been great to have made a film that had more of
Michael Hordern and Ian in it. They had a fantastic bond and were
very much at ease with each other. There were a lot of young actors
in *Diamond Skulls* and we were all huge fans of Ian and Sir Michael.

When you're working with somebody like that, you want to
make a whole film with them. In a way I felt there were almost two
different films going on: there was this rather smart Lucan story
with Gabriel Byrne's wife [Ginny, played by Amanda Donohoe]
and then there was this rather comedic statement on the ruling class,
and I felt that these two sides were almost working against each
other.

Ian was an incredible professional, an absolute pleasure to work
with. He was a lovely guy. He was super prepared and super
professional; I was super unprepared and super unprofessional,
probably, and very insecure about what I was doing. He brought a
certain attitude to the British film industry which I think was, 'We're
going to get though anything and we're going to get through it with
a great deal of wit.' There was a bravery to him and a great civility.
He acted the cartoon character some of the time, but he had a very

strong integrity and a sense of who he was and what the bigger picture was. All of that was in his persona. I think he represented something that helped people get through the war, that sort of optimism.[19]

Broomfield's misgivings about *Diamond Skulls* were shared by the press. In *Midweek*, Derek Malcolm criticised the film for not making 'up its mind which of its three elements to concentrate upon and ... not adding up to the sum of its parts,'[20] a view shared by the *Financial Times*, which bemoaned a film that faltered 'from scene to scene with neither momentum nor conviction.'[21] Despite this, Broomfield's debut feature film comes across as a dark and visually stylish, if flawed, drama about the decadent British officer class. Its critical eye on an acquisitive, selfish Britain followed the trend established by other notable 1980s conspiracy thrillers inspired by the harsh politics of the Margaret Thatcher government, such as *Edge of Darkness* (BBC TV, 1985), *Defence of the Realm* (1986, starring Gabriel Byrne, the lead in *Diamond Skulls*) and *The Whistle Blower* (1987). Ian had very few scenes as Exeter the butler, calmly taking care of Lord Hugo Bruckton's family on their sprawling country estate, enthusiastically banging the dinner gong and vigorously announcing the guests at a dinner party. There was a certain delicious irony that in his last film he was playing a dutiful manservant, when in the past he had been the one ordering them around. Ian's best scene is where the two grand old gentlemen of *Diamond Skulls*, Exeter and Lord Crewne (Sir Michael Hordern), sit quietly talking and drinking in the kitchen while the eighteenth birthday party of His Lordship's youngest daughter Rebecca (a young Sadie Frost) is in full swing.

Lord Crewne: Rebecca.
Exeter: Rebecca.

They toast each other.

Lord Crewne: An afterthought if ever there was one.

Exeter: (*Mildly drunk*) I can't think what you must have been thinking of when you thought of her.

Lord Crewne: I must have been out of my mind when I thought of her ... Must have lost my mind.

They continue drinking quietly.

In what proved to be Ian's last ever scene as a movie actor, the mixture of warmth, humour, mild melancholia and the upper-class *milieu* was a low-key, poignant coda to a film career that had included all those elements, together with a slightly bitter taste caused by Ian's unofficial blacklisting.

Bowing to increasing international pressure, the South African regime released Nelson Mandela from prison after twenty-seven years on 11 February 1990, and shortly afterwards, the machinery of apartheid began to be dismantled, with Mandela becoming president in 1991. With these positive changes taking place in South Africa, the attitude of those influential members of the British acting establishment who had punished, so they thought, Ian's transgression, slowly began to soften and he started getting more substantial work, beginning with *Strathblair*, a Sunday night family drama set in 1950 that BBC1 commissioned to fill the gap left by *All Creatures Great and Small*. The popular TV adaptation of James Herriot's books about his life as a vet in the Yorkshire Dales in the 1930s had finished its run in 1990. Ian took on the part of the benevolent Sir James Menzies, the laird of the local manor who ran an estate in Scotland that supported several tenant farmers. The veteran actor now had over twenty hours' of filming on the first series to look forward to.

Before this, Ian took the time to pay tribute to his old friend and colleague in *A Tribute to Terry-Thomas*, shown on ITV on 16 September 1990. Terry had died from Parkinson's disease, a terrible end for such a talented, funny and charming man. Also before commencing the long run of filming on *Strathblair*, Ian was offered a script for the prestigious *The Play on One* slot called *Obituaries*, a clear sign that his days in the acting wilderness were over. Originally written by David Conville to be performed in a London pub by two actors, *Obituaries* concerned two bored old men living in a nursing home, who compete with each other to be granted an audience with a visiting member of the Royal family, duelling in wheelchairs and fighting each other with rolled-up copies of the *Tatler*. They write exaggerated biographies of each other: Bartholomew 'Chalky' White (Ian), in reality a bank clerk, becomes a Second World War Spitfire pilot and marries Tallulah Bankhead. Timothy Apear (Ronald Fraser), a music-hall novelty act and electric-kettle salesman, in his fantasy life has a heroic career in the Indian army, is the first man up Everest and redesigns Lutyens' Viceregal Lodge. Their language is both baroque and colourful:

Apear: A catheter for thy catamite kingdom!
White: A condom for the copulating cuckoldry!

The *Daily Mail* noted the Samuel Beckett-style mixture of comedy and tragedy in the play, and that 'unreality was sustained until the fateful visit which brought out the fatal flaws in both men – showing just how fragile their absurd code of honour was, and leading rapidly to the denouement of cheating, lying, poisoning and death.'[22] The play brought out something almost visceral in Ian's performance, possibly a release of his frustration through White at the way he had been treated over the previous decade. Flatteringly, the *Daily Telegraph* recognised that with *Obituaries* both actors had achieved new heights of acting excellence: 'Ronald Fraser, who played Apear, and Ian Carmichael, who played Chalky, have delighted TV audiences as Evelyn Waugh's Apthorpe, P.G. Wodehouse's Bertie Wooster, and uncounted other comic characters over several decades. This was, quite possibly, their finest hour. If, unthinkably, it were also to be their last on our screens, the obit notices would surely read: "Gloriously … Hilariously …"'[23]

Playing Sir James Menzies' Korean War veteran son Andrew in *Strathblair* was David Robb. The actor had a distinctly military bearing and had been born in England but brought up in Edinburgh. *Strathblair* begins just as Andrew returns from fighting Communists in South-East Asia. Robb had been a formidable Germanicus in the highly regarded 1976 BBC adaptation of Robert Graves's *I, Claudius* directed by Herbert Wise, the effete Edgar Linton in *Wuthering Heights* (BBC TV, 1978) and, perhaps most famously, Robin in 1981's *The Flame Trees of Thika* for ITV. '*Strathblair* was all shot in Scotland,'[24] Robb explains.

> The location stuff was all shot in and around Blair Atholl in Perthshire. It was a social triumph, I have to say, because we were up there for *months* as the storylines had to go from spring to autumn, so we were there from April until October and it was a very, very nice job to do in that respect. *Strathblair* wasn't a great critical success, but it was a very nice unit, we all got on very well and I've got very fond memories of it.
>
> I was Ian's son in the series, and the funny thing is that my wife played Ian Carmichael's daughter in a series that he did in the '70s called *Bachelor Father*. It was about this chap bringing up children on his own and Briony [McRoberts] was the eldest foster daughter. We stayed in touch and he used to send us cards addressed to 'My children', which was very sweet.[25]

Briony herself remembers making the pilgrimage to Blair Atholl and enjoying Ian's company again after a gap of over twenty years: 'From playing his daughter, it was really nice when David got *Strathblair* – coincidence of coincidences as his son! – that I was able to go up there, no longer a young thing, and get arseholed with them all. That brought [my relationship with Ian] to a lovely close.'[26]

Spending so much time with Ian gave Robb an insight into the man's gentle and bright personality:

> He was very redolent of that immediate post-war thing of the slightly 'silly ass' character. Which he wasn't, of course, he was a

very bright guy. If I remember rightly, David Blair, one of the directors on *Strathblair*, just came up with the idea [of casting him]. He thought we should get somebody who was well known to the audience and he came up with Ian Carmichael. I wasn't there at the time, but I think it was one of those things of, 'Let's offer it to him and see whether he bites.' And he did; I think he felt that it wasn't too far away to get home for weekends when he wanted to. He took to it, he was very keen and everyone was very fond of him.

I remember very distinctly one evening having supper with him, just the two of us, and getting quite merry, and deciding that we should have a couple of malts after dinner. It was delightful; it was really, *really* delightful. Because he'd nailed a couple of those 'silly ass' parts early in his career he had been fine with it, but it wasn't what he was actually like at all. He was a much sharper individual than those slightly daft parts that he played, and I think in later life he enjoyed playing people that weren't as silly.

The thing about Ian's generation was that they did have a degree of influence. They had a kind of cushion that we [younger actors] didn't get as everything had exploded by the time the late 1960s came along. There were loads and loads of actors, the style was changing and all the rest of it. Gordon Jackson was another one: they actually made very good money – not in the same league as American stars – but good, steady money. That sort of middle ground has been eroded now, it doesn't really exist, except for the half-dozen home-grown British TV stars: Martin Shaw, Martin Clunes – apparently you have to be called Martin – those kind of guys. There's very few of them and a lot of the youngsters now go to America anyway.

Ian was a delightful man. He did sort of represent an era that was fading but he wasn't old fashioned in himself. I'd forgotten how old he was, actually; because he kept his hair and everything he never really looked like an old bloke, he just looked progressively middle-aged. He was a very nice chap and had a very long and good and full life. It was very sad when he died because he was one of those guys who personified another generation.[27]

Another member of the cast who got to know Ian well on the Blair

Atholl shoot was Francesca Hunt, who with Derek Riddell played the married couple Jenny and Alec Ritchie, the newly weds who rent a farm from Sir James. Francesca was a recent drama graduate before being cast in *Strathblair* and, confined to the Highlands for several months in the company of her fellow actors and the production team, she was just as impressed with and intrigued by Ian as Robb had been. 'He was quite extraordinary,'[28] Francesa remembers.

> He was such a classic English gentleman – that was exactly how he behaved. One had no idea whether he'd perfected it over the years or he was genuinely one of nature's smoothies. He was *incredibly* nice, because this was mine and Derek Riddell's first job: we were straight out of drama school, had never been in front of a camera before and [Ian] was *charming* and gentle and very helpful. There were quite a lot of knowing looks between some of the other people, which is slightly off-putting when you're new, seeing them catch each other's eye when you do something patently foolish. And Ian *never* did it. Absolutely charming. He was a sweet being.[29]

In the company of one of the most experienced actors in England, Francesca made the most of the opportunity to learn from a master craftsman.

> Ian was certainly somebody you watched. It was quite an intensive learning period, because the schedule was incredibly fast, so there wasn't much time for the coaching of a newbie. The only way of learning really was watching, and yes, there were these two grand old folks, him and Andrew Keir [as Macrae of Balbuie] – an extraordinary being, similarly. You just sat there, watched the way they did it and you thought, 'Yeah, that works.' I'd come out of a very classical drama school that had only really trained you for the stage – two years of learning how to project your voice so it was loud and how to wear a cloak without tripping over furniture and that sort of thing. To come across that minute, focused style of telly acting, almost immediately out of drama school, was quite interesting. Yes, Ian and Andrew were the old school and in that

they were much less intense about it – very much just 'Get on and do it' – but there was also something rather gracious about the acting, something rather more stylised.

The main difference between the younger and the older generation of actors was that as a young member you felt you were part of the whole production team, whereas Ian was very definitely 'just' the actor. That generation weren't entitled to query a director's notes or comment on the lighting or any of the other things that, actually, the modern young actor does tend to do.

Ian was also very funny. A very witty man. His humour was slightly dry, and my goodness *Strathblair* needed it! He injected it with a lovely sense of almost taking the piss. He had an archness. There were times when you thought he was ever so slightly doing a bit of revue. His *bonhomie* shone through. It's quite interesting how quite often what kind of person you are shines through in the acting. You can hide a nasty nature for so long, but I think it comes out and Ian had *such* a sunny nature. He was so gently good humoured, and clever too. He never pushed it or showed off about it but he was a very, very bright man. It startled you because you assumed he was Bertie Wooster and actually Jeeves was a bit closer to how he really was. He was a very smart being.

As a first job, you couldn't have come across someone better to work with. I've heard so many bad stories of people being unpleasant, bitchy and luvvy and all that sort of thing, but having that guy at the helm just set the tone for the whole thing. He was very gracious, very professional and *just* charming too.[30]

Despite the avuncular mood of the production, enhanced by a healthy drinking culture among some of the younger members of the unit, *Strathblair* quickly ran into trouble due to rights problems with the scripts that had long-term consequences for the making of the series. Veteran producer Leonard White, who had last worked with Ian nearly twenty years before on *The Importance of Being Earnest* for ITV, was brought in to oversee the second block of ten episodes and was highly concerned about what he found: 'The extraordinary thing is they started work and, in the true, good old BBC way of not believing anybody was going to turn them down, they didn't have the rights [to adapt the stories they wanted]. I mean, it was as critical as that. So in the middle of doing it, the writers had to go back and change the whole thing.'[31]

'It was a bit of a hybrid really,' says Robb, speculating on the reasons for *Strathblair*'s troubled production.

> They never really did much with it. It was very strange ... There were a lot of politics going on at the time. BBC Scotland was still trying to fight its corner with home-grown drama and they came up with the idea for this series which was a bit *Dr Finlay's Casebook*, a bit *Upstairs, Downstairs*, but they never really had the scripts. The scripts were only half developed and the first one, the very first episode, was adapted from a kid's story about a sheepdog. So in the first episode there was this bloody dog that seemed to be the leading character!
>
> Because the scripts on *Strathblair* became quite wobbly – and I don't advertise this as a general rule – some of us were changing them quite a lot. You'd get a script and you'd think, 'God, this speech is *appalling*,' and my character was meant to be ex-army, or in the army and going back to Korea, and I had this speech that was just *drivel*. It was completely and utterly unmilitary. I had a friend who was in the army at the time and I said to him, 'This is all wrong, isn't it, that would never happen?' and he said, 'No, no, no.'
>
> We actually cobbled together a completely different and far better speech. Ian was in the scene and he said, 'Look, old boy, it doesn't affect me cue-wise, does it, because I've learnt my bit.' And I said 'No, no, I wouldn't dream of changing anything that you're going to do, Ian, I'm just saying that this is what I'm going to say.' This was quite a surprise to him, I think, that a script was more malleable, whereas in his day a script was like a Bible, you didn't change anything.'[32]

Robb was making an unintentionally ironic comment, as he didn't know how much rewriting of his own Ian had done on his one Rank film, *The Big Money*, in 1955.

Francesca remembers Robb's rewrites very well. 'He was outrageous,'[33] she says with a laugh. 'He's a writer anyway, and luckily what he writes is very good. He'd quite happily say, "No, I can't be saying *that*!" and back would come great sheets of new dialogue, which was slightly alarming. As a newbie you were completely unused to someone changing your script three days before [shooting], and I think Ian found the same thing as well! Both of us would be going, "Wait a minute, wait a minute, you want to say *what*?"'[34] His concern about a rapidly changing script aside, it must have been heartening for Ian to see a new generation of younger actors involved in the writing process, just as he had been on *The World of Wooster* and *Lord Peter Wimsey* earlier in his own career. Happily, high standards still clearly prevailed for some of his thespian successors.

Transmitted from June 1992 on BBC1, *Strathblair* garnered a mixed response from critics. 'With its swirling orchestral music and familiar plots, here is a vehicle that has been designed for comfort,'[35] observed the *Daily Mail*. 'The real trick, I suspect, has been to ensure that every character in the entire series has a heart of gold.'[36] The *Sun* was rather less charitable in its reaction: '*Heartbeat* [ITV's Sunday night family drama set in the 1960s] was a tender reconstruction of an upbeat era but *Strathblair* paints a dowdy picture of post-war Scotland. A plodding Highland soap that's about as much fun as mohair underpants.'[37] The *New Statesman*, meanwhile, was positively scathing in its assessment of Ian's performance: 'Sir James, for some unexplained reason, is English. Very. In fact, Sir James' English is even more incomprehensible than the Scots dialect. He has a son whom he calls "Aindrew", a word he manages to evacuate from his throat despite the three pounds of plums in his mouth.'[38]

'There were only one and a half scripts I could look at, and one of those was the first one with the dog,'[39] recalls Leonard White, reflecting on the situation when he arrived at the *Strathblair* production offices. 'Unfortunately for me, it was almost like I was running something that had just started, as the team making the first block of episodes were still in production at the same time that we started to roll [on the next ten episodes, which became the second series for 1993]. It was hairy, but I was trying to make it less hairy by trying to do something different. When I wanted to get in touch with those writers who had done some of the early stuff, [script editor] Bill Craig didn't want to know anything about it. So we had to go and write it from a different angle. I knew quite a few Scottish writers, so I went chasing round and got them all interested in the possibility of now making the whole thing about the Strathblair village and the village characters, and this was the trick which I think made it interesting from my point of view. We set it all in one year and that was 1951, Festival of Britain year. We'd see how Scotland, through a little village, would relate to those twelve months. I also hoped that the follow on would be 1952.'[40]

White's strategy paid dividends, as the TV critic in the *Mail on Sunday* noted: 'There have been signs of life in the second series with dour drama replaced by soap opera situations. There was the unidentified assailant who clobbered Italian ex-POW Umberto. Then young laird Andrew Menzies (pronounced Mingies, please) chased art thieves with a shotgun. And last week motorbikers from Clydebank gave the villagers something to gossip about.'[41] However, all White's hard work and ingenuity couldn't prevent *Strathblair* being axed at the end of its second year.

'To be perfectly honest I think *Strathblair* finished because it had something to do with [the quality of] the scripts,'[42] Francesca says, thinking back on the many desperate rewrites. 'The BBC did *Monarch of the Glen* about five years later and it was the same format but slightly better done. *Strathblair* was the prototype, I reckon. The BBC seems to work like that; it'll come up with something, have a go at it, take it off, have another look at it and come back with a different version. And actually *Monarch of the Glen* was pretty much the same, only quite obviously funnier. I think [*Strathblair*] needed a bit more wit. If you do it too straight it becomes a bit like a historical lecture and it can come a bit unstuck that way.'[43]

'South of the Border [*Strathblair*] was never really publicised,'[44] Robb states. 'It was put out on a Sunday evening and nobody seemed to take much notice, so consequently while the audience appreciation figures were quite high, the actual viewing figures were quite poor. You've got to advertise something and get people's arses on the sofa to watch it.' He agrees with Francesca about *Monarch of the Glen* being a reboot of the same basic idea as their own series: 'I still find it a completely wacky programme, though. I don't know *what* it was supposed to be, I don't know *who* it was aimed at. There you had Susan Hampshire wafting through the whole thing exuding Surrey all over the place, and Richard Briers ...! I know Ian was English, but he was very proud of his Scottish surname, whereas Richard Briers is ineffably suburban. I never understood the whole *Monarch of the Glen* thing.'[45]

In the same year that *Strathblair* began its two-year run on BBC1, Ian made a happy announcement. He was to marry again, the woman in question being one Kate Fenton, born on the 14 October 1954 in Failsworth on the outskirts of Manchester. Thirty-three years Ian's junior, she had met him when she was working as a producer at the BBC in 1984: 'To be accurate, I'd employed him, to read some stories I was producing for Radio 4.'[46] The couple's marriage coincided with Kate's decision to leave the BBC in 1985 and settle in North Yorkshire with Ian.

With interests in theatre, cabaret and developing a second career as a novelist – *The Colours of Snow* (1990), *Lions and Liquorice* (1996) and *Too Many Godmothers* (2002) numbering among her books – Kate was the ideal partner for Ian. The age gap was a source of amusement for both of them and didn't make any difference to their relationship; when Kate felt like teasing him good naturedly, she would call him the 'old boy.' With this well-deserved revitalisation of his personal life, Ian would be inspired to some fine performances in the late stages of his career.

Ian's status in his autumnal years as a quality character performer continued with an appearance in John Mortimer's ITV auction drama *Under the Hammer*, designed as a vehicle for the actor

Richard Wilson, who was beginning to feel typecast as his most famous creation, the grumpy pensioner Victor Meldrew in the BBC sitcom *One Foot in the Grave*. Ian was one of a distinguished guest cast that also included Sir John Gielgud and the name of his character, Sir Bertie Wednesbury, was something of an in joke for those who remembered watching his turn as Wooster in the 1960s.'

'I started as a writer in an ad agency, about nineteen or twenty, and met this guy about ten years my senior called Terry Winsor,'[47] says Julian Dyer, the lively scriptwriter behind Ian's next project *The Great Kandinsky* who has a taste for colourful language.

> There was something about his fucking energy, man; we kind of warmed to one another. He said, 'I'm a film director, I'm looking for material outside of the adverts we make. Would you be interested in writing a B-picture for a film feature?' I'd fallen into advertising, did a year's course at Watford, got a job in a shit agency, then eleven months later got a job in a good agency which had a reputation for being left of centre. That's where I met Terry. I was, like, 'Yeah, yeah, I'll do it.' Pretty soon, the advertising guy I was working with dropped out as he couldn't commit the time. I fell into working with Terry and it became apparent that he already had the idea to do a film about escapology and someone like Harry Houdini.
>
> During the time that it took us to write anything at all, a year or two, B-movies had stopped happening, but we realised we were on to something and decided that we'd expand *The Great Kandinsky* into a feature. It languished on 'options' with various production companies that did very little with it. One in particular suggested that if we could incorporate the Queen music catalogue, they could get it financed the next day. I chose to walk out of that meeting, but Ben Elton obviously didn't and look at him now! We did so many drafts of the script, but eventually, Simon Channing Williams of *Imagine* film fame came on board. It was green-lighted and I bawled my eyes out. [The film became a made-for-television production, partly funded by the BBC's *Screen Two* division.]
>
> Richard Harris, who was playing Ernest Kandinsky, had major problems with this, as it turned out that he'd had some huge falling-out with Simon back in the late sixties over some other picture. He

wouldn't fucking work with him, blah, blah, blah. That's how we ended up with Tom Bell as the professor and Richard Harris as his assistant [Kandinsky]. Mr Carmichael was on it from the beginning; there wasn't any doubt about that. We even wrote it with him in mind. The person that plays the role of Kandinsky's mate in the old people's home, we thought, should be someone from the navy or the army. Somebody like Ian Carmichael, who was the proper English gent with the simmering anger and the uncomfortableness about being British. Right from the beginning I don't think there was any uncertainty that we wanted him if we could get him. Everybody said 'Yes!' We hadn't actually approached him, but when we were writing it was as if we already knew we'd get him. I tell you what, he was a fucking gent, mate!

Dyer's refreshingly direct enthusiasm about Ian was in stark contrast to the dismissive denial of him that still prevailed among some of his peers because of his work in South Africa. 'There was a scene in a ballroom where Kandinsky had this conflict about being in an old people's home,' Dyer remembers, warming to his theme.

He still wants to perform tricks and can't really retire as he still doesn't know the secret of this one special illusion. His best mate is this sea captain called Patrick McCormick, that was Ian Carmichael, but their relationship is all about challenges and one trying to trump the other. This old lady played by Dorothy Tutin comes along, and plays one off against the other. There was a scene where there was a dance and Ian turns up as a very British naval officer all in white. Richard was there and Dorothy was dropping big hints about having a dance, but Richard was thinking about himself and his trick and so on, so Ian walks up and he goes, 'May I have the pleasure of this dance?' and Richard goes, 'I was about to ask,' and Ian says, 'Time and tide, my old friend, wait for no man,' and started dancing with her. Harris stands there simmering, so I said to him, as I was watching him when it was shot, 'That was fucking brilliant, I could see all the jealousy and nastiness in your eyes, what were you thinking about? Was it 'cos you read the script and you were so into the part?' He said, 'No, I was thinking about my ex-wife and how much money she owes me!' I'm like, 'OK, that's what acting is, then.' When that sequence was actually cut together, the thing that makes it brilliant is not Richard's simmering jealousy. It was just one little look from Ian Carmichael – and he could dance, he could proper dance. He took Dorothy in his hands, waltzed away with her and he just casts his eye at Richard Harris with a look that said in my language, 'Fucking hell, I got the bird!'[48]

Terry Winsor had begun his feature-film directing career with the irreverent *Party Party* (1983), a raucous comedy about a house party that gets out of hand. He enjoyed a close working relationship with another Yorkshire actor, Sean Bean, directing him in *Fool's Gold: The Story of the Brinks-Mat Robbery* (1992) and later in the thriller *Essex Boys* (2000), also based on a true story. 'I knew instinctively, on meeting Ian, that something terrible had happened in his life,'[49] the restrained and thoughtful Winsor says. 'You can just tell with people. I mean, he had all the confidence in the world but there was just something behind those eyes that was sad. In a way, it actually made him that much more interesting, though that sounds selfish in terms of what I was trying to do. The character he played was at the end of his life; he actually dies quite early on in the film, and it has an amazing impact on Kandinsky and the fact that they had found the only "life" in the old people's home together. Maybe Ian used that life experience, I don't know, but he was a very talented man. Richard Harris is big and bold, and Ian does everything that makes you want to look at him, he makes you look at him in a completely different way to Richard Harris. Richard could read you the phone book in a way that could make it interesting. What Ian offered was something different. Ian made you want to look at his face. The camera liked him a lot and whichever way he turned, he could cleverly turn into profile; he knew exactly how he looked, even at that age. He had that fantastic hair and had so much experience of how to use the camera. I can't actually remember having to do more than two takes on anything he ever did because it was always spot on. Richard was much more exploratory, which was very interesting. So the combination of the two of them did make it fascinating to deal with on the set, as Ian was very, very contained and would go off to his caravan where I'd go and talk to him, whereas Richard had to make a drama out of everything. They were each from a completely different mould. There was no friction as they both respected each other's talent, but they were very different men.

'I think the camera liked Ian,'[50] Winsor affirms. 'That's what makes actors special in my opinion. An actor can have all the talent in the world but when an actor can suck in the camera in that way, that's what enables them to go up onto the big screen. Sean Bean has that same relationship with the camera. It's all in the eyes, it's about what they can do with them, they've both got big eyes and they can both use them in exactly the right way with a fantastic sense of timing. Every actor knows how to use their straight, forward, three-quarter profile etc., but to be able to use something that is in silhouette or just pure profile, to know your face that well, to be able to do that, that's talent. Ian had worked out how he was going to do it and he didn't want some silly sod coming along and changing the script for him. I think he did a lot of preparation. He thought about the moment in the sentence construction when he was going to move into profile. To do that, somebody has to study and think about what they are going to do and how they're going to do it.

'There's one scene that Ian did that is particularly memorable. The idea is that Richard Harris is supposed to be an illusionist and his character always wants to be, and is up for, being challenged. Ian's character challenges him to stay on the track of an approaching train and as the train is getting closer and closer and closer and they talk about death and whether it makes any difference to go now or later. We see Richard Harris jump aside as the train goes whistling past and obviously we cut to the rails and see a body and then Ian just gets up, looks across to Richard and says, "A little challenge, eh, Kandinsky?" He's actually proved to Kandinsky that he's better at defeating death, though quite quickly after that his character dies and because he dies, it sends Kandinsky on this journey to find all the people he worked with as an escapologist.

'The film is interesting but I have to say, as the director and co-writer, there is still something that's not quite right about it,' Winsor considers. 'There were a lot of difficulties, mainly after Ian had done his part on it. Richard went on a bit of a bender. He had a suite in the Savoy and his doctor lived next door to him and he used to send Richard off every six weeks to a detox clinic in Austria or Switzerland. So I managed to do three weeks shooting and then he went off on the piss. It was very hard to get your head around. A lot of not particularly happy memories.'⁵¹

As it transpired, *The Great Kandinsky* was actually one of the underrated highlights of Ian's whole career. None of the unhappiness or compromise Winsor had to deal with is evident in the finished film, which was first shown on Good Friday, 14 April 1995. It was a sweet comic fantasy, gorgeously photographed by director of photography Dick Pope, in a style somewhere between *The Prisoner* and *The Avengers* that presented a surreal England of bearded ladies who worked in public libraries, the world's tallest man, randy pensioners, psychic identical twins living in a tepee in the middle of an English field and duelling magicians tightrope-walking across the skyline of London. Intentionally or not, it also looked like a colour *homage* to Ian's equally quirky Boulting brothers films of the 1950s. *The Great Kandinsky* was modishly self-aware too, with 'Mrs Bader' (Gabrielle Hamilton) constantly trying to escape from the old people's home in her turbo-charged wheelchair. Every time she appears, the theme tunes from films about heroic RAF crews *The Dam Busters* (1955) or *633 Squadron* (1964) break out on the soundtrack, wittily indicating that her surname was deliberately referencing the Second World War air ace Douglas Bader. The film also broke down the 'fourth wall' – the illusion that what viewers were seeing on their televisions at home was happening in a sealed fictional environment – by having the great Tom Bell, in a strikingly nasty, feral performance as Kandinsky's nemesis The Professor, address the audience directly.

Although he dies early on in the film, McCormick's passing energises Kandinsky and his influence permeates the whole film. Speaking just before making his comeback recital, the escapologist gives a moving eulogy to his old friend: 'On a more serious note, I would like to dedicate tonight's performance to an old friend of mine, sadly not with us tonight, but without whom I would not be standing here now. A man who refused to give up. The saltiest old sea dog of them all – Patrick McCormick.'

It was a shame that on the whole the press largely missed the point of *The Great Kandinsky*, *Time Out* dismissively concluding 'it barely holds your interest for its ... 84 minutes'[52] and the *Guardian* glibly noting that it 'attracted a remarkable constellation of stars ... momentarily Ian Carmichael ... none of them shining to great advantage.'[53] Balancing views came from the *Evening Standard*, which rightly applauded the film as 'extraordinarily entertaining'[54] and *Today*, praising it as 'BBC1's zippy Good Friday treat.'[55] The *Guardian* was right about one thing: it was indeed an opportunity to enjoy a plethora of vintage actors who belonged to the same generation as Ian – Dorothy Tutin, Earl Cameron and Stephen (*On the Buses*) Lewis among them. *The Great Kandinsky* also tapped into the same *Zeitgeist* that had recently produced the defiant pensioner comedies *One Foot in the Grave*, *My Good Friend* and *Waiting for God*, which saw 'the spirited and independent elderly [refusing] to meet the wishes of the impatient young by sitting quietly and tidily in the corner before, as soon as possible, dying.'[56]

Later in 1995, in what would be his final stage performance, Ian took on the major role of Sir Peter Teazle in the Restoration comedy *The School for Scandal* by Richard Brinsley Sheridan for the Chichester Festival. At seventy-five, there was no denying that Ian had enjoyed a good run, and *The School for Scandal*, which the title of *School for Scoundrels*, Ian's finest film, had deliberately referenced, was a fitting epitaph to his work in the English theatre. The play was praised by William Hazlitt as 'if not the most original, perhaps the most finished and faultless comedy which we have.

When it is acted, you hear people all around you exclaiming, "Surely it is impossible for anything to be cleverer?" The scene in which Charles sells all the old family pictures but his Uncle's, who is the purchaser in disguise, and that of the discovery of Lady Teazle when the screen falls, are among the happiest and most highly wrought that comedy, in its wide and brilliant range, can boast. Besides the wit and ingenuity of this play, there is a genial spirit of frankness and generosity about it, that relieves the heart as well as clears the lungs. It professes a faith in the natural goodness as well as habitual depravity of human nature.'[57]

Says the play's director Richard Cottrell:

I had a good relationship with Ian both professional and personal and I liked him as a man. However, he was notorious for having the greatest difficulty in learning lines. I realised after the event that this is why [producer] Duncan Weldon opened Scandal at the Crucible in Sheffield for a month. If he hadn't done that, we'd have had a complete disaster at Chichester where we faced the national press on the opening night. Ian did, indeed, arrive at rehearsals having done a lot of work on the lines. But he was very, very easily thrown. In fact, I realised early on that one wouldn't be able to rehearse with him but only repeat [what he'd learned], as the slightest variation on what had been done last time threw him and made him dry up.

As you may imagine, this is not what one does in rehearsals, which are a number of weeks devoted to a process of discovery. It was very hard on those actors who had a lot to do with him, particularly Abigail McKern who played Lady Teazle. She behaved like an angel from beginning to end and never expressed the frustration I know she felt. The opening night in Sheffield was not a happy one. Ian was very nervous and dried several times, I think, while Frank Middlemass, who played Rowley, developed a migraine as he went into a rather long speech of explanation and dried at the end of every line! I sent the stage manager on in the interval to explain to the audience what was happening [with Frank] and he said that he would continue holding the book rather than cancel the performance. The audience responded sympathetically and this encouraged everyone, including Ian. But the next night [Ian] asked to see me in his dressing room and told me he couldn't continue and wanted to withdraw as soon as possible.

Now, though the cast was a rock solid one of leading supporting actors – Frank, Dinsdale Landen and Edward de Souza – and had two other stars in Honor Blackman and, more importantly, Dora Bryan, Ian was the draw card, a star for many years and someone who hadn't done a play for quite a while, so his dropping out before Chichester would have been a major blow. But I knew why he wanted out – terror – and knew too that he'd get better as the Sheffield run progressed. I managed to persuade him that he was marvellous, that he was going to be marvellous and obviously gave him the encouragement he desperately needed and he agreed to continue. By the time he opened in Chichester, he'd pretty much conquered it and had a personal success that I always hope gave him much pleasure. He certainly wrote me a very sweet and appreciative note after the Chichester opening.

His performance, I thought, was a fine one and very true – his great quality as an actor was his truthfulness, even when playing the 'silly ass' with which he had such success – and the discovery in the famous 'screen scene', as all the critics pointed out, was deeply moving and ranks him as one of the memorable Sir Peters. He would have gone into London with the show had Duncan Weldon not insisted on a nine-week provincial tour before opening in the West End. Ian simply didn't want to be away from his wife for that long (which I understood, the more so I'm now at the age he was then: as the end of your life approaches it becomes easier to see what your priorities are) so he left the company, which made Honor leave too and though their replacements were admirable (Moray Watson in Ian's part and Barbara Jefford, who was much better than Honor, as Lady Sneerwell) nobody really expected Duncan to bring the show in with only Dora as a name. And indeed he didn't.

Ian was always co-operative, not at all vain or 'starry' and we all liked him and wanted him to succeed. No one had any idea he wouldn't do another play, though it doesn't surprise me that he didn't. Being at home and with his wife was what he wanted to do the most, which is fair enough. I don't think we had contact later on beyond the odd Christmas card, but that's the nature of and one of the wonderful things about the theatre: you get very close to someone, then you don't see them for years perhaps but when you do, you pick up exactly where you left off before. I hope this is helpful and I hope, too, that you won't downplay the difficulties Ian had. The fact that he had them and managed to overcome them (all through his career) makes his achievement all the greater.[58]

Tim Wallers remembers Ian well. Now an established character actor in television, film and on the stage, with roles in the iconoclastic teenage drama *Skins*, as the father of the famous game show host in *Hughie Green: Most Sincerely* and in *Doctor Who*. Like many of the actors who worked with Ian late in his career, Wallers was part of a generation who had grown up in thrall to the charming man of British entertainment. 'We used to drive back to London on a Sunday night and my mum and dad always had *Lord Peter Wimsey* on the radio. We listened to it every single Sunday – I adored it. My dad was a big Wodehouse fan. My dad even looked like Ian Carmichael!'[59] Wallers continues:

I'd been [an actor] about five years. It was 1995 and [*The School for Scandal*] was one of my first jobs. I was thrilled – I really was *thrilled* – when I found out I was going to be working with Ian Carmichael. He was a big cricket fan as I am and I have since become a member of the club that he was wearing the tie for. He and I started talking cricket in rehearsals as all the cricketers find each other out. We all relied on Ian to know the score. I admired him not only for his love of cricket, but just generally he was everything I wanted him to be. If you chose to tap him on subjects that you wanted anecdotes about he could do it just like that. He was a very modest man.

I think he was very nervous of doing it, it was a big part. There was a lot of difficult language … I mean Ian was terrific in it but he *was* nervous. Even though he was nervous about the amount of lines, he had a lot of soliloquies he had to deliver to the audience and when he came on stage he had that same amiable quality that he had off stage and the audience loved him. I remember Ian was wearing his green tailcoat with the doily cuffs. He brought a lot of history with him, particularly to an audience such as at Chichester who were going to know all of it; they're going to know him from the Wooster days right forward. It was a great shame that he didn't do the tour and as a result we didn't go into town. Ian was that big a name that at seventy-five, if he decided not to do it, then the likelihood was that it might not go into the West End.

It was his amiable effortlessness that I liked, the way he was just able to do it ... I'm a great fan of that – I think it's wonderful. He had a terrific stage presence. There was a very famous scene in *The School for Scandal* where a screen comes down and behind it is Lady Teazle; Ian just used to stand there with one eyebrow raised just staring at her and it was priceless; the audience would just fall about: just the look, then the line. You're not going to get anyone who times a line better than Ian Carmichael.[60]

Like a lot of contemporary actors, Wallers recognised that Ian was the last of his kind.

Today the gentleman actor, of which he was the epitome, doesn't exist in the same way. I remember him telling me he used to film by day at Ealing and then go and do *The Gazebo*, or some other comedy play at night. That just doesn't happen very much now. His reputation, the prestige that comes with him is enormous. I fear, without getting too sentimental about it, we won't see his like again. We'll never have the insouciant Ian Carmichael or the bounder Terry-Thomas or the 'ding-dong' Leslie Phillips in the same way. We don't live in those times anymore.[61]

By now firmly re-established on television, both at the BBC *and* ITV, Ian saw out the 1990s with guest appearances in the historical drama *Branwell* and in Andrew Davies's adaptation of Elizabeth Gaskell's novel *Wives and Daughters* (on which he was reunited with a delighted Tim Wallers), playing Lord Cumnor. As with *Diamond Skulls*, Ian's part was a small, almost a background one, but the director Nichols Renton needed to cast someone who would be instantly identifiable as a reassuring symbol of the English Establishment. By now the elder statesman of British entertainment, Ian Carmichael was the only man in the running.

CHAPTER 17

At The Royal

Recognition as a national treasure and a television Indian summer

ON 8 DECEMBER 2002 at the National Film Theatre on the South Bank of the Thames, Ian finally received the kind of recognition that was long overdue, appearing for an on-stage interview that was the climax to a season of his film and television work billed as 'Ian Carmichael: A Man of Wit and Wimsey'. After a sold-out screening of *School for Scoundrels* and a selection of clips which encompassed *Tottie True*, *Private's Progress*, *I'm All Right Jack*, *Lucky Jim*, *The World of Wooster* and *Lord Peter Wimsey: Murder Must Advertise*, he was interviewed by the journalist and broadcaster Clive Jeavons, who introduced him as one of England's 'most endearing, most versatile and best-loved actors'[1] who had enjoyed an 'extraordinarily varied, eclectic career'[2]. To rapturous applause, Ian took the stage to reminisce with his customary charm, wit and insight about his personal odyssey through nearly fifty years of show business.

'I always had a bit of a buzz to do some performing,'[3] he recalled, going on to reflect on the people who inspired him: Jack Buchanan, Fred Astaire and Cary Grant. 'For a long time I wanted to be a musician and run a dance band, then I realised I didn't know anything about music, and I thought it'd be easier to become an actor.'[4] Asked later which Ian preferred, film or theatre, he replied:

In my early days in the '50s and '60s there was much more discipline in the [film] studios. Everybody worked to rule, you only worked a five-day week, you knocked off at 5.30 or whatever it was, you didn't work Bank Holidays. It was a much more ordered life so you were able to see your chums in the evening or at the weekend if you wanted to. With the theatre, you've got to be there every night, and you've got to keep yourself in check the *whole perishing day* for that two-and-a-half or three hours in the evening – watch you don't get tired, watch you don't have an extra drink. It's *very* restricting. So I think the answer is, for the actual work on the stage – THAT IS IT, nothing beats it, the live audience. But the life that went with it … I preferred the films, but all that's been changed now, because all those hours are gone; the union's strict control has gone.[5]

Being a discreet gentleman Ian politely refused to discuss 'corpsing', the actor's habit of bursting into uncontrollable laughter on stage, even though Dora Bryan had mentioned in the 1987 edition of her autobiography *According to Dora* her and Ian's tendency so to do during the run of *The Lyric Revue*. There then followed a lively, respectful and nostalgic journey through Ian's personal life and times, covering his adventures in the army, his rise to prominence as a revue artist, the Boulting brothers, the erratic behaviour of Hal E. Chester, through to his latter success at the BBC with *The World of Wooster*, *Bachelor Father* and *Lord Peter Wimsey*. Along the way there were mentions of old friends and colleagues Terry-Thomas, Peter Sellers, Moira Lister and Leo Franklyn, among others. Asked why he had never released an updated edition of his autobiography *Will the Real Ian Carmichael* …, he thoughtfully replied:

There are reasons I didn't want to continue. First of all, I had retired by then, and I wasn't doing much work. And if you haven't got a lot of work to tell anecdotes and stories about, people aren't interested. 'I went down to Tesco's today and bought this and that' – people aren't interested. And the other thing was I would have to go into my second marriage and I didn't particularly want to do that and open up that side. My second wife is here and she's an absolute darling, but I just didn't want to open that side [up]. Those two things put together is why I didn't want to go on.[6]

At the end of the evening, Ian informed the audience about his next project:

I've just done this series for Yorkshire Television which doesn't come out until early next year called *The Royal*. It's a spin-off from *Heartbeat* ... it's another hospital drama. It's a cottage hospital on the East Coast of Yorkshire at that period of 1969. Now at that [time], cottage hospitals were all run by the local GPs' practice, but it was the time that the National Health were trying to get in and get rid of all those little hospitals, so that gives it something a little bit different. And in the first series we do, a lot of the *Heartbeat* characters have occasion to come into the hospital, so it very much dovetails.[7]

Although, inexplicably and rather rudely, there was a ripple of laughter through the audience at the mention of *Heartbeat*, Ian's comments were followed by a clip from his upcoming series. Just before this intriguing preview, Jeavons brought proceedings to a close and thanked 'your present wife Kate Fenton for giving us a huge amount of help [with] your life story. We've been very dependent on her to get the dirt for this interview.'[8] Following a good-natured chuckle at Jeavons' quip from the audience, he concluded, 'Ian Carmichael, this has been an honour and a great pleasure,' to which Ian replied with an endearingly modest, 'It's been a great honour for me, I tell you,'[9] and the rapturous applause began again as this charming man left the stage to join friends and family for a celebratory drink in the green room.

The final vindication of Ian's standing as one of the best-loved actors in Britain came on 23 October 2003, when, in what could not have been a more fitting honour for a man who was such a committed and loyal patriot, he was awarded the Order of the British Empire. In one moving gesture of recognition from the Queen, any residual bitterness relating to Ian's blacklisting in the 1980s was completely erased. Asked what he would do if his grand new status increased his earning potential significantly, Ian replied that he would buy 'some absolutely *spiffing* clarets.'[10] Of course.

On 19 January 2003, *The Royal* began transmission on ITV with the episode 'First Impressions'. It was a conscious attempt by ITV to try and reclaim some of the ground they had lost to the BBC in the Sunday-night battle for ratings. The *Stage* reported, 'It is hoped that once the series is aired … it will help wrestle the initiative from BBC1 which last year [2001] attracted more viewers than ITV1 for the first time in the commercial channel's 50-year history.'[11]

TV writers John Flanagan and Andrew McCulloch were busy in the 2000s. Both had begun their careers as actors, with Flanagan notably featuring as Detective Sergeant Mathews in the first series of the iconoclastic 1970s police series *The Sweeney*. Up until the call came to work on *The Royal*, their writing commissions had included the fondly remembered sword-and-sorcery series *Robin of Sherwood* in the 1980s, the Sunday night 1990s community dramas *Ballykissangel* and *Heartbeat* and, in 1979, their first commission, devising a shape-changing cactus nemesis called Meglos for Tom Baker's last season as *Doctor Who*. The life of a TV writer is nothing if not varied.

Flanagan and McCulloch were something of a unique case: before becoming an actor, the latter had trained as a doctor, making the duo ideal candidates as writers on a medical drama. Ruminating on the philosophy behind *The Royal*, Flanagan remembers:

> Producer Ken Horn had a particular philosophy which was to use established, well-known, almost national treasures for a Sunday night-type audience and the casting of Wendy Craig and Ian Carmichael fell into that category. They were looking for people who had a resonance from earlier success on television and wanted to show the audience that they were still around. In setting something back in the 1960s and using actors who were around at that time, the feeling was that it would help to bridge the fact of setting it in the past. There was a conscious decision to try and get actors from that period. Honor Blackman played an occasional character that was a

patient in two or three episodes. I know the producer was keen on that kind of casting.

As it turned out, Ian was an excellent choice because he was perfect for the role, representing another era within something that was set in the 1960s. His character, T.J. Middleditch, represented the founders from an earlier era than the '60s when all the changes were afoot. The cottage hospital was under threat from the way the NHS was evolving at that time and he represented the values of an earlier part of the century, so in that sense, it was a perfect piece of casting. On a practical level, Ian lived, at that time, relatively close to Scarborough where the series was filmed and I think that was a consideration as well, because he must have been approaching 80.

My writing partner Andrew McCulloch and I were associated with *The Royal* throughout. Ian, obviously, wasn't getting any younger and we were cautioned not to give him too much towards the end of his time on the show, and not to be too taxing in what we wanted of the character. Scenes of him sitting in the office were fine, but we were not to give him too much activity because I think by that stage he was feeling the strain a bit. I think it was a mutual decision; he was never, as it were, killed off, he was only ever retired from the role that he had in the hospital and he was still in the background, he was still talked about and he still did make the odd guest appearance. He was never written out, he was only ever semi-retired. I think it was all due to the practicalities of filming with someone who was reaching an age where the rigours of TV production become too demanding on them. Filming can be an extremely tedious process, but it can also be very tiring for an actor of that age. You can be standing about for long periods waiting and then suddenly called into action and have to hit marks and hit lines. Its 'stop' for a long period of the day and then its 'go, go, go!' That kind of demand is particularly heavy on elderly actors. Ian didn't need to work, it was only a question of doing it if he enjoyed it, and I think he wanted to do it occasionally rather than all the time.

Ian had such a wonderful ease and charm as an actor. What I would describe it as is – and it's not an original phrase of mine, a theatre director used it – that he was an actor who'd got something like a 'comic bubble'. It's where they walk around in a 'bubble' that is comic rather than tragic. My director friend didn't say this about Ian; I'm using it in relation to him as he had a twinkle, which was akin to a 'comic bubble', and he would play the undercurrent of humour magnificently. When, as Middleditch, he was dealing with some escapade that had gone on in the hospital that was of a slightly comic nature, he played those scenes terrifically. Equally, he had wonderful scenes with Wendy Craig – he could easily be the mature man of wisdom. He was very good to write for. Once we saw what he was giving us, we liked to use him quite a lot and I think a lot of the other writers did that too. The problem was, the more you gave him the more demanding it was and you could be putting too much pressure on him. It was, 'Yes, use him, get as much as you can out of him, but don't overdo it.' Whenever we wrote something that he was in, we gave him a slightly humorous take because he could deliver it. He was a master of understated humour, and he had real warmth as a performer as well.

Andy and I are both still acting, actually, when the writing jobs dry up – I'm getting fairly ancient now – but I was actually cast in *The Royal* as the father of the leading female doctor played by Amy Robbins [Jill Weatherill]. I turn up for the wedding and I had to act with Ian, though there was only one scene. The character I was playing was a bit of a know-all, a self-made businessman from the Midlands who was a bit pompous. Middleditch found my character a bit of a strain, and Ian was superb because he was listening to me with this glazed expression and he was making the crew fall about because they vaguely know me with my writer's hat on and to see this elderly professional actor taking the piss, as it were, out of a slightly younger actor … I remember the scene very well. He was very good at conveying his utter boredom at what I was saying. I enjoyed that and it was a privilege to work with him as an actor as well, albeit briefly. Andy and I were very fond of him. Anyone who lived to that age and had a career like him had a few theatrical stories that always went down well. He was always good value; as far as I recall he still had the odd glass of wine. Once you got it in the can for the day, he didn't hang around for too long, but if you caught him for a glass of wine in the unit hotel he was always very sparky. He was a hugely professional guy. When he did work, he worked, he didn't let anyone down at all, he knew his lines, he knew his marks, he got tired sometimes but he certainly was a consummate professional.

He didn't have the sort of clout he would have had on *Lord Peter Wimsey* on *The Royal*, but he was still rather good and beady on the odd line. One of the things that Andy and I, being actor/writers, always feel we deliver is dialogue that actors can say. Which I think is a slight advantage of an actor/writer as opposed to just writers, who sometimes deliver a very good scene but some of the dialogue has got a syllable too many or a word too many in the sentence for the breathing pattern or for the delivery. Well, Ian had all the instincts and, without having stuff rewritten, if he found a way to deliver a line he would just deliver it. If it was pointed out to him by the Production Assistant that it wasn't exactly the line as written, he would say, 'Oh, is it not?' and he would still say it his way. If it was queried again, he would say 'I know it's not exactly what was written, but I *do* feel what I am saying sounds so much better, don't you? I think it's so much clearer.' He was very good at saying, 'If you move this word here and put it at the end it's funnier than if you leave it where it is, buried in the middle of the sentence.' He was very on the ball like that. Andy and I prided ourselves that he didn't move our words around too much, and we used to take that as a compliment. He would occasionally say something like, 'Jolly good script, liked that scene there, well done', which we always took as praise indeed. We do know from other writers he would occasionally, with a great deal of courtesy, change lines. He was the opposite of Hollywood's stamp-the-foot-and-slam-the-Winnebago-door brigade. There was this wonderful innocence of, 'Oh, is it not the right line?' His *modus operandi* was to actually say it his way and just get his way very gently. There was always method in his madness. What I'm saying is, his choices weren't out of ego – they actually made the line better and most people agreed with that.

I remember that the lead actor Robert [Daws] who played the main doctor Gordon Ormerod used a certain phrase when working with Ian. Robert wanted to get things right and was quite known for being particular about his scenes, except when he worked with Ian. If Ian made a suggestion he would go along with him. And Robert's phrase to us was, 'Well, what I've discovered is, it's rather like being in the navy – you should always give way to sail,' which I thought was lovely, as Ian Carmichael represented our 'sail', as it were. There comes a time that if you've been around the block as many times as Ian had and you've done all that stuff, anyone who's got any 'nous' will give way to sail or the equivalent thereof, because you don't survive that long in this business unless you're doing something right.[12]

Derek Fowlds was well known for playing opposite the Terry-Thomasesque puppet Basil Brush as 'Mr Derek' in the 1960s and 1970s and had played a civil servant who regularly helped bamboozle Jim Hacker (Paul Eddington) in *Yes Minister* and *Yes, Prime Minister*. Latterly Fowlds had been Sergeant and then publican Oscar Blaketon in *Heartbeat* throughout the 2000s. He came from a generation of actors who grew up watching Ian on the big screen. He recalls:

I was interested, like any kid in the '50s, in films, and I lived in a small country town where there were two cinemas which changed films every three days. Apart from playing football, cricket and ballroom dancing, and as there wasn't any television about in those days, the Rex and the Court cinemas were very important to me. I thought Ian Carmichael, in those films that he made in the fifties, was a brilliant comedy actor and I became an enormous fan of him in films like *School for Scoundrels*, *I'm All Right Jack* and *Simon and Laura*, so if he was in anything new, I always used to make certain that I saw the film.

So we cut now to years later when I'm doing *Heartbeat* and sitting in the pub with Ann Reid who was a guest artist and I said, 'Where have you been?' and she said, 'I've just had tea with Ian Carmichael' and I said, '*What*? *The* Ian Carmichael?' and she said, 'Yes, he lives in Grosmont', which was just down the road, and I said, 'I'd give anything to meet him' and she said, 'Well, I'll arrange it.' When she told him that I wanted to meet him, he said I was in his favourite programme *Yes, Prime Minister*, and that he would love to meet me. So we met. William Simons, who I worked with in *Heartbeat* was also a great fan of his, so Bill and I became presidents of the Ian

Carmichael Fan Club and we often went up and had lunch and dinner with him. We *so* enjoyed his company.'

With an actor of Ian's quality languishing virtually just down the road from a *Heartbeat* spin-off in the making, it was only a matter of time before the powers that be asked him to become involved. 'We couldn't think who to cast for Middleditch in *The Royal*. We'd been racking our brains,'[13] says Ken Horn, who had produced *Heartbeat* and was now preparing *The Royal*. 'We all went to the funeral for Bill Simons' wife, and Ian was there. Immaculately dressed, he walked up to the front of the church and did a reading. The authority, the dignity, the command, the warmth and the humanity we wanted were all there right in front of us.'[14]

'I think he got very tired towards the end,' Fowlds reflects, thinking about Ian's years on *The Royal*. 'I think he really enjoyed working again and he was wonderful in [*The Royal*]. I mean, he was in his eighties, he still had incredible energy and he was a great raconteur. He was very funny and witty, very warm and extremely kind to both Bill and myself, and we became very good friends with Ian and his lovely wife, Kate. She adored Ian and they were very, very happy. She called him the "old boy!"'

'There isn't a lot of work for the older actor,' Fowlds suggests. 'I think Ian was thrilled to go to work again. Once you get into your seventies like my contemporaries and I, where do you find the really good parts to play? They don't write them, and if they do, Jim Broadbent and Michael Gambon play them all.'[15] Perhaps surprisingly, Fowlds is critical of the direction *The Royal* ultimately took: 'In the end, they never wrote storylines for the older characters, they were just there as token characters. It developed into a soap for the younger actors, instead of developing stories for Ian and Wendy Craig.'

It's easy to be cynical about Sunday night family TV dramas. Screened around 7 p.m. or 8 p.m. before a large percentage of the audience are preparing for work the next day, they are designed as escapism – particularly those set in the past – lionising a perhaps mythical golden age of British community spirit. Gary Leboff, writing in the *Sun* and discussing *The Royal*'s predecessor *Strathblair*, observed that 'TV bosses seem to think that turning the clock back several decades each Sunday night is the best way to deal with the terrifying prospect of Monday morning. Turning it back to Friday night would do for me.'[16]

The Royal bucked this trend to some extent. Among the comedy escapades that usually involved the accident-prone hospital porter Ken Hopkirk (Michael Starke) and later Jack Bell (Gareth Hale), their gormless assistant Alun Morris (Andy Wear) and the gobby receptionist with a heart of gold Lizzie Hopkirk (Michelle Hardwick), there were storylines about a Swinging London photographer who poisoned his models with magic mushrooms, a child being born to a nun's unmarried Catholic sister and a mentally unstable woman who pretended to be pregnant so she could steal a baby from the Royal. In particular, there was a running storyline set during the vicious Nigerian-Biafran War of 1967–1970 that had one of the hospital's young doctors volunteering for aid work in the besieged refugee camps in Africa.

The *Guardian*'s TV critic recognised what *The Royal* was doing. 'It may sound ghastly, but *The Royal* was actually great. How could you fail to warm to a show that features Wendy Craig as a plain-speaking matron in a frilly white cap, ably assisted by a nursing nun called Sister Brigid?'[17] the reviewer wrote enthusiastically, noting 'Ian Carmichael was suavely camp as the harassed hospital secretary'[18]. The writer continued, 'Maybe it's cynical of ITV to produce such genre TV, and it's true that *The Royal* is breaking no new ground. It's nostalgic, it's reactionary, but it's also strangely sophisticated. There were enough in-jokes about "the new commercial channel" to show that someone at ITV has a sense of humour; the episode ended with [an] entire ward gathering around for *Coronation Street*. TV eating itself again.'[19]

Ian's character T.J. Middleditch (first introduced in the 2002 *Heartbeat* episode 'Out of the Blue' to trail the spin-off series) was the moral compass and the moral arbiter of the series. Wearing a slightly foppish bow tie, ambling along the Royal's corridors and greeting the staff on a first-name basis, he harnessed all the arresting qualities Flanagan, Horn and Fowlds had so admired. Like Ian himself, Middleditch radiated warmth, wit and wisdom, making an appealing double act with Wendy Craig's stern matron (who, needless to say, deep down also had a heart of gold).

As the series developed, there is something to Derek Fowlds' criticism that the younger characters started becoming more prominent. In the eighth series, Adam Carnegie (Robert Cavanah) the proto-yuppie administrator who replaced Middleditch, began secretly dating Matron's sexy but thoughtless niece Susie Dixon (Sarah Beck Mather) who worked at the Royal as a nurse. This coincided with Ian being relegated to a recurring guest role; the really frustrating thing was that as *The Royal* ended its run on ITV so abruptly, there was no resolution to Middleditch's ongoing story.

After a lengthy absence due to internal politics at ITV, *The Royal* returned to ITV1 on Sunday 5 June 2011 with the episode 'Any Old Iron' which featured the last scene that Ian shot before he died. No one knew when the episode was written and filmed that it would be the last acting performance he would ever give. Like the cameo he made in *Diamond Skulls*, Ian is very much in the background and has very little dialogue. Attention is focused on Middleditch's wife Elizabeth (Susan Hampshire), in hospital for an operation. Ian hovers at the side of the doctors and consultants, concerned, dutiful and supporting, all qualities that the audience would have recognised from his previous roles. When Mrs Middleditch is given the wrong blood by Susie Dixon in a transfusion, her husband is mortified: Middleditch doesn't say anything, just sits in the corridor outside his wife's room, looking into the distance with an unreadable expression on his face as Matron, lost for words, sits down beside him. It's a refined, dignified and subtle end to Ian's screen career. 'Wendy was so moved by his performance that she burst into tears,' Horn remembers.

As a tribute to Ian, the closing credits were followed by a portrait of him with the simple testimonial, 'In memory of Ian Carmichael: 18th June 1920 – 5th February 2009.'

Alison Graham, the rather caustic ex-editor of and reviewer in the *Radio Times*, welcomed the return of *The Royal*'s generic feel-good factor: 'There's still the same laboured farce, the same creaking slapstick, the same cloying sentiment liberally applied with a trowel, and the same literal use of music. (Someone leaves, so Dusty Springfield croons "If You Go Away" on the soundtrack.) All are thrown together with the subtlety of a cement mixer to produce the wonder that is *The Royal*. I will miss it, I really will.'[20] *Metro* agreed with her: 'It's hard to come down too hard on a show that shoehorns Joni Mitchell, Cream and vintage Rolling Stones into the action. Though what Cream's "I Feel Free" had to do with a lifeboat rescue is anyone's guess: a coded message from the music picker?'[21]

'When Ian left we presented him with the portrait of Middleditch that used to hang on the set,' Horn says with a smile. 'He took it home and, as far as I know, it's still hanging up in his house somewhere.'[22] The producer recalls one particular incident that, in retrospect, is a heart-warming summation of Ian's entire career:

> We were in the editing suite one day, and we'd just got to the part of the scene we were working on where Ian was doing one of his marvellous surprised looks that everyone loved so much. Now, Yorkshire Television used to run old films during the afternoon. And I swear this is true, but when we freeze-framed [the part of the scene] we wanted to work on, on the monitor opposite that showed what was being transmitted on Yorkshire TV Ian was doing *exactly* the same expression in *I'm All Right Jack*! Amazing and, in a strange way, quite moving.[23]

Horn concludes simply, 'We [the cast and production team] all went to his funeral. It was very sad.'[24]

CHAPTER 18

Goodbye, Old Man

Ian passes on but his legacy endures

On 8 February 2010, it was announced in the British press that Ian Gillett Carmichael had died at the age of eighty-nine after falling ill over the previous Christmas, his long and happy life curtailed at the eleventh hour by cancer, just as Pym's had been.

Tributes to the man were legion. Speaking in the *Guardian*, his *Simon and Laura* co-star Richard Briers praised Ian as 'a splendid straight man surrounded by eccentrics. I think he played that best with Peter Sellers and Terry-Thomas in *I'm All Right Jack*. He was an excellent foil for others and particularly good at playing a sort of dim but very well-mannered English gentleman. He was never pushy, he sort of wandered through the world of film.'[1] In the same paper Brian Blessed, the oversized actor best known for the series *I, Claudius* and the 1980 film *Flash Gordon*, celebrated Ian as 'a national treasure and a consummate artist,'[2] while Michael Parkinson, who had enjoyed the company of Ian on his BBC chat show in 1979, simply said 'he was a charming man and a very good comedy actor.'[3] Elsewhere, Ann Reid sweetly commented that Ian had 'a lot of style. He belonged to an age of elegance.'[4]

Ian did, indeed, come from a distinguished club of gentlemen actors that included Richards Attenborough and Todd, Terry-Thomas, Laurence Olivier, Jack Hawkins, Ralph Richardson, John Mills, Patrick Macnee, John Gielgud, Richard Burton, Dennis Price,

Jon Pertwee, Roger Moore, John Le Mesurier, Patrick McGoohan, Herbert Lom, Richard Todd, Peter Wyngarde and John Gregson, among others. Before they achieved fame, often well into their thirties, they'd already lived the kind of lives today's young men would only recognise from improbable action films or violent computer games. Most of Ian's generation had fought a war in their early twenties, and inspiring examples of Britain's 1940s youth under fire are many: Ian was in command of a unit of the flail tanks which detonated mines on the killing fields of Normandy, Todd parachuted into battle on D-Day itself and Macnee had been a lieutenant on a Motor Torpedo Boat, fighting German E-Boats at sea and rescuing survivors of the ill-fated Arnhem raid behind Nazi lines from the Dutch coast. Such experiences made a man grow up extremely fast, so by the time these gentleman actors slapped on the greasepaint, they brought a seasoned, mature authenticity to whatever role they were playing, which often included army officers. That's why they were so special.

Ian Ogilvy as Grayson, the 'School Bully' in Michael Palin and Terry Jones' 1975 *Ripping Yarns* pilot show *Tomkinson's Schooldays*, is clearly an affectionate take on Ian's Wooster and Wimsey but, as a whole, the series pastiched the defiantly old-fashioned English genres Ian became famous in, such as country house mysteries, wartime prison breaks and colonial epics. *Ripping Yarns'* gleeful lampooning, casting an irreverent, knowing eye on Britain's imperial and cultural past, showed just how passé Ian's patriotic values had become by the mid-1970s. Ian's allegiance to Queen and country, something he was proud of throughout his whole life, was distinctly unfashionable between 1970 and 1979, when Britain couldn't have fallen further from its status as the imperial nation that his characters were synonymous with. Nevertheless, Ian remained extremely loyal to his wartime regimental comrades in the 22nd Dragoons, attending without fail every year the Remembrance Day service at Helmsley, where the 22nd had been stationed at Duncombe Park during the war.

In recent years, Colin Firth, Simon Pegg, Martin Freeman and

David Tennant (who delivered the memorable bounder Sir Piers Ponsonby in *St Trinian's 2: The Legend of Fritton's Gold*) have all played lovable, well-educated losers who triumph in the final reel and endear themselves to the audience in the process, just as Ian did. Number one in this category is Hugh Grant, who is funny, self-effacing *and* posh, playing roles that would have fitted Ian like one of Bertie Wooster's cashmere gloves in *Four Weddings and a Funeral* (1994), *Notting Hill* (1999) and *Love, Actually* (2003). *Little Britain*'s David Walliams, as well as being a very clever, chameleonic funny man, is equally well-spoken and well turned-out, no matter what time of the morning or which nightclub he happens to be leaving.

On YouTube, a well put-together spoof of the popular 1980s US action show *The A Team* called *The I Say! Team* – 'In 1945, four bounders left the British army ...' – 'starring' Kenneth Williams, Leslie Phillips and Terry-Thomas (no Ian, sadly) with, naturally, Sid James as B.A. Barracus, showed that, in the Britain of 2011, there remained a fondness for the kind of impeccably tailored, upright and, crucially, amusing fellow who had been an integral part of British society from the Second World War up until 1970.

Nicholas Parsons sums up Ian the man and Ian the actor very movingly:

> As someone who was really very fond of Ian and had huge respect for his talent, I think his memory has somewhat been eclipsed and I think that's probably because he wasn't working until the day he died. I do think Ian was one of our most exceptional comedy actors with the most impeccable timing and he created some of the most memorable, memorable roles. But he wasn't what we would call a personality actor; in other words, his personality didn't shine through at the expense of the role, he brought the character, the part, to life – he was it. It was superb acting, wonderful interpretive character-acting with, I think, some of the best comedy timing anybody could possibly have had. And a lovely fellow, utterly natural and so easy to get along with.[5]

The last word goes to Derek Fowlds, who towards the ends of his life got to know Ian perhaps better than anyone during his semi-retirement in Yorkshire:

> I always sent him a card on his birthday and at Christmas and he always replied (I've got all his notes), 'Hello, Fowlds, old boy!' He was charming, a true gentleman, a wonderful actor. He was honoured later in life, but I felt he should have been honoured long before he was. He was underrated. He was a huge star of the British cinema, all through the fifties and the early sixties. He got top billing in films that included Peter Sellers and other luminaries. Ian was *very* special and I was so pleased to meet him and just thrilled, really. We had many happy hours together. I had favourite actors like Montgomery Clift and Marlon Brando when I was growing up, but the British actor, the one that I *always* looked forward to seeing, was Ian Carmichael, as I thought he was a genius. Always nervous and diffident, but the true English gent.[6]

Notes

Introduction

1 Quoted in Laing, *Representations of Working-Class Life*, p.89

Chapter 1

1 Carmichael, *Will the Real Ian Carmichael* ..., p.ix, Book Club Associates, 1979
2 *Ibid.*, p.14
3 *Ibid.*
4 *Ibid.*, p.15
5 *Ibid.*, p.16
6 *Ibid.*
7 *Ibid.*, p.17
8 *Ibid.*
9 *Ibid.*
10 *Ibid.*, p.17
11 *Ibid.*
12 *Ibid.*, p.18
13 *Ibid.*
14 *Ibid.*, p.20
15 *Ibid.*
16 *Ibid.*, pp.20–21
17 *Ibid.*
18 *Ibid.*
19 *Ibid.*, p.23
20 *Ibid.*, p.23
21 *Ibid.*

Chapter 2

1 Carmichael, *Will the Real Ian Carmichael* ..., p.24, Book Club Associates, 1979
2 *Ibid.*, p.27
3 *Ibid.*
4 *Ibid.*, p.31
5 *Ibid.*
6 *Ibid.*, p.31
7 *Ibid.*, p.35

Chapter 3

1 Carmichael, *Will the Real Ian Carmichael* ..., p.40, Book Club Associates, 1979
2 *Ibid.*
3 *Ibid.*, p.43
4 *Ibid.*, p.46–47
5 Ian Carmichael National Film Theatre interview, 8 December 2002
6 Carmichael, *Will the Real Ian Carmichael* ..., p.47, Book Club Associates, 1979
7 *Ibid.*, p.48
8 *Ibid.*, p.49
9 *Ibid.*, p.49
10 Ian Carmichael National Film Theatre interview, 8 December 2002
11 Quoted in Carmichael, *Will the Real Ian Carmichael* ..., p.58, Book Club Associates, 1979
12 Quoted in Carmichael, *Will the Real Ian Carmichael* ..., p.62, Book Club Associates, 1979
13 *Ibid.*, p.63
14 *Ibid.*
15 *Ibid.*, pp.64–65
16 *Ibid.*, p.65
17 *Ibid.*
18 *Ibid.*, p.69
19 *Ibid.*
20 *Ibid.*, p.69
21 *Ibid.*, p.70
22 *Ibid.*, p.71

Chapter 4

1 Carmichael, *Will the Real Ian Carmichael* ..., p.72, Book Club Associates, 1979
2 *Ibid.*, p.73
3 *Ibid.*, p.74
4 *Ibid.*

5 *Ibid.*
6 *Ibid.*, p.75
7 *Ibid.*
8 *Ibid.*, p.77
9 Ian Carmichael National Film Theatre interview, 8 December 2002
10 *Ibid.*, p.78
11 *Ibid.*, p.80
12 *Ibid.*, p.86
13 Macnee, Patrick, with Marie Cameron, *Blind in One Ear*, pp.12–13. Harrap, 1988
14 Carmichael, *Will the Real Ian Carmichael* …, p.97, Book Club Associates, 1979
15 *Ibid.*, p.100
16 *Ibid.*, p.102
17 *Ibid.*, p.105
18 *Ibid.*, p.107
19 *Ibid.*, p.109
20 Carmichael, *Will the Real Ian Carmichael* …, p.115, Book Club Associates, 1979
21 *Ibid.*, p.117
22 *Ibid.*, p.118
23 *Ibid.*
24 *Ibid.*
25 *Ibid.*, pp.118–119
26 *Ibid.*, p.120
27 *Ibid.*, p.127
28 *Ibid.*, p.150
29 *Ibid.*
30 *Ibid.*, p.159
31 *Ibid.*, p.160
32 *Ibid.*, p.162
33 *Ibid.*, p.164
34 *Ibid.*, p.166
35 *Ibid.*, p.174
36 *Ibid.*, pp.174–175
37 *Ibid.*, p.181
38 *Ibid.*, pp.182–183
39 *Ibid.*, p.183
40 *Ibid.*, p.184
41 Ian Carmichael National Film Theatre interview, 8 December 2002
42 *Ibid.*
43 *Ibid.*
44 Carmichael, *Will the Real Ian Carmichael* …, p.188, Book Club Associates, 1979
45 *Ibid.*, p.190
46 *Ibid.*, p.192

Chapter 5

1 Carmichael, *Will the Real Ian Carmichael* …, p.195, Book Club Associates, 1979
2 *Ibid.*, p.199
3 Ian Carmichael National Film Theatre interview, 8 December 2002
4 *Ibid.*
5 Carmichael, *Will the Real Ian Carmichael* …, p.204, Book Club Associates, 1979
6 *Ibid.*
7 The *Stage*, 4 December 1947
8 Carmichael, *Will the Real Ian Carmichael* …, p.205, Book Club Associates, 1979
9 The *Stage*, 9 October 1947
10 *Ibid.*
11 Carmichael, *Will the Real Ian Carmichael* …, p.208, Book Club Associates, 1979
12 *Ibid.*
13 Nicholas Parsons interview with author, 9 August 2010

Chapter 6

1 Memo from Television Bookings Manager to IC c/o Richard Stone, 21 May 1947
2 Letter from Ian Carmichael to Television Bookings Manager, 23 May 1947
3 Ian's BBC Television audition card, 2 June 1947
4 Letter from BBC Television Bookings Manager to Ian Carmichael, 16 July 1947
5 Carmichael, *Will the Real Ian Carmichael* …, p.212, Book Club Associates, 1979
6 Author Interview with Valerie Leon, 19 September 2010
7 *Ibid.*
8 Carmichael, *Will the Real Ian Carmichael* …, p.214, Book Club Associates, 1979
9 Ian Carmichael National Film Theatre interview, 8 December 2002
10 *Ibid.*
11 *Ibid.*
12 Ian Carmichael interview at the National Film Theatre, 8 December 2002
13 Carmichael, *Will the Real Ian Carmichael* …, p.223, Book Club Associates, 1979
14 Ian Carmichael National Film Theatre interview, 8 December 2002

15 Carmichael, *Will the Real Ian Carmichael* ..., p.223, Book Club Associates, 1979

16 Ian Carmichael National Film Theatre interview, 8 December 2002

17 Quoted in Carmichael, *Will the Real Ian Carmichael* ..., p.226, Book Club Associates, 1979

18 The *Stage*, 1 September 1949

19 Ian Carmichael National Film Theatre interview, 8 December 2002

20 *Ibid.*

21 Carmichael, *Will the Real Ian Carmichael* ..., p.231, Book Club Associates, 1979

22 Ian Carmichael National Film Theatre interview, 8 December 2002

23 Carmichael, *Will the Real Ian Carmichael* ..., pp.206–7, Book Club Associates, 1979

24 *Ibid.*

25 Nash, *Star*, 27 November 1953

26 Carmichael, *Will the Real Ian Carmichael* ..., p.241, Book Club Associates, 1979

27 Letter from Ian Carmichael to BBC Head of Light Entertainment Ronald K. Waldman, 5 November 1950

28 Programme listings, *Radio Times* for the week 31 December 1950

29 Ian Carmichael National Film Theatre interview, 8 December 2002

30 Internal BBC memo, 19 February 1952

31 *Ibid.*

32 Carmichael, *Will the Real Ian Carmichael* ..., p.244, Book Club Associates, 1979

33 Quoted in Carmichael, *Will the Real Ian Carmichael* ..., p.246, Book Club Associates, 1979

34 Author interview with Nicholas Parsons, 9 August 2010

35 Quoted in Carmichael, *Will the Real Ian Carmichael* ..., p.248, Book Club Associates, 1979

36 *Ibid.*, p.249

37 *Ibid.*, p.250

38 *Ibid.*

39 Bryan, *According to Dora*, pp.73–74, Hodder and Stoughton, 1987 edition

40 *Ibid.*

41 Ian Carmichael National Film Theatre interview, 8 December 2002

42 Quoted in Carmichael, *Will the Real Ian Carmichael* ..., p.256, Book Club Associates, 1979

43 *Ibid.*

44 *Ibid.*, p.262

45 Ian Carmichael National Film Theatre interview, 8 December 2002

46 *Ibid.*

47 *Ibid.*

48 Mosley, 'Fade out: gone with the years is the gay-guy Gable I knew', *Daily Express*, 19 August 1954

49 Nash, the *Star*, 20 August 1954

50 Majdalany, *Time and Tide*, 28 August 1954

51 Carmichael, *Will the Real Ian Carmichael* ..., p.265, Book Club Associates, 1979

52 'The New Films by Peter Burnap', *Evening News*, 13 November 1954

53 Nash, the *Star*, 11 November 1955

54 Powell, *Sunday Times*, 13 November 1955

55 Graham, *Spectator*, 11 November 1954

56 *The Dam Busters* review, *Time Out Film Guide: Eighth Edition*, Penguin Books, 1999

57 Carmichael, *Will the Real Ian Carmichael* ..., p.266, Book Club Associates, 1979

58 *Ibid.*

59 Bullock, 'Going Up the Ladder: Ian Carmichael's work in Revue', the *Stage*, 18 February 1954

60 Carmichael, *Will the Real Ian Carmichael* ..., p.273, Book Club Associates, 1979

61 Johnson, *Evening News*, 27 November 1955

62 Conway, *Daily Sketch*, 25 November 1955

63 Maydaley, *Daily Mail*, 26 November 1955

64 'Oh! What a bash at the Telly', *Daily Herald*, 25 November 1955

65 'Television's Ideal Married Couple', *The Times*, 24 November 1955

Chapter 7

1 *Movie Memories*, Anglia Television, 1985

2 Carmichael, *Will the Real Ian Carmichael* ..., p.280, Book Club Associates, 1979

3 Lindsay Anderson, quoted in Sinyard, '1950s British Cinema', *Screenonline*, 2011

4 Carmichael, *Will the Real Ian Carmichael* ..., p.280, Book Club Associates, 1979

5 Ian Carmichael National Film Theatre interview, 8 December 2002

6 *Ibid.*

7 Carmichael, *Will the Real Ian Carmichael…*, p.280, Book Club Associates, 1979

8 Ian Carmichael National Film Theatre interview, 8 December 2002

9 *Movie Memories*, Anglia Television, 1985

10 Roy Boulting, quoted in McFarlane, *An Autobiography of British Cinema*, p.79

11 'The Army won't aid Army film by *Daily Mail* Reporter', *Daily Mail*, 8 September 1955

12 Griffith, *The Fool's Pardon* p.175, Warner Books, 1994

13 Mosley, 'Army satire', *Daily Herald*, 17 February 1956

14 Harman, 'Gad, Sir! Is THIS the army?', *Evening News*, 16 February 1956

15 Dehn, 'A satire', *Northern Chronicle*, 17 February 1956

16 Nash, *Star*, 17 February 1956

17 Schulman, 'So THIS is the Army', *Sunday Express*, 19 February 1956

18 'The Army as a film joke – *Private's Progress*', *The Times*, 20 February 1956

19 Harman, 'Gad, Sir! Is THIS the army?', *Evening News*, 16 February 1956

20 White, 'Don't blame star for shelved film', *Daily Sketch*, 24 July 1956

21 Thompson, *Tribune*, 4 May 1956

22 'Army cooperation in film show stopped', *The Times*, 6 March 1956

23 *Ibid.*

24 Carmichael, *Will the Real Ian Carmichael …*, p.282, Book Club Associates, 1979

25 Wilson, 'Rank boss says it is not funny enough', *Daily Mail*, 23 July 1956

26 Ian Carmichael National Film Theatre interview, 8 December 2002

27 *Ibid.*

28 Carmichael, *Will the Real Ian Carmichael …*, p.283, Book Club Associates, 1979

29 Ian Carmichael National Film Theatre interview, 8 December 2002

30 *Ibid.*

31 White, 'Don't blame star for shelved film', *Daily Sketch*, 24 July 1956

32 Wilson, 'Rank boss says it is not funny enough', *Daily Mail*, 23 July 1956

33 White, 'Don't blame star for shelved film', *Daily Sketch*, 24 July 1956

34 *Brothers in Law* press release, early 1957

35 Quoted in Hinxman, 'Britain's Conquering Clown' part 1, *Picturegoer*, 9 March 1957

36 *Ibid.*

37 Hinxman, 'Britain's Conquering Clown' part 1, *Picturegoer*, 9 March 1957

38 *Ibid.*

39 *Ibid.*

40 Hinxman, 'Britain's Conquering Clown' part 1, *Picturegoer*, 9 March 1957

41 *Ibid.*

42 'An outstanding British comedy – Boulting Brothers take a look at the law by our London film critic', *Manchester Guardian*, 2 March 1957

43 Conway, 'They make an ass of the Law, and the Boulting brothers prove you can – take the mickey – make money', *Daily Sketch*, 1 March 1957

44 Oakes, 'Laughter in court – and this is the Boulting brothers creating it', *Evening Standard*, 28 February 1957

45 Carthew, 'Justice has been done – by the terrible twins', *Daily Herald*, 1 March 1957

46 'An outstanding British comedy – Boulting Brothers take a look at the law by our London film critic', *Manchester Guardian*, 2 March 1957

47 Dehn, *News Chronicle*, 1 March 1957

48 Conway, 'They make an ass of the Law, and the Boulting brothers prove you can – take the mickey – make money', *Daily Sketch*, 1 March 1957

49 Author correspondence with Lucy Boulting, 21 February 2011

50 Carmichael, *Will the Real Ian Carmichael …*, p.286, Book Club Associates, 1979

51 Pritchett, *New Statesman*, 20 August 1955

52 Waugh, *Encounter*, December 1955

53 Maugham, *Sunday Times*, 25 December 1954

54 Quoted in Ross, *The Complete Terry-Thomas*, p.98, Reynolds and Hearn, 2002

55 Ian Carmichael National Film Theatre interview, 8 December 2002

56 *Ibid.*

57 Quoted in Ross, *The Complete Terry-Thomas*, p.98, Reynolds and Hearn

58 Lewin, '*Lucky Jim* film chiefs quit', *Daily Express*, 3 December 1956

59 Wilson, 'Two quit in row over film', *Daily Mail*, 3 December 1956

60 Lewin, '*Lucky Jim* film chiefs quit', *Daily Express*, 3 December 1956

61 Carmichael, *Will the Real Ian Carmichael* ..., p.289, Book Club Associates, 1979

62 Myers, 'Satire gone in *Lucky Jim*', *Daily Telegraph*, 19 August 1957

63 Wilson, 'Brewer's Dray? On a Sunday? Unthinkable', *Daily Mail*, 19 August 1957

64 Myers, 'Satire gone in *Lucky Jim*', *Daily Telegraph*, 19 August 1957

65 Frank, '*Lucky Jim* is film fun', *News Chronicle*, 19 August 1957

66 Anderson, 'Dismal Jimmy', *New Statesman*, 5 October 1957

67 Ian Carmichael National Film Theatre interview, 8 December 2002

68 Quoted in Ross, *The Complete Terry-Thomas*, p.98, Reynolds and Hearn, 2002

69 Quoted in 'Not so *Lucky Jim* – comments by critics', *Daily Telegraph*, 2 September 1958

70 Carmichael, *Will the Real Ian Carmichael* ..., p.289, Book Club Associates, 1979

71 McCalren, *Time and Tide*, 1 March 1958

72 Watson, 'So chaotic so noisy so English', *Daily Mail*, 21 February 1958

73 *News of the World*, 23 February 1958

74 Dixon, 'No strangers', *Daily Telegraph*, 22 February 1958

75 Quoted in Ross, *The Complete Terry-Thomas*, p.101, Reynolds and Hearn, 2002

76 Janette Scott interview with author, 22 November 2010

77 *Ibid.*

78 *Ibid.*

79 *Ibid.*

80 *Ibid.*

81 *Ibid.*

82 *Ibid.*

83 *Ibid.*

84 Memo from Eric Maschwitz, Head of Light Entertainment Television, BBC, to Kenneth Adam, Controller of Programmes, 1 July 1960

85 *Ibid.*

86 Frank, '*Lucky Jim* is film fun', *News Chronicle*, 19 August 1957

Chapter 8

1 Carmichael, *Will the Real Ian Carmichael* ..., p.295, Book Club Associates, 1979

2 *Ibid.*, p.294

3 Tynan, *Observer*, 13 May 1956

4 Carmichael, *Will the Real Ian Carmichael* ..., p.295, Book Club Associates, 1979

5 *Ibid.*

6 *Ibid.*, p.295

7 *Movie Memories*, Anglia Television, 1985

8 Quoted in Carmichael, *Will the Real Ian Carmichael* ..., p.296, Book Club Associates, 1979

9 *Ibid.*

10 *Ibid.*, p.297

11 *Ibid.*, p.297

12 'Happy baby hunting in *The Tunnel of Love*', the *Stage*, 5 December 1957

13 Marriott, 'Ian Carmichael only wants to play in comedy', the *Stage*, p.8, 27 December 1957

14 *Ibid.*

15 *Ibid.*

16 *Ibid.*

17 *Ibid.*

18 Marriott, 'Ian Carmichael only wants to play in comedy', the *Stage*, p.8, 27 December 1957

19 *Ibid.*

20 Letter from Ian Carmichael to Leslie Bridgemont, 7 May 1958

21 Carmichael, *Will the Real Ian Carmichael* ..., p.301, Book Club Associates, 1979

22 Ian Carmichael National Film Theatre interview, 8 December 2002

23 Sandbrook, *You've Never Had It So Good: A History of Britain from Suez to the Beatles*, p.442, Abacus, 2008 edition

24 Barker, *Evening News*, 29 May 1958

25 Oates, *Sunday Dispatch*, 1 June 1958

26 *Manchester Guardian*, 31 May 1958

27 *Ibid.*

28 Oates, *Sunday Dispatch*, 1 June 1958

29 Betts, *The People*, 1 June 1958

30 Powell, *Sunday Times*, 1 June 1958

31 Ian Carmichael National Film Theatre interview, 8 December 2002

32 Carmichael, *Will the Real Ian Carmichael* ..., p.298, Book Club Associates, 1979

33 *Ibid.*, p.299

34 Robinson, *Financial Times*, 20 July 1959

35 *Ibid.*

36 Powell, *Sunday Times*, 19 July 1959

37 Carthew, *Daily Herald*, 17 July 1959

38 Ian Carmichael National Film Theatre interview, 8 December 2002

39 *Ibid.*

40 Shanks, *The Stagnant Society*, p.85, Harmondsworth, 1961, quoted in Sandbrook, *You've Never Had It So Good: A History of Britain from Suez to the Beatles*, p.351, Abacus, 2008 edition

41 Hibbin, *Daily Worker*, 28 February 1959

42 Sandbrook, *You've Never Had It So Good: A History of Britain from Suez to the Beatles*, p.351, Abacus, 2008 edition

43 Ian Carmichael National Film Theatre interview, 8 December 2002

44 Waterman, 'What will Cousins say?', *Evening Standard*, 13 August 1959

45 Ian Carmichael National Film Theatre interview, 8 December 2002

46 Dehn, *News Chronicle*, 14 August 1959

47 Adams, *The Star*, 13 August 1959

48 Betts, *The People*, 16 August 1959

49 *Time*, 2 May 1960

50 Dehn, *News Chronicle*, 14 August 1959

51 Adams, *Star*, 13 August 1959

52 *Media Guardian*, 15 August 1959

53 Robinson, *Financial Times*, 17 August 1959

54 Robinson, *Financial Times*, 17 August 1959

55 Mallory, '*I'm All Right Jack* breaks the record,' 11 December 1959

56 'Films by Jympson Harman', *Evening News*, 13 August 1959

57 Dehn, *News Chronicle*, 14 August 1959

58 Carthew, 'Shop steward Sellers shows us up,' *Daily Herald*, 14 August 1959

59 Hibbin, *Daily Worker*, 28 February 1959

60 Vyse, *Daily Worker*, 15 August 1959

61 *Ibid.*

62 Waterman, 'What will Cousins say?', *Evening Standard*, 13 August 1959

63 Adams, *The Star*, 13 August 1959

64 Delaney, *Daily Mail*, 14 August 1959

65 'Films by Jympson Harman', *Evening News*, 13 August 1959

66 Ian Carmichael National Film Theatre interview, 8 December 2002

67 Moseley, 'I've just seen Peter Sellers finally escape from the Goons!', *Daily Express*, 12 August 1959

68 Burnap, 'Big Business gets the works', *News of the World*, 16 August 1959

69 Quigley, *The Spectator*, 21 August 1959

70 Ian Carmichael National Film Theatre interview, 8 December 2002

71 Carmichael, *Will the Real Ian Carmichael* ..., p.303, Book Club Associates, 1979

Chapter 9

1 Carmichael, *Will the Real Ian Carmichael* ..., p.303, Book Club Associates, 1979

2 *Ibid.*

3 Thomas, quoted in Quoted in Ross, *The Complete Terry-Thomas*, p.110, Reynolds and Hearn

4 Powell, *Sunday Times*, 27 March 1960

5 Author interview with Janette Scott, 22 November 2010

6 *Ibid.*

7 *Ibid.*

8 Scott, quoted in Quoted in Ross, *The Complete Terry-Thomas*, p.116, Reynolds and Hearn

9 Carmichael, *Will the Real Ian Carmichael* ..., Book Club Associates, 1979

10 Author interview with Janette Scott, 22 November 2010

11 Ian Carmichael National Film Theatre interview, 8 December 2002

12 Carmichael, *Will the Real Ian Carmichael* ..., p.304, Book Club Associates, 1979

13 Ian Carmichael National Film Theatre interview, 8 December 2002

14 Ian Carmichael National Film Theatre interview, 8 December 2002

15 *Ibid.*
16 Carmichael, quoted in Ross, *The Complete Terry-Thomas*, p.118, Reynolds and Hearn
17 Janette Scott interview with author, 22 December 2010
18 Lewis, *Southern Dispatch*, 27 March 1960
19 *Ibid.*
20 Robinson, *Financial Times*, 28 March 1960
21 Hackerer, *Time And Tide*, 2 April 1960
22 Janette Scott interview with author, 22 December 2010
23 Patrick Macnee correspondence with author, 3 August 2010
24 *School for Scoundrels* Associated British Elstree press pack, 1960
25 Adams, *The Star*, 24 March 1960
26 Powell, *Sunday Times*, 27 March 1960
27 Monsey, *Sunday Express*, 27 March 1960
28 Hudis, quoted in Ross, *The Carry On Story*, p.27, Reynolds and Hearn, 2005
29 Phillips, *Hello: The Autobiography*, p.215, Orion Books Ltd, 2007 edition
30 'Ian Carmichael in Molière musical', the *Stage*, p.17, 3 September 1959
31 *Ibid.*
32 Carmichael, *Will the Real Ian Carmichael* ..., p.305, Book Club Associates, 1979
33 *Ibid.*, p.306
34 *Ibid.*
35 *Ibid.*, p.306
36 *Ibid.*, p.307
37 Marriott, 'If only *The Love Doctor* had been a hit!', the *Stage*, p.17, 3 September 1959
38 Carmichael, *Will the Real Ian Carmichael* ..., p.307, Book Club
39 *Ibid.*
40 *Ibid.*
41 *Ibid.*
42 *Guardian*, 9 July 1960
43 Harman, 'What Dad did in the war', *Evening News*, 6 July 1960
44 Hibbin, *Daily Worker*, 9 July 1960
45 Gibbbs, *Daily Telegraph*, 9 July 1960

Chapter 10

1 Carmichael, *Will the Real Ian Carmichael* ..., p.309, Book Club Associates, 1979
2 *Ibid.*

3 *Ibid.*, p.310
4 *Ibid.*
5 *Ibid.*
6 *Ibid.*
7 Ian Carmichael National Film Theatre interview, 8 December 2002
8 Carmichael, *Will the Real Ian Carmichael* ..., p.311, Book Club Associates, 1979
9 Marriott, 'Ian Carmichael pivot of *The Gazebo*', the *Stage*, 31 March 1960
10 *Ibid.*
11 Carmichael, *Will the Real Ian Carmichael* ..., p.313, Book Club Associates, 1979
12 *Ibid.*, p.313
13 Janette Scott interview with author, 22 November 2010
14 *Ibid.*
15 *Ibid.*
16 *Ibid.*
17 Perrick, 'The worst for my money', *Daily Mail*, 30 March 1961
18 *Ibid.*
19 *Evening News*, 30 March 1961
20 Dent, *Sunday Telegraph*, 2 April 1961
21 'The new films by Peter Burnap', *News of the World*, 2 April 1961
22 Hibbin, *Daily Worker*, 2 April 1961
23 Gilliatt, *Observer*, 2 April 1961
24 Ian Carmichael National Film Theatre interview, 8 December 2002
25 *Ibid.*
26 *Ibid.*
27 Carmichael, *Will the Real Ian Carmichael* ..., p.314, Book Club Associates, 1979
28 *Ibid.*, p.316
29 *Ibid.*, p.318
30 *Ibid.*
31 *Ibid.*
32 Programme listings, *TV Times*, 1 September 1961
33 'Laughter in the City', *TV Times*, 1 September 1961
34 *Ibid.*
35 *Ibid.*
36 *Ibid.*, p.325
37 *Ibid.*, p.320
38 *Ibid.*, p.321
39 *Ibid.*, p.322
40 *Ibid.*, p.320

41 *Ibid.*, p.323
42 'Notes on Broadcasting: How to lure the floating viewer. From our special correspondent', *The Times*, 6 January 1962
43 Author interview with Bridget Armstrong, 24 May 2011
44 *Ibid.*
45 *Ibid.*
46 Kaplan, *Time*, 8 November 1962
47 *Guardian*, 10 November 1962
48 Breen, *Observer*, 11 November 1962

Chapter 11

1 Carmichael, *Will the Real Ian Carmichael* …, p.323, Book Club Associates, 1979
2 *Double Bunk* press pack, 1961
3 Ian Carmichael National Film Theatre interview, 8 December 2002
4 Carmichael, *Will the Real Ian Carmichael* …, p.324, Book Club Associates, 1979
5 Ian Carmichael National Film Theatre interview, 8 December 2002
6 Carmichael, *Will the Real Ian Carmichael* …, p.324, Book Club Associates, 1979
7 *Ibid*, p.304
8 Ian Carmichael National Film Theatre interview, 8 December 2002
9 *Ibid.*
10 *Ibid.*
11 Powell, *Sunday Times*, 21 June 1964
12 Pacy, *Daily Herald*, 19 June 1964
13 Hibdin, *Daily Worker*, 20 June 1964
14 Walker, 'Twisting', *Evening Standard*, June 1964
15 Barker, *Evening News*, 18 June 1964
16 Wilson, 'On the difference between Hitchcock and halfcock', *Daily Mail*, 20 June 1964
17 Pacy, *Daily Herald*, 19 June 1964
18 Oakes, 'Drab Hybrid', *Sunday Telegraph*, 21 June 1964
19 *The Times*, 18 June 1964
20 Hamilton, *Daily Express*, 20 June 1964
21 *Ibid.*
22 Carmichael, *Will the Real Ian Carmichael* …, p.304, Book Club Associates, 1979
23 *Hide and Seek* press sheet, British Empire Films, 1964

24 Carmichael, *Will the Real Ian Carmichael* …, p.330, Book Club Associates, 1979
25 *Case of the 44's* press release, 1965
26 Ian Carmichael National Film Theatre interview, 8 December 2002
27 *Screen International*, March 1964
28 Letter from Ian Carmichael to Robin Whitworth, BBC Drama Booking Manager, 17 August 1964
29 Letter from Richard Stone to the BBC's Bill Ward, 5 May 1949
30 Quoted in Rogers, *The Avengers*, p.13, ITV Books and Michael Joseph, 1983
31 Leonard White interview with author, 8 November 2010
32 Richard, *Oscar Wilde*, Vintage Books. 1988
33 Fenella Fielding interview with author, 2010
34 *Ibid.*
35 *Ibid.*
36 *Ibid.*
37 Susannah York interview with author, 26 July 2010
38 *Ibid.*
39 *Ibid.*
40 Carmichael, *Will the Real Ian Carmichael* …, p.330, Book Club Associates, 1979
41 Reviews, *Television Today*, 26 November 1964
42 Fenella Fielding interview with author, 2010
43 Susannah York interview with author, 26 July 2010
44 Lockwood, 'Television – Importance of being Oscar Wilde', *Daily Telegraph*, 16 November 1964
45 Quoted in White, *Armchair Theatre – The Lost Years*, p.125, Kelly Publications, 2003
46 Leonard White interview with author, 8 November 2010
47 Macnee, Patrick, with Marie Cameron, *Blind in One Ear*, page 236. Harrap, 1988
48 Ian Carmichael National Film Theatre interview, 8 December 2002
49 Telegram from Laurence Olivier to Ian Carmichael, 1 November 1964
50 Carmichael, *Will the Real Ian Carmichael* …, p.333, Book Club Associates, 1979

51 *Ibid.*, p.331

52 *Ibid.*, p.332

53 Ian Carmichael National Film Theatre interview, 8 December 2002

54 Gerald Harper interview with author, 9 February 2011

55 *Ibid.*

56 *Ibid.*

57 Carmichael, *Will the Real Ian Carmichael* ..., p.335

58 Gerald Harper interview with author, 9 February 2011

59 *Ibid.*

60 *Ibid.*

61 *Ibid.*

62 Carmichael, *Will the Real Ian Carmichael* ..., p.336

63 Gerald Harper interview with author, 9 February 2011

64 Nicholas Parsons interview with author, 9 August 2010

65 Gerald Harper interview with author, 9 February 2011

66 Carmichael, *Will the Real Ian Carmichael* ..., p.337

Chapter 12

1 Quoted in Collins, 'I learn my lines while the children are at school', *Radio Times*, 9 September 1971

2 Pollock, 'Ian Carmichael and the World of Wooster', *Radio Times*, 17 June 1965

3 Memo from Eric Maschwitz, Head of Light Entertainment Television, BBC, to Kenneth Adam, Controller of Programmes, 1 July 1960

4 Memo from Dennis Main Wilson to Michael Mills, 15 July 1963

5 Pollock, 'Ian Carmichael and the World of Wooster', *Radio Times*, 17 June 1965

6 *Ibid.*

7 Letter from Ian Carmichael to Michael Mills, 15 February 1965

8 Telegram from producer Michael Mills to Ian Carmichael at the Hotel Algonquin, 59 West 44th Street in New York, 19 February 1965

9 Wodehouse, *The World of Jeeves*, p.295, Arrow Books, 2008 edition

10 *Ibid.*, p.302

11 BBC memo, 8 March 1965

12 Letter from Constance Chapman to Michael Mills, 5 April 1965

13 Letter from composer Sandy Wilson to Michael Mills, 21 April 1965

14 Letter from Robin Lowe of Christopher Mann Ltd to Michael Mills, 6 April 1965

15 Carmichael, *Will the Real Ian Carmichael* ..., p.340, Book Club Associates, 1979

16 Ian Carmichael National Film Theatre interview, 8 December 2002

17 Pollock, 'Ian Carmichael and the World of Wooster', *Radio Times*, 17 June 1965

18 Wright, 'Points from the Post', *Radio Times*, 17 June 1965, 19–25 June 1965 issue

19 Banks-Smith, 'The World of Wooster', *The Sun*, 15 January 1966

20 Letter from P.G. Wodehouse to the *The World of Wooster* team, 19 July 1965

21 Note from Joe McGrath to Michael Mills, date unknown

22 Carmichael, *Will the Real Ian Carmichael* ..., p.342, Book Club Associates, 1979

23 *Ibid.*, p.340

24 Letter from Sandy Wilson to Michael Mills, 2 March 1966

25 'What Would I Do Without Jeeves?', words and music by Sandy Wilson, 1965

26 Winsor, 'Acting It up on the Esk: at 50 plus, Ian Carmichael decided it was time to enjoy himself', *Sunday Telegraph*, 27 May 1979

27 *Ibid.*

28 'This is where I switch off. By Ian Christie', *Daily Express*, 29 December 1967

29 *Ibid.*

30 'One late wish for Santa: Films by Ann Pacey', *The Sun*, 28 December 1967

31 Prowse, *Sunday Times*, 31 December 1967

32 Bean, 'Robin Bean finds the Swingers in squeezy-land', *Films and Filming*, February 1968

33 *Ibid.*

34 Marriott, 'Fifty Years', the *Stage*, 23 May 1968

35 Ian Carmichael obituary, the *Daily Telegraph*, 8 February 2010

36 *TV Times* for the week of 22 October 1968
37 Milne, *The Times*, 3 December 1971
38 *Ibid.*
39 Malcolm, *Guardian*, 2 December 1971
40 *Ibid.*
41 Barker, 'The New Film', *Evening News*,
   2 December 1971
42 Melly, *Observer*, 5 December 1971

Chapter 13

1 Carmichael, *Will the Real Ian Carmichael*
   ..., pp.371–2, Book Club Associates, 1979
2 *Ibid.*, p.373
3 Author interview with Nicholas Parsons, 9
   August 2010
4 Briony McRoberts interview with the
   author, 11 July 2010
5 Carmichael, *Will the Real Ian Carmichael*
   ..., p.368, Book Club Associates, 1979
6 *Ibid.*
7 *Ibid.*, p.369
8 *Ibid.*
9 Quoted in Collins, 'I learn my lines while
   the children are at school', *Radio Times*,
   9 September 1971
10 *Ibid.*
11 *Ibid.*
12 Briony McRoberts interview with the
   author, 11 July 2010
13 *Ibid.*
14 Briony McRoberts interview with the
   author, 11 July 2010
15 *Ibid.*
16 Quoted in Richmond, 'How I stopped
   being frightened of television', *Radio
   Times*, 12–18 September 1970
17 *Ibid.*
18 *Ibid.*
19 *Ibid.*
20 *Ibid.*
21 Carmichael, *Will the Real Ian Carmichael*
   ..., p.370, Book Club Associates, 1979
22 Jackson, 'Farewell party for the bachelor',
   Daily Express, 11 November 1971
23 Briony McRoberts interview with the
   author, 11 July 2010
24 Carmichael, *Will the Real Ian Carmichael*
   ..., p.370, Book Club Associates, 1979
25 *Ibid.*

26 Briony McRoberts interview with the
   author, 11 July 2010
27 Banks-Smith, 'Alma Mater', *Guardian*, 8
   January 1971
28 Black, 'This Founder's Day Farce went on
   a bit too long', *Daily Mail*, 8 January 1971
29 Banks-Smith, 'Alma Mater', *Guardian*, 8
   January 1971
30 Black, 'This Founder's Day Farce went on
   a bit too long', *Daily Mail*, 8 January 1971
31 *Ibid.*
32 Author interview with Linda Thorson, 26
   June 2011
33 Author correspondence with Ann
   Holloway, 27 May 2011

Chapter 14

1 Carmichael, *Will the Real Ian Carmichael*
   ..., p.380, Book Club Associates, 1979
2 *Ibid*, p.345
3 Winsor, 'Acting It up on the Esk: at 50
   plus, Ian Carmichael decided it was time
   to enjoy himself', *Sunday Telegraph*, 27
   May 1979
4 Sayers, *The Unpleasantness at the Bellona
   Club*, pp.31–32, New English Library,
   2003 edition
5 Sayers, *Murder Must Advertise*, p.2, New
   English Library, 2003 edition
6 Carmichael, *Will the Real Ian Carmichael*
   ..., p.380, Book Club Associates, 1979
7 *Ibid.*, p.381
8 Memo from John Ecclestone, Head of
   Programme Planning (Forward)
   Television to Ronald Marsh, Head of
   Serials, 30 June 1970
9 Memo from Donald Wilson, Senior
   Producer Drama Serials, to Ronald Marsh,
   Head of Serials, 21 September 1970
10 Letter from Angela Hepburn at Ian's
   agents London Management to Ronald
   Marsh, 16 October 1970
11 Memo to Ronald Marsh, Head of Serials,
   29 October 1970
12 Letter from writer John Brason to Ian
   Carmichael, 13 November 1970
13 Note from Ian Carmichael to Shaun
   Sutton, 18 December 1971

14 Letter from Angela Hepburn to Shaun Sutton, 30 April 1971

15 Memo from Shaun Sutton, Head of Drama Group, Television, to Ronald Marsh, Head of Serials, 6 January 1971.

16 Letter from Ian to Head of Serials Ronald Marsh, 14 January 1971

17 Letter from Angela Hepburn to Shaun Sutton, 30 April 1971

18 Letter from Angela Hepburn at London Management to Shaun Sutton, 30 April 1971

19 Memo from Betty Willingale, Television Script Unit, to Ronald Marsh, 7 may 1971

20 Memo from Shaun Sutton, Head of Drama Group, to Ronald Marsh, Head of Serials, 12 May 1971

21 Letter from Richard Beynon to Ronald Marsh, 1 August 1971

22 Letter from Ian via London Management to Ronald Marsh, 15 September 1971

23 Letter from Ian via London Management to Ronald Marsh, 15 September 1971

24 *Ibid.*

Chapter 15

1 Amis, 'Whodunnit, Lord Peter?', *Radio Times*, p.7, 30 March 1972

2 *Ibid.*

3 *Ibid.*

4 *Ibid.*

5 *Clouds of Witness* episode 4, BBC1, TX. 26 April 1972

6 Author interview with cast member, 20 January 2011

7 *Ibid.*

8 *Ibid.*

9 Author interview with cast member, 20 January 2011

10 Author interview with Rachel Herbert, 1 October 2011

11 Quoted in Phillips, 'Wimsey's a stuck-up snob, says his valet', *The Sun*, 1 September 1973

12 *Ibid.*

13 *Ibid.*

14 Letter from Ian via London Management to Ronald Marsh, 15 September 1971

15 'Letters', *Radio Times*, 25 May 1972

16 *Ibid.*

17 *Ibid.*

18 'Letters', *Radio Times*, 8 June 1972

19 Alpert, 'Will You Take Breakfast in Bed, My Lord?', *Saturday Review*, 9 October 1973

20 *Ibid.*

21 *Ibid.*

22 *Ibid.*

23 *Ibid.*

24 Ian Carmichael National Film Theatre interview, 8 December 2002

25 Ian Carmichael National Film Theatre interview, 8 December 2002

26 Dignam, *Morning Star*, 22 February 1973

27 Banks-Smith, 'Sayers Thriller', *Guardian*, 1 February 1973

28 *Ibid.*

29 Last, *Daily Telegraph*, 16 February 1973

30 Due to lack of studio allocations at the BBC TV centre in London, production of the second *Wimsey* serial was moved to the BBC's Pebble Mill facilities in Birmingham

31 Memo from Ronald Marsh, Head of Serials, Drama, to producer Richard Beynon, 6 July 1972

32 *Ibid.*

33 *Ibid.*

34 Greenwood, 'Lord Peter is angry about his lost cases', *The Sun*, 30 November 1973

35 *Ibid.*

36 *Ibid.*

37 *Ibid.*

38 Memo from Shaun Sutton

39 *Ibid.*

40 Penn, 'A typical auntie', *Radio Times*, 22 November 1973

41 James, 'Television: Redeeming appearances', *Observer*, 2 February 1973

42 Author correspondence with Paul Darrow, 9 September 2010

43 Author interview with Bridget Armstrong, 24 May 2010

44 *Ibid.*

45 Author interview with Rodney Bennett, 8 November 2010

46 *Ibid.*

47 *Ibid.*

48 Ian Carmichael National Film Theatre interview, 8 December 2002

49 Usher, *Daily Mail*, 24 April 1974

50 Reynolds, 'The Nine Tailors', *The Times*, 7 May 1974

51 *Ibid.*

52 Letter from London Management to John Moore, contracts manager for *Five Red Herrings*, 19 August 1974

53 Ian Carmichael National Film Theatre interview, 8 December 2002

54 Author interview with Phyllida Law, 3 March 2011

55 *Ibid.*

56 *Ibid.*

57 Donovan, 'Stiff upper fillip. Bounders beware ... the 'silly ass' Englishman is back with a vengeance. By Paul Donovan', *Daily Mail*, 21 November 1978

58 *Ibid.*

59 *Daily Mail*, 10 November 1978

60 *Ibid.*

61 Author interview with Gerald Harper, 9 February 2011

62 Donovan, 'Stiff upper fillip. Bounders beware ... the 'silly ass' Englishman is back with a vengeance. By Paul Donovan', *Daily Mail*, 21 November 1978

63 *Ibid.*

64 *Ibid.*

65 *Ibid.*

66 *Ibid.*

67 Simons, *Daily Express*, 12 May 1979

68 *Ibid.*

69 Malcolm, *Guardian*, 10 May 1979

70 Andrews, *Financial Times*, 11 May 1979

71 Winsor, 'Acting it up on the Esk: At 50 plus, Ian Carmichael decided it was time to enjoy himself', *Sunday Telegraph*, 27 May 1979

72 *Ibid.*

73 Winsor, 'Acting it up on the Esk: At 50 plus, Ian Carmichael decided it was time to enjoy himself', *Sunday Telegraph*, 27 May 1979

74 Ian Carmichael National Film Theatre interview, 8 December 2002

75 *Ibid.*

76 *Ibid.*

77 Winsor, 'Acting it up on the Esk: At 50 plus, Ian Carmichael decided it was time to enjoy himself', *Sunday Telegraph*, 27 May 1979

78 *Ibid.*

79 *Ibid.*

Chapter 16

1 Hepple, 'Haymarket: *Overheard*', the *Stage*, 2 April 1981

2 *Ibid.*

3 Braun, 'Richmond: *Overheard*', the *Stage*, 14 May 1981

4 *Ibid.*

5 Author Interview with Robert Putt, 15 February 2011

6 *Ibid.*

7 Attenborough and Hawkins, *Entirely Up to You, Darling*, p.251, Windsor Paragon, 2009

8 Paton, *Daily Express*, 28 December 1983

9 David, *The Times Educational Supplement*, 27 April 1984

10 Ian Carmichael National Film Theatre interview, 8 December 2002

11 *Ibid.*

12 Ian Carmichael National Film Theatre interview, 8 December 2002

13 The *Stage*, 16 July 1987

14 *Ibid.*

15 The *Stage*, 16 July 1987

16 Author interview with Nick Broomfield, 31 January 2011

17 *Ibid.*

18 Author correspondence with Lucy Boulting, 21 February 2011

19 Author interview with Nick Broomfield, 31 January 2011

20 Malcolm, *Midweek*, 7 June 1990

21 Andrews, *Financial Times*, 7 June 1990

22 Kupfermann, 'A gem of hope and vainglory', *Daily Mail*, 17 August 1990

23 'Playing the obituaries game', *Daily Telegraph*, 17 August 1990

24 Author interview with David Robb, 10 July 2010

25 *Ibid.*

26 Author interview with Briony McRoberts, 11 July 2010

27 *Ibid.*

28 Author interview with Francesca Hunt, 19 July 2010

29 *Ibid.*

30 *Ibid.*

31 Author interview with Leonard White, 20 July 2010

32 Author interview with David Robb, 10 July 2010

33 Author interview with Francesca Hunt, 19 July 2010

34 *Ibid.*

35 Berkmann, *Daily Mail*, 20 July 1992

36 *Ibid.*

37 Leboff, *The Sun*, 28 June 1993

38 Stephen, *New Statesman & Society*, 2 July 1993

39 Author interview with Leonard White, 20 July 2010

40 *Ibid.*

41 'Glen gets its act together', *Mail on Sunday*, 8 August 1993

42 Author interview with Francesca Hunt, 19 July 2010

43 *Ibid.*

44 Author interview with David Robb, 10 July 2010

45 *Ibid.*

46 Kate Fenton website, 28 May 2011

47 Author interview with Julian Dyer, 10 January 2011

48 *Ibid.*

49 Author interview with Terry Winsor, 15 January 2011

50 *Ibid.*

51 Author interview with Terry Winsor, 15 January 2011

52 Morrow, 'The great escape – losing touch with the march of time', *Time Out*, 12–19 April 1995

53 Banks-Smith, *Guardian*, 15 April 1995

54 Phillips, *Evening Standard*, 13 April 1995

55 Day-Lewis, *Today*, 15 April 1995

56 Day-Lewis, *Sunday Telegraph*, 9 April 1994

57 Hazlitt, *Lectures of the English Poets and the English Comic Writers*, George Bell and Sons, 1876

58 Author correspondence with Richard Cottrell, 28 February 2011

59 Author interview with Tim Wallers, 21 February 2011

60 Author interview with Tim Wallers, 21 February 2011

61 *Ibid.*

Chapter 17

1 Ian Carmichael National Film Theatre interview, 8 December 2002

2 *Ibid.*

3 *Ibid.*

4 *Ibid.*

5 *Ibid.*

6 *Ibid.*

7 *Ibid.*

8 *Ibid.*

9 Ian Carmichael National Film Theatre interview, 8 December 2002

10 Obituary, *Daily Telegraph*, 8 February 2010

11 Dowell, 'Hospital drama is *Heartbeat* "sister"', the *Stage*, 23 May 2002

12 Author interview with John Flanagan, 11 November 2010

13 Author interview with Ken Horn, 8 May 2011

14 *Ibid.*

15 Author interview with Derek Fowlds, 24 November 2010

16 Leboff, *The Sun*, 28 June 1993

17 *Guardian*, 20 January 2002

18 *Ibid.*

19 *Ibid.*

20 Graham, 'Drama: *The Royal*', *Radio Times*, 4–10 June 2011

21 *Metro*, 6 June 2011

22 *Ibid.*

23 *Ibid.*

24 *Ibid.*

Chapter 18

1 Obituary, *Guardian*, 8 February 2010

2 *Ibid.*

3 *Ibid.*

4 Obituary, *The Times*, 8 February 2010

5 Author interview with Nicholas Parsons, 8 August 2010

6 Author interview with Derek Fowlds, 24 November 2010

Bibliography

Archive

The British Film Institute, 21 Stephen Street, London W1T 1LN

BBC Written Archives Centre, Peppard Road, Caversham Park, Reading RG4 8TZ

Ian Carmichael interview at the National Film Theatre, chaired by Clive Jeavons, 8 December 2002 (courtesy of the BFI)

Interviews, phone conversations and correspondence

Bridget Armstrong, London, 24 May 2011

Rodney Bennett, 8 November 2010

Lucy Boulting, 21 February 2011

Nick Broomfield, Santa Monica, 31 January 2011

Richard Cottrell, Australia, 28 February 2011

Paul Darrow, 9 September 2010

Julian Dyer, London, 10 January 2011

Fenella Fielding, London 2010

John Flanagan, Castle Cary, 11 November 2010

Derek Fowlds, Wiltshire, 24 November 2010

Gerald Harper, London, 9 February 2011

Rachel Herbert, London, 1 October 2010 and 20 January 2011

Ann Holloway, 27 May 2011

Ken Horn, Cheshire, 23 April 2011

Francesca Hunt, 19 July 2010

Phyllida Law, London, 3 May 2011

Valerie Leon, London, 19 September 2011

Abigail McKern, 22 February 2011

Briony McRoberts, Manchester, 11 July 2010

Patrick Macnee, 2 August 2010

Nicholas Mcardle, 12 July 2010

Nicholas Parsons, Edinburgh, 8 August 2010

Robert Putt, London, 15 February 2011

Robert Rietti, Birmingham, 20 November 2010

David Robb, Manchester, 10 July 2010

Janette Scott, Runcorn, 17 November 2010

Linda Thorson, Chichester, 26 June 2011

Susannah York, London, 26 July 2010

Leonard White, Newhaven, 20 July 2010

Tim Wallers, London, 21 February 2011

Terry Winsor, London, 15 January 2011

Biographies

Attenborough, Richard and Hawkins, Diana, *Entirely Up to You, Darling* (Windsor Paragon, 2009)

Bryan, Dora, *According to Dora* (Hodder and Stoughton, 1987)

Carmichael, Ian, *Will the Real Ian Carmichael . . .* (Book Club Associates, 1979)

Fisher, John, *Tony Hancock: The Definitive Biography* (Harper Collins, 2009)

Eden, Mark, *Who's Going to Look at You?* (Matador, 2010)

Griffith, Kenneth, *The Fool's Pardon* (Warner Books, 1995)

Lewishon, Mark, *Funny, Peculiar: The True Story of Benny Hill* (Pan Books, 2003)

McCann, Graham, *Bounder! The Biography of Terry-Thomas* (Aurum Press, 2008)

McCann, Graham, *Is That Wise? The Biography of John Le Mesurier* (Aurum Press, 2010)

McCann, Graham, *Spike and Co* (Hodder & Stoughton, 2006)

Phillips, Leslie, *Hello: The Autobiography* (Orion Books, 2007)

Rietti, Robert, *A Forehead Pressed Against a Window* (Ari Scharf Publishing, 2010)

Ross, Robert, *The Complete Terry-Thomas* (Reynolds and Hearn, 2002)

Sykes, Eric, *If I Don't Write It Nobody Else Will* (Harper Perennial, 2006)

Background

Barnes, Alan and Hearn, Marcus, *Kiss Kiss Bang! Bang! The Unofficial James Bond Film Companion* (Batsford, 2000)

Coward, Simon, Down, Richard and Perry, Christopher, *The Kaleidoscope British Independent Television Drama Research Guide 1955–2005* (Kaleidoscope Publishing, 2005)

Coward, Simon, Down, Richard and Perry, Christopher, *The Kaleidoscope BBC Television Drama Research Guide 1936–2006* (Kaleidoscope Publishing, 2006)

Crawford, Steve, *Strange but True Military Facts* (Pen & Sword Military, 2010)

Docherty, Mark J. and McGown, Alistair D., *The Hill and Beyond: Children's Television Drama: An Encyclopedia* (BFI, 2003)

Fairclough, Robert, *The Prisoner: The Official Companion to the Classic TV Series* (Carlton Books, 2002)

Fairclough, Robert (editor), *The Prisoner: The Original Scripts, Volume 2* (Reynolds and Hearn, 2006)

Fairclough, Robert and Kenwood, Mike, *Sweeney! The Official Companion* (Reynolds and Hearn, 2002)

Ganzal, Kurt, *Musicals* (Carlton Books, 1995)

Geldof, Bob, and Vallely, Paul, *Is That It?* (Penguin Books, 1986)

Hazlitt, William, *Lectures of the English Poets and the English Comic Writers* (George Bell and Sons, 1876)

Lewishon, Mark, *Radio Times Guide to TV Comedy* (BBC Worldwide, 1998)

Marsh, Graham and Nourmand, Tony, *Film Posters of the 60s* (Aurum Press, 1997)

Miles, Barry, *The Beatles Diary, Volume 1: The Beatles Years* (Omnibus Press, 2001)

Nourmand, Tony, *James Bond Film Posters* (Boxtree, 2001)

Pym, John (editor), *Time Out Film Guide, Eighth Edition* (Penguin Books, 1999)

Rogers, Dave, *The Avengers* (ITV Books and Michael Joseph, 1983)

Ross, Robert, *The Carry On Story* (Reynolds and Hearn, 2005)

Sandbrook, Dominic, *You've Never Had It So Good: A History of Britain from Suez to the Beatles* (Abacus, 2008)

Screen International (May 1964)

Sandbrook, Dominic, *White Heat: A History of Britain in the Swinging Sixties* (Abacus, 2009)

Sheridan, Simon, *Keeping the British End Up: Four Decades of Saucy Cinema* (Reynolds and Hearn, 2005)

Turner, W. Alwyn, *The Man Who Invented the Daleks: The Strange Worlds of Terry Nation* (Aurum Press, 2011)

Various, *National Film Theatre Programmes 2002* (BFI, 2002)

Various, *Variety Film Reviews, Volume 9: 1954–1958* (R.R. Bowker, 1983)

Various, *Variety Film Reviews, Volume 10: 1959–1963* (R.R. Bowker, 1983)

Various, *Variety Film Reviews, Volume 11: 1964–1967* (R.R. Bowker, 1983)

Winnert, Derek (editor), *The Ultimate Encyclopedia of the Movies* (Carlton, 1995)

White, Leonard, *Armchair Theatre: The Lost Years* (Kelly Publications, 2003)

Williams, George and Kenwood, Mike, *Fags, Slags, Blags and Jags: The Sweeney* (Uslag, 1998)

Wood, Tat, *About Time: The Unauthorized Guide to Doctor Who 1970–1974, Seasons 7 to 11* (Mad Norwegian Press, 2009 expanded edition)

Fiction

Sayers, Dorothy L., *Clouds of Witness* (New English Library, 2003)

Sayers, Dorothy L., *Five Red Herrings* (New English Library, 2003)

Sayers, Dorothy L., *Murder Must Advertise* (New English Library, 2003)

Sayers, Dorothy L., *The Nine Tailors* (New English Library, 2003)

Sayers, Dorothy L., *The Unpleasantness at the Bellona Club* (New English Library, 2003)

Sayers, Dorothy L., *Whose Body?* (New English Library, 2003)

Wodehouse, P.G., *The World of Jeeves* (Arrow Books, 2008)

Selected articles

Anonymous, 'Ian Carmichael: Unassuming star of 1950s light comedies who found fresh fame on television as Wooster and Wimsey', *Daily Telegraph* obituary (8 February 2010)

Bullock, George, 'Going up the ladder: Ian Carmichael's work in revue', the *Stage*, 18 February 1954

Dacre, Richard, 'Great Britons: Ian Carmichael', *Video Times*, November 1989

Alpert, Hollis, 'Will You Take Breakfast in Bed, My Lord?', *Saturday Review*, 9 October 1973

Hinxman, Margaret, 'Britain's Conquering Clown', *Picturegoer*, 2 March 1957

Hinxman, Margaret, 'A private's progress of his own. Ian Carmichael: Britain's Conquering Clown Part II', *Picturegoer*, 9 March 1957

Fiddy, Dick, 'The Archive Presents: The Boulting Brothers', 'Ian Carmichael: A Man of Wit and Wimsey', National Film Theatre programme, December 2002

Fiddy, Dick, 'Carmichael on TV', National Film Theatre programme, December 2002

Kupfermann, Jeanette, 'A gem of hope and vainglory', *Daily Mail*, 17 August 1990

Marriott, R.B., 'Ian Carmichael just wants to play comedy', the *Stage*, 27 December 1957

Slade, Alison, 'By Royal Appointment', *TV Times*, 19 January 2003

Periodicals

Picture Show & Film Pictorial, Volume 69, No. 1,805, 2 November 1957

The Danger Man Collection (DeAgostini, 2004; 2005–2006)

Ian's plays and musicals

RUR (1938)
Nine Sharp (1940)
Springtime for Henry (1942)
Between Ourselves (1947)
She Wanted a Cream Front Door (1947)
The Late Joys (1947)
Out of the Frying Pan (1947)
Cupid and Mars (1947)
Tomorrow is a Lovely Day (1948)
What Goes On (1948)
The Lagoon Follies (1948)
The Lilac Domino (1949)
Wild Violets (1949)
The Lyric Revue (1951)
The Globe Revue (1952)
High Spirits (1953)
At the Lyric (1954)
Going to Town (1954)
Simon and Laura (1951)
The Tunnel of Love (1958)
The Love Doctor (1959)
The Gazebo (1960)
Critic's Choice (1961)
Devil May Care (1963)
Sunday in New York (1963)
March Hares (1964)
Boeing-Boeing (1964)
Say Who You Are (1965–66)
Getting Married (1967)
I Do! I Do! (1968)
Birds on the Wing (1969)
Ridgeway's Late Joys (1969)
Springtime for Henry (1974)
Out on a Limb! (1976)
Overheard (1981)
Pride and Prejudice (1987)
The School for Scandal (1995)

Ian's films

Bond Street (1948)
Trottie True (1949)
Dear Mr Prohack (1949)
Time, Gentlemen, Please! (1952)
Ghost Ship (1952)
Miss Robin Hood (1952)
Meet Mr Lucifer (1953)
Betrayed (1954)

The Colditz Story (1955)
Simon and Laura (1955)
Private's Progress (1956)
Brothers in Law (1957)
Lucky Jim (1957)
Happy is the Bride (1958)
The Big Money (1958)
Left, Right and Centre (1959)
I'm All Right Jack (1959)
School for Scoundrels (1960)
Light up the Sky! (1960)
Double Bunk (1961)
Heaven's Above! (1963)
The Amorous Prawn (1962)
Hide and Seek (1964)
Case of the 44s (1965)
Smashing Time (1967)
The Magnificent Seven Deadly Sins (1971)
From Beyond the Grave (1973)
The Lady Vanishes (1979)
Diamond Skulls (1989)

Ian's main TV productions

New Faces (1947, BBC)
Twice Upon A Time (1948, BBC)
Tricks of the Trade (1948, BBC)
The Passing Show (1948, BBC)
Tell Her the Truth (1948, BBC)
Old Songs for New (1948, BBC)
Lady Luck (1948, BBC)
First Time Ever (1948, BBC)
Give My Regards to Leicester Square (1948, BBC)
Jill Darling (1949, BBC)
Regency Room (1950, BBC)
Alfred Marks Programme (1950, BBC)
Carmichael's Night Out (1957, BBC)
The Girl at the Next Table (1957, BBC)
Gilt and Gingerbread (1961, ITV)
Compact: first episode (1962, BBC)
Armchair Theatre: The Importance of Being Earnest (1964, ITV)
The World of Wooster (1965–67, BBC)
The Morecambe and Wise Show (1970, 1972 BBC)
Bachelor Father (1970–71, BBC)
Play for Today: Alma Mater (1971, BBC)
Father, Dear Father: 'An Affair to Forget' (1971, ITV)

Lord Peter Wimsey (1972–75, BBC)
Three More Men in a Boat (1983, BBC)
The Wind in the Willows (1983–89, ITV)
All for Love: 'Down at the Hydro' (1983, ITV)
Movie Memories (1985, ITV)
A Day in Summer (1989, ITV)
Oh! Mr Toad (1990, ITV)
The Play on One: Obituaries (1990, BBC)
A Tribute to Terry-Thomas (1990, ITV)
Strathblair (1991–92, BBC)
Under the Hammer: 'Wonders in the Deep' (1994, ITV)
Bramwell (1995, ITV)
Wives and Daughters (1999, BBC)
The Royal (2003–2011, ITV)

Background film and television (movies and DVD)

A Very Peculiar Practice: The Complete First Series (Network, 2004)
Adam Adamant Lives! The Complete Collection (BBC/2 Entertain, 2006)
The Avengers: The Complete Series 3 (Optimum Home Entertainment, 2010)
The Avengers: The Complete Series 5 (Optimum Home Entertainment, 2010)
Bachelor Flat (1961)
Black Narcissus (1947)
Campion: The Complete Second Series (Madman, 2010)
Casino Royale (1967)
Danger Man: 45th Anniversary Special Edition (Umbrella Entertainment, 2005)
Danger Man: The Complete 1964–66 Series (Madman Television, 2008)
Darling (1965)
Dr No (1962)
Doctor Who: Beneath the Surface (BBC/2 Entertain, 2008)
Doctor Who: Mara Tales (BBC/2 Entertain, 2011)
Doctor Who: New Beginnings (BBC/2 Entertain, 2007)
Doctor Who: Resurrection of the Daleks Special Edition (BBC/2 Entertain, 2011)
Doctor Who: The Talons of Weng-Chiang Special Edition (BBC/2 Entertain, 2010)
From Russia with Love (1963)

The Forsyte Saga (BBC, 2004)
Goldfinger (1964)
The Great Rock and Roll Swindle (Shout!, 2005)
The Innocents (1961)
The Life and Death of Colonel Blimp (1943)
The Naked Truth (1957)
North by Northwest (1959)
Ripping Yarns (Network, 2004)
The St Trinian's Collection (Optimum Classic, 2006)
St Trinian's 2: The Legend of Fritton's Gold (Entertainment by Video, 2009)
Too Many Crooks (1959)
A Year to Remember: The War Years 1939–1945 (Pathé, 2010)

CDs

The Boomtown Rats, *Best of The Boomtown Rats* (Eagle Records, 2003)
The Clash, *London Calling* (CBS, 1979)
The Jam, *Setting Sons* (Polydor, 1979)
The Ruts, *The Crack* (Virgin, 1979)

Internet

AMC Filmsite
BFI Screenonline
Kate Fenton
The Dorothy L. Sayers Society
The P.G. Wodehouse Society
The *Stage* Archive
YouTube

Index